■◆■◆■◆■

Embedded Symmetries, Natural and Cultural

■◆■◆■◆■

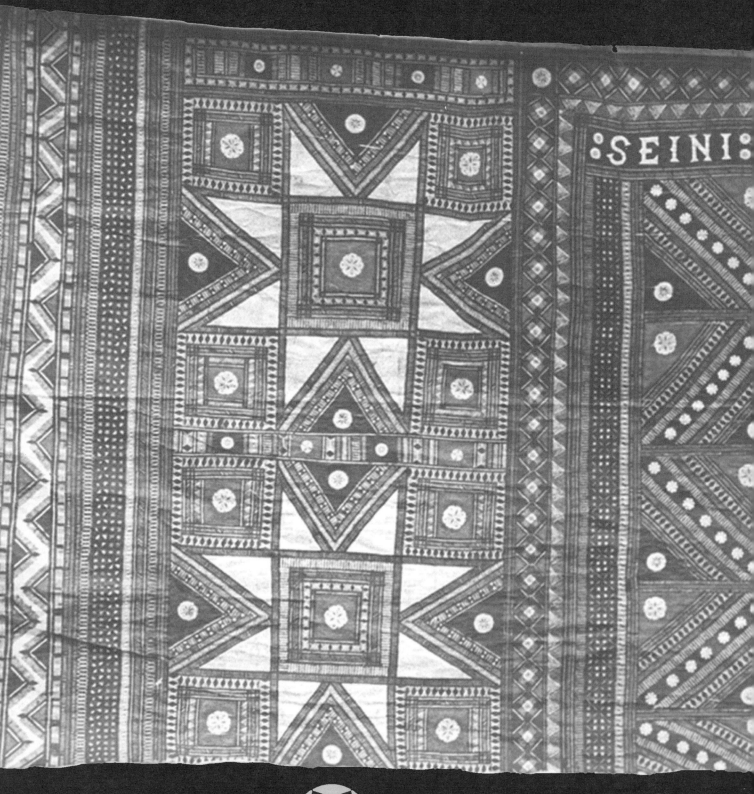

:SEINI:

Number Six in the   Amerind Foundation New World Studies Series

EMBEDDED SYMMETRIES
Natural and Cultural

Dorothy K. Washburn, Editor

University of New Mexico Press ■ Albuquerque

Published in cooperation with the Amerind Foundation

To Anne Paul, and Ed Franquemont.
Their groundbreaking work has opened our eyes
to the language of symmetry.
They are greatly missed.

■ ◆ ■ ◆ ■ ◆ ■

©2004 by the University of New Mexico Press
All rights reserved. Published 2004
Printed in the United States of America
10 09 08 07 06 05   2 3 4 5 6 7

Library of Congress Cataloging-in-Publication Data

Embedded symmetries, natural and cultural / Dorothy K. Washburn, editor.
p. cm. — (Amerind Foundation New World studies series ; no. 6)
"Published in cooperation with the Amerind Foundation."
Includes index.
ISBN 0-8263-3152-1 (cloth : alk. paper)
1. Symmetry. 2. Symmetry (Art) 3. Material culture.
4. Culture—Semiotic models. I. Washburn, Dorothy Koster.
II. Amerind Foundation. III. Series.
BH301.S9E63 2004
117—dc22

2004011782

DESIGN AND COMPOSITION: Mina Yamashita

Contents

List of Figures

Acknowledgments

I AM GRATEFUL TO DOROTHY WASHBURN for bringing together this group of scholars. The late Joseph Hester's generosity was instrumental in providing sound financial support for the seminars. Special recognition for the support of the Amerind Foundation New World Studies Series is extended to the foundation's board of directors: Wm. Duncan Fulton, Peter L. Formo, Michael W. Hard, Elizabeth F. Husband, Marilyn Fulton, George J. Gumerman, Peter Johnson, Sharline Reedy, and Lawrence Schiever. Their friendship is much appreciated.

—*Anne I. Woosley*
The Amerind Foundation, Inc.

Foreword

THE AMERIND FOUNDATION NEW WORLD STUDIES seminars were initiated almost fifteen years ago with the conviction that interesting ideas, those that move a discipline into new directions, are best generated through the intellectual interaction of individuals actively participating in research. All too often in our fast-paced, segmented lives, when we gather at national meetings, the opportunity to talk with one another for any length of time is lacking. The intent of Amerind seminars, in contrast, was to create the environment in which scholars could meet in small groups to discuss, to argue, to question but always in a spirit of mutual exploration. Seminars were dedicated to the investigation of topics and issues not restricted by geographic or temporal barriers. This might be a synthesis of Hohokam and Salado prehistories or might involve comparatively fledgling areas of anthropological studies such as the anthropology of technology. Seminars brought together researchers who, under ordinary circumstances, would probably not speak directly to each other, such as the archaeologists analyzing political systems of the prehistoric U.S. Southwest and Southeast or those debating the nature of Mesoamerican influences on the Southwest. Amerind seminars were intended to break through boundaries of anthropological discourse and subject matter by traversing new paths rather than following well-established thoroughfares of inquiry. *Embedded Symmetries, Natural and Cultural* represents one of these efforts to integrate research presently considered to be more or less tangential to generally accepted studies of culture into the broad discipline of anthropology.

Dorothy Washburn proposed the topic and a potential list of participants during the course of a Society for American Archaeology meeting. The multidisciplinary character of the scholars that included expertise in the subdisciplines of anthropology, archaeology, sociology, biology, psychology, and the arts boded an interesting mix. This was not simply to be a discussion that symmetries exist, but how and why they are such integral components of social life, as a means of communicating cultural principles, for encoding social thought, and expressing a variety of cultural information. The nine chapters that follow pursue these and related topics employing diverse methodologies and bodies of data.

On a personal note, completion of *Embedded Symmetries* is somewhat poignant as it represents my final Amerind seminar volume. My own path has taken a new direction leading me to the Arizona Historical Society.

—Anne I. Woosley

Introduction

Embedded Symmetries

Dorothy K. Washburn

THIS VOLUME RESULTED FROM THE SYMPOSIUM Embedded Symmetries held at the Amerind Foundation from April 13 through 17, 2000. The intent was to gather a group of scholars who consider symmetrical relationships central to human existence and who have explored how cultures make these relationships manifest through patterning of their material culture as well as through other kinds of culturally constructed relationships and activities. The participants explored the cultural saliency of nonrepresentational pattern from perceptual and cultural perspectives. The coverage ranged widely, from laboratory studies of how humans perceive repeated geometric arrays to field studies of the varied ways prehistoric and contemporary non-Western societies use pattern as a form of visual communication. Although most participants were ethnographers and archaeologists, the hope is that with the input here of experimental psychologists, the symposium will presage the first of many multidisciplinary investigations of this domain.

Geometry describes the measurement, properties, and relationships of points, lines, angles, surfaces, and solids in space. Symmetry is perhaps the ultimate mathematical relationship, for it describes correspondences in size, shape, and position between parts of a whole. The sciences study symmetries of form, such as the symmetries underlying the lattice packing of crystalline solids or the symmetries of organic molecules. Typically, nonmathematicians have a more limited concept of symmetry, thinking of it as mirror reflection across a central axis. The human body, for example, is generally vertically bilaterally symmetric.

However, there are symmetries in many other domains. The authors in this volume explore how symmetries pervade social relationships as well as the physical representations we make of these relationships that shape and enable our daily lives. These symmetries have multiple dimensionalities, from the symmetries in the radial layout of a Navajo hogan to the planar symmetries in the design on a Persian carpet. These cultural symmetries can be described by the same series of motion classes that describe the symmetries for discrete three-dimensional objects as well as for finite, one- and two-dimensional patterns in the plane developed by mathematicians and crystallographers to characterize solids and crystals. Mathematician Don Crowe developed flowcharts to help non–mathematically sophisticated users see the symmetries in their materials (Washburn and Crowe 1988).

In this symposium we went beyond these methodological considerations to explore how symmetry characterizes conceptual relationships among people and between people and the natural world and to describe some of the different ways that the symmetries of these relationships are made manifest in pattern. Far from being an imposed, abstract, mathematical construct, the symmetry of human relationships in all its visual, verbal, and kinesthetic manifestations deserves our careful study. In this volume, the authors present a number of different views on how symmetrical relationships are presented in visual formats for the consumption of one's cultural peers as well as for the outside world.

Imagery that "communicates" is often said to be, by analogy, a form of visual language. The nature of this semiotic role has been actively debated (see the discussion in Hanson and in Ewins, this volume). It is probably more accurate to say that pictures fall at one end of an informational continuum of marks that move through signs and notations to lettered texts (Elkins 1998). Beginning sometime during the Paleolithic, artists began developing different formats to express ideas or represent things. Each format is explicitly designed to focus on a particular kind of information being presented. It is one of the cognitive hallmarks of human beings that we can endlessly create different kinds of visual modes in which to communicate. Here we explore how symmetrical pattern is one of these modes.

The volume begins with two chapters on the perception of symmetry that offer the anthropologist important reasons to abandon the superorganic perspective and incorporate observations about human biology into our understanding of human behavior. For years, study of the perception of symmetry has been thought to be irrelevant to cultural behavior because, since all humans have the same perceptual system, this property should not be related to cultural differences. These two studies show that although all human perceptual systems use fundamental properties such as symmetry (Washburn 1999) and color (Zeki 1999) to identify form, differences in gender as well as cultural enculturation may result in different *perceptual experiences* of the same symmetrical pattern. They are but the beginning of many different avenues of research that will be necessary to redefine the interface between the capacities of the human organism at birth and its ontogeny relative to the varieties of ways individuals and cultures perceive and respond to the world.

In Chapter 1, Diane Humphrey sets the stage by pointing out that while we are born with a visual and vestibular system that seeks symmetry, our kinesthetic and representational skills in achieving symmetry in walking and image making must be developed. She supports this with developmental studies of children and adults of both sexes that cry for cross-cultural tests. Anthropologists who study child-rearing practices and art production by children would do well to review their data to see if cultural preferences for symmetry appear as early as infant self-soothing practices and extend to the different kinds of symmetries that appear in the art productions of the two sexes.

One of the most interesting observations is that in the laboratory, individuals who are asked to observe an array of symmetries and indicate preferences for certain kinds of symmetry do not use those same preferred symmetries when asked to produce a symmetrical pattern. This disjunction between observation and production is reiterated in a different set of sensory media—between language and behavior. Field anthropologists have long observed that what people say they do is not, a high percentage of the time, what they actually do. Our visual and linguistic activity is not reflected in our behavior. For both of these domains, there is a learning curve in the cognitive understanding and use of symmetry and language. Just as babies must verbally practice babbling to achieve comprehensible speech, they

also must physically practice moving their legs by glide reflection in order to walk. Thus, while we are born with the ability to see and prefer symmetry, it takes time for each individual to learn that symmetrical motions are the most productive in terms of locomotion. Unfortunately, these disjunctions, which argue for the importance of understanding the interface between biological and cultural ontogeny, are too often overlooked because only one domain—the perceptual (physiological) or the production (cultural)—is examined.

Michael Kubovy and Lars Strother (Chapter 2) focus on the important disjunction between mathematically based descriptions and perceptually based understandings of symmetry. The Gestalt principles of grouping and closure active in the perception of patterns result in perceptual responses that differentiate patterns with different spatial groupings of the constituent elements even if they have the same symmetry. Kubovy and Strother show how different perceptions can occur where the elements are combined or separated, where some symmetries suppress other symmetries, and where symmetries within a motif are observed over those between motifs. Although they assert that these perceptual effects should be universal, they urge cross-cultural studies to test how these observations might appear in different cultural contexts. Indeed, given the cases explored in this volume alone where cultures preferentially use different symmetries, one might well wonder whether, tested on their perception of different kinds of element and motif groupings, these different cultures would discriminate among them differently. Kubovy and Strother's observations again remind us how important it is to study the interface between what humans perceive in their world and how they act on these perceptions.

Moving from considerations of perception to production of symmetry, Thomas Wynn (Chapter 3) demarcates the acquisition of two distinct competencies in the production of symmetrical tools. The first evolved about 500,000 years ago during the Acheulean, when hominids began making bifaces, tools that were clearly more symmetrical than those made during the Oldowan. It appears that a more advanced conceptualization of symmetry, as manifest in the production of more symmetrical tools, evolved quite late, perhaps in tandem with language. Wynn argues that the high degree of consistency in tool shape at this late time reflects cognitive understanding and use of algorithms—rule systems for tool production that result in highly similar objects.

For symmetrical productions in the two-dimensional plane, I (Chapter 4) consider, from a perceptual perspective, what might have been the trajectory in the development of different modes of representation in an effort to place symmetrical pattern within the scope of representational systems. I argue that the first representational style to appear focused on re-creating realistic shapes in three-dimensional sculpture and then in two-dimensional drawings with a minimal set of visual primitives—line, angle, and curvature. The contour outlines of animals from Upper Paleolithic cave walls are well-studied examples of such early representational imagery. Subsequent culture history has preserved an explosion of different ways these form primitives have been combined to create different realistic styles. But in tandem with realism, as early as the Neolithic, human cultures were developing nonrepresentational ways to visually represent—ways that are as diverse as cuneiform records, symmetrical pattern, or Abstract Expressionism. I further suggest that these different formats were created in order to best express different kinds of information.

Perhaps one of the most sophisticated uses of symmetry to encode social thought is found on the textiles of pre-Columbian and present-day Andean peoples. However, the intricate juxtapositions of the weaving techniques, coloring systems, and iconographic referents call for highly sensitive analytical methodologies. While most people think of symmetry as bilateral reflection, the Andean symmetries surpass even the standard crystallographic classes (Washburn and Crowe 1988). Textile analysts will be indebted to mathematician Branko Grünbaum's (1990; reprinted in Washburn and Crowe [2004]) expansion of the seventeen classes of two-dimensional plane patterns to account for directionality and orientation of patterns that occur in fixed positions in real-world situations.

In this volume, Anne Paul (Chapter 5) effectively uses Grünbaum's (1990) classification to find the combinatorial logic in the color and structure systems of Paracas textiles. She notes that although 97 percent of the textile patterns in her sample are based on two motions—glide reflection and bifold rotation—the Andean visual communication system was so highly complex and many layered that it required the development of numerous variants of these two basic symmetrical relationships to encode all the different kinds of information. It will be up to other scholars to decode the wealth of information about Andean thought and culture embedded in this color-weave structure-iconographic system. In some cases, as on border patterns, the symmetries used to repeat the design units replicate those in the weave structure. In other cases, as on center field patterns, neither the coloring of the iconographic units nor the symmetry used to repeat the iconographic units is isomorphic with the symmetry of the weave structure. Of the 142 color block patterns studied by Paul, only three have arrangements that map onto the underlying structural symmetry. Surely, such disjunction indicates a complexly layered hierarchy of intersecting but not isomorphic informational systems. The "mavericks" that do not follow this system might be indicative of attempts by outsiders to copy the Paracas style (cf. Washburn 2001), perhaps because they have married in or have been moved to the area as laborers within the *mita* system. Or, as Paul suggests, since they appear late in the sequence, they may be indicative of a system about to "unravel."

Ed Franquemont (Chapter 6), writing from years of apprentice instruction with weavers in the village of Chinchero, Peru, explains how textiles are the dominant form of conceptual expression. Andean weavers have capitalized on their character of mirror reversibility and figure/ground enhancement so that the same image appears in a complementary state on the two sides of the textile. The textiles seem to be visible material markers of Andean social structure that is built on a hierarchy of reciprocal exchanges. The woven base is a perfect format in which to present these interconnected hierarchical systems of color and weave structure. In effect, this inextricable mix of textile structure, color, and pattern is a metaphor for the way the Andean peoples think about human interrelationships. However, within this complex nesting of systems is ample room for variation, a character Franquemont compares to the improvisation that is found in jazz. The Andean world is not a static bilateral world, but is full of fluid and dynamic relationships that are embodied in the rotational and glide symmetries.

In Chapter 7, Peter Roe presents evidence that the Amerindian worldview is embodied in design organization on ceramic vessels. He examines the body metaphor in vessel form as well as the designs applied to the vessels. Roe argues that the overall symmetry of the vessel and design as well as the asymmetry in detail embodies the Amerindian perspective of the world: "What you see is not what you get." That is, what is hidden is what is real. In contrast, the rule in the West is: "What you see is what you get"; that is, what is on the surface is reality. Since the Renaissance, artists in the West devised many ways of showing reality until Picasso averred, teaching us to see, through African art, that there are other ways of representing reality. Roe deftly outlines how symmetry reflects the evolution of the Amerindian worldview as seen in Saladoid Antillean ceramics and petroglyphs.

Both F. Allan Hanson and Rod Ewins investigated the symmetries of art in cultures that have long been subjected to outside influences, such that the patterns today present only general referents to what was probably formerly a larger, more complex body of traditional knowledge and ways of representing that knowledge. Hanson (Chapter 8) observes that although both reciprocities in feast exchanges and revenge warfare as well as complementarities in the cycle of creation and disintegration in the union and production of men and women may be signified in the general two-part nature of Maori decorative patterns, further significances are no longer discernable. Likewise, Ewins (Chapter 9) found that traditionally, different clans, phratries, and villages could be distinguished by the different element arrangements of tapa cloth patterns. Today tapa making preserves only a general pan-Fijian identity; village identities are no longer differentiated in tapa patterns. Some cultural specifics, such as the contrast between the black/white elements in the tapa patterns, continue to replicate the male/female, spirit world/temporal world distinctions that pervaded traditional society. Further, the tapa patterns use symmetries, such as glide reflection, to characterize the passage of time between traditional ritual exchanges and mirror reflection to characterize equivalent exchanges that occur in markets and other nonritual interactions. However, over time these cultural signs have become "detached signifiers." Fijian tapa and perhaps Maori rafter design of today are

fragments—generalized and simplified symbols of what was once a complex, many-layered semiotic system.

In sum, these chapters not only substantiate the existence of symmetries in cultural relationships but, more importantly, demonstrate that the bearers of these symmetries are fully aware of how to use them to shape their concepts and behavior to effective and adaptive ends. In order to establish these points, many of the chapters present densely argued and evidenced cases and so require careful reading. Yet the new insights and understandings will richly reward readers' efforts.

Finally, one of the things I wanted to achieve in this symposium was to move the study of cultural symmetries beyond noticing their existence and variety toward looking at ways we can explore how and why symmetry is such an important component of social life. It is now time to address these complex issues.

No discipline grows by adhering rigidly to a set of algorithms. At any given time, we may think we have found all the solutions until new questions arise that cannot be accounted for by the existing set. The classic set of seven and seventeen one- and two-dimensional plane pattern classes is an excellent example. Defined in the nineteenth century, these classes were the classificatory standard until the work of Grünbaum (1990) expanded the two-dimensional classes to account for directionality; Paul, in this volume, has shown how useful they are. Similarly, Roger Penrose discovered exceptions to the standard array of periodic tilings composed of the same shape arranged in different crystalline formation such that a whole subgroup of these quasi-periodic tilings composed of two or more different shapes is now being defined (Steinhardt 1986). Similarly, we must ask if there are cultural examples of these "quasi-symmetric" patterns. Moreover, how should we understand them? Are they visual signs of a transition between two different symmetric states that are, in turn, representative of different structural states in systems of cultural relationships?

We must also ask why there are significant departures from symmetry in preference and production. This is a much harder task. Evolution surely has taught us that symmetrical form seems to be the most adaptive. This state seems to be the most adaptive in cultural relationships. Perhaps periods of symmetry breaking throughout the social network are manifestations of adaptation to change and reorganization. It will be interesting to study the sequence in which cultural systems manifest these shifts to new structural adaptations: I predict art forms will be among the first.

Finally, in the interests of understanding the evolutionary, adaptive significance of the perception and production of symmetric human relationships as well as of the presence of broken symmetries, we need to link our studies with those of primatologists who are studying the kinds of activities and cognitive responses enabled by the things chimps and apes see, process, and respond to (cf. Bradshaw and Rogers 1993). It has been suggested that although the prototypical model of reality coded in the human brain is one of symmetric form, the real sign of the superior cognitive processing abilities of human brains lies in our ability to detect deviations from symmetry that may be maladaptive (Enquist and Arak 1995). For example, studies of facial preferences suggest that men prefer women with average (i.e., symmetric) faces (Thornhill and Gangestad 1993). Given the suggestion that healthy individuals are symmetric in body form, it may be that the ability for men to detect departures from symmetrical faces enables them to select females who will be able to pass along the fittest genes. It will be important to link our studies of culturally produced pattern asymmetries to the growing body of data from the paleoanthropological and primatological domains. Interestingly, the phylogenetic and neurobiological bases for cerebral asymmetry that exist in humans but not nearly as strongly in other primates have been attributed by some to the perceptual system but by others to the motor system (see review in Corballis 1998), which Humphrey (Chapter 1, this volume) has shown to be asymmetric at birth.

Clearly, we have come a long way from initial studies that fought the assumption that decorative styles merely decorate (cf. David et al. 1988) toward in-depth studies of the precise features that do the communicating and the mechanisms through which communication is accomplished. In this volume, the authors admirably present a wonderfully diverse introduction to the many ways symmetry embodies and communicates cultural principles as well as raise issues that should be the subject of future studies.

I have just described this symposium and resultant volume as if the study of symmetry were a standard chapter of cultural studies. Actually, whereas the mathematics of symmetry has been understood for many years and psychological studies of the perception of symmetry have been conducted for some decades now, the acknowledgment by anthropologists that cultures actually recognize, use, and prefer certain kinds of symmetrical orders has not had widespread currency in cultural studies. It is for this reason that I want to especially thank Amerind Foundation director Anne Woosley for having the foresight to support such a fringe perspective by financially enabling the conference and making the fine facilities and hospitality of the Amerind available for this interdisciplinary gathering. It is through conferences such as these that isolated researchers share observations, formulate new ideas, and make plans for further explorations. I hope that the following series of papers from this conference will bring the importance of symmetry in culture to greater attention and stimulate others to explore its presence and meaning in other cultural situations and contexts.

The entire staff at the Amerind made our stay comfortable, not the least of which was the chef's incredible food. Allan McIntyre has been a scrupulously careful editor, standardizing formats, coordinating the voluminous illustrations, and attending to other countless details. We thank the University of New Mexico Press, which has continually supported the publication of the Amerind seminar series and has added our volume to their book list. Editors Evelyn Schlatter and Karen Taschek and designer Mina Yamashita gave dedicated and yeoman attention to preparing the book in its final form and shepherding it into publication. I cannot thank them enough. ■

References Cited

Bradshaw, J. L., and L. J. Rogers
1993   *The Evolution of Lateral Asymmetries, Language, Tool Use
            and Intellect*. Academic Press, New York.

Corballis, M. C.
1998   Cerebral Asymmetry: Motoring On. *Trends in Cognitive
            Science* 2:152–157.

David, N., J. Sterner, and K. Gavua
1988   Why Pots Are Decorated. *Current Anthropology* 29:365–389.

Elkins, J.
1998   *On Pictures and the Words That Fail Them*. Cambridge
            University Press, Cambridge, UK.

Enquist, M., and A. Arak
1995   The Illusion of Symmetry? *Afterwards: The Journal of NIH
            Research* 7:54–55.

Grünbaum, B.
1990   Periodic Ornamentation of the Fabric Plane: Lessons from
            Peruvian Fabrics. *Symmetry* 1:45–68.

Steinhardt, P. J.
1986   Quasicrystals. *American Scientist* 74:586–597.

Thornhill, R., and S. W. Gangestad
1993   Human Facial Beauty. *Human Nature* 4:237–269.

Washburn, D. K.
1999   Perceptual Anthropology: The Cultural Salience of
            Symmetry. *American Anthropologist* 101:547–562.
2001   Remembering Things Seen: Experimental Approaches to
            the Process of Information Transmittal. *Journal of
            Archaeological Method and Theory* 8:67–99.

Washburn, D. K., and D. W. Crowe
1988   *Symmetries of Culture: Theory and Practice of Plane Pattern
            Analysis*. University of Washington Press, Seattle.

Washburn, D. K., and D. W. Crowe (editors)
2004   *Symmetry Comes of Age: The Role of Pattern in Culture*.
            University of Washington Press, Seattle.

Zeki, S.
1999   *Inner Vision: An Exploration of Art and the Brain*. Oxford
            University Press, Oxford, UK.

CHAPTER ONE

Symmetries in Development

The Eye Is Quicker Than the Hand

Diane Humphrey

PERCEPTUAL SYSTEMS are symmetrically organized, both morphologically and functionally, in the body and in the brain. Representational and praxic systems, on the other hand, are asymmetrically organized. This difference seems to account for the differential development of the perception and production of symmetries. The development of sensitivity to structure is based on the organization of vestibular and kinesthetic systems. Because of the symmetrical organization of these systems, the newborn is especially soothed by symmetrical stimulation and seeks to maintain symmetry of sensory input in orientation, reaching, and locomotion patterns. The development of visual pattern discrimination and preference in infancy also shows this proclivity for symmetries, particularly for vertical reflection and "multiple" symmetries. Production of symmetries in drawings and constructions by both children and adults lags behind perception of symmetries, perhaps because of the asymmetrical organization of the praxic system. Experience and brain organization both seem to have a role in the ability to represent symmetries.

In this chapter, I will examine evidence that visual preferences for symmetry patterns are related developmentally to the structural sensitivities of the sensory systems. I propose that early experience coordinates the symmetries of the vestibular, kinesthetic, and visual systems. Production of symmetrical patterns, on the other hand, develops long after visual preferences for symmetries can be seen, perhaps due to the inherent asymmetries of manual motor control. Even adults trained in drawing do not frequently produce spontaneously the kinds of symmetry patterns that they prefer to look at. In terms of superiority of symmetrical structuring,

between the eyes and the hands, the eyes have it.

Previously, on Symmetry

Adult perception of symmetry has been investigated as a Gestalt principle (e.g., Bertamini et al. 1997; Kubovy and Wagemans 1998; Labonte et al. 1995; Palmer 1991; and Kubovy and Strother, this volume) ultimately important in object perception (Shepard 1994) but also as it is related to the "goodness" of patterns (van der Helm and Leeuwenberg, 1999). Visual search tasks are purported to reveal the basic features that are detectable by the visual system (Treisman 1986) but have failed to yield evidence for automatic feature extraction of symmetry per se (e.g., Wolfe and Friedman-Hill 1992), suggesting that symmetry may be processed at some higher level than as a basic detectable feature.

Much of the literature on symmetry perception deals with a limited range of types of symmetries, and much of it is concerned with reflection about a vertically oriented axis. This may be related to the fact that only some classes of symmetry patterns have precedence over others (see Kubovy and Strother, this volume, for a discussion). Symmetry has been studied in relation to a variety of other perceptual phenomena, including orientation judgments of objects and patterns (Beh and Latimer 1997; Palmer and Hemenway 1978; Wenderoth 1997a); as an indicator of elongation (Sekuler 1996), as an indicator of a center (Bingham and Muchinsky 1993; Davi et al. 1992); as related to vernier judgments (Patel et al. 1999), depth (Szlyk et al. 1995), motion and optical flow (Telford and Howard 1996; te Pas et al. 1998), haptics (Ballesteros et al. 1997; Ballesteros et al. 1998), and seeing honesty in faces (Zebrowitz et al. 1996); and as part of locomotion (Amazeen et al. 1998; Berthenhal and Pinto 1993). In summary, symmetry seems to be an important aspect of self-motion as well as in the perception of a variety of kinds of objects in the world.

Developmentally, sensitivity to various forms of symmetry is seen both in the infant's remarkable early abilities to orient to the world around her and in rapidly developing preferences for symmetrical stimuli, including static visual patterns. In this chapter I would like to explore the possibility that both of these aspects of perceptual development are based on self-movement as well as on pattern and object perception and are related to early attempts by the infant to symmetrize her world. Thus, I suggest that the symmetrical structure of the visual system is based on both kinesthetic structures and vestibular structures.

Development of Sensory Systems

Sensory development begins long before birth. At birth, then, development of sensory systems is a continuation of processes already under way (see Bronson 1974 for a discussion of neonatal sensory systems). Of all the possible varieties of sensory experience, the newborn comes into the world with vestibular and kinesthetic experience in particular, which must then be related to profoundly novel types of stimulation in her other senses. Indeed, vestibular stimulation is at the top of a textbook (Berk 2000) list of techniques for soothing a crying newborn. Newborn infants are particularly comforted by being raised in an upright position to the shoulder, combined with rocking or walking. Other soothing techniques also serve to make the infant's world more symmetrical. Swaddling prevents the uncoordinated, asymmetrical movements of limbs that the newborn finds difficult to control. A pacifier in the infant's mouth promotes symmetrical, rhythmic sucking behaviors. Soft rhythmic sounds can soothe. A ride in a car, a carriage, or a swing produces symmetrical changes in the optical flow on the retina and the kinesthetic experience of the infant as well as symmetrical stimulation of the semicircular canals and utricles of the vestibular system. I argue that soothing stimulation is often symmetrical relative to the infant's body and the sensory organs that are already developed at birth.

Development of Movement

Gradually, motor patterns emerge in the infant's repertoire (Bayley 1961, 1993) that serve to make the world symmetrical with respect to the activation of sensory receptors and therefore also the distributed activity of the brain. I will return to a discussion of sensory and brain organization later in this chapter. The competent newborn can soothe herself by bringing her own hand to her mouth at the midline (Brazelton and Nugent 1995). Newborns orient with their eyes and heads to sounds (Muir and Field 1979), voices, faces, and touch on the cheek or arm (see Muir et al. 1994 for a review),

which, in turn, brings visual and auditory receptors into a symmetrical position with regard to the source of stimulation. Very young infants at or before two weeks of age will sometimes extend both of their arms toward an object or picture that is visually fixated at the midline (DiFranco et al. 1978). Visual fixation and tracking abilities continue to develop, of course, into childhood (Kowler and Martins 1983). I am arguing that the process of visual orientation control is a process of symmetrizing the stimulation of sensory receptors in several modalities. Gradually, reaching and grasping, crawling, and walking build on earlier motor and sensory abilities in an ever-expanding dynamic spiral of development (Thelen and Smith 1994).

Self-Motion Makes the World Symmetrical

A symmetrically changing pattern of optical flow on the retina (Gibson 1950) is an important indicator of one's relation to the world, whether the objective is to grasp or to avoid the symmetrically expanding or contracting optical flow. The developing child's own movements thus create changes in the stimulation of the perceptual systems that are symmetrically structured. Fixation at the center of a visual pattern allows for looming or receding of the pattern. Fiddler crabs, chicks, monkeys, and human infants have all long been known to avoid looming objects (Schiff 1965). Regan and Cynader (1979) have found single cells in the visual cortex of the cat that respond to symmetrical expansion of a visual stimulus. Indeed, asymmetrical movement of optical flow can produce vestibular illusions, even with one illuminated dot in the periphery (Johansson 1977), and make you dizzy, even sick.

The development of locomotion in a necessarily symmetrical organism (see Gardner's [1979] classic discussion) brings about another level of complexity in symmetrical movement. The glide reflection pattern of footprints reveals the symmetrical movements of the human body in normal walking (for a discussion of symmetry in locomotion see Bertenthal and Pinto 1993). Even early crawling by infants shows this same glide reflection of movements, where the diagonally symmetrical hand and knee are moved forward at the same time (Adolph et al. 1998). The biomechanical constraint of keeping balance keeps the center of mass moving forward with minimal destabilizing torques.

Other researchers (Corballis and Roldan 1975; Julesz 1971) have suggested that there is a developmental relationship between upright walking and the human's visual advantage for vertical reflective symmetry. I would argue, to the contrary, that vertical reflective symmetry becomes important for the visual system long before walking emerges. The visual cliff apparatus (Gibson and Walk 1960) is used to study the development of locomotion. The apparatus consists of a large, raised, transparent surface that has a visible shallow checkerboard bottom surface on one side of a bridge and a visible deep checkerboard bottom surface on the other side of the bridge. Around the sides of the apparatus parents and others can stand and be seen by the infant. When babies graduate to walking, their approach and avoidance behavior on a visual cliff changes (Adolph et al. 1993). Crawlers at around eight months of age would plunge right over the edge (if it were a real edge), but walkers at fourteen months will at least prepare to slide and will usually avoid the deep side of the cliff. This new skill of locomotion over slopes may begin by babies' using the new types of asymmetries in the optic flow that are produced by changes in locomotion from crawling to walking. The change from crawling to walking does indeed bring about new variations in optical flow patterns, but these must be symmetrized during approach and avoidance even during crawling. Furthermore, adjustment of the infant's movement to optic flow has been demonstrated long before walking or even crawling has begun. As soon as infants can sit up, they will adjust their posture to a moving visual field (Bertenthal and Bai 1989; Lee and Lishman 1975).

In summary, even the earliest movements show the need to map stimulation in one sensory modality onto other sensory modalities, producing spatially coordinated structures of stimulation. For example, early reaching to the midline, bringing of hands to mouth, and orientation of head and eyes serve to produce symmetrical translations and rotations of visual patterns. This sensitivity of the visual system to rotations and translations may also be related to the inherent structure of another, more basic sensory system: the vestibular system.

The vestibular system, in particular, responds to changes in movement of a linear or a rotary nature, with the movement of hair cells in the utricles and semicircular canals, respectively. The physiological structure of the vestibular system, located in the inner ear, is such that it responds to the acceleration or deceleration of self-motion of two basic types: rotary motion and linear motion. The three semicircular canals are oriented in three different planes at right angles to each other in order to respond maximally to rotary self-motion in any plane. The two utricles respond best to linear self-motion. Poincaré (1952) suggested that the structure of the vestibular system, as a reference frame for movements of the body, might provide a physiological basis for the three axes in space that are the basis of Euclidian geometry. As Einstein pointed out in 1911, the vestibular system is an egocentric system that cannot distinguish self-movement from gravity (Berthoz 2000). As such, it is an inertial system, which provides an independent spatial frame of reference for the orientation of the body.

Reaching and Grasping

At around four months of age infants are sitting up independently and beginning to attempt to reach consistently toward objects within grasping distance using one hand, although not preferentially with the left or the right until at least five months of age or older (Humphrey and Humphrey 1987). I filmed reaching behavior in my son once a week over the first year of life. At around four months of age, he could maintain upright posture in an infant seat and attempted to reach toward a ball on the end of a stick with one hand at a time. When lying on his back, however, many more reaches toward objects were made with both hands. In this position, he used two hands to reach toward suspended objects that were presented at the midline but were too far away to grasp. As an object was brought toward him, he closed his hands together at the midline, bringing them into his mouth before the object arrived within his grasping distance. His arm movements in this position were mirror-symmetrically coordinated with respect to his body and with respect to gravity although inappropriate for the distance of the object. Although he was unable to reach and grasp objects accurately at four months, these attempts revealed symmetrical behaviors. Likewise, perception of symmetries of visual patterns seems to be

salient by four months of age. Perhaps the emergence of preferences for symmetrical visual patterns is related to the symmetry of movements and the accompanying symmetrical kinesthesis.

Development of Pattern Discrimination

Just as moving patterns are structured by the sensory systems, the development of sensitivity to visual static patterns likewise reveals an increasing affinity for structured, symmetrical patterns. As Arnheim (1974) and others have argued, the basis for perception of dynamic structure in visual patterns lies in the structure of self-movement perception, or kinesthesis. Arnheim goes further. In *The Power of the Center,* he (1988) suggests that two structural principles, centric and eccentric, organize visual patterns. These two structural principles appear to resemble the basic structures of the vestibular system. Although Arnheim himself does not comment on this, Berthoz (2000), among others, as discussed above, has noticed this similarity between translation and rotation in geometry and the two basic structures of the vestibular system. Let us look at the development of sensitivity to visual structure in static patterns to see what pattern perception has to do with how we come to perceive and process the structures of symmetries.

Beginning with the work of Fantz (1961), it has become clear that infants can discriminate even static visual patterns that have particular forms of structure. In our own studies, infants were tested in a habituation paradigm, where a stimulus pattern is shown repeatedly and looking times on each exposure of the stimulus are measured. If the infant habituates to the stimulus pattern, her looking time duration will decrease over trials. Thus, we can present a pattern repeatedly until some criterion looking time demonstrates that habituation has occurred. On presentation of a different stimulus pattern, the infant may look longer at the new pattern. If she increases her looking time to the new pattern by some criterion, we can say that she has dishabituated and can thus infer that she can tell the difference between the two patterns. At four months of age, infants were shown vector patterns based on mathematical Lie groups (Dodwell 1983) (Figure 1.1) in a habituation paradigm (Humphrey et al. 1988). When the infants were shown unstructured patterns first, followed by structured patterns, looking time did not increase. With the reverse sequence, however, where structured patterns were shown first, looking time did increase, suggesting that there was some discrimination of structured patterns but only when they were seen first. In another study (Humphrey et al. 1986) four-month-olds were shown patterns that varied in "goodness" (Figure 1.1) according to Garner's (1974) criteria of number of patterns that can be obtained with reflection and rotation, called R&R subsets. "Good" patterns have the smallest number of alternatives, while "poor" patterns have the greatest number. A pattern that has several classes of symmetry, such as the center (a) dot pattern in Figure 1.1, does not produce a new pattern by being rotated in 45-degree steps or by reflection around four axes. Thus, Garner calls these kinds of reflection and rotation subsets "good" patterns. "Poor" patterns do change with reflection and rotation. In our study, infants showed dishabituation (longer looking durations) to changes in orientation and location of the patterns but not to change in the internal structure, that is, the "goodness" per se of the patterns. However, keep in mind that habituation is not the only methodology that can be used to demonstrate the infant's ability to discriminate patterns.

Development of Pattern Preferences

A study of visual preferences (Humphrey and Humphrey 1989), again with four-month-old infants, revealed longer looking times to dot patterns (Figure 1.1) with specific symmetries compared to dot patterns with no symmetries. One group of infants preferred twofold or fourfold symmetry when the patterns had sixteen dots while another group of infants showed longer looking times to patterns with vertical reflection, twofold, fourfold, eightfold symmetry or vertical reflection when the patterns had thirty-two dots. Studying the childhood years, Mendelson and Lee (1981) have found that kindergarteners and prekindergarteners can recognize reflective symmetries, particularly oriented vertically with higher levels of contour, especially in the younger group.

I have studied the visual symmetry preferences of children (Humphrey 1997). In one experiment I asked children at the London Regional Children's Museum from two to twelve years of age to tell me which dot pattern they preferred, presented two at a time on cards.

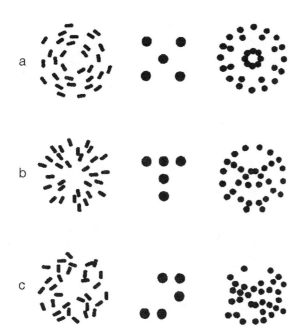

Figure 1.1 Examples of patterns shown to infants. Left: vector patterns: (a) concentric circles, (b) radial lines, (c) random; center: Garner patterns: (a) good, (b) medium, (c) poor; right: symmetry patterns: (a) eightfold, (b) vertical reflection, (c) asymmetrical.

The dot patterns were like those used in Humphrey and Humphrey (1989) (see Figure 1.1). Younger children and girls, in particular, preferred symmetry patterns with several axes of reflectional symmetry (multiple symmetries). Some researchers (e.g., Royer 1981; Wenderoth 1997b) have found that multiple symmetries are easier to detect than are patterns with a single axis of reflection, even when the axis is vertical. Although other researchers have not found an advantage for multiple symmetries under all conditions (e.g., Locher and Wagemans 1993), the special status of vertically oriented reflectional symmetry remains clear. In another experiment I showed the same dot patterns as above to children and adults and found that girls preferred both vertical and horizontal reflections.

The perception of symmetry can also be studied when symmetry is seen as a continuous feature. For example, Zabrodsky and Algom (1994) have investigated the relationship between perception and "symmetry distance." Their continuous symmetry measure can compare the "amount" of symmetry of different shapes and can compare the "amount" of different symmetries of a single shape. The "symmetry distance" is defined as the minimum effort required to transform a given

object into a symmetric object. When they presented shapes varying in symmetry distance from mirror symmetry and rotational symmetry, they found that subjects' ratings of "goodness" of the shapes were highly negatively correlated with symmetry distance.

In my own study (Humphrey 1997) children and adults were asked to rate "how much" symmetry was in the dot patterns. Adults showed a wider spread of these amount-of-symmetry ratings than did children. These adults seem to show greater differentiation of types of symmetries than do children in these ratings.

Symmetry in Drawings and Constructions

Nonetheless, it is clearly established that from early infancy, certain types of symmetries are preferred visually with greater statistical frequency. If these visual preferences are related to productions, drawings and constructions should show comparable proclivities. Specifically, people should draw and construct vertical reflections and multiple symmetries more often than other symmetries. While Washburn and Crowe (1988) and many others, including contributors to this volume, have documented the use of a range of symmetry types in various materials (e.g., pottery and textiles) in a variety of cultures, I will restrict my discussion here to material produced for the benefit of an experimenter in a somewhat controlled situation. This is not to argue that preference is best studied in the laboratory. Rather, the types of productions considered here are of interest because they are generated in a situation that attempts to encourage spontaneous, individual choice of pattern, motif, or both.

Children's drawings have been studied in a variety of ways. Typically, researchers look at the representational aspects of drawings. Golomb (1983, 1987), on the other hand, has studied overall composition in children's drawings. She has found evidence for the use of Arnheim's (1988) centric and eccentric organizational principles in children's drawings (Golomb 1987). My own students (Stothers 1997; Vance 1999) have investigated centric and eccentric distribution of visual weight in children's drawings using a method developed by Locher, Gray, and Nodine (1997). Application of a compositional scale (Golomb 1983) has further revealed the use of, among other strategies, symmetrical compositional structures in children's drawings. None of these studies has attempted to quantify local details in drawings.

Quantification of freehand drawings, while possible (see Shimaya 1997 for an analysis of Gestalt principles in line drawings), poses certain problems. I chose to analyze drawings made with colored markers by children and adults using a single marker stroke as the unit of analysis. I could then count symmetries or near symmetries between marker strokes. The drawings of girls, especially, showed a great deal of vertically oriented reflection as well as translation. Adult females also used vertical reflections more often than did adult males and, furthermore, used other types of symmetries, including multiple symmetries, more often than did males (Humphrey 1993). Mortensen (1990) has also noted the production of symmetrical drawings by girls, particularly in frontal representations of the human figure. Boys are more likely to draw in profile, resulting in a less symmetrical figure. Stothers (1997) has further noted a preponderance of symmetries in the representational drawings of girls from two to twelve years of age, but both boys and girls used vertical reflections as well as translations. Younger children who drew scribbles did not produce symmetrical drawings.

It is noteworthy that like the drawings of apes and chimps (see Wynn, Chapter 3, this volume), the early scribbles of young children are typically centered on the page. Perhaps, in older children's drawings, the choice of themes influences the symmetry of the drawings. Plante (1995), for example, found that six-year-old boys drew more monsters, vehicles, and military activities than did girls, who drew more plants, buildings, natural objects, hearts, and surrealistic scenes.

Adults too vary the kind of symmetry they use in a line drawing according to the particulars of the drawing task. Humphrey and Washburn (2002) asked art students and students untrained in art to draw four different pictures with black markers, each from life, memory, fantasy, and a diagram. While drawings by art students were clearly more complex and used many more marker strokes, there were some similarities to the drawings of students untrained in art. Drawings from memory, in particular, showed greater use of vertical than horizontal reflections, especially when made by untrained females or by art students of either gender.

Diagrams also showed a preponderance of the use of reflection, but both vertical and horizontal. It appears that adults, just as do children trained and untrained in art, produce many vertical reflections in their drawings.

Art students and untrained students were also asked to make constructions of one-dimensional band designs by arranging right-triangular shapes. Female art students, in particular, used predominantly vertical reflections in their drawings, while untrained females used bifold rotations most often. The bifold rotations produced by untrained females may have been the result of a preference for specific groupings of these rotations (see Kubovy and Strother, Chapter 2, this volume, for a discussion of grouping). Again the preference for "multiple" symmetries seen in visual tasks is not seen in the production of designs, whether by children or adults, trained or untrained in art, with the possible exception of spontaneous drawings by untrained women. Perception and production of symmetries are not identical.

Symmetry and the Brain

The development of visual perception of symmetry must be inextricably tied to the development of the whole, coordinated organism. As the infant makes sense of her world, she brings patterns of stimulation into line with her own symmetries by orienting, reaching out, crawling, locomoting, and using other, more complex modes of action. Julesz (1971) has suggested that reflectional symmetry is perceived by point-to-point mapping across the two cerebral hemispheres of the brain, joined by the corpus callosum. Van der Helm and Leeuwenberg (1996) have subsequently proposed a holographic modeling of such a process that would account for the superiority of detection of vertical reflective symmetry over other types of symmetries. Their approach implies a different structure for mirror symmetry than for other transformations. While mirror symmetry can also be considered as a transformation, a holographic analysis sees it as a graded rather than all-or-nothing property. A holographic analysis uses identity chains, which describe identities of sequences of symbols. These are more basic than rigid invariance transformations that require the existence of identities, not the other way around. Identity chains in this model are categorized into identity structures that may or may not have holographic regularity, attained when the subchains of an identity chain all describe a same identity structure. Herbert and Humphrey (1996), testing acallosal patients (born without a corpus callosum), suggested that the corpus callosum, which connects the two cerebral hemispheres, plays a role in the detection of vertical mirror symmetry at the midline. This accounts for the ubiquitous salience of vertical reflection but does not explain sensitivity to other symmetry types.

As experience must play a role in all perceptual capacities, various types of symmetry processing abilities must depend on various types and timings of experience. It may also be the case that some symmetries require another level of processing. Symmetry, as studied by authors in this volume in terms of metaphor (Hanson, Chapter 8, and Washburn, Chapter 4), semiotics (Ewins, Chapter 9), iconography (Paul, Chapter 5), algorithm (Wynn, Chapter 3), skill (Franquemont, Chapter 6), and grammar (Roe, Chapter 7), exemplify other levels of processing beyond the ability to see symmetry as a Gestalt (see Kubovy and Strother, Chapter 2).

Sex and Symmetry

While it would be appealing to say that sex differences in symmetry perception, preference, and production are related to the structure of the corpus callosum, which has been found to differ morphologically in male and female infants (deLacoste-Utamsing and Holloway 1982), it is not at all clear that this is true. Furthermore, hemispheric differences between the human sexes are notoriously elusive. Nonetheless, recent research described by Kimura (1999) on body asymmetry and cognitive sex differences suggests that individuals with specific body asymmetries (finger ridge counts, that is, the number of the ridges on fingertips that produce fingerprints) show cognitive test results resembling typical female patterns. Specifically, people with higher numbers of finger ridges on their left hands tend to have better fluency, worse math, less asymmetry on dichotic listening, and better interhemispheric connections. It is tempting to speculate that better interhemispheric connections might be related to preference for vertical reflection patterns, especially since such a hypothesis would fit with Julesz's (1971) framework and related

findings by others already discussed (e.g., Herbert and Humphrey 1996).

Very little is known about sex differences in perception other than vision (Kimura 1999). We know that women have better stereoscopic vision than men do (Petersen 1993), probably making them better at fine movements within personal space, as Kimura (1999) has pointed out. Women also have superior "perceptual speed" in identifying differences between designs (for a description see Kimura 1999). Women may also be better at reading facial and body expression and tone of voice (Hall 1984). Taken together, the evidence with regard to visual perception suggests that women may be more sensitive to visual dynamic structures, particularly at close range. Plane pattern symmetries are important examples of such structures.

Why the Eye Precedes the Hand

The studies reviewed here suggest that visual perception of symmetry patterns long precedes their production. Young children cannot make marks or mold materials into intentional shapes or designs until at least the second year of life. The development of manual specialization (see Young 1977) is gradual, although at birth, motor and perceptual rightward biases are usually present, except for some lower-body reflexes that may be stronger on the left in male neonates (Grattan et al. 1992). Children's first productions are asymmetrical scribbles, although attempts at symmetrical shapes quickly follow (Kellogg 1970). Perhaps the asymmetry of the motor system, not to mention of the representational system, must be overcome in order to produce a symmetrical graphic shape. If this is true, then we should see girls (who may be more symmetrically organized) producing symmetrical constructions earlier and more frequently than boys. This seems to be the case in the research reviewed here, done by my students and myself as well as by Mortensen (1990). Wynn (Chapter 3) provides evidence for gradual evolution of the production of symmetrical objects in the form of knapping stones. Early hand tools are less symmetrical than later productions, suggesting a parallel with the ontogeny of symmetry production in children's drawings. Brain and culture, of course, evolve together, just as they develop together across the individual life span.

The perception of symmetry, particularly vertical reflection, seems to be related to the structure of the human perceptual systems, which must orient the person on a planet that has gravity. The production of representations of such patterns requires the development of those asymmetrically organized systems (for relevant discussions see Arnold 1984; Corballis 1991; and Trevarthan 1978, 1986) that are required to produce a pattern having symmetry. To produce a symmetrical pattern, these systems must operate, despite their own inherent lack of symmetry. In sum, symmetry is a fundamental aspect of perception and action. The asymmetry of the praxic, gestural, and communications systems militates against early symmetrical graphic productions and continues into adulthood to make perception and production of symmetries inherently different. ■

Acknowledgments

The writing of this paper was supported by grants from King's College and the Social Sciences and Humanities Research Council of Canada. The author thanks Lavlet Forde and Kimberly Leung for typing and Jonah Humphrey for producing figures as well as for serving as the subject of filming, although he doesn't remember the latter. ■

References Cited

Adolph, K. E., M. A. Eppler, and E. J. Gibson
1993　Crawling Versus Walking Infants' Perception of Affordances for Locomotion over Sloping Surfaces. *Child Development* 64:1158–1174.

Adolph, K. E., B. Vereijken, and M. A. Denny
1998　Roles of Variability and Experiences in Development of Crawling. *Child Development* 69:840–848.

Amazeen, P. G., E. L. Amazeen, and M. T. Turvey
1998　Breaking the Reflectional Symmetry of Interlimb Coordination Dynamics. *Journal of Motor Behavior* 30:199–216.

Arnheim, R.
1988　*The Power of the Center: A Study of Composition in the Visual Arts.* University of California Press, Berkeley.
1974　*Art and Visual Perception: A Psychology of the Creative Eye, the New Version.* University of California Press, Berkeley.

Arnold, M.
1984　*Memory and the Brain.* Erlbaum, Hillsdale, NJ.

Ballesteros, S., D. Manga, and J. M. Reales
1997　Haptic Discrimination of Bilateral Symmetry in Two-Dimensional and Three-Dimensional Unfamiliar Displays. *Perception & Psychophysics* 59:37–50.

Ballesteros, S., S. Millar, and J. M. Reales
1998　Symmetry in Haptic and in Visual Shape Perception. *Perception & Psychophysics* 60:389–404.

Bayley, N.
1961　*Bayley Scales of Infant Development.* Psychological Corporation, New York.
1993　*Bayley Scales of Infant Development,* 2nd edition. Psychological Corporation, New York.

Beh, H. C., and C. R. Latimer
1997　Symmetry Detection and Orientation Perception: Electro-cortical Responses to Stimuli with Real and Implicit Axes of Orientation. *Australian Journal of Psychology* 49:128–133.

Berk, L.
2000　*Child Development.* Allyn and Bacon, New York.

Bertamini, M., J. D. Friedenberg, and M. Kubovy
1997　Detection of Symmetry and Perceptual Organization: The Way a Lock-and-Key Process Works. *Acta Psychologica* 95:119–140.

Bertenthal, B., and D. Bai
1989　Visual-Vestibular Integration in Early Development. In *Childhood Powered Mobility: Developmental, Technical, and Clinical Perspectives,* edited by K. Jaffe, pp. 43–61. RESNA, Washington, DC.

Berthenthal, B., and J. Pinto
1993　Complementary Processes in the Perception and Production of Human Movements. In *A Dynamic Systems Approach to Development: Applications,* edited by L. B. Smith and E. Thelen, pp. 209–239. MIT Press, Cambridge, MA.

Berthoz, A.
2000　*The Brain's Sense of Movement.* Harvard University Press, Cambridge, MA.

Bingham, G. R., and M. M. Munchinsky
1993　Center of Mass Perception: Perturbation of Symmetry. *Perception & Pychophysics* 54:633–639.

Brazelton, T. B., and J. K. Nugent
1995　*Neonatal Behavioral Assessment Scale.* MacKeith Press, London, UK.

Bronson, G.
1974　The Postnatal Growth of Visual Capacity. *Child Development* 45:873–879.

Corballis, M.
1991　*The Lopsided Ape: Evolution of the Generative Mind.* Oxford University Press, New York.

Corballis, M., and C. E. Roldan
1975　Detection of Symmetry as a Function of Angular Orientation. *Journal of Experimental Psychology: Human Perception and Performance* 1:221–230.

Davi, M., M. A. Doyle, and D. R. Proffitt
1992　The Role of Symmetry in Determining Perceived Centers within Shapes. *Perception &Psychophysics* 52:151–160.

deLacoste-Utamsing, M. C., and R. L. Holloway
1982　Sexual Dimorphism in the Human Corpus Callosum. *Science* 216:1431–1432.

DiFranco, D., D. Muir, and P. Dodwell
1978　Reaching in Very Young Infants. *Perception* 7:385–392.

Dodwell, P.
1983　The Lie Transformation Group Model of Visual Perception. *Perception & Psychophysics* 34:1–16.

Fantz, R. L.
1961　The Origin of Form Perception. *Scientific American* 204:66–72.

Gardner, M.
1979　*The Ambidextrous Universe: Mirror Asymmetry and Time-Reversed Worlds.* Scribner, New York.

Garner, W.
1974　*The Processing of Information and Structure.* Erlbaum, Hillsdale, NJ.

Gibson, E. J., and R. D. Walk
1960　The "Visual Cliff." *Scientific American* 202:64–71.

Gibson, J. J.
1950　*The Perception of the Visual World.* Houghton-Mifflin, Boston.

Golomb, C.
1983   On Imaginary or Real Decalage in Children's Representations: Compositional Trends in Drawings, Completion and Selection Tasks. *Visual Arts Research* 9:71–81.
1987   The Development of Compositional Strategies in Children's Drawings. *Visual Arts Research* 13:42–52.

Grattan, M., E. De Vos, J. Levy, and M. McClintock
1992   Asymmetric Action in the Human Newborn: Sex Differences in Patterns of Organization. *Child Development* 63:273–289.

Hall, J.
1984   *Nonverbal Sex Differences*. Johns Hopkins University Press, Baltimore.

Herbert, A., and G. K. Humphrey
1996   Bilateral Symmetry Detection: Testing a "Callosal" Hypothesis. *Perception* 25:463–480.

Humphrey, D.
1993   Sex Differences in Adults' Drawings. Paper presented at the Canadian Society for Brain, Behavioral, and Cognitive Science, Toronto, July 1993.
1997   Preferences in Symmetries and Symmetries in Drawings: Asymmetries between Ages and Sexes. *Empirical Studies of the Arts* 15:41–60.

Humphrey, D., and G. K. Humphrey
1987   Sex Differences in Infant Reaching. *Neuropsychologia* 25:971–975.

Humphrey, D., and D. Washburn
2002   Pictures in the Mind. King's College, unpublished MS.

Humphrey, G. K., and D. Humphrey
1989   The Role of Structure in Infant Visual Pattern Perception. *Canadian Journal of Psychology* 43:165–182.

Humphrey, G. K., D. Humphrey, D. Muir, and P. Dodwell
1986   Pattern Perception in Infants: Effects of Structure and Transformation. *Journal of Experimental Child Psychology* 41:128–148.

Humphrey, G. K., D. Muir, P. Dodwell, and D. Humphrey
1988   The Perception of Structure in Vector Patterns by 4-Month-Old Infants. *Canadian Journal of Psychology* 42:35–43.

Johansson, G.
1977   Studies on Visual Perception of Locomotion. *Perception* 6:365–376.

Julesz, B.
1971   *Foundations of Cyclopean Perception*. University of Chicago Press, Chicago.

Kellogg, R.
1970   *Analyzing Children's Art*. Mayfield Publishing Company, Palo Alto, CA.

Kimura, D.
1999   *Sex and Cognition*. MIT Press, Cambridge, MA.

Kowler, E., and A. J. Martins
1983   Eye Movements of Preschool Children. *Science* 215:997–999.

Kubovy, M., and J. Wagemans
1998   Grouping by Proximity and Multistability in Dot Lattices: A Quantitative Gestalt Theory. *Psychological Science* 6:225–236.

Labonte, F., Y. Shapiro, P. Cohen, and J. Faubert
1995   A Model for Global Symmetry Detection in Dense Images. *Spatial Vision* 9:33–55.

Lee, D. N., and J. R. Lishman
1975   Visual Proprioceptive Control of Stance. *Journal of Human Movement Studies* 1:87–95.

Locher, P., S. Gray, and C. Nodine
1997   The Structural Framework of Pictorial Balance. *Perception* 25:1419–1436.

Locher, P., and J. Wagemans
1993   The Effects of Element Type and Spatial Grouping on Symmetry Detection. *Perception* 22:565–587.

Mendelson, M., and Lee, S.
1981   The Effects of Symmetry and Contour on Recognition Memory in Children. *Journal of Experimental Child Psychology* 32:373–388.

Mortensen, K. V.
1990   *Forms and Content in Children's Human Figure Drawings*. New York University Press, New York.

Muir, D., and J. Field
1979   Newborn Infants Orient to Sounds. *Child Development* 50:431–436.

Muir, D., D. Humphrey, and G. K. Humphrey
1994   Pattern and Space Perception in Young Infants. *Spatial Vision* 8:141–165.

Palmer, S.
1991   Goodness, Gestalt, Groups and Garner: Local Symmetry Subgroups as a Theory of Figural Goodness. In *The Perception of Structure: Essays in Honor of Wendell Garner*, edited by G. Lockhead and J. Pomerantz, pp. 23–39. American Psychological Association, Washington, DC.

Palmer, S., and K. Hemenway
1978   Orientation and Symmetry: Effects of Multiple, Rotational, and Near Symmetries. *Journal of Experimental Psychology: Human Perception and Performance* 4:691–702.

Patel, S. S., H. E. Bedell, and M. T. Ukwade
1999   Vernier Judgements in the Absence of Regular Shape Information. *Vision Research* 39:2349–2360.

Petersen, R.
1993   *A Sex Difference in Stereoscopic Depth Perception*. Unpublished Master's thesis, Department of Psychology, University of Western Ontario, London, Canada.

Plante, D.
1995   *Contents and Themes of Boys' and Girls' Drawings.* Unpublished Senior Honors thesis, Department of Psychology, University of Western Ontario, London, Canada.

Poincaré, H.
1952   *Science and Hypothesis.* Dover, New York.

Regan, D., and M. Cynader
1979   Neurons in Area 18 Cat Visual Cortex Selectively Sensitive to Changing Size: Non-Linear Interactions between Responses to Two Edges. *Vision Research* 19:699-711.

Royer, F.
1981   Detection of Symmetry. *Journal of Experimental Psychology: Human Perception and Performance* 7:1186–1210.

Schiff, W.
1965   Perception of Impending Collision. *Psychological Monographs* 79:1–26.

Sekuler, A. B.
1996   Axis of Elongation Can Determine Reference Frames for Object Perception. *Canadian Journal of Experimental Psychology* 50:270–279.

Shepard, R. N.
1994   Perceptual—Cognitive Universals as Reflections of the World. *Psychonomic Bulletin & Review* 1:2–28.

Shimaya, A.
1997   Perception of Complex Line Drawings. *Journal of Experimental Psychology: Human Perception and Performance* 23:25–50.

Stothers, M.
1997   *Spatial Analysis, Perception of Stability, and Fluency: Cognitive Sex Differences in Children's Drawings.* Unpublished Senior Honors thesis, Department of Psychology, University of Western Ontario, London, Canada.

Szlyk, J. P., I. Rock, and C. B. Fisher
1995   Level of Processing in the Perception of Symmetrical Forms Viewed from Different Angles. *Spatial Vision* 9:139–150.

Telford, L., and I. P. Howard
1996   Role of Optical Flow Field Asymmetry in the Perception of Heading During Linear Motion. *Perception & Psychophysics* 59:37–50.

te Pas, S. F., A. M. L. Kappers, and J. J. Koenderink
1998   Detection of Spatial Discontinuities in First-Order Optical Flow Fields. *Perception & Psychophysics* 59:567–579.

Thelen, E., and L. Smith
1994   *A Dynamic Systems Approach to the Development of Cognition and Action.* MIT Press, Cambridge, MA.

Treisman, A.
1986   Features and Objects in Visual Processing. *Scientific American* 225:114–125.

Trevarthan, C.
1978   Manipulative Strategies of Baboons and Origins of Cerebral Asymmetry. In *Asymmetrical Function of the Brain*, edited by M. Kinsbourne, pp. 329–391. Cambridge University Press, Cambridge, UK.
1986   Form, Significance, and Psychological Potential of Hand Gestures of Infants. In *The Biological Foundations of Gestures: Motor and Semiotic Aspects,* edited by J. L. Nespoulous, P. Perron, and A. Lecours, pp. 149–202. Erlbaum: Hillsdale, NJ.

van der Helm, P. A., and E. L. J. Leeuwenberg
1996   Goodness of Visual Regularities: A Nontransformational Approach. *Psychological Review* 103:429–456.
1999   A Better Approach to Goodness: Reply to Wagemans. *Psychological Review* 106:622–630.

Vance, A.
1999   *Perception of Pictorial Balance in Untrained Adult and Children's Drawings.* Unpublished Senior Honors thesis, Department of Psychology, University of Western Ontario, London, Canada.

Washburn, D., and D. Crowe
1988   *Symmetries of Culture: Theory and Practice of Plane Pattern Analysis.* University of Washington Press, Seattle.

Wenderoth, P.
1997a   The Role of Implicit Axes of Bilateral Symmetry in Orientation Processing. *Australian Journal of Psychology* 49:176–181.
1997b   The Effects on Bilateral-Symmetry Detection of Multiple Symmetry, Near Symmetry and Axis Orientation. *Perception* 26:891–904.

Wolfe, J. M., and S. R. Friedham-Hill
1992   On the Role of Symmetry in Visual Search. *Psychological Science* 3:194-198.

Young, G.
1977   Manual Specialization in Infancy: Implications for Lateralization of Brain Development and Neurological Theory. In *Language Development and Neurological Theory*, edited by S. J. Segalowitz and F. A. Guber, pp. 289–311. Academic Press, New York.

Zabrodsky, H., and D. Algom
1994   Continuous Symmetry: A Model for Human Figural Perception. *Spatial Vision* 8:455–467.

Zebrowitz, L. A., L. Voinesuc, and M. A. Collins
1996   "Wide-Eyed" and "Crooked-Faced": Determinants of Perceived and Real Honesty across the Life Span. *Personality & Social Psychology Bulletin* 22:1258–1269.

CHAPTER TWO

The Perception of Band Patterns

Going Beyond Geometry

Michael Kubovy and Lars Strother

THE PURPOSE OF THIS CHAPTER is to bring the psychology of perception to bear on the characterization of regular patterns that repeat themselves in one dimension, that is, band designs. This classification of patterns does not concern the shape of motifs or their arrangement but the isometries that move a pattern along an axis or around a point. Our study concerns the perception of the isometries that characterize a band design. We show that the perception of the symmetries of a band design is exquisitely sensitive to changes in the spatial arrangement of motifs even when these changes do not change its formal classification.

In this chapter, we argue for a perception-based description of band designs. We show that the group-theoretic description of patterns fails to capture the way band designs are perceived and propose some explanations for this discrepancy. Before we go any further, let us state our working assumption: that the phenomena we discuss here are universal, that is, not culture dependent. In other words, we believe that all humans see patterns in the same way, even though they may interpret them differently.

The designs we encounter rarely conform precisely to the rules of geometry (Washburn and Crowe 1988:53). Actual designs deviate from the mathematical ideal in at least three ways: (1) the designs we encounter are finite, whereas for the mathematician, one- and two-dimensional patterns must be infinite; (2) copies of a design's motif are often imprecise; and (3) isometries may be imperfectly executed: for example, motifs related by translation may not be equally spaced. So we are forced to exercise "some imagination and good will" (Grünbaum and Shephard 1987:Figure 5.2.12) to decide which pattern underlies an actual design. Although the

remainder of this chapter will focus on designs that conform to the rules of geometry, we have no doubt that our discussion can be generalized to real-world designs in which we can recognize an underlying mathematical ideal.

Patterns that conform to geometry pose a different problem: two patterns of the same formal type (Grünbaum and Shephard 1987:Section 5.2) may *look* different for reasons that cannot be captured by group theory. These differences can only be explained by reference to the workings of the visual system. We have not found many discussions of such perceptual effects; Shubnikov and Koptsik (1974:81–82) are a notable exception. They point out that in many band designs of type *p111*[1] (Figure 2.1)

Figure 2.1 A *p111* band design.

the translation axis is polar . . . [which] gives the impression of forward motion. . . . [These bands are] often encountered in applied art and architecture . . . in cases in which it is desired to use the disposition of the figures to emphasize forward motion in one particular direction, e.g., in the decoration of underground subway passages and intersections intended to produce a flow of people in one direction.

To start our exploration, we need to distinguish between mathematical descriptions of patterns and perceptual descriptions of patterns. This move is common in psychology. We often distinguish between events that occur in the physical world and how they are experienced. To use a familiar example, the conundrum (due to Berkeley), If a tree fell in the forest and no one was there to hear it, did it make noise? makes clear that we must distinguish between two aspects of noise: a physical event (the pressure wave caused by the falling of the tree)—which we call ϕ–noise—and the corresponding mental event (the *effect* of such a wave on the experience of a person)—ψ–noise. So, of course, the answer to the conundrum is, Yes, the tree made a noise, but it was a ϕ–noise.[2]

Figure 2.2 A *pm11* band design.

Figure 2.3 The *pm11* band design of Figure 2.2, with symmetry elements indicated. The vertical lines are lines of reflection (transverse mirrors). The mirrors fall into two transitivity classes, *r* and *s*. The arrow represents the direction and the length of the translational symmetry of the pattern.

In this chapter, we will restrict ourselves to the perception of one-dimensional patterns (band designs). We will focus on two issues, both involving discrepancies between the mathematical description of patterns and the way patterns are perceived. The first deals with the way symmetries such as reflection and rotation are perceived in all band designs. It is the phenomenon of *locality* (rather than *globality*) of perceived symmetries. The second deals with the effect of changes in the location of copies of the motif of a band design while its symmetry elements remain unchanged—and therefore its formal description remains fixed—on the perception of its symmetries. Such changes can have a striking effect on the appearance of a band design.

The Local Nature of Perceived Symmetries
Description of the Problem

Consider a *pm11* band design (Figure 2.2).[3] Figure 2.3 shows its group diagram—a diagram that represents its symmetry elements: the translation vector and transverse mirrors[4] (we discuss the letters that label the mirrors in the next paragraph). The first, and perhaps most fundamental, way our perception of a *pm11* band design deviates from group theory involves the perception of its mirror symmetry. Mathematically, the mirror symmetry of a *pm11* pattern maps the pattern onto itself. As we will see in a moment, this implies that the symmetries of a band design are global. But of course, we can never encounter an infinite pattern, and if we did, we could never see it. It is not even clear how to

imagine it. Therefore, for our perceptual system, transformations are necessarily *local*.

To present the distinction between global and local transformations, we have labeled some of the mirrors in Figure 2.3 *r* and others *s*. If you translate the band design by one (or more) times the length of the translation vector, the *r* mirrors move onto *r* mirrors while the *s* mirrors move onto *s* mirrors. That is why Grünbaum and Shephard (1987:Figure 1.4.1) say that the *r* mirrors form one *transitivity class,* whereas the *s* mirrors form another.

It will be easier for us to present our argument if we think of these mirrors not as optical devices, but as axes of rotation (hinges if you will) in the plane of the pattern, around which patterns can be rotated 180 degrees in depth. Focus on the third mirror from the right, an *s* mirror. To make the group-theoretic conception of the reflection symmetry of this band design concrete, we can imagine the entire band design rotating about this axis. This means that none of the other mirrors is "active" at the time; they are merely "carried along" in this rotation. We have illustrated this in the top panel of Figure 2.4. One can think of the mirrors as being alternative ways to map the band design onto itself. The mathematician's view of multiple mirrors is that they are disjunctive operations: r_1 or s_1 or r_2 or . . .

The group-theoretic representation of patterns does not capture how the untutored person sees mirror symmetry. We *see* mirrors as multiple concurrent transformations of parts of the pattern. We see a *pm11* band design as if it consisted of multiple pairs of motifs concurrently rotating in depth around vertical axes (Figure 2.4, bottom). Why pairs? Because we cannot visualize *all* the mirrors operating concurrently. Consider the second motif from the right in Figure 2.3. To its left there is an *r* mirror, to its right, an *s* mirror. Only the unhinged will put hinges on both the right and the left side of the motif: it must turn toward you or away from you. You cannot imagine it rotating both ways at the same time. If you see the symmetry that relates the two rightmost motifs as a rotation about an *s* mirror, they must rotate *together* about this axis. Consequently, these two motifs must form a perceptual pair. If we propagate this pairing from right to left, all the other motifs will join into pairs, and the mirror symmetry of the pattern will be seen as a collection of *local* transformations about the *s* mirrors. If we had started our

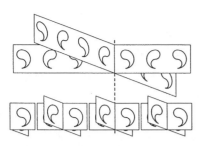

Figure 2.4 Top: A mirror symmetry of *pm11* as conceived by mathematicians. Bottom: how we see rotational symmetry in *pm11*.

Figure 2.5 A *p112* band design, with symmetry elements indicated. The diamonds are centers of rotation, which fall into two transitivity classes, *a* and *b*. The arrow represents the direction and the length of the translational symmetry of the pattern.

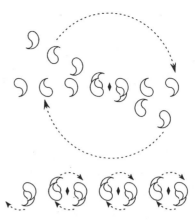

Figure 2.6 Top: a rotational symmetry of *p112* as conceived by mathematicians. Bottom: how we see rotational symmetry in *p112*.

Figure 2.7 The Gestalt principle of grouping by proximity.

construal of the pattern from the motif on the left, we would have seen the mirror symmetry of the pattern as a collection of local transformations about the *r* mirrors.

Let there be no misunderstanding: we are not claiming that we see the symmetry of this band design as if it involved multiple concurrent rotations; the notion of rotation is a convenient device for our exposition. What we are claiming is that we perceive more than one axis of mirror reflection at a time, all belonging to the same transitivity class.

Therefore, in a *pm11* band design we either see reflections about *r* mirrors or about *s* mirrors. In that sense, our perception is disjunctive. But once some psychological process (attention, for example) determines which of these two classes will be suppressed—say, *s*—we see all the mirrors of the salient class—in this case *r*—operating conjunctively: r_1 and r_2 and r_3 and . . .

An analogous argument holds for the local nature of perceived rotational symmetry, as you can see in Figures 2.5 and 2.6.

Grouping and the Salience of Transitivity Classes

In the preceding section, we wrote as if the two transitivity classes of symmetry elements were equally salient to start with. The reader may have gathered that the only difference between them is that they cannot coexist

perceptually. In many band designs, however, the two transitivity classes might not be equally salient. This is because the *Gestalt principles of grouping* organize the way we see collections of visual objects.

Of these principles, grouping by proximity (Figure 2.7) is most relevant to our discussion. Compare the two band designs in Figure 2.8 to the one in Figure 2.2. In the latter, pairs of motifs are approximately equidistant from the mirrors: the two transitivity classes of mirrors are about equally noticeable. However, in each of the band designs in Figure 2.8 only one transitivity class is readily perceived. There is a discrepancy between the mathematician's description, the ϕ and the perceiver's description, the ψ Therefore, we need two notations: a crystallographic notation of the form *pxyz* and a notation of what we see. In the latter, we replace the usual notation with π*uvw* to denote the perceived symmetries of the pattern. If we modify the standard crystallographic notation slightly, we can emphasize the two transitivity classes of mirrors in *pm11* by writing $pm_{(2)}11$. In Figure 2.2 the two transitivity classes are about equally salient, so we notate its perceived structure $\pi m_{(2)}11$. But in the band designs of Figure 2.8 we do not see the transitivity class equally, so we notate their perceived structure $\pi m_{(1)}11$.

The reason that grouping by proximity can cause

Figure 2.8 Two *pm11* band designs. In each, one transitivity class of mirrors is suppressed.

Figure 2.9 Two *p112* band designs. In each, one transitivity class of centers of rotation is suppressed.

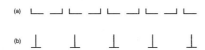

Figure 2.10 Grünbaum and Shephard's (1987) refinement of pattern *pm11*. Panel (a) represents the primitive version of the band design. Panel (b) represents its refinement.

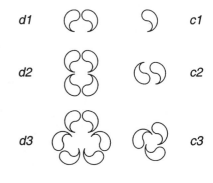

Figure 2.11 Examples of finite patterns.

Figure 2.12 A *pmm2* band design.

the suppression of a transitivity class of symmetry elements lies in the fact that it creates *compound motifs*. These compound motifs are treated by the visual system *as if they were connected*.[5] We see a similar effect in the salience of centers of rotation in Figure 2.9.

To better understand how grouping by proximity decreases the salience of one class of mirrors, we draw on Grünbaum and Shephard's (1987:Figure 5.2.6, Table 5.2.2) refinement of the mathematical classification of patterns. We focus our discussion on the refined pattern they built on the *pm11* band design. Both band designs in Figure 2.10 are properly described as *pm11,* and neither belongs in one of the other categories of band designs. Nevertheless, they are perceptually and, as Grünbaum and Shephard (1987) show, mathematically different. In panel (a), the motif is asymmetric. In panel (b), the motif has one axis of mirror symmetry: its symmetry is *d1* (*d* stands for "dihedral symmetry"; see Figure 2.11). For our purposes, Grünbaum and Shephard's procedure for refining patterns simulates the effects of perceptual grouping.

Rules of Symmetry Precedence
The Precedence of Mirrors over Half Turns
Grouping has another effect on the perception of band

designs, more profound than the suppression of transitivity classes: it can cause the suppression of *symmetries*. Consider the *pmm2* band design in Figure 2.12.[6] Only a person who has been exposed to group theory is likely to say that a half turn is one of its symmetries. Again we have found a discrepancy between the mathematician's description, the φ–pattern, and the perceiver's description, the ψ–pattern. We see *pmm2* band designs as π*mm1*.[7] How shall we explain the diminished salience of the half turn in *pmm2* band designs? First, we note that just as in *pm11* band designs, there are two transitivity classes of transverse mirrors and that we tend to see only one class of them at a time. Second, recall that as soon as one transitivity class of mirrors is selected, the symmetry operations are local, that is, they seem to operate concurrently. That is why the phenomenon has nothing to do with the fact that it appears in a band design. It is a phenomenon that characterizes the *individual compound motifs* formed by perceptual grouping in the band design. Consider the finite pattern in Figure 2.13. It has the same symmetry as one compound motif in *pmm2* (Figure 2.12), that is, *d2* (Figure 2.11), which has two perpendicular mirrors and a center of a twofold rotational symmetry (a half turn) that falls on the intersection of these two mirrors. As we conjectured, here as in the band design,

Figure 2.13 A finite pattern whose symmetry elements are two orthogonal mirrors and a half turn. The half turn is not likely to be seen spontaneously.

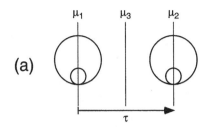

(a)

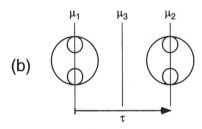

(b)

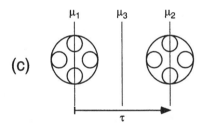

(c)

Figure 2.14 (a) Two copies of a *d1* motif whose mirrors are parallel. These two copies can be mapped onto each other either by translation or by reflection. The reflection is suppressed. (b) Same for copies of a *d2* motif. (c) Same for copies of a *d4* motif.

the half turn is suppressed, and we spontaneously notice only the two mirrors. We think of this observation as an instantiation of a general rule of symmetry precedence.

Perceived Symmetry Precedence 1: Let f be a finite pattern whose symmetry group is d2. The half turn is suppressed; the mirrors are perceived (Figure 2.13).

The Precedence of Translation over Reflection

In our earlier discussion of *pm11* band designs, we noted that only one transitivity class of mirrors is perceived at one time. We then compared the *pm11* band design in Figure 2.2 to the *pm11* band designs in Figure 2.8 and

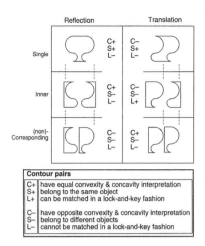

	Reflection		Translation	
Single		C+ S+ L−		C− S+ L−
Inner		C+ S− L−		C− S− L+
(non-) Corresponding		C− S− L−		C+ S− L−

Contour pairs	
C+	have equal convexity & concavity interpretation
S+	belong to the same object
L+	can be matched in a lock-and-key fashion
C−	have opposite convexity & concavity interpretation
S−	belong to different objects
L−	cannot be matched in a lock-and-key fashion

Figure 2.15. Summary of the conditions in the experiments of Baylis and Driver (1995) and Bertamini et al. (1997).

observed that grouping by proximity suppresses one transitivity class of mirrors. In this section, we will show that the suppression of one class of mirrors goes hand in hand with the increased perceptibility of translation.

In Figure 2.14a we have replaced two compound motifs from Figure 2.8 with two copies of a *d1* finite design. It is easy to see that because the axes of reflection of the two copies of the finite pattern (μ_1 and μ_2 in Figure 2.14a) are parallel, two isometries can map each one of these motifs onto the other: translation (indicated by τ) and reflection (indicated by μ_3). It is immediately apparent that the reflection is suppressed. From Figure 2.14b and 2.14c it is also easy to see that it is sufficient that the two copies of the motif have parallel mirrors: regardless of their order of dihedral symmetry, mirror μ_3 is suppressed.

Perceived Symmetry Precedence 2: Let f_1 and f_2 be copies of a finite pattern with dihedral symmetry, and let a mirror in f_1, μ_1, be parallel to a mirror in f_2, μ_2. Then the mirror that reflects f_1 onto f_2, μ_3, will be suppressed and the translation, τ, will be salient.

Data collected by Baylis and Driver (1995) followed by a series of experiments by Bertamini et al. (1997) support the claim we have just made: we often more readily see mirror symmetry within objects than between them. Figure 2.15 summarizes the conditions of some of the relevant experiments. Observers were asked to detect—as rapidly as they could—whether two curved contours were related by translation or by reflection. Pairs of contours were either equal or opposite in

Figure 2.16 Band design *p1a1*, with its symmetry elements. The dashed horizontal line is the axis of glide reflection.

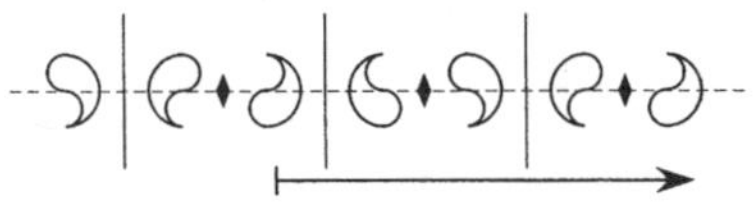

Figure 2.17 Band design *pma2*, with its symmetry elements.

Figure 2.19 Two *pma2* band designs grouped so that the most salient symmetry is rotation.

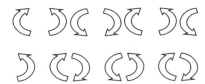

Figure 2.20 Our interpretation of the way Figure 2.19 is seen.

Figure 2.18 Two *pma2* band designs grouped so that the most salient symmetry is reflection.

convexity and concavity and belonged either to a single object or to two different objects. In some of the cases in which contours belonged to separate objects, the contours could be matched in a lock-and-key fashion.

The contours in the figures in the left column of Figure 2.15 were related by reflection. The observers detected the mirror symmetry of contours belonging to a single object (Figure 2.15, left-upper panel) more easily than the mirror symmetry of contours belonging to two objects (left-center panel). The contours in the right column were related by translation. The observers detected the parallelism (translation symmetry) of contours belonging to two objects (Figure 2.15, right-lower panel) more easily than the parallelism of contours belonging to one object (right-upper panel).

The Case of Glide Reflection
Glide reflection is easy to see when it is not accompanied by other symmetries (Figure 2.16). But when it is accompanied by other symmetries, as in the *pma2* band design (Figure 2.17), we will see that under some conditions it is suppressed and under other conditions it is salient.

The Precedence of Glide Reflection over Rotation
When we group motifs by proximity in the *pma2* band design so that the motifs are close to each other on either side of a mirror, the most salient symmetry is reflection

(Figure 2.18). The band design has three other symmetries: glide reflection, rotation, and translation. Glide reflection is perhaps more salient than rotation. We believe that this is the case because the compound motifs, with symmetry *d1*, alternate between facing up and down.

The Precedence of Reflection over Glide Reflection
When we group motifs by proximity in the *pma2* band design so that the motifs are close to each other on either side of a center of rotation, the most salient symmetry is rotation (Figure 2.19).[8] Here the compound motifs suggest rotation in opposite directions, clockwise and counterclockwise, as illustrated in Figure 2.20. The compound motifs appear to be related by reflection, and the glide reflection that links them is suppressed.

Conclusion
Before mathematicians began to apply the tools of crystallographic classification to patterns collected from a variety of cultures, most patterns were described according to the appearance of the motifs (Chapman 1995; Christie 1969). When authors such as Washburn and Crowe (1988) introduced formal crystallographic methods, much was gained. However, something was also lost: the *perceptual effect* of the pattern.

The product of this first attempt to extend the mathematics of pattern description takes a step back toward the analysis of motifs because it draws attention to the local structure of patterns. Nevertheless, our approach does not abandon the idea that understanding symmetry is central to the understanding of patterns. It requires a careful analysis of the perceptual effects of variations in patterns, to which crystallography-based methods of analysis are blind.

The perceptual effects we have uncovered are best considered second-order effects. The first-order effects on which they are based are the result of Gestalt phenomena, primarily grouping by proximity. When asymmetric motifs are brought into proximity, they form compound motifs that are not asymmetric. The emergence of compound motifs brings forth second-order effects: the suppression of symmetries. Symmetries that are perceptible in band designs where grouping does not occur are often suppressed in less uniform ones.

We are not the first to show that some symmetries are easier to see than others. Mach (1996) demonstrated that mirror symmetry is more salient than translation and easier to detect when the axis of symmetry is vertical. Our observations of band designs have taken this further. We believe that in patterns with multiple symmetries or multiple axes of symmetry, the salience of symmetries is largely determined by the formation of subjective compound motifs: grouping is pivotal to symmetry salience in band designs. We have proposed two general rules of precedence and have showed that the relative salience of symmetries can be strongly influenced by grouping, especially grouping by proximity.

The analyses we have presented here have implications for basic research in perception. The phenomena we have described are no less compelling than the classic Gestalt principles of grouping. Nevertheless, they probably occupy a different place in the machinery of what is often called middle-level perception. The function of the Gestalt principles is probably to suggest to the visual system putative objects that could be formed from discrete arrays of input elements. Mechanisms of symmetry perception have probably evolved in the service of object recognition and comparison.

Our work may not only be of value to those who study perception, but also to those who study patterns in cultural contexts. As we stated at the beginning of this chapter, our working assumption has been that the phenomena we have discussed are universal, that is, not culture dependent. We have no empirical evidence in support of this assumption beyond our inevitably limited personal experience and our knowledge of the cross-cultural invariance of other perceptual phenomena. It is therefore possible that our assumption is mistaken. For example, the relative prevalence of different symmetries decorating artifacts in a particular culture and the relative salience of these symmetries may be a reflection of the culture's ways of thinking. That is why a cross-cultural inquiry into the validity of our assumption is of considerable importance. ■

Notes

1. We use the standard crystallographic notation as summarized by Washburn and Crowe (1988:Figure 2.26).

2. This, of course, was not Berkeley's position: he claimed that *esse* is *percipi* or *percipere*; that is, to exist is to be perceived or to perceive. Thus, according to him, "there is no ϕ noise without ψ noise."

3. We have chosen a strongly asymmetric motif. We believe that our conclusions would not have been different if we had chosen a different motif. We suspect that if we had chosen a motif that looked less asymmetric, the effects we discuss here would be less striking.

4. In this chapter, all translation vectors are drawn horizontally, and therefore all transverse mirrors are vertical.

5. See Grünbaum and Shephard's (1987:205, Figure 5.1.1g) discussion of discrete patterns and connected motifs.

6. According to Cesàro (1992:81–82), this is the most common type of frieze, representing 41 percent of the friezes among the 135 sampled by Lehmann (1920) from fifty-five cultures.

7. Let there be no misunderstanding: we are not claiming to have discovered a group *pmm1*. The notation π*mm1* amounts to no more than a listing of the symmetries perceived in *pmm2*. A *pmm1* group cannot exist because the corresponding set of isometries is not closed under the product of the transverse and the longitudinal reflections, which violates the closure axiom of group theory. The relevant theorem: *A half turn about a point P is the product (in any order) of the two reflections in any two lines perpendicular at P* (Martin 1982:Theorem 6.12, slightly paraphrased).

8. We have looked for examples of such groupings in *pma2* band designs but found none in Grünbaum and Shephard (1987), Stevens (1980), or Shubnikov and Koptsik (1974).

References Cited

Baylis, G., and J. Driver

1995   Obligatory Edge Assignment in Vision: The Role of Figure and Part Segmentation in Symmetry Detection. *Journal of Experimental Psychology: Human Perception and Performance* 21:1323–1342.

Bertamini, M., J. D. Friedenberg, and M. Kubovy

1997   Detection of Symmetry and Perceptual Organization: The Way a Lock-and-Key Process Works. *Acta Psychologica* 95:119–140.

Cesàro, A. L.

1992   *Simmetrie, Ordine Percettivo e Arte Ornamentale.* Unpublished Master's thesis, Università degli studie di Trieste, Italy.

Chapman, K. M.

1995   *Pueblo Pottery Designs.* Dover, New York.

Christie, A. H.

1969   *Pattern Design: An Introduction to the Study of Formal Ornament.* Dover Publications, New York.

Grünbaum, B., and G. C. Shephard

1987   *Tilings and Patterns.* Freeman, New York.

Lehmann, J.

1920   *Die Ornamente der Natur—und Halbkulturvölker, mit einem Beitrag zur Entwicklung der Ornamente und ihrer Verwertung für Kunstgewerbe und Architektur. Selbstverlag,* Frankfurt, Germany.

Mach, E.

1996   *The Analysis of Sensations and the Relation of the Physical to the Psychical.* Thoemmes Press, Bristol, UK.

Martin, G. E.

1982   *Transformation Geometry: An Introduction to Symmetry.* Springer-Verlag, New York.

Shubnikov, A. V., and V. A. Koptsik

1974   *Symmetry in Science and Art.* Plenum Press, New York.

Stevens, P. S.

1980   *Handbook of Regular Patterns: An Introduction to Symmetry in Two Dimensions.* MIT Press, Cambridge, MA.

Washburn, D. K., and D. W. Crowe

1988   *Symmetries of Culture: Theory and Practice of Plane Pattern Analysis.* University of Washington Press, Seattle.

CHAPTER THREE

Evolutionary Developments in the Cognition of Symmetry

Thomas Wynn

SYMMETRY IS UBIQUITOUS in human material culture. It appears in the form of artifacts, buildings, and built environments all over the world. It is a central component of decorative systems in almost all human culture and also a component of games (e.g., string games) and mathematical puzzles (e.g., tessellations). In many of these cases, the symmetry results from the application of transformational rules: simple figures repeated and "moved" to produce intricate patterns. Symmetry is so fundamental in Western culture, at least, that it is often a metaphor for balance and regularity (e.g., the "symmetrical" arrangement of keys in *The Marriage of Figaro*). Moreover, it is often endowed with meaning, carrying explicit and implicit information about fundamental values of a culture (Washburn 1999). This kind of symmetry is part of the cultural knowledge carried by every artisan of a community and as such must be learned from earlier artisans. Humans do not come endowed with specific rules of symmetrical transformations: we must learn them.

Symmetry is also ubiquitous in the natural world. It is a well-known feature of crystal growth, resulting from the chemical structures of the molecules themselves. It also acts as a principle in biological growth and development, as in the symmetrical duplications of supernumerary appendages in beetles (Bateson 1972); here the source probably lies in the genes regulating growth. Symmetry is a feature of the overall body plans of many organisms, from microscopic foraminifera to large vertebrates. Natural selection has even worked to attune the perceptual and cognitive structures of organisms to the detection of symmetry. Asymmetry of body plan signals poor health, poor reproductive potential, and low evolutionary prospects (Gangestaad 1997). In this sense, natural symmetry is also endowed with meaning: the individual most sensitive to symmetry may have had greater reproductive success.

How are cultural symmetry and natural symmetry related? Do the complex tessellations of modern decorative systems result simply from a heightened or exaggerated ability to perceive and detect symmetry? Is it a feature of neurologically based pattern recognition ability? Or is something else needed, some transformational knowledge or ability unknown in any other living being?

The following argument will suggest that it is a bit of both. Human cognition has evolved a cognitive/perceptual system that is finely attuned to the detection of symmetry and, importantly, to the production of symmetry. It is a development that can be traced archaeologically over fifteen hundred millennia of human evolution. However, this development, as interesting as it is, is not sufficient to account for the symmetrical patterns of modern culture. For these we must invoke another cognitive mechanism for which there is no evidence until very late in human evolution, something we can term *algorithmic thought*.

The evidence I will employ is primarily archaeological, and some discussion of the archaeology of mind is necessary to set the stage.

The Archaeology of Mind

The products of minds can provide clues to the organization and working of the minds themselves. Most commonly, the products of minds are actions of some kind, and as action is ephemeral, it is necessary to observe or record it if we want to make inferences about the mind itself. This places obvious limits on our ability to make inferences about the minds of individuals who lived long ago: we cannot observe their actions. Some actions do affect material things, which consequently "record" some features of the original action. Archaeology consists of a set of methods for reconstructing past action from patterns of material things that exist in the present. If our reconstructions of past action are reliable, we should be able to make inferences about the minds behind the action.

There are some obvious methodological caveats to an archaeology of cognition. The first is the problem of resolution. Most interpretations in cognitive science are based on experiments, in which particular problems are posed directly to subjects or, in the case of ethology, on extensive observation of individuals in natural settings. In both methods, emphasis is on control and replicability, both of which require a large number of examples from similar, if not identical, circumstances. There is considerable disagreement in cognitive ethology, for example, about the usefulness of anecdotal evidence. If a primatologist observes a single instance of a chimpanzee smashing a rock and using the sharp pieces to cut a vine, must we add stone tool use to the natural repertoire of chimpanzees? Archaeologists confront just this problem regularly because archaeological evidence is largely anecdotal. We have no control over the circumstances in which the actions occurred. We cannot take controlled samples of action streams or attempt to duplicate circumstances except in the most global sense (for example, we can sometimes determine that a stone tool was used for a particular class of task, say, butchery, but cannot reconstruct the circumstances of that particular use). We must accept a great deal of latitude when we conclude that two tools or two reconstructed actions are the same. This problem is exacerbated by the problem of preservation. The vast majority of the material evidence of action is rapidly destroyed, leaving a nonrandom representation for later examination. Moreover, what is not destroyed is subject to the serendipity of discovery. We do not have a continuous, coherent record of past action. An apt metaphor for the archaeological record is a jigsaw puzzle, most of whose pieces are missing. When archaeologists do a good job, we can describe one piece and place it somewhere in the vicinity of its position in time. If we are very lucky, this piece may fit with another. However, local sequences or small-scale patterns of pieces are very rare. This does not mean that we cannot make interpretations of the past, but it does mean that our interpretations must always be relatively coarse grained. We can often reconstruct the "big" picture but can rarely detect fine-grained images.

A second caveat, with particular relevance to the archaeology of mind, is the problem of minimum necessary competence. Archaeologists can only assess the minimum abilities required to produce a particular pattern. We cannot logically eliminate the possibility

that our prehistoric subjects employed simple reasoning when producing and using stone tools and much more complex reasoning in archaeologically invisible domains. Our assessment becomes more reliable, however, if several lines of evidence point to the same abilities. If our reconstructions of foraging, tool manufacture, tool use, raw material selectivity, group size, and size of home range all point to the same levels of cognitive ability, then our interpretation of minimum competence becomes more reliable. It is not always necessary to kowtow to the catchy phrase "absence of evidence is not evidence of absence." Sometimes absence of evidence is a very persuasive argument for absence.

The advantage that the archaeological record holds over other evolutionary methodologies is that it is able to provide long sequences of evolutionary development. These sequences are not predictions from comparative evidence or interpolations from the spotty fossil record but actual, chronologically ordered sequences of hominid[1] products. The record of hominid tools is by far the most voluminous record we have from human evolution: archaeologists have recovered millions of stone tools. True, the record is not complete. There are chronological gaps, especially for the early periods, and there are geographic gaps, in areas where little or no archaeology has been done. Nevertheless, despite these gaps the archaeological record is more complete than the fossil record. The archaeological record presents a picture of technological change over a period of almost 2.5 million years. From this picture, we can detect the appearance of technological innovations, identify periods of change and stasis, and even assess rates of change (in some ideal cases of preservation, archaeologists can make reliable interpretations of tool function, but these situations tend to be rare).

The following discussion will begin with a summary of the relevant evidence, being as atheoretical as possible. I will begin with examples of chimpanzee drawing. Though not archaeological in the usual sense of the word, these drawings and paintings are products of the minds of our nearest relatives. As such, they can act as a basis for comparison. What can humans do that chimpanzees cannot, and when and perhaps why did these developments occur? After this, I will present a chronological sequence of prehistoric products, starting with the earliest stone tools of our Pliocene forbearers.

The Ability of Apes

Nonhuman primates do not produce symmetries. The only possible example of symmetry produced by apes in the wild is the chimpanzee sleeping nest, which has a kind of radial symmetry that is produced when the individual reaches out from a central position and pulls branches inward. Here the symmetry is a direct consequence of a motor habit pattern, and one need not posit some idea of symmetry. There are no other ethological examples, at least to my knowledge. However, there has been a significant amount of research with captive apes, especially chimpanzees, including a fascinating literature about chimpanzee art and drawing, from which one can examine the ways apes arrange elements in space.

Work with ape art has been of two kinds. In the first, researchers present an ape with appropriate media (finger paints, brushes and paint, etc.) and encourage it to create. In the second, researchers control the productions by supplying paper with predrawn patterns. The former is the more "archaeological" in that researchers have not tried to coax particular pattern productions. Perhaps not surprisingly, these spontaneous productions are patterned primarily by motor patterns. Fan shapes are common, as are zigzags produced by back and forth arm motion (Figure 3.1a). Desmond Morris (1962), the most well-known researcher in ape art, thought that these productions may demonstrate a sense of balance and tried to coax it out with a series of experiments using sheets with stimulus figures already printed on (Figure 3.1b), following the earlier lead of Schiller (1951). Morris's work led to a number of subsequent experiments by others using similar techniques. The results have been enigmatic at best. Most chimpanzees presented with a figure that is offset from the center of the paper will mark on the opposite side or on the figure itself (Figure 3.1b). Morris suggested, cautiously, that this confirmed a notion of balance. Later Smith (1973) and Boysen (Boysen et al. 1987) confirmed these results but argued that the pattern resulted from the chimpanzee's placing marks toward the center of the vacant space: balance was an accident.

It is hard to know what to make of this evidence. First, even with the few experimental subjects, there was a lot of individual variability. Indeed, each chimpanzee had an idiosyncratic approach to both the controlled

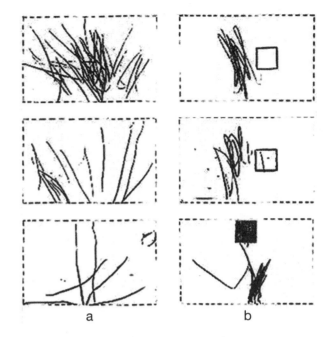

a   b

Figure 3.1 Chimpanzee drawings (Morris (1962). The fan patterns on the left reflect the prevailing biomechanics of the task, a pull stroke. The patterns on the right exemplify the chimpanzees' tendency to fill spaces and mark on stimulus figures. A sense of balance is not necessary for any of these compositions but cannot be ruled out.

and uncontrolled drawing. Second, most repetitive patterns resulted from repetitive motor actions. Nevertheless, the individuals did appear to place their marks nonrandomly and did attend to features of the visual field. Other, nongraphic experiments have indicated that chimpanzees can be taught to select the central element of a linear array (Rholes and Devine 1967), so chimpanzees can clearly perceive patterns in which balance is a component. However, they do not appear able to produce symmetrical patterns.

The Archaeological Record
The Biomechanics and Cognitive Prerequisites of Stone Tool Manufacture

To make a stone tool, the knapper[2] must control actions directed at a relatively small spatial field. In the simplest kind of knapping,[3] the knapper strikes a cobble with another, usually harder stone (termed a *hammer*) (Figure 3.2). This basic action of knapping yields two potentially useful products. The first is a smaller, thin piece (termed a *flake*) that has a very sharp edge. The second is the larger piece from which the flake was removed (termed a *core*). This large piece now has at least a few sharper edges than it did before, edges that are also potentially useful. Even this simple hammering technique requires that the knapper direct blows toward particular locations on the target core. The physics of stone fracture and the limitation of a knapper's strength preclude fracturing edges that form an angle greater than 90 degrees: one must place a blow over an acutely angled edge. This proscription had important consequences for the development of knapping techniques. Eventually knappers developed core preparation techniques in which the removal of small flakes modified the edges of a core in order to permit the removal of larger flakes. After removing one flake, a knapper can further modify the shape of the core by removing more flakes and can modify the shape of the flakes by removing even smaller flakes from their edges. All such modifications require directing the hammer blows to particular locations. Some knapping techniques that appeared late in human evolution require very precise placement indeed, such that a minor error can destroy the entire tool.

Knapping requires both strength in delivering blows and precision in the placement of blows. Not surprisingly, some features of human anatomy appear to have evolved as an adaptation to stone knapping. The human hand presents the most salient of these: long thumbs relative to fingers, broad fingertip pads, and a suite of features in the central palm that make it more robust and stable compared to the hands of apes (Marzke 1996:131). Marzke argues that these features are an adaptation to the "intrinsic and extrinsic forces associated with the grasp and manipulation of stones in pounding"(Marzke 1996:131) and has identified many of these features on two-million-year-old hominid fossils, suggesting that selection had been in place for some time before then. Toth (personal communication) has suggested, based on his own experience in knapping and his observation of knapping done by a bonobo chimpanzee (see below), that there must also be anatomical features of the human shoulder that are adapted to delivering powerful directed blows with a handheld object.

Unfortunately, little has yet been published on the cognition of stone knapping. Mithen (1996) has argued for the existence of a cognitive module tied to general tool manipulative abilities, and there is at least some support for this hypothesis from studies of modern technology. It is clear, for example, that people learn

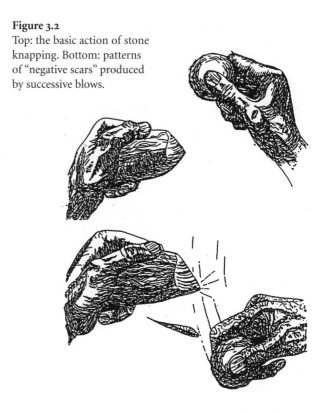

Figure 3.2
Top: the basic action of stone knapping. Bottom: patterns of "negative scars" produced by successive blows.

tool use largely by observation, replication, and repetition (apprenticeship) and that language plays a minor role (Gatewood 1985; Keller and Keller 1996; Wynn 1991), so it is reasonable to suppose that there is some cognitive discreteness. This is, however, a long way from a detailed description of a cognitive module. Moreover, no attempt has been made to incorporate spatial cognition into a model of technical cognition, even though spatial knowledge had to have been incorporated from the very beginning of stone knapping. After all, knapping is a directed action in space. Studies of the evolution of spatial cognition have instead borrowed directly from psychology, where there is an extensive literature, and have modified the concepts for use in studying stone tools (Wynn 1979, 1989).

Whatever the cognitive requirements of stone knapping are, they are within the abilities of apes, at least at the basic level of using a hammer to remove a flake. Nick Toth and Sue Savage-Rumbaugh have taught a bonobo to flake stone, and the results of their research help identify what might have been different about the cognition of the earliest stone knappers (Toth et al. 1993). Kanzi, a bonobo also known for his ability to

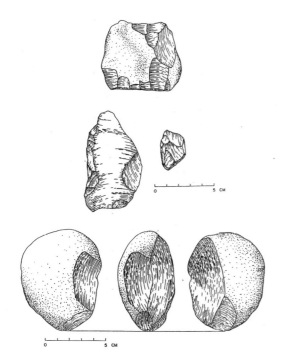

Figure 3.3 Stone tools that are 1.8 millions years old, from Olduvai Gorge, Tanzania (after Leakey 1971). The knapper placed blows adjacent to earlier blows, but there is no reason to believe that the overall shape of the artifact was the result of intention.

understand spoken English and use signs (Savage-Rumbaugh et al. 1998), learned how to remove flakes from cores by observing a human knapper; he also learned to use the sharp flakes to cut through a cord that held shut a reward box. After observing the procedure, Kanzi perfected his technique by trial and error. His initial solution, interestingly, was not to copy the demonstrator's action, but to hurl the core onto a hard surface and then select the sharp pieces from the shattered remnants. He clearly understood the notion of breakage and its consequences. When experimenters padded the room, he then copied the hammering technique used by the knapper. From this experiment (and an earlier one by Wright [1972]), it is clear that fracturing stone is within the cognitive abilities of apes. However, Kanzi is not as adept as human knappers: "as yet he does not seem to have mastered the concept of searching for acute angles on cores from which to detach flakes efficiently, or intentionally using flake scars on one flake of a core as striking platforms for removing flakes from another face" (Wright 1972:89). These abilities are basic to modern knapping and, more telling, are evident in the tools made two million years

ago. Toth et al. (1993) suggest that this represents a significant cognitive development, though they do not specify just what cognitive ability may have evolved. Elsewhere (Wynn et al. 1996), I have suggested that it may represent an evolutionary development in *spatial visualization,* which is the ability to discriminate patterns in complex backgrounds. If true, this would represent a minor cognitive development, of interest primarily because it is a cognitive ability tied to tool manufacture and use.

Kanzi's inability to recognize acute angles is a feature of his spatial perceptual/cognitive repertoire. He is also not very accurate in delivering blows, and this is harder to assess. These problems could simply be a matter of biomechanical constraint: he does not have the necessary motor control, or they could also result from his inability to organize his action on the small spatial field of the core. The organization of such action, fossilized as patterns of flake scars, developed significantly over the two million years following the first appearance of stone tools. While spatial perceptual/cognitive abilities affected many characteristics of stone tools, the development of symmetry as an imposed pattern most clearly documents the evolution of this component of human cognition.

The Earliest Stone Tools

The earliest stone tools exhibit no convincingly symmetrical patterns. Archaeologists assign these tools to a category termed *Oldowan* because of their first discovery at Olduvai Gorge in Tanzania. A better label was proposed several decades ago by Graham Clark (1977), who termed them a *Mode 1 technology,* a term based on technological characteristics, with no time-space implications. Mode 1 tools first appeared about 2.5 million years ago in what is today Ethiopia and were the only kind of stone technology in evidence for the next million years. After 1.5 million years ago, Mode 1 technologies continued to be produced in many areas and, indeed, were made into historic times. As such, Mode 1 represents a common, "generic" stone tool industry. It was also the earliest (Figure 3.3).

The emphasis of Mode 1 tools is on the edges. Simple stone flakes can have very sharp edges and are useful cutting tools without further modification. The

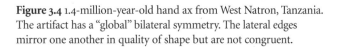

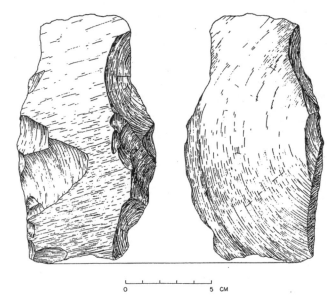

Figure 3.4 1.4-million-year-old hand ax from West Natron, Tanzania. The artifact has a "global" bilateral symmetry. The lateral edges mirror one another in quality of shape but are not congruent.

Figure 3.5 1.4-million-year-old cleaver from Olduvai. The position of negative flake scars indicates overall shape was probably intentional.

cores from which the flakes were removed also have useful edges. These are not as sharp as the flakes, but the cores are usually heavier, and the result is a tool that can be used for chopping, crushing, and heavy cutting. Mode 1 tools exhibit little or no attention to the overall shape of the artifact. The only possible examples of a shaped tool occur in relatively late Oldowan assemblages, where a few flakes have trimmed projections (termed *awls*). Here a two-dimensional pattern of sorts has been imposed on the artifact, but it is a "local" configuration, one that is very much tied to the nature of the edge itself.

Nothing about the tools required a concept of symmetry or even of balance. The topological concepts of boundary, proximity, and order constitute the minimum spatial concepts necessary to produce these tools. All are in the spatial repertoire of apes (Wynn and McGrew 1989).

The First Hominid-Imposed Symmetry

The earliest-possible examples of a hominid-imposed symmetry occur on artifacts termed *bifaces*. These are core tools that have bifacial trimming around much or all of the margin. This trimming results in a single edge that is usually sinuous in profile, at least on the early examples. Bifaces are longer than they are wide. The core was often a very large flake that had been removed

from a boulder-size core by a two-handed hammering technique (Jones 1981). There are two major types of bifaces: (1) hand axes, whose lateral edges converge to a rounded or pointed tip, and (2) cleavers, whose lateral edges define a transverse bit.

Some of the earliest bifaces are bilaterally symmetrical, with one lateral edge appearing to mirror the other. Others are not at all symmetrical, except to the extent that any artifact with a continuous edge and that is longer than it is wide will be vaguely symmetrical (Figure 3.4). Must the maker have had an idea of symmetry, or is the symmetry only in the mind of the archaeologist? This is a knotty problem about which there is considerable disagreement and about which I have myself flip-flopped on several occasions. I now maintain that there is intentional symmetry here, but that it is a very simple kind. On several of the bifaces, the trimming appears to have been placed in order to produce the symmetry, that is, one lateral edge has been trimmed to copy the other (Figure 3.5). However, the inverted copy is not a metrically precise duplicate. It reproduces the qualitative characteristics of shape but is not a quantitative duplicate. Nevertheless, the knapper employed a motion of symmetry in executing the artifact, and this is the important thing, for it marks the first evidence for the imposition of symmetry.

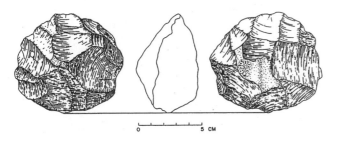

Figure 3.6 1.4-million-year-old "discoid" from Olduvai. The regularity of diameter suggests attention to a "local" spatial quantity.

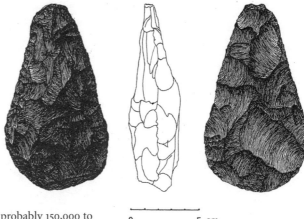

Figure 3.7 A late European hand ax (age uncertain, probably 150,000 to 300,000 B.P). This artifact has congruent symmetry in three dimensions.

Some evidence exists for radial symmetry contemporary with these early bifaces. These artifacts are termed "discoids" precisely because they have regular diameters (Figure 3.6). One could also term them "round" bifaces because they differ from hand axes and cleavers only in having radial rather than bilateral symmetry. Several discoids have been very extensively trimmed, and their shape was almost certainly intentional.

These earliest symmetrical artifacts first appeared about 1.4 million years ago in East Africa. They are the hallmarks of Clark's Mode 2 technology, which is also known as the Acheulean industry. Artifacts similar to these early African bifaces of similar age have been found in Israel, but they were not as widespread geographically as the Mode 1 industries, which have been found not only in Africa, but also in Asia. Over the next thousand millennia, there were few, if any, developments in hominid-imposed symmetry. Sometime after 500,000 years ago, some hominids began producing bifaces with a much more striking symmetry.

Congruent and Three-Dimensional Symmetries
Three developments in hominid imposed symmetry appear in the archaeological record sometime after 500,000 years ago: (1) true congruency, (2) three-dimensional symmetries, and (3) broken symmetry.

While the bilateral symmetry of early bifaces was rough and imprecise, the symmetry of late examples clearly suggests attention to congruency. The mirrored sides are not just qualitative reversals, but quantitative duplicates, at least to the degree that this is possible given the constraints of stone knapping. Many, but

certainly not all, late hand axes and cleavers present such congruent symmetries, and this is one of the features that makes them so attractive to us. Such symmetry was not limited to a single shape. Late bifaces demonstrate a considerable amount of variability in overall plan shape. Some are long and narrow, others short and broad. Some have distinct shoulders, while others are almost round. Although some evidence exists that this variability was regional (Wynn and Tierson 1990), much of it is related to raw material, and much appears to have been idiosyncratic. But in almost every assemblage of this time period a few bifaces will have fine congruent symmetry, whatever the overall shape.

The second development in symmetry was the appearance of bilateral symmetry in three dimensions. Many of these bifaces are bilaterally symmetrical in profile as well as in plan. In the finest examples, this symmetry extends to all of the cross sections of the artifacts, including cross sections oblique to the major axes, as we would define them (Figure 3.7). Once again, this feature is not universally true, and many, many bifaces do not have it, but it is present on at least a few artifacts from most assemblages.

The third development in symmetry was the appearance of broken symmetry. Here a bilateral pattern appears to have been intentionally altered into a nonsymmetrical but regular shape. Several cleavers from the Tanzanian site of Isimila appear "bent," as if the whole plan symmetry, including the midline, had been warped into a series of curved, parallel lines. These are invariably extensively modified artifacts, whose cross sections are symmetrical, and the pattern is almost certainly the result

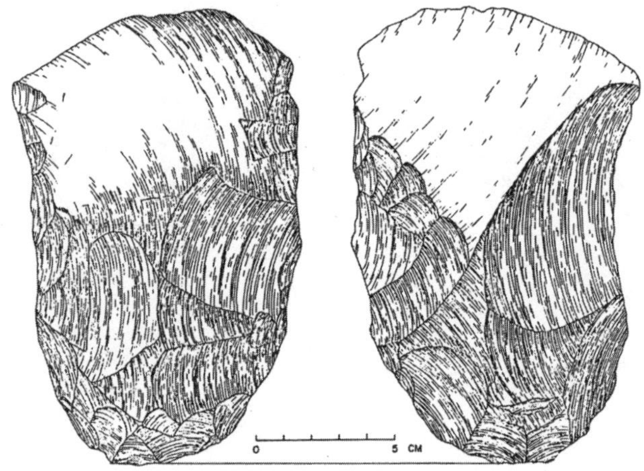

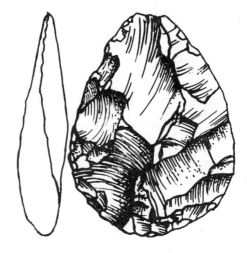

Figure 3.8 A "bent" cleaver from the Tanzanian site of Isimila (ca. 300,000 B.P.).

Figure 3.9 A "twisted profile" hand ax (ca. 200,000 B.P.) from the English site of Swanscombe (after Roe 1970).

of intention (Figure 3.8). A better-known example is the twisted profile, or "S twist," hand axe. The artifacts give the appearance of having been twisted around the central pole. The result is an S shape to the lateral edges, as seen in profile (Figure 3.9). Again, these are extensively modified artifacts, and we must conclude, I think, that the pattern is the result of intention.

Several caveats complicate interpretation of these three developments. One is the problem of individual skill: some prehistoric stone knappers must have been more adept than others and better able to achieve congruent, three-dimensional symmetries in the intractable medium of stone. We have no way of knowing how common highly skilled knappers were. A second caveat is raw material. Some stone is much easier to work than others. I do not think it is entirely coincidental that twisted profile hand axes are invariably made of flint or obsidian, two of the most prized knapping materials. On the other hand, raw material is not as tyrannical as one might think. The "bent" cleavers from Isimila are made of granite.

It is impossible to date these developments in symmetry at all precisely. Archaeological systematics place all of the examples in the late Acheulean (sometimes on morphological grounds alone, which leads to a circular argument). All were probably made after 500,000 years ago, perhaps even after 400,000 years ago. The Isimila artifacts, for example, date to between 170,000 and 330,000 years ago (Howell et al. 1972). The twisted profile

hand axes are probably no earlier than 350,000, and most may be much later. Although 300,000 years is a long time in a historical framework, it represents only the final 12 percent of technological evolution.

Symmetry in New Materials

The examples I have used thus far have all been knapped stone artifacts. While symmetry clearly can be and was imposed on many knapped stone artifacts, the medium is not ideal for the imposition of form. It is not plastic, and shaping can only be done by subtraction. Indeed, after the appearance of the symmetrical patterns just discussed, no subsequent developments in symmetry can be recognized in knapped stone. There were developments in technique and perhaps skill, but the symmetries imposed on even very recent stone tools are no more elaborate than those imposed on 300,000-year-old hand axes. Consequently, we must turn to other materials.

Artifacts made of other materials—bone, antler, skin, wood, fiber, etc.—were undoubtedly part of the technical repertoire of many early hominids (although see Mithen 1996 for a countersuggestion). Because such materials are far more perishable than stone, the archaeological record contains few of them until relatively late in prehistory. A few examples almost certainly predate 100,000 years ago, but all are controversial, either as to age or as to significance. One is a pebble from the Hungarian site of Tata, on which someone engraved a line perpendicular to a natural crack (Bednarik 1995). While one might be tempted to

Figure 3.1o Two bison from Lascaux (ca. 17,000 B.P.), a composition with reflection of elements.

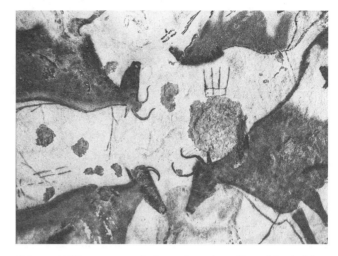

Figure 3.11 Three cows and a horse from the ceiling of the Axial Gallery, Lascaux. Rotational symmetry may have guided the composition.

Figure 3.12 "Swimming" stags from Lascaux. This is an example of translational symmetry. (All after Bataille 1955)

argue from it that the maker had some notion of rotation or radial symmetry, this is too heavy an interpretive weight to be born by a single, isolated artifact. More to the point, even if true, this would tell us little more about symmetry than is supplied by contemporary bifaces. However, it would be symmetry in a new context, a fact that if confirmed would have possible implications for cognitive evolution.

It is not until very close to the present, indeed, after 100,000 years ago, that the archaeological record presents extensive evidence of artifacts made of perishable materials. Some archaeologists see this timing as entirely a reflection of preservation; others see it as evidence of new behaviors and abilities. The earliest such evidence is African and dates from before 90,000 years ago (Yellen et al. 1995). These are worked bone points from a site in the eastern Congo. While these

artifacts are quite important to several current arguments about prehistory, they reveal nothing new about hominid-imposed symmetry.

The European Upper Paleolithic provides the best-documented examples of hominid-imposed symmetries for the period between 40,000 and 10,000 years ago. Here we find extensive evidence of symmetry in materials other than stone. Perhaps most widely known are the cave paintings of Franco-Cantabrian art, especially in compositions that are about 15,000 years old. Here we can see possible symmetries as patterns of elements in a composition, not just inherent in a single object. The example of bison from Lascaux is one of the better examples of reflection within a composition (Figure 3.10). There are also examples of rotational symmetry (Axial Gallery cattle, Figure 3.11) and translational symmetry (swimming stags, Figure 3.12). In addition to the art, there are examples of symmetry imposed on bone tools. The best examples are Magdalenian antler harpoons, some of which have barbs arranged in a translation, glide reflection and mirror reflection symmetries (Figure 3.13, left to right). In these examples, the motion of symmetry is more apparent than in the earlier bifaces. Translation and glide reflection have been used to arrange elements that are figural in their

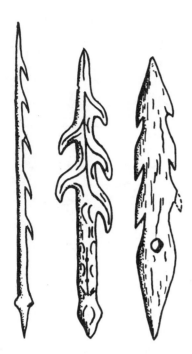

Figure 3.13 Magdalenian harpoons, similar in age to the Lascaux painting. The center artifact exemplifies glide reflection symmetry (after Peterkin, Bricker , and Mellars 1993).

own right. Whereas the symmetry of bifaces appears static, the symmetry of these artifacts is dynamic and, more telling, very like the symmetries we encounter in the modern world. These artifacts appear to have resulted from the application of a compositional rule.

The Appearance of Modern Symmetry

On the scale of human evolution, 15,000 years was not long ago. Nevertheless, most prehistorians and historians acknowledge that a great deal has happened since then. Certainly major technological developments have occurred, and it is appropriate to ask if there have been any developments in symmetry as an imposed pattern. Of course, the closer to the present an artifact was made, the more likely it is to be preserved and discovered. Perhaps more importantly, certain new technologies are more amenable to the imposition of form because they are based on a malleable medium: ceramics and metallurgy come immediately to mind. People living during recent millennia simply have been more able to impose form on artifacts.

Modern symmetrical patterns appear in the archaeological record with the Neolithic. Of the numerous examples, Ban Chiang pottery was produced in what is today Thailand about 5,000 years ago. By then pottery had a long history in East Asia, and techniques of construction and firing were well established. Ban Chiang pottery is painted with elaborate designs that

cover the surface of the pot. The designs consist of simple forms—curves, loops, line segments—applied and transformed into symmetrical patterns, including bifold rotation and glide reflection (Van Esterik 1979). From southeastern Europe, Neolithic pottery presents similar patterns of simple elements transformed by the iterative application of symmetrical rules (Figure 3.14; Washburn 1983). These examples are sufficient to make my point: by 5,000 years ago the symmetrical patterns imposed on artifacts were as complex as those imposed in modern culture. If we accept the evidence that the reflective/translational pattern of barbs on Magdalenian harpoons must also have resulted from the iterative application of a symmetrical rule, then we can push this date back to 15,000 years ago. In either case, modern symmetry appeared late in human evolution.

Discussion

At the outset of this discussion, it is important to reiterate several of the caveats mentioned at the beginning of the chapter. Foremost among these is the imperfection of the archaeological record. The examples used in this chapter are a tiny sample of the objects produced in the past. We have no assurance that they present a picture that is typical for any point in time. The second caveat is related to the first. Any cognitive interpretation of these patterns can assess only the minimum necessary competence. Archaeologically invisible domains might well have had patterns requiring different, and more complex, forms of reasoning.

I believe it is possible to make two generalizations about the evidence. First, there is a real trend in the nature of symmetry over time. By real, I mean that it is not a trend created by my interpretation, nor is it a trend in the concepts defined by cognitive psychology. Rather, it is an identifiable trend in the pattern itself. Over time, artifactual symmetry became more regular and more complex. "More regular" simply means that the symmetry more closely approximates an ideal of duplication and reflection. "More complex" means that more elements came into play. Early symmetry was less regular and less complex than the symmetry of modern artifacts. I do not see this as resulting from some kind of inevitable progress. Rather, I believe that the evolution of symmetry reflects, but was not central to, developments in hominid cognition. The second generalization that can be derived from the evidence is that symmetry does not seem to have developed in a slow, continuous way. During immense spans of time, no development occurred. For over one million years, for example, the symmetry of bifaces remained unchanged.

The First Million Years

The vast majority of the archaeological record of symmetry, chronologically speaking, reflects the evolution of hominid spatial perception/cognition. This evolution included both developments in perceptual/cognitive abilities and developments in skill. The earliest stone tools have no imposed symmetries. Basic spatial patterns such as proximity and boundary are the minimum necessary concepts. In this, the early stone knappers were very apelike. Recall that apes can attend to the nearness of existing elements and the boundaries of figures but have never produced a symmetrical construct. Enigmatic, anecdotal evidence exists that chimpanzee artists have a sense of balance, but "space filling" seems a more parsimonious explanation. Concluding that the spatial patterns imposed by early stone knappers lacked symmetry and was therefore apelike does not mean that these hominids were indistinguishable from chimpanzees. They may well have had, probably did have, biomechanical abilities not possessed by modern apes, but this is not the point. Their spatial abilities are indistinguishable from those of a chimpanzee.

The first arguably symmetrical artifacts appeared about 1.4 million years ago, which, interestingly, postdated the appearance of *Homo erectus* by several hundred thousand years. This early symmetry is not regular and indeed seems more akin to a balance of the halves of a spatial field. It marks an imposition of overall form unknown in earlier artifacts, and this may well reflect developments in spatial perception/cognition. Much later, about one million years later in fact, this rough symmetry was augmented with a fine congruent symmetry in three dimensions. These bifaces are very pleasing to the modern eye, and their quality of symmetry has never really been improved on in stone knapping.

It is hard not to interpret this evidence in Gestaltist terms. The symmetrical target became more regular and refined over time, and one possible interpretation is that a neurologically based "good Gestalt" of bilateral

Figure 3.14 Ban Chiang pots from Thailand, dating to about 3000 B.C. (Van Esterik 1979).

symmetry had evolved as a feature of the hominid perceptual/cognitive repertoire. Symmetry is an especially salient pattern in human perception (Uttal 1996). Infants as young as four months discriminate symmetrical patterns better than asymmetrical patterns. Moreover, the pattern perceptual abilities that children use to detect and remember symmetry develop during ontogeny. Initially children attend to the global pattern characteristic of symmetries; that is, they recognize and reproduce from memory the qualitative features of the pattern. Later they attempt to reproduce the pattern with precision (Bornstein and Stiles-Davis 1984). There is a similar sequence of development in the symmetry imposed on stone tools. Initially it was a global symmetry of reflected shape, later precise congruent symmetries appeared, but the motion of symmetry is evident even in the earliest bifaces. Children attend earliest to symmetries around a vertical axis, followed by recognition of symmetry around a horizontal axis, and only much later to symmetries across oblique axes (Bornstein and Stiles-Davis 1984). Once again, stone tools document a similar sequence. For a million years, stone tools had only bilateral symmetry around a longitudinal axis; later there are symmetrical cross sections across imagined oblique (and invisible) axes. "Symmetry, a higher order organizing principle in pattern perception, aids children in both discrimination and memory"(Bornstein and Stiles-Davis 1984:647). As a principle organizing perception, it clearly develops in ontogeny. Stone tools indicate that it also evolved significantly between two million and 500,000 years ago.

The archaeological evidence also corroborates the predictions of Piagetian psychology (which has some affinities with Gestaltist theory). Many aspects of Piaget's theory have been challenged over the last two decades, especially his ideas on infancy, but the basic outlines of his account of spatial development remain sound. Piaget and Inhelder (1967) argued that Euclidean concepts, including congruency and precise symmetries, appear late in childhood and are built out of earlier projective and topological concepts as the child reorganizes his spatial conception of the world. Among these earlier concepts is the ability to reverse a configuration (the basic motion of symmetry), so that the earlier appearance of roughly symmetrical artifacts in technological evolution is predictable from a Piagetian developmental perspective. In addition, Piaget and Inhelder argued that the ability to conceive of regular cross sections resulted from a child's ability to imagine a visual perspective not directly available to the perceiver and that this projective ability develops in later childhood. Such ability is obviously required to conceive of and produce the three-dimensional symmetries of later bifaces.

We can also use symmetry to recognize developments in other spatial abilities. For example, symmetries imposed on artifacts document the development of ability in visual projection and mental rotation. Reith and Dominin (1997) have recently documented children's ability to remember scenes projected onto a two-dimensional screen. The results corroborate, in general, some of the results of Piaget and Inhelder. Not until the age of eight or nine do children reliably remember how a scene appears from a specific point of view; earlier they recall global relations, ignoring changes in masking

and size inherent in the view from a specific perspective. The ability to conceive of the invisible cross sections of artifacts requires the same ability to "record a projection mentally" that the eight- and nine-year-olds reliably employ, but it is an ability that appeared relatively late (after 500,000 years ago) in the archaeological record. A related ability is that of mental rotation (Linn and Petersen 1986), which is the ability to rotate a three-dimensional image in the mind (e.g., the rotated block task on many intelligence tests). Success at these tasks varies greatly, even late in ontogeny. It is one of the spatial abilities that consistently demonstrate gender difference in performance (Wynn et al., 1996). The ability to rotate an image in the mind was almost certainly required for the manufacture of the very fine three-dimensional and broken symmetries true of some bifaces after 500,000 years ago.

Other specific spatial abilities required for the imposition of some symmetries are frame independence (also known as spatial perception) and spatial quantity. Even the earlier bifaces, with only a global symmetry, required that the stone knapper "see past" the local spatial frame constituted by the core blank. This ability to impose a shape was not required for the earliest artifacts and is nowhere clearly evident in the products of nonhuman primates. It also develops in ontogeny. The concept of spatial quantity also clearly evolved. Early symmetries were global, qualitative reversals of a shape; later bifaces with congruent symmetry add a notion of equivalent spatial quantity.

Models of the neurological underpinnings of imagery corroborate this important distinction between shape and spatial quantity. Kosslyn (e.g., 1994) has used PET scan studies and evidence from brain trauma patients to investigate the neural basis of visual recognition and imagery. One of the most reliable conclusions of his study is that recognition of shapes is largely independent of the recognition of spatial relations. The brain processes shape information in the lower temporal lobe but spatial information (size, left-right, etc.) in the parietal lobe. While there appears to be some direct neural connectivity between these regions, it is minimal. In other words, at the level of visual recognition, there are two separate neural networks. Information from these networks passes to associative regions of the frontal lobe, where they are available for higher-level processing. Complicating the picture further is the brain's apparent reliance on two spatial subsystems. The first, linked anatomically to the left parietal, processes "categorical" spatial information such as left-right, above-below, and inside-outside. Most of the "topological" concepts discussed earlier in this chapter (boundary, proximity, etc.) fall under this rubric. The second subsystem, which is linked more to the right parietal, processes metrical relations of size, coordinates, and so on. While the two subsystems are more directly linked than either is to the shape recognition network, they process information separately and, again, pass it to higher functions. The processing of global symmetry appears to occur in the shape recognition subsystem and does not require higher-level processing. Congruent and three-dimensional symmetry is considerably more complex. In order to generate an image of a congruent symmetry, the brain must coordinate information from the shape recognition network (temporal lobe) with information from the spatial network, the metrical subsystem in particular (right parietal). This coordination probably occurs in the associative regions of the frontal lobe.

In sum, the archaeological record of symmetry documents a clear development of spatial cognition over the million-year period between 1.5 million and 500,000 years ago. Indeed, the archaeological record indicates that, in essence, modern spatial cognition, in the sense of a perceptual/cognitive system, evolved relatively early in human evolution, certainly prior to the appearance of anatomically modern humans and perhaps earlier than the first *Homo sapiens*. This development included a clearly enhanced ability to produce symmetry. However, what was the context of this evolution? What selected this impressive ability to conceive of and manipulate complex three-dimensional patterns? We can attempt to answer these questions at three different levels. First, the enhanced ability to perceive and conceive of symmetry itself might have been selected. Alternatively, perhaps enhanced spatial ability in general was under selective pressure. Finally, these apparently enhanced spatial abilities might have been a by-product of selection operating on the level of general intelligence.

What is the perceptual saliency of symmetry good for? Some evidence exists that body symmetry is related to reproductive success for males (Gangestad 1997). According to Gangestad, observable phenotypic asymmetry (separate from the bilateral symmetry coded genetically) correlates with developmental stress, so that asymmetry marks lower health. If a potential mate could detect this, he or she could avoid a reproductively costly (in an evolutionary sense) mating. Presumably, however, this is generally true for vertebrates and not just for humans, so why would our hominid ancestors have acquired such an exquisitely fine sense for symmetry, beyond that known for other animals? Perhaps symmetry gained added importance as a clue to general health when hominids lost thick body hair. Condition of coat is also a good indicator of general health, and its absence may have led to selection for a heightened ability to detect variations away from symmetry. Another possibility is that more refined symmetries came to mark technological skill. An individual who could produce a more regular (symmetrical) artifact would be cuing his or her skill and worth as a potential mate. Other things being equal, the stone knapper who produced the fine three-dimensional bifaces was smarter and more capable, with better genes, than one who couldn't. Especially if knapping skill correlated with other technological abilities, this would be one means of identifying mates with future potential as providers. Kohn and Mithen (1999: 521) take this argument even further, framing it in terms of sexual selection and emphasizing abilities other than technological:

> Those hominids . . . who were able to make fine symmetrical handaxes may have been preferentially chosen by the opposite sex as mates. Just as a peacock's tail may reliably indicate its "success," so might the manufacture of a fine symmetrical handaxe have been a reliable indicator of the hominid's ability to secure food, find shelter, escape from predation, and compete within the social group. Such hominids would have been attractive mates, their abilities indicating "good genes."

Here the saliency of symmetry has been transferred out of the domain of the phenotypic to that of cultural signaling, but the selective advantage is the same. In this scenario, both the ability to detect and produce symmetry would have had reproductive consequences. While it is extremely difficult to test this hypothesis, two factors lend it greater credence than pure speculation. First, modern people certainly do use material culture to mark their individual success, and it is not far-fetched to extend this behavior into the past, perhaps even to the time of late *Homo erectus* or early *Homo sapiens*. Second, symmetry does have evolutionary value, as mentioned above. A perceptual system attuned to detection of body symmetry would presumably be sensitive to artifactual symmetry. Of course, the transference of mate assessment from aspects of physical appearance to aspects of cultural products must have been a very significant development in human evolution. That it may have first occurred via the production and perception of symmetry is perhaps not surprising, given the saliency of symmetry itself.

Rather than selection operating on symmetry, it may have operated on general spatial ability. Projective ability, mental rotation, and other spatial abilities tied to the production of symmetrical artifacts might also have been under selection. They are essential components of an ability to manipulate images and scenes, so perhaps selection acted on navigational abilities (Silverman et al. 2000). Here the paleoanthropological evidence provides some clues. The initial evolution of hominid spatial thinking appears to have coincided with an important shift in adaptive niche. About 1.8 million years ago, with the advent of *Homo erectus,* hominids finally broke from the woodland/riparian adaptations of their predecessors and moved out onto the open grasslands. Not only did they invade more open country, with dramatic anatomical consequences (Walker and Leakey 1993), they also invaded higher and colder terrain (Cachel and Harris 1995). The choice of *invade* is apt because the most striking feature of this new niche was that it was expansionistic. *Homo erectus* rapidly spread to occupy much of the tropical and subtropical Old World (e.g., Asian Georgia at 1.6 million years ago, Java as early as 1.8 million years ago). Cachel and Harris have described *Homo erectus* as a "weed" species—never numerous as individuals but able to expand into new areas very rapidly. For *Homo erectus* the generalized adaptation required of a weed species was partially technological

(reliance on tools and fire), but evidence also exists of a more sophisticated array of spatial concepts than any known for apes, including global symmetry imposed on artifacts and a rudimentary concept of spatial quantity (regular diameters of discoids, a round biface). These spatial patterns appeared on artifacts *after* the shift in niche, suggesting that something in the new niche selected for spatial thinking.

While this correlation between a development in spatial thinking and a change in niche is provocative, it does have several serious weaknesses. First, many animals are fine navigators without relying on the enhanced spatial abilities in question. Second, the more impressive developments in spatial thinking, including the imposition of three-dimensional symmetrical patterns, occurred long after this niche shift and in fact do not correlate well with any changes in hominid foraging. Third, when modern people navigate, they rarely use the spatial abilities in question. For example, when modern hunters and gatherers move across the landscape, they use established trails and routes that often follow waterways or animal trails (Bahuchet 1992; Gamble 1999). The cognitive underpinning of such navigation is largely topological and does not rely on the kind of spatial abilities necessary for stone tools. Yes, it is possible to imagine a form of navigation that relies on such abilities, but this is not the way people actually move about. Finally, the navigation hypothesis does not match up well with the neurological evidence.

Kosslyn's study of perception and imagery, discussed above, challenges the facile conclusion that navigation of any sort could have selected for the spatial abilities in question. While Kosslyn rarely addresses evolution, the implications of his results for evolutionary reconstructions are significant. If the brain processes information about space independent of information about shape, then selection for navigational ability is unlikely to have had a direct effect on shape recognition skills. Shape recognition (and probably imagery) must have been an aspect of the neural processing invoked in tool manufacture, especially edges and angles, but also symmetry. Here the archaeological record presents a puzzle for cognitive science. Eventually metrical considerations came into play in the production of tools, and in Kosslyn's scheme, metrics are processed by the spatial net in the right parietal. If Kosslyn's model is at all reliable (and there is strong evidence that its general features are, at least), then application of spatial information to shape images must occur in the higher processing regions of the brain, associative memory in particular.

This conclusion has implications for a modular view of intelligence and for the evolution of a modular mind in particular. At first blush, developments in symmetry would appear to document the evolution of the hominid visual input system, to use Fodor's (1983) classic definition of a cognitive module. Even incorporating Kosslyn's more detailed characterization of visual recognition and imaging (1994), it is possible to conceive of an encapsulated visual imaging module that is made up of shape and spatial subsystems. If true, what the archaeological record may document is the increasing complexity of the outputs of this cognitive module. However, there are good reasons for rejecting this idea. Features of "advanced" symmetry, congruency in particular, simply do not fulfill the requirements laid out by Fodor (1983). Congruency, for example, is not fast, mandatory, or limited in access. Even modern adults trained in geometry cannot automatically compute congruency, and when they do make such an assessment, it is not a rapid, at-a-glance recognition. It is a conscious cognitive process. All of this implies the operation of a central processor to some degree. Whether this is Kosslyn's associative memory, Fodor's diffuse central processor, or Mithen's (1996) cognitive fluidity is perhaps simply a difference in semantics. What seems clear is that the ability to recognize and conceive three-dimensional, congruent symmetries is not simply the output of an encapsulated visual system: it also requires the services of a more general neural processor that can integrate the outputs of several information subsystems. In other words, the archaeological evidence of symmetry documents the evolution of higher brain function, not just spatial ability or shape imagery. In addition, what selected for a more powerful general intelligence may have been very different, even unrelated, to what selected for spatial ability or shape recognition ability.

Algorithmic Thought

The application of developmental theories has led to a paradoxical conclusion: by 300,000 years ago spatial perceptual/cognitive thinking was modern. The ability to conceive and execute regular three-dimensional congruent symmetries in flaked stone was in place 300 millennia ago at least. However, very little else about the archaeological evidence from this time period looks modern. Despite having a repertoire of modern spatial abilities, these hominids did not produce modern culture. Perhaps, as I once argued, cognition was modern, but culture was not (Wynn 1979). I now suspect that this conclusion was naive and that cognition continued to evolve after 300,000 years ago but that spatial perception/cognition was not an important component of this evolution. Once again, symmetry gives us a clue, not as an element of spatial thinking, but rather as a transformational rule.

When we examine the basic forms of patterns produced by modern people, they are often very simple. Modern people continue to produce artifacts with regular three-dimensional symmetry very like that of 300,000-year-old bifaces. However, we also delight in complex patterns produced by the iterative application of transformational rules. This results in symmetries, yes, but the underlying cognition is very different from that of spatial perception and cognition. I believe that the complex symmetries discussed by Ewins, Paul, Roe, and others in this volume represent a very different kind of thinking from that underpinning hand axes.

Modern thinking often relies on algorithms, which are sets of rules used to solve problems. Calculus is an especially telling example. It is a sophisticated set of rules and conventions that are learned and used by a very small percentage of people (not including this author). It allows them to solve problems that would be otherwise unsolvable, certainly well beyond the ability of naive judgment, intuition, or trial and error. There are many, many other examples. Sheldon Klein (e.g., 1983) has argued that the Chinese I Ching is a computational system based on the iterative application of an "appositional transformation operator (ATO)," which is a set of analogical rules. Here again we have a complex algorithm, the mastery of which allows the solving of complex problems (in this case divination), making the user "smarter." Algorithms need not be so formalized. They can also be "rules of thumb." A good example is that of the Micronesian Etak (Gladwin 1970), a system of navigation based on sidereal observations and the interesting convention of conceiving of invisible target islands that move against the background of the sky. This learned algorithm allows successful navigation between low-lying islands that are situated over the horizon from one another, occasionally hundreds of miles apart, a truly impressive feat of intelligence.

Algorithms are clever devices that mark a very important development in the evolution of human intelligence, an understanding of which is crucial to an understanding of the modern cultural world. There are two ways to interpret this development. First, it may represent the ultimate step in the organic evolution of humans, a final rewiring of the brain that produced the modern mind. Second, it may represent a cultural development, the discovery or invention of a very valuable psychological tool that yielded immediate benefits to human action and consequently spread rapidly.

The ability to reason by applying a system of contentless rules may result from the evolution of some feature of brain anatomy and/or physiology. We may be seeing here Mithen's "cognitive fluidity," the ability to evaluate and coordinate the content of the several discrete intelligences of the human mind (Mithen 1996). Use of algorithms is, after all, not tied to specific content. It is a kind of shorthand general intelligence, an intelligence that is flexible in application and allows unique solutions to unique problems regardless of the domain of action. A neuroanatomical development that produced such ability would have spread rapidly through natural selection: enhanced problem-solving ability would have had reproductive consequences.

While persuasive on the surface, this scenario does have weaknesses. Is the ability to reason algorithmically universal, that is, characteristic of all normal adults? Arguments for a general intelligence do not, as far as I know, specify algorithmic thought as the key feature. A second weakness lies in evolutionary timing. The earliest evidence for algorithmic thought is only about 15,000 years old, which is tens of thousands of years after the appearance of anatomically modern humans (with modern brain size and shape and modern vocal structure). One could, of course, argue that "absence of evidence is not evidence of absence," that anatomically modern humans (AMHs) have possessed algorithmic reasoning for 100,000 years but that it simply left no

trace. The alternative is even more problematic. One could argue that the earliest AMHs were not in fact modern in all respects. They lacked the key neural reorganization that lay behind algorithmic thought. This evolved very late, long after the appearance of AMHs, but had no outward effect on the size and shape of the brain. This scenario, too, has a serious weakness. How could one explain the current global distribution of the ability without positing a late, worldwide diaspora for which there is no evidence whatsoever?[4]

The difficulties with these "organic" hypotheses vanish if one considers algorithmic thought to be an invention, a cultural tool for thinking that spread very rapidly by learning, not by genes. After all, the example that initiated this section, calculus, is just such a cultural tool. Vygotsky's (1986) theory of child development provides a useful and powerful basis for such an interpretation. Like Piaget, Vygotsky's focus was the intellectual development of the child, but he differed from Piaget in the emphasis he placed on the context of development, especially language. Vygotsky's ideas are relevant to both levels of the current analysis—the nature of symmetry in modern culture and the significance of algorithmic thinking.

Symmetry as manifested on Quichua pots or Fijian bark cloth is clearly a Vygotskian *concept:* "To form such a concept it is also necessary *to abstract, to single out* elements, and to view the abstracted elements apart from the totality of the concrete experience in which they are embedded" (1986:135, emphasis in original). For Vygotsky, such concepts do not develop spontaneously in the thinking of children. Their development depends on the "ready made meaning of words," which are supplied by the parent or teacher. Without such a model, the child may develop complexes of concrete, factual-linked ideas that are not abstract and general.[5] In other words, without the model, abstract concepts will not appear: the neurological equipment cannot generate them outside of a specific cultural context. Such a cultural context of abstract concepts of symmetry was clearly in place in the Neolithic and perhaps for the Magdalenian people who lived 15,000 years ago. The earlier symmetry of bifaces was not a "concept" in the Vygotskian sense because it was not abstract. Rather, it was a concrete, "fact-based" perceptual pattern.

As an algorithmic rule, symmetry is an example of what Vygotsky termed a *psychological tool*—artificial formulations used to "master natural forms of individual behavior and cognition." "Vygotsky noted such psychological tools as gestures, language and sign systems, mnemonic techniques, and decision-making systems—for example, casting dice" (Kozalin 1986:xxv). Klein's ATOs, Micronesian Etak, and calculus all clearly fall under this rubric. They are artificial formulations used to master cognitive problems. The transformational rules of decorative traditions, including rules of symmetry, are also psychological tools. They are real, they solve problems, but they are not organic. In characterizing the role of psychological tools in child development, Vygotsky (1986:94) observed that the "nature of development itself changes, from biological to sociohistorical."

The same can be said for the evolution of culture. Certainly by 15,000 years ago evolutionary development had become sociohistorical rather than biological.[6] It was not until this late date, for example, that material culture began to change in the volatile fashion so familiar to us. This was not a coincidence, but almost certainly resulted from the concept-based nature of modern culture.

The late development of what I am terming *algorithmic thought* is congruent with William Noble and Iain Davidson's argument for the late appearance of language. Noble and Davidson base their argument on what they acknowledge as a minority position in cognitive science (Noble and Davidson 1996), a position with which I do not usually agree. In essence (though I risk oversimplification), they maintain that minds cannot exist in the absence of symbolic communication and that one can speak of "concepts" only in the context of such mindedness. Concepts are symbolic representations; indeed, they require words in the narrow sense. If we have convincing evidence of conceptual thought, which we do in the guise of algorithmic thinking, then language is implicated as well. Noble and Davidson's argument about the origin of symbols hinges on archaeological evidence for such abstract, conceptual thought, which abounds after 40,000 years ago but is virtually absent earlier. Algorithmic thought is clearly conceptual in Noble and Davidson's sense and appears at a time that can be predicted from their theoretical position. Noble and Davidson also advocate a Vygotskian position vis-à-vis the importance of words in the milieu of development, and, as I have tried to show, a Vygotskian approach is perhaps the best way to understand real developments in the archaeological record of the last 100,000 years.

General Conclusion

The archaeological record of symmetry documents two threads in the evolution of human cognition. The first, and earlier, was the evolution of spatial perception/cognition. Between 1.5 million and 500,000 years ago hominid ability to recognize and conceive of spatial patterns evolved away from a generalized ape ability and acquired the features of modern human spatial thinking. These included such specific spatial abilities as projection of shapes from alternative perspectives, mental rotation, and congruency. While it is possible that the ability to detect and produce symmetries was itself selected, developments in central neural processing were almost certainly necessary as well. This evolutionary story is not simply one of developments within a single cognitive module. Whatever evolutionary process lay behind human spatial thinking, it worked relatively early in human evolution, certainly long before the appearance of anatomically modern humans.

The second thread is altogether different. Relatively late in human evolution, around 15,000 years ago, evidence exists for symmetry as an iteratively applied transformational rule. This brand of symmetry exemplifies algorithmic thought, in which a small set of transformation rules generate a multitude of problem solutions. This style of thinking is ubiquitous in the modern mind. The evolutionary mechanisms behind this critical development may have been organic, but it is also possible, even likely, that it was a cultural invention. Language was almost certainly required. Regardless of cause, it marks the advent of truly modern thought. ■

Acknowledgments

Of the many scholars who have provided useful comments on the matter of symmetry, I note especially Charles Keller, Iain Davidson, Peter Carruthers, and Dorothy Washburn. ■

Notes

1. Chimpanzees might well also have such a record, but it has never been recognized in the field.

2. Knapping is the controlled fracture of stone by hand.

3. One can fracture stone by simply throwing a core down onto a hard surface. While this can produce useful products and may well have preceded more formal techniques, it is not knapping per se and reveals little about spatial cognition.

4. The "absence of evidence" hypothesis has the advantage here, for evidence exists for the rapid spread of AMHs beginning about 100,000 years ago.

5. Cf. Piaget's concrete operations.

6. This interpretation is also in line with that of Donald (1991), who sees later human evolution as one of "externalization."

References Cited

Bahuchet, S.
1992   Spatial Mobility and Access to Resources among the African Pygmies. In *Mobility and Territoriality,* edited by J. Casimer and A. Rao, pp. 205–258. Berg, Oxford, UK.

Bataille, Georges
1955   *Prehistoric Painting: Lascaux or the Birth of Art.* Skira, Lausanne

Bateson, G.
1972   A Re-examination of "Bateson's Rule." In *Steps to an Ecology of Mind,* edited by G. Bateson, pp. 379–398. Ballantine, New York.

Bednarik, R.
1995   Concept-Mediated Marking in the Lower Palaeolithic. *Current Anthropology* 36:605–634.

Bornstein, M., and J. Stiles-Davis
1984   Discrimination and Memory for Symmetry in Young Children. *Developmental Psychology* 20:637–649.

Boysen, S., G. Berntson, and J. Prentice
1987   Simian Scribbles: A Reappraisal of Drawing in the Chimpanzee (*Pan troglodytes*). *Journal of Comparative Psychology* 101:82–89.

Cachel, S., and J. Harris
1995   Ranging Patterns, Land-Use and Subsistence in *Homo erectus* from the Perspective of Evolutionary Biology. In *Evolution and Ecology of* Homo erectus, edited by J. Bower and S. Sartono, pp. 51–66. Pithecanthropus Centennial Foundation, Leiden, Netherlands.

Clark, G.
1977   *World Prehistory.* Cambridge University Press, Cambridge, UK.

Donald, Merlin
1991   *Origins of the Modern Mind.* Harvard University Press, Cambridge, MA.

Fodor, J.
1983   *The Modularity of Mind: An Essay on Faculty Psychology.* MIT Press, Cambridge, MA.

Gamble, C.
1999   *The Palaeolithic Societies of Europe.* Cambridge University Press, Cambridge, UK.

Gangestad, S.
1997   Evolutionary Psychology and Genetic Variation: Non-Adaptive, Fitness-Related, and Adaptive. In *Characterizing Human Psychological Adaptations,* edited by G. Bock and G. Cardew, pp. 212–230. Ciba Foundation Symposium #208. Wiley, New York.

Gatewood, J.
1985   Actions Speak Louder Than Words. In *Directions in Cognitive Anthropology,* edited by J. Dougherty, pp. 199–220. University of Illinois Press, Urbana.

Gladwin, T.
1970   *East Is a Big Bird.* Harvard University Press, Cambridge, MA.

Howell, F., G. Cole, M. Kleindienst, B. Szabo, and K. Oakley
1972   Uranium Series Dating of Bone from the Isimila Prehistoric Site, Tanzania. *Nature* 237:51–52.

Jones, P.
1981   Experimental Implement Manufacture and Use: A Case Study from Olduvai Gorge, Tanzania. In *The Emergence of Man,* edited by J. Young, E. Jope, and K. Oakley, pp. 189–195. The Royal Society and the British Academy, London.

Keller, C., and J. Keller
1996   *Cognition and Tool Use: The Blacksmith at Work.* Cambridge University Press, Cambridge, UK.

Klein, S.
1983   Analogy and Mysticism and the Structure of Culture. *Current Anthropology* 24:151–180.

Kohn, M., and S. Mithen
1999   Handaxes: Products of Sexual Selection? *Antiquity* 73:518–526.

Kosslyn, S.
1994   *Image and Brain: The Resolution of the Imagery Debate.* MIT Press, Cambridge, MA.

Kozulin, A. (translator)
1986   Vygotsky in Context. *Preface in Thought and Language* by Lev Vygotsky. MIT Press, Cambridge, MA.

Leakey, M.
1971   *Olduvai Gorge,* Vol. 3. Cambridge University Press, Cambridge, UK.

Linn, M. C., and Petersen, A. C.
1986 A Meta-analysis of Gender Differences in Spatial Ability: Implications for Mathematics and Science Achievement. In *The Psychology of Gender,* edited by J. Hyde and M. Linn, pp. 67–101. Johns Hopkins University Press, Baltimore.

Marzke, M.
1996   Evolution of the Hand and Bipedality. In *Handbook of Human Symbolic Evolution,* edited by A. Lock and C. Peters, pp. 126–154. Oxford University Press, Oxford, UK.

Mithen, S.
1996   *The Prehistory of the Mind.* Thames and Hudson, London.

Morris, D.
1962   *The Biology of Art.* Methuen, London.

Noble, W., and I. Davidson
1996   *Human Evolution, Language, and Mind: A Psychological and Archaeological Inquiry.* Cambridge University Press, Cambridge, UK.

Peterkin, G., H. Bricker, and P. Mellars
1993   Hunting and Animal Exploitation in the Later Palaeolithic and Mesolithic in Eurasia. *Archaeological Papers of the American Anthropological Association* No. 4. American Anthropological Association, Washington, DC.

Piaget, J., and B. Inhelder
1967   *The Child's Conception of Space.* Translated by F. Langlon and J. Lunzer. Norton, New York.

Reith, E., and D. Dominin
1997   The Development of Children's Ability to Attend to the Visual Projection of Objects. *British Journal of Developmental Psychology* 15:177–196.

Roe, D.
1970   *Prehistory: An Introduction.* University of California Press, Berkeley.

Rohles, F., and J. Devine
1967   Further Studies of the Middleness Concept with the Chimpanzee. *Animal Behavior* 15:107–112.

Savage-Rumbaugh, S., S. Shanker, and T. Taylor
1998   *Apes, Language, and the Human Mind.* Oxford University Press, Oxford.

Schiller, P.
1951   Figural Preferences in the Drawings of a Chimpanzee. *Journal of Comparative and Physiological Psychology* 44:101–110.

Silverman, I., J. Choi, A. Mackewn, M. Fisher, J. Moro, and E. Olshansky
2000   Evolved Mechanisms Underlying Wayfinding: Further Studies on the Hunter-Gatherer Theory of Spatial Sex Differences. *Evolution and Human Behavior* 21:201–213.

Smith, D.
1973   Systematic Study of Chimpanzee Drawing. *Journal of Comparative and Physiological Psychology* 82:406–414.

Toth, N., K. Schick, E. Savage-Rumbaugh, R. Sevcik, and D. Savage-Rumbaugh
1993   Pan the Tool-Maker: Investigations into the Stone Tool-Making and Tool-Using Capabilities of a Bonobo (*Pan paniscus*). *Journal of Archaeological Science* 20:81–91.

Uttal, D.
1996   Angles and Distances: Children's and Adults' Reconstruction and Scaling of Spatial Configurations. *Child Development* 67:2763–2779.

Van Esterik, P.
1979   Symmetry and Symbolism in Ban Chiang Painted Pottery. *Journal of Anthropological Research* 35:495–508.

Vygotsky, L.
1986   *Thought and Language.* Translated by A. Kozulin. MIT Press, Cambridge, MA.

Walker, A., and R. Leakey (editors)
1993   *The Nariokotome* Homo erectus *Skeleton.* Harvard University Press, Cambridge, MA.

Washburn, D. K.

1983   Symmetry Analysis of Ceramic Design: Two Tests of the Method on Neolithic Material from Greece and the Aegean. In *Structure and Cognition in Art,* edited by D. Washburn, pp. 140–164. Cambridge University Press, Cambridge, UK.

1999   Perceptual Anthropology: The Cultural Salience of Symmetry. *American Anthropologist* 101:547–562.

Wright, R.

1972   Imitative Learning of a Flaked Tool Technology: The Case of an Orangutan. *Mankind* 8:296–306.

Wynn, T.

1979   The Intelligence of Later Acheulean Hominids. *Man* 14:371–391.

1989   *The Evolution of Spatial Competence.* University of Illinois Press, Urbana.

1991   Tools, Grammar, and the Archaeology of Cognition. *Cambridge Archaeological Journal* 1:191–206.

Wynn, T., and W. McGrew

1989   An Ape's View of the Oldowan. *Man* 24:283–298.

Wynn, T., and F. Tierson

1990   Regional Comparison of the Shapes of Later Acheulean Handaxes. *American Anthropologist* 92:73–84.

Wynn, T., F. Tierson, and C. Palmer

1996   Evolution of Sex Differences in Spatial Cognition. *Yearbook of Physical Anthropology* 39:11–42.

Yellen, J., A. Brooks, E. Cornelissen, M. Mehlman, and K. Stewart

1995   A Middle Stone Age Worked Bone Industry from Katanda, Upper Simliki Valley, Zaire. *Science* 268:553–556.

CHAPTER FOUR

The Genesis of Realistic and Patterned Representations

Dorothy K. Washburn

In this chapter, I address the nature of pattern as a visual form of communication and contrast this mode to other kinds of imagery formats. By *pattern,* I mean an arrangement of marks that repeats in systematic fashion. Such patterns can be distinguished by the geometries that are used to repeat the marks. They appear on many forms of material culture made by cultures throughout the world and have generally been thought to function as decorative embellishments. In this chapter, I suggest that patterns communicate many kinds of culturally important information.

While intuitively we might suppose that realistic depictions would be a clearer and more direct way to communicate, I survey how the formats of the various forms of representational and nonrepresentational imagery serve to transmit different kinds of information in different kinds of transfer situations. I argue that we should complement our cultural explanations for the presence of certain forms of imagery with insights from experimental psychology and neuroscience about how the eye and brain see and process fundamental parts and properties of things. This latter information will enhance our understanding of why and how the different formats of representation present, clarify, and enhance different kinds of information.

The Nature of Representation

Geometric patterns that are painted on ceramics, carved on house posts, or woven into cloth or baskets have usually been interpreted as decorative embellishment. This interpretation probably arose in Western contexts, where meaning is principally transmitted via alphabetic

scripts and pattern is left to function as attractive adornment. Indeed, Owen Jones titled his monumental survey of designs from different civilizations *The Grammar of Ornament* (1987 [1856]) and likewise, Flinders Petrie titled his survey *Decorative Patterns of the Ancient World* (1974 [1930]). Both titles imply that pattern embellishes rather than informs.

It is true, from technological considerations, that geometric shapes, rather than realistic depictions, are more easily produced on woven materials such as textiles and basketry due to structural constraints. In the weaving process, the wefts and warps interlock at angles, producing a two-dimensional grid. This base offers the perfect support for an endless variety of weave combinations and supplementary weft additions that can result in one-dimensional designs (banded designs along a single linear axis) and two-dimensional patterns (wallpaperlike designs that repeat in two directions).

It may also be true, from physiological considerations, that some of these geometric designs are visual records of the patterns "seen" by shamans during drug-induced trancelike states. These images tend to be geometric in form. In a provocative article, Lewis-Williams and Dowson (1988) suggest that the spaghetti meanders and other such "unidentifiable" markings found on Upper Paleolithic cave art as well as some rock art, for example that of the San of southern Africa and of the Shoshonean Coso of the Great Basin, may have been produced during altered states of consciousness. Patterns drawn from the visions experienced by the Tukano after taking a liquid preparation from a hallucinogenic vine (Reichel-Dolmatoff 1978) support this interpretation.

Nevertheless, nonrepresentational patterns are not limited to woven designs or drug-induced illusions. They are found on almost every kind of material culture made and used by literate and nonliterate societies. More importantly, in nonliterate societies peoples communicate through pattern. The specific geometries manifest in the patterns act as a kind of metaphoric shorthand to embody cultural information (Washburn 1999). Thus, the serving dish and shirt on which they appear function not only in practical ways for eating and clothing the body, but also as "billboards" that carry metaphorical messages about the central concepts of that society. That the meaning of such patterns appears as

undecipherable code to outsiders may merely mean that outsiders have not yet understood the important underlying premises of that culture and how they are embedded in pattern.

In this chapter, I consider why human beings communicate in such a patterned format. To best address this issue, I pose it within a more inclusive question— why do representations[1] take the various forms that they do? I explore why imagery takes these various forms from evolutionary, physiological, and cultural perspectives. That is, I ask, What are the perceptual and cultural factors that relate to imaging formats that range from those with almost photographic realism to the geometric constructions of the kind we are considering here?

I have diverged from other researchers[2] and enveloped nonrepresentational pattern within the notion of representation, centering it around the idea that images of all format types act as a visual language. In this capacity, they communicate by representing. Thus, although most analysts of images would make an initial distinction between realistic images and those that are nonrepresentational, I use the term "representational" to refer both to images that attempt to "look like" their subject as well as to images that are about their subject although they do not convey the way the subject appears to the eye.[3] Morphy (1980, 1989), for example, has discussed how Australian aboriginal images exemplify these two ways of representing: iconic or figurative images that attempt to represent what an object looks like and noniconic or nonrepresentational images that encode meaning in what appears to the outsider as ambiguous or unreadable combinations of geometric shapes.

From a cultural perspective, we need to consider the kinds of information best conveyed by each type of representational system. For example, to identify an object or to convey emotional state, age, role, or other information, realistic images of animals and portraits of people clothed befitting their status are the most direct means of conveying this information. However, it is difficult to imagine what cosmologies and moiety organizations "look like" and thus how to represent such ideas and institutional constructs realistically. Indeed, concepts and principles do not look like anything, for they are relationships, not things. Although it is possible to depict some kinds of relationships indirectly, such as in scenes

that indicate status through spatial and positional and size arrangements (cf. the positioning of Christ and his disciples in Leonardo da Vinci's painting *The Last Supper*), other kinds of relationships can actually be better embodied in pattern symmetries. To clarify this issue, I review the different formats that underlie the more prevalent representational systems as well as the properties of nonrepresentational pattern and discuss how these formats and properties best serve the communication of different kinds of information.

From a perceptual perspective, we need to know how the human eye and brain process the visible world and, in particular, whether and how different kinds of representations are differently processed. Brain-imaging studies now allow us to identify the specific areas of the visual cortex that are stimulated when objects are viewed. Preliminary studies indicating that color is differently perceived on abstract and representational art (Zeki 1999a, b) should inspire us to take a closer look at how manipulation of such basic properties as color or form are used by artists and cultures on different art formats to engender certain responses. The importance of integrating insights from experimental psychology and the neurosciences about how images are processed in the brain with anthropological interpretations of the culturally mediated responses to these images cannot be understated.

If, as Zeki suggests (1999a, b), imagery is a visual display of information about the world *as it is stored in the brain,* then, from an evolutionary perspective, our earliest systematic, organized representations are evidence of fully sapient human beings. It is notable that many of the representations on the walls of Upper Paleolithic caves in France and Spain appear to be superimposed, as if the cave walls were some sort of blackboard on which the artists were "thinking about" and sketching out their subjects (cf. illustrations in Ucko 1977). This kind of activity appears analogous to the way the brain stores multiple views of objects in "sketch pad" fashion (Harth 1999), allowing us to think about what we have "seen" in the same way that talking to ourselves allows us to mull over an idea. Harth proposes that representing arose as the concrete, permanent form of this kind of mental activity.

The largest body of systematically produced representations appears to be realistic depictions of animals painted and engraved on walls of caves during the last ice age. I briefly review how the cave paintings of the Upper Paleolithic exhibit the features essential for representational depictions that would have been cognitively meaningful to the Magdalenians of the Franco-Cantabrian world.[4] However, as populations grew and social institutions arose to organize these larger communities, other kinds of representational formats were developed to communicate different kinds of information (see survey in Jablan 1989). Some representations became more abstract and nonrepresentational, adopting a shorthand format that was intended principally for in-group consumption. As the chapters in this book clearly demonstrate, especially in cultures without writing, such nonrepresentational patterns not only decorate, but also act as visual voices that, in conjunction with verbalized speech and song, communicate important cultural information.

The Cognitive/Perceptual Baseline

One perspective on why representation developed at all among human groups may be gained from comparing human to nonhuman primate modes of communication. Studies of primate behavior in the wild (Tomasello and Call 1997) offer the best comparative benchmarks against which to consider the kinds of contexts and adaptive pressures in which hominid cognitive capabilities for image making probably evolved.

Summaries of the literature found in Hauser (1996) and Tomasello and Call (1997) indicate that the capability to produce markings that have meaning is a distinctly human capacity. No other nonhuman primate has the same set of cognitive skills that enable the various kinds of communicative forms produced by human beings. Although many primates live in social groups and have amazing displays of intraspecies communication, such as vocal calls, coloration, and bodily gesture, only humans have developed forms of communication that are *external* to their bodies and permanent beyond the moment of expression. There is no evidence that nonhuman primates produce permanent depictions with the intent to communicate this recorded information to an audience not present. In contrast, humans, by making permanent representational translations of reality, gain enormous communicative

power that transcends the immediacies of face-to-face or auditory interactions.

Such representational transcriptions of ideas and things fall at the end of Donald's proposed (1991) sequence of human cognitive development. He has suggested that the first formalized communication began with the miming of information and ideas not immediately at hand. This gestural format was augmented with verbalized expressions and then with permanent external recordings of actions and ideas that we call art and writing. The coordinated and complementary use of all these different sensory modes to preserve and transfer information to succeeding generations is one of the cognitive hallmarks of the human mind.

Although visual forms of permanent representation appear relatively late in the cognitive development of *Homo sapiens,* once developed, they exploit every facet of the highly developed perceptual system possessed by human beings. Indeed, humans everywhere have used these capabilities to distinguish themselves, advertise their wares, intimidate their enemies, and convince their peers through visual representation of information. What has been unrecognized heretofore is that the most effective of these visual statements are those that have targeted, manipulated, and highlighted the very primitive features and holistic properties of form that the human visual system evolved to detect and use in the basic processes of recognition, identification, and categorization. The thesis that the earliest art highlights these fundamental primitives of visual perception has been most elegantly elaborated by Halverson (1992), who has described how Upper Paleolithic cave representations were created almost solely by incised or painted outline contour drawings. Latto has further argued that works of art deemed "great" are considered so precisely because the artists have embedded their messages in visual primitives and properties that our perceptual system evolved to detect (1995).

What are these basic features and properties of form? Neuroscientists are beginning to unravel the immensely complex human visual process (Zeki 1999b). In the human brain the cells relating to vision are highly specialized: different cells respond to different kinds of features—some to color, some to line, etc.[5] When identifying an object, the brain only selects information about

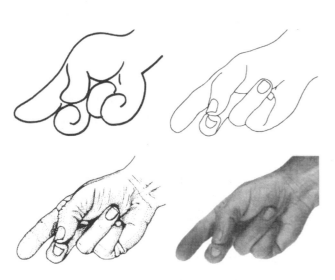

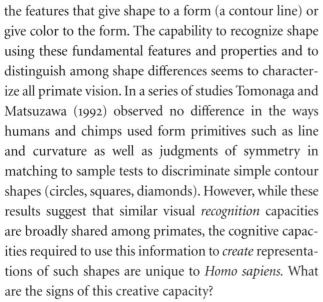

Figure 4.1 Four representational formats for depicting a hand (after Ryan and Schwartz 1956).

Figure 4.2 Tadpole figures (illustration courtesy of the artist).

the features that give shape to a form (a contour line) or give color to the form. The capability to recognize shape using these fundamental features and properties and to distinguish among shape differences seems to characterize all primate vision. In a series of studies Tomonaga and Matsuzawa (1992) observed no difference in the ways humans and chimps used form primitives such as line and curvature as well as judgments of symmetry in matching to sample tests to discriminate simple contour shapes (circles, squares, diamonds). However, while these results suggest that similar visual *recognition* capacities are broadly shared among primates, the cognitive capacities required to use this information to *create* representations of such shapes are unique to *Homo sapiens.* What are the signs of this creative capacity?

The visual preeminence of contour in human vision was demonstrated long ago by Ryan and Schwartz (1956), who presented subjects with four representations of an object: a black-and-white photograph, a detailed drawing, an outline drawing, and a cartoon drawing (Figure 4.1). They found that the photograph, which contained the greatest amount of detail, took the longest to identify, while the cartoon and simple outline drawings were recognized more quickly. Such outline images, stripped of embellishing distracters, allow the eye to focus directly on the essential features. Hochberg (1978) called them "canonical" features. Thus, it is precisely because contour line is one of the primitive features and properties that the brain recognizes and

processes that images created solely by line are easily read. Successful outline representations, from Upper Paleolithic cave art to Picasso drawings, in fact, are a material demonstration of the distinctly human cognitive ability to abstract from many details these defining characteristics of an entity and then to make a representation of that entity with only those essential characteristics.

It has been shown that other features, such as color, texture, or depth, can be eliminated from an outlined form without diminishing the ability of the viewer to detect the form (Pomerantz et al. 1989). Minimalist art exemplifies how form can be reduced to canonical geometric elements and still be recognizable. In Piet Mondrian's sketches for *Pier and Ocean* or his series *Apple Trees,* the forms become increasingly abstracted until they are nothing more than a series of horizontal and vertical short lines.

Researchers who study developmental issues related to art making have noted that a child's first representations are simplified versions of reality that focus on these form primitives. Their "tadpole" figures of people in frontal views composed of form primitives—circles for the head and two parallel lines for the legs—indicate their recognition of the basic defining aspects of the human figure. In short, in their earliest representational drawings children distill figures to their most canonical features (Figure 4.2). Only later do they add detail and begin to learn how to specify size differences and spacing relationships in order to combine separate figures into scenes (Golomb 1992).

The most canonical view for human figures is a frontal outline or silhouette, such as are found on many petroglyphs. In these views, foreshortening, shading, or shape indicators are not necessary to create identifiable form. Other information, such as that indicative of age, role, or status, can be economically and recognizably superimposed by using the three primitives—dots, lines, and regions—to create clothing or accessories.

In contrast, the most canonical view for animals is silhouette or contour profile, such as are found on the early Upper Paleolithic cave paintings. Profile views clearly show overall body shape as well as appendages that indicate the identity of the animal. The effectiveness of the profile view is confirmed by Palmer, Rosch, and Chase's study of viewer response to pictures of horses in many poses (1981). They found that of all the poses, recognition was fastest and most accurate when the horse was seen from the side.

The human visual system also focuses on contrasts between light and dark areas to differentiate figure from ground. Mithen (1996) has suggested that such perceptual acuity in detecting contrast would be useful in the detection of faintly indicated forms such as animal tracks. In fact, Hewes (1986:204 response to Davis 1986) makes the important point that the ability to visually read animal tracks appears to be uniquely human since other animals follow tracks by their sense of smell. Certainly the light contrast between the native rock and the freshly pecked or incised petroglyph would have enhanced the visual recognition of these early views of human and animal images.

The First Representations

The making of representations is a revolutionary cognitive achievement. As we have observed, no other primate intentionally makes images, either transitory or permanent, with the purpose of communicating information to another member of his social group. In this activity, humans have been exceedingly creative. Visual representations, like languages, appear in an incredible array of forms and formats. Some, like declarative sentences, attempt to capture reality directly, as in a portrait. Others, like poetry, depart from "photographic" equivalence, projecting intangible concepts in abstract pattern. Indeed, it is likely that in the lengthy

period before the development of formal writing systems, visual forms of representation were the most important vehicles for the recording of information and the spread of ideas.

The first representations were undoubtedly transitory, made of and/or on perishable materials, and we will probably never be certain what form they took. Among our earliest extant representations, many are three-dimensional sculptures, such as the famous Venus figurines and the postulated carved vulvas. It may be that making three-dimensional copies of three-dimensional forms that could be tangibly felt and visibly observed represented a cognitively easier process than re-creating the image of a three-dimensional form on a two-dimensional surface. Indeed, Halverson (1987) has argued that the first art took its inspiration from stone knapping and thus was sculptural (see also Wynn's chapter in this volume). Thus, I would argue that one of the pivotal breakthroughs that ultimately led to the diversity in forms of notation and representation involved learning how to depict three-dimensional entities on flat, two-dimensional surfaces.

Given the perceptual salience of line, it is not surprising that many of the earliest images on two-dimensional surfaces are outline profiles of animals made on cave walls in France and Spain during the Upper Paleolithic (cf. Ucko 1977). These incised and painted depictions demonstrate that these artists understood how to use simple line outline to create realistic likenesses of something (cf. Davis 1986). Outline emphasizes the most canonical aspects of the animals necessary for accurate recognition and identification. In the case of these cave images, the features represented—horns, hooves, and distinctive profile shapes—indicate that the artists clearly intended to identify the animal. Mithen (1988) observed that Upper Paleolithic artists explicitly used such drawings to record species information, citing examples where, although the bodies are outlined in profile, the feet are often drawn as one would see them as tracks. This is a format surely intended to indicate the specific species to the viewer.

Likewise, it is not surprising that early two-dimensional images of humans appear as frontal silhouettes, as exemplified on petroglyphs and pictographs. These images preserved on rock faces are probably the permanent counterparts of the kinds of similar but impermanent images drawn in the dirt, sand, or snow that preceded them. The outline and silhouette character of such images is ethnographically exemplified by the sand story drawings made by Walbiri women (Munn 1973). As a woman tells a story, she makes and then erases a series of activity scenes, much like the successive frames in a comic strip, using a minimal "alphabet" of thirteen different curved and straight lines, dots, and circles. For example, the simple wavy line that represents a snake and the vertical line with crosspieces that represents ribs serve, for all Walbiri viewers, as the most salient, canonical aspects that identify these objects. While many such figures drawn with these form primitives may appear unidentifiable to those outside the Walbiri culture, the meanings of these forms are known and shared by all Walbiri viewers.

However, if imagery was to communicate more than the identity of single objects, it had to become a formalized and complex system equal in communicative strength but different in format from the rules and meanings of spoken and written language. Thus, just as separate words are combined into sentences that have specific meanings, so too did people have to devise imagery formats that combined separate images into scenes that had specific meanings. While we have a very incomplete record of the early history of the development of imagery, it is likely that artists first began adding detail to separate images that would give these images additional informational power. Superpositional evidence in the sequence of line drawings indicates that Upper Paleolithic artists soon not only began to add detail to the simple outline contour representations, but also juxtaposed lines in ways that indicated efforts to capture the three-dimensionality of the animals. Willets (1997) has defined two pictorial devices that indicate dimensionality—*T junctions,* the points where an edge or a contour passes behind a surface, and *end junctions,* the points where contours end. These simple manipulations of line frequently appear in cave art. However, most of these early depictions were separate, often randomly placed on the cave walls. Relatively few were arranged in compositions that have internal structure and external limits (a frame). This early representational activity may be analogous to a similar stage in the developmental sequence toward fully structured language communication. Harth has suggested that language first consisted of unstructured separate words (1999).

From these early separate depictions, artists began to combine them into scenes; that is, compositions that used pictorial conventions to systematically relate things within a single image. It appears that if compositions are to communicate more than object identity, they require the development of a consistent set of rules, analogous to language grammars, for object arrangement in order for them to be "read" and understood by a community of viewers. For "look like" representations, the history of the development of different projection formats by different cultures is, in essence, a history of different solutions to the problem of how to make two-dimensional representations of a composition of three-dimensional objects that exist in three-dimensional space. The fact that this problem was solved at all is an important cognitive milestone. I shall briefly review such representational efforts.

Realistic Representations

Both Hagen (1986) and Willets (1997) describe the different kinds of projection systems that have been developed for representations in the two-dimensional plane. Willets most directly addresses the different forms of representation in terms of the picture primitives that are important in form perception. He shows how these primitives are used to create separate representations of form and then how these different forms are composed into scenes using different projection formats. I summarize here a few of the most frequently used projective systems to emphasize how each format highlights different canonical features of form.

Three primitives are used to create separate forms. *Optical denotation systems* use juxtaposed dots to create images. Pointillist paintings or digitized newspaper images are twenty-first-century examples. *Line drawings* use line to create the edges or contours of objects. Caricatures are classic examples. *Silhouettes* are solid regions in the form of objects. A simple example is the female restroom sign of a frontal figure in a dress.

A number of projective formats arose to arrange separate forms into scenes.

Perspective preserves the illusion of depth in a scene but distorts the shape and size of objects in the foreground and background. Developed by Renaissance artists, who sought a "realistic" way to capture the "actual" relationships among things in the everyday world, such images have become the sine qua nom of Western art. Art education in the West consists of moving children away from their elementary school projections of frontal views of houses on linear grass baselines (see Figure 4.2) to drawings that more "realistically" project depth and shape.

Oblique projection highlights the shape of the front face of objects, typically the most canonical view. The front face is placed parallel to the plane of projection and the sides of the other faces of the object diverge along parallel lines that run in the same oblique direction across the picture. This system typifies Chinese landscape painting, in which depth is achieved by tilting the picture plane so that objects in the background appear farther away.

Orthogonal projection places the most typical face of an object perpendicular to the picture plane. No effort is made to project depth or volumetric shape. Classic examples of orthogonal projections are children's drawings where all the objects are depicted as views of only one of their sides spaced along a horizontal ground line.

Other kinds of projection systems are variants of these principal formats. For example, in the genre of Indian miniature paintings, the ground plane is folded down to give the viewer a more complete view of everything depicted. Byzantine mosaics and Russian icon paintings are typically based on inverted perspective, where the orthogonals along the faces of objects diverge instead of converge to the edges of the picture. Even less "realistic" formats are topological transformations that alter the shape, scale, and dimensions of things but preserve the relative spatial relationships among them. For example, subway maps or circuit diagrams indicate the correct arrangement of the places or parts, but they are schematic, plan view representations that reproduce relationships rather than "realistic" appearances.

Willets argues that each representational system was developed to highlight certain features and thus to serve a specific communicative purpose. For example, he suggests that the Byzantine Orthodox Church purposely had artists use inconsistent combinations of vertical and horizontal oblique projections and inverted perspective in order to emphasize that the figures depicted were not of this world. Other depiction devices, such as the lack of shadows to suggest that "the Divine light permeates all things" and the floating placement of figures who have no "attachment to earthly time and space" to separate the everyday "real" world of humans from the anomalous world of the saints (Willets 1997:339ff) emphasized this perspective.

In sum, since the earliest representational forms of imagery, artists have developed many formats that focus the viewer's eye on certain canonical aspects of the image. None convey photographic realism, yet each is a fully adequate representation in the sense that the meaning is clear to the intended viewers. Indeed, images that attempt to precisely copy nature represent only a relatively small fraction of artistic output throughout human history (Hochberg 1979). Most formats simply highlight the canonical, prototypical characteristics of an object or the metaphoric essence of an idea in such a way that the correct identity and intended meaning is transferred to the viewer.

In the final analysis, each representational system is honed to be at the service of a specific communicative purpose. Throughout the history of visual representation, different kinds of representational formats were developed because each served as the best instrument to most effectively communicate certain kinds of information. From this perspective, some image formats are "better than others" not because they are "realistic," but because they more effectively serve the function of communicating the necessary information within a given social setting. There is no "best" representational system but simply many different systems that have been developed by different cultures in different times and places to serve different needs.

Pattern Representations

We have seen how meaningful "realistic" representations exploit features of the human perceptual system and adhere to compositional rules in order to communicate certain kinds of information. I now want to consider the features of pattern that enable it to be a vehicle for communicating. The appearance of nonrepresentational patterns appears to coincide with the need to message different kinds of information than simple identity—indeed, it coincides with the need to message concepts that cannot be represented in "look like" formats, such as cultural ideas and relationships. I focus on how the property of symmetry not only creates the pattern, but also metaphorically carries information about cultural relationships.

Patterns are representations in the two-dimensional plane composed of motifs repeated systematically by four geometric motions: translation, rotation, mirror reflection, and glide reflection. Such patterns can be symmetric in three dimensions as finite or point designs; one-dimensional, or linear banded designs; or two-dimensional, overall or wallpaper patterns. A pattern can be repeated by rotations or mirror reflections an infinite number of times around and through the central point on finite designs. However, there are only seven ways that the four motions can be combined in one-dimensional bands and only seventeen ways that the four motions can be arranged along the five kinds of grids in two-dimensional patterns. A more detailed explanation of the mathematics of symmetry and how this property is used to create and study cultural pattern is found in Washburn and Crowe (1988).

One of the essential features of a scene is the presence of meaningful relationships among the entities in the composition. Indeed, the human visual system, when analyzing scenes (Marr 1982), looks for properties that define these relationships. Lower primates, such as rhesus monkeys, focus on individual elements when confronted with a discrimination task (Polidora 1966). In contrast, human viewers, when confronted with tasks that attempt to force them to focus on parts of a design, persist in processing the entire array holistically (Clement and Weiman 1970).

One of the basic properties of pattern that allows humans to view such representations holistically is its symmetry. A substantial body of research has explored how humans use the property of symmetry in the perceptual process (reviewed in Washburn 1999). Unfortunately, most of this work has investigated symmetry as a property of single geometric shapes rather than as a property of patterns created by repeating these shapes. Thus, for example, we know that symmetry in single forms is perceived and identified faster and remembered and reproduced more accurately than asymmetrical form (Attneave 1955; Deregowski 1978), and we know that humans most easily detect symmetries about a vertical axis, then across a horizontal axis, and finally, with difficulty, across a diagonally placed axis (Corballis and Roldan 1975). Indeed, Shepard and Metzler (1971) demonstrated how individuals rotated nonsense forms to a vertical orientation in order to identify them. This preference for vertical orientation may be a hardwired adaptation related to the human bipedal stance perpendicular to the earth.

Unfortunately, some research has confused symmetries in single form with symmetries in pattern. Both Corballis and Roldan (1974) and Bruce and Morgan (1975), for example, erroneously fail to understand that repetition, that is, translation, is a symmetry. They also fail to distinguish finite forms, which can have only mirror reflection and rotational symmetries, from patterns that repeat along one or two axes using all four motions of rotation: mirror reflection, glide reflection, and translation. Indeed, the perception of and preferences for *all* the different symmetrical combinations of these four motions have not been examined systematically and in cross-cultural perspective. Future reinvestigations of the perception of all classes of symmetrical pattern in various cultural contexts should be given high priority.

In contrast to our more sophisticated understanding of the pictorial devices that are tied to the visual processing of representational imagery discussed above, our understanding of the critical features involved in visual processing of nonrepresentational pattern is still in its infancy. Studies (e.g., Washburn 2000) that attempt to define the kinds of pattern features that are noticed and that might carry culturally salient information are sorely needed. We do know from ethnographic studies that although patterned representational systems do not "look like" what they represent, pattern appears to be a compositional format that represents cultural ideas by metaphorically embedding cultural relationships in specific pattern symmetries (cf. Guss 1989; Washburn 1999; Witherspoon and Peterson 1995). That is, particular symmetrical arrangements of motifs are metaphorical statements of important cultural relationships and concepts. The chapters in this book describing ethnic affiliations among prehistoric groups in the Antilles (Roe, Chapter 7) and the social relationships in Andean (Franquemont, Chapter 6), Fijian (Ewins, Chapter 9), and Maori (Hanson, Chapter 8) societies attest to the many ways symmetries in pattern are involved in the representation of cultural ideas and activities. Pattern is truly an important visual medium of communication.

Conclusion

During hominid evolution, a networked array of neural, cognitive, and physical capacities coalesced that enabled human beings to develop many rich formats for communication—verbal, visual, and kinesthetic—possessed by no other members of the animal kingdom. This capacity to represent things and ideas in a variety of communicative modes is a hallmark of fully sapient human beings.

Although the record of humankind's earliest representational imagery is woefully incomplete, we can argue from knowledge of our perceptual system's capacities that the first efforts may well have been three-dimensional sculptures. The subsequent development of various ways to represent three-dimensional forms on a flat surface was a cognitive triumph, which, once mastered, was repeated and varied endlessly.

I have argued in this chapter that the earliest planar representations were simple, single realistic depictions. Images of animals were rendered in their canonical pose—a side profile that gives the most information about the animal's identity. Images of people and things were in frontal pose. During the subsequent explosion of culture, concurrent with the changing needs of more complex social groups, artists developed a variety of projection systems that enabled the creation of scenes of things in order to serve greatly expanded information storage and communication needs.

But as populations of hominids became larger and more socially and spatially differentiated, the associated changes in frequency, magnitude, and nature of human interactions within and among these social groupings prompted a greater diversity of imaging formats, some of which did not so directly and simply represent the visible world. Some population groups organized and packaged information about themselves and their world in formats as visual metaphors in patterned design rather than realistic depictions.

I have further suggested that the most effective of these realistic representations and patterned representations gain their communicative power because they highlight fundamental visual primitives and holistic properties that are perceived by the human visual system. The earliest realistic representations of form were outlined images of animals that focused on the basic form primitives of line to depict their canonical features. Patterns also "represent" relationships metaphorically through the holistic property of their symmetries. Far from being merely "decorative," patterns are powerhouses of information and knowledge.

Finally, I am urging that future studies include interdisciplinary collaborations with disciplines that study imaging from other perspectives. Some of the most interesting reinterpretations of image making that will expand our understanding about this uniquely human capacity are now coming from psychology and neuroscience. For example, Zeki (1999b) has contrasted observer response to realistically colored and Fauvist-colored objects and observed that different areas of the brain are activated. Will similar differences be observed when realistic and geometric images are observed? And how are such activation differences related to other cognitive processing activities that eventually interface with culturally mediated choices, preferences, and responses?

The symposium that resulted in this book was convened to begin the sharing and brainstorming process that will eventually lead to new insights about a very old human activity—the making of many kinds of visual representations, each of which communicates important but different aspects of human thought and activity. The intent of this chapter was to place nonrepresentational pattern within the spectrum of the many different formats in which information is visually communicated. ■

Notes

1. I do not use the term *art* here as this term is a Western category. Halverson (1987) astutely comments that the Magdalenian painters did not know they were creating art, but they certainly knew they were creating representations.

2 Davis's discussion of representational art excludes "other 'artistic' phenomena, such as ornament or architecture" (Davis 1986, n.2). Ittelson (1996) also separates markings that are depictions of things, from designs, writing, and diagrams, failing, it seems, to understand that nonrepresentational forms can also be representations even if they lack realism.

3. I do not include various forms of notation, such as the Upper Paleolithic lunar notation described by Marshack (1972), the clay token marks of the Sumerians (Schmandt-Besserat 1992) or even the knotted strings of the Inca (Ascher and Ascher 1981) within this representational scope, since they appear to be kinds of abstract symbolization for recording, rather than representing.

4. Most of the studies of Paleolithic art have centered around its meaning, dating, and spatial distribution, as well as how it functioned in the service of the earliest *Homo sapiens* (cf. Conkey et al. 1997 for a review of these issues). This chapter focuses, rather, on the way these very early representations demonstrate that *Homo sapiens* possessed certain kinds of perceptual capacities.

5. Overviews of the perception process can be found in Pinker (1984) and Hendee and Wells (1993). Overviews of the ways form primitives and holistic properties pertain to art can be found in Kennedy (1974), Parker and Deregowski (1990), Solso (1994), and Gregory et al. (1995).

References Cited

Ascher, M., and R. Ascher
1981   *Code of the Quipu: A Study in Media, Mathematics, and Culture.* University of Michigan Press, Ann Arbor.

Attneave, F.
1955   Symmetry, Information, and Memory for Patterns. *American Journal of Psychology* 68:209–222.

Bruce, V. G., and M. J. Morgan
1975   Violations of Symmetry and Repetition in Visual Patterns. *Perception* 4:239–249.

Clement, D. E., and C. F. R. Weiman
1970   Instructions, Strategies, and Pattern Uncertainty in a Visual Discrimination Task. *Perception & Psychophysics* 7:333–336.

Conkey, M. W., O. Soffer, D. Stratmann, and N. G. Jablonski (editors)
1997   Beyond Art: Pleistocene Image and Symbol. *Memoirs of the California Academy of Sciences,* No. 23, San Francisco.

Corballis, M. C., and C. E. Roldan
1974   On the Perception of Symmetrical and Repeated Patterns. *Perception & Psychophysics* 16:136–142.
1975   Detection of Symmetry as a Function of Angular Orientation. *Journal of Experimental Psychology: Human Perception and Performance* 1:221–230.

Davis, W.
1986   The Origins of Image Making. *Current Anthropology* 27:193–215.

Deregowski, J. B.
1978   Role of Symmetry in Pattern Reproduction. *British Journal of Psychology* 69:217–224.

Donald, M.
1991   *Origins of the Modern Mind: Three Stages in the Evolution of Culture and Cognition.* Harvard University Press, Cambridge, MA.

Golomb, C.
1992   *The Child's Creation of a Pictorial World.* University of California Press, Berkeley.

Gregory, R., J. Harris, P. Heard, and D. Rose
1995   *The Artful Eye.* Oxford University Press, Oxford, UK.

Guss, D. M.
1989   *To Weave and Sing: Art, Symbol, and Narrative in the South American Rain Forest.* University of California Press, Berkeley.

Hagen, M. A.
1986   *Varieties of Realism: Geometries of Representational Art.* Cambridge University Press, Cambridge, UK.

Halverson, J.
1987   Art for Art's Sake in the Paleolithic. *Current Anthropology* 28:63–89.
1992   The First Pictures: Perceptual Foundations of Paleolithic Art. *Perception* 21:389–404.

Harth, E.
1999   The Emergence of Art and Language in the Human Brain. *Journal of Consciousness Studies* 6:97–115.

Hauser, M. D.
1996   *The Evolution of Communication.* MIT Press, Cambridge, MA.

Hendee, W. R., and P. N. T. Wells (editors)
1993   *The Perception of Visual Information.* Springer-Verlag, New York.

Hewes, G. W.
1986   Response to W. Davis, the Origins of Image Making. *Current Anthropology* 27:204.

Hochberg, J.
1978   Art and Perception. In *Perceptual Ecology,* edited by E. C. Carterette and M. P. Friedman, pp. 225–258. *Handbook of Perception,* Vol. X, Academic Press, New York.
1979   Some of the Things That Paintings Are. In *Perception and Pictorial Representation,* edited by C. F. Nodine and D. F. Fisher, pp. 17–41. Praeger, New York.

Ittelson, W. H.
1996   Visual Perception of Markings. *Psychonomic Bulletin and Review* 3:171-187.

Jablan, S.
1989   Geometry in the Pre-Scientific Period. *History of Mathematical and Mechanical Sciences,* Book 3, Mathematical Institute, Belgrade, Serbia.

Jones, O.
1987   [1856] *The Grammar of Ornament.* Day and Son, London. Dover, New York.

Kennedy, J. M.
1974   *A Psychology of Picture Perception.* Jossey-Bass, San Francisco.

Latto, R.
1995   The Brain of the Beholder. In The Artful Eye, edited by R. Gregory, J. Harris, P. Heard, and D. Rose, pp. 66–94. Oxford University Press, Oxford, UK.

Lewis-Williams, J. D., and T. A. Dowson
1988   The Signs of All Times: Entoptic Phenomena in Upper Paleolithic Art. *Current Anthropology* 29:201–245.

Marr, D.
1982   *Vision.* Freeman, San Francisco.

Marshack, A.
1972   Upper Paleolithic Notation and Symbol. *Science* 178:817–828.

Mithen, S. J.
1988   Looking and Learning: Upper Paleolithic Art and Information Gathering. *World Archaeology* 19:297–327.
1996   *The Prehistory of the Mind: The Cognitive Origins of Art, Religion and Science.* Thames and Hudson, New York.

Morphy, H.
1980   What Circles Look Like. *Canberra Anthropology* 3:17–36.
1989   On Representing Ancestral Beings. In *Animals into Art,* edited by H. Morphy, pp. 144–160. Unwin Hyman, London, UK.

Munn, N. D.
1973   *Walbiri Iconography.* Cornell University Press, Ithaca, NY.

Palmer, S. E., E. Rosch, and P. Chase
1981   Canonical Perspective and the Perception of Objects. In *Attention and Performance,* edited by J. Long and A. Baddeley, Vol. IX. Earlbaum, Hillsdale, NJ.

Parker, D. M., and J. B. Deregowski
1990   *Perception and Artistic Style.* North-Holland, Amsterdam.

Petrie, F.
1974   [1930] *Decorative Patterns of the Ancient World.* Dover, New York.

Pinker, S.
1984   Visual Cognition: An Introduction. *Cognition* 18:1–63.

Polidora, V. J.
1966   Stimulus Correlates of Visual Pattern Discrimination by Monkeys: Multidimensional Analyses. *Perception & Psychophysics* 1:405–414.

Pomerantz, J. R., E. A. Pristach, and C. E. Carson
1989   Attention and Object Perception. In *Object Perception: Structure and Process,* edited by B. E. Shepp and S. Ballesteros, pp. 53–89. Erlbaum, Hillsdale, NJ.

Reichel-Dolmatoff, G.
1978   Drug-Induced Optical Sensations and Their Relationship to Applied Art among Some Columbian Indians. In *Art in Society: Studies in Style, Culture and Aesthetics,* edited by M. Greenhalgh and V. Megaw, pp. 289–304. St. Martin's Press, New York.

Ryan, T. A., and C. Schwartz
1956   Speed of Perception as a Function of Mode of Presentation. *American Journal of Psychology* 69:60–69.

Schmandt-Besserat, D.
1992   *Before Writing: From Counting to Cuneiform.* University of Texas Press, Austin.

Shepard, R. N., and J. Metzler
1971   Mental Rotation of Three-Dimensional Objects. *Science* 171:701–703.

Solso, R. L.
1994   *Cognition and the Visual Arts.* MIT Press, Cambridge, MA.

Tomasello, M., and J. Call
1997   *Primate Cognition.* Oxford University Press, New York.

Tomonaga, M., and T. Matsuzawa
1992   Perception of Complex Geometric Figures in Chimpanzees (*Pan troglodytes*) and Humans (*Homo sapiens*): Analysis of Visual Similarity on Basis of Choice Reaction Time. *Journal of Comparative Psychology* 106:43–52.

Ucko, P. J.
1977   *Form in Indigenous Art: Schematisation in the Art of Aboriginal Australia and Prehistoric Europe.* Prehistory and Material Culture Series No. 13. Australian Institute of Aboriginal Studies, Canberra. Duckworth, London and Humanities Press, NJ.

Washburn, D. K.
1999   Perceptual Anthropology: The Cultural Salience of Symmetry. *American Anthropologist* 101:547–562.
2000   An Interactive Test of Color and Contour Perception by Artists and Non-Artists. *Leonardo* 33:197–202.

Washburn, D. K., and D. W. Crowe
1988   *Symmetries of Culture: Theory and Practice of Plane Pattern Analysis.* University of Washington Press, Seattle.

Willets, J.
1997   *Art and Representation: New Principles in the Analysis of Pictures.* Princeton University Press, Princeton.

Witherspoon, G., and G. Peterson
1995   *Dynamic Symmetry and Holistic Asymmetry in Navajo and Western Art and Cosmology.* Peter Lang Publishing, New York.

Zeki, S.
1999a   Art and the Brain. *Journal of Consciousness Studies* 6:76–96.
1999b   *Inner Vision: An Exploration of Art and the Brain.* Oxford University Press, Oxford, UK.

Figure 5.1 Detail of mantle MNAA 18-2, EIP 1B, ca. A.D 50–100. The field symmetry pattern is D-HHHH (see Figure 5.12); in the border, figures repeat in glide reflection. There are four color blocks in the field, arranged in two bicolor S diagonals with tetracolor Z diagonals, rows, and columns. This type of color block alternation is coded as 2 bi.s, 1 tetra.zrc (Paul 1997:Pattern 19).

Figure 5.2 Mantle 290-14, EIP 1B, ca. A.D. 50–100. The field symmetry and color patterns are the same as those in the mantle illustrated in Figure 5.1.

Figure 5.3 Mantle 89-16, EIP 1B/2, ca. A.D. 75–150. The field symmetry pattern is D-TTVV, illustrated in Figure 5.17b. There are five color blocks arranged to form the color configuration 1 penta.szcr (Paul 1997:Pattern 28).

Figure 5.4 Mantle 382-9, EIP 1B, ca. A.D. 50–100. Figures have a nonegalitarian symmetry pattern (shown in Figure 5.57) and are stitched in five color blocks arranged so that all diagonals, rows, and columns are different (coded szrc.all different; Paul 1997:Pattern 32)

CHAPTER FIVE

Symmetry Schemes on Paracas Necrópolis Textiles

Anne Paul

THE CULTURAL ARTIFACT PAR EXCELLENCE of the ancient Central Andes is cloth: generations of Andeans used cloth as a symbol of identity and distinction, as the most precious accessory to rituals, and as an item for sacrifice. Since many important ideas were expressed through this medium, textiles are a source of information about the people who produced them. This interest in Andean fiberwork as a means of understanding the past is not the exclusive domain of art historians, archaeologists, or anthropologists, as the following quotation makes clear: "It is rather remarkable that the ancient Peruvian fabrics were able to inspire—thousands of years after their creation—new mathematical points of view on orderly patterns" (Grünbaum 1990:67).[*] These "orderly patterns" are the subject of this chapter. I will describe and discuss the system of organization that underlies the orientation of images on garments made by one of the early participants in this long weaving tradition, a culture today called Paracas/Topará (Figures 5.1 to 5.5).[1] In addition, I will comment on the logic behind the color patterns on the same textiles.

---

[*]Editor's note: This article has been reprinted in *Symmetry Comes of Age*, edited by Dorothy Washburn and Donald Crowe, University of Washington Press, Seattle, 2004

Paracas/Topará communities buried their dead in cemeteries on the arid Paracas Peninsula of south coastal Peru from at least Early Horizon epoch 10 through Early Intermediate period epoch 2 (approximately 100 B.C. to A.D. 200).[2] In preparation for interment, the deceased were carefully wrapped to form bundles; the largest of the bundles excavated from a burial zone called the Necrópolis de Wari Kayan were packed with cloth, including woven garments. The majority of Paracas Necrópolis-style textiles are structurally simple, comprising a plain weave ground cloth that acts as the support for stem-stitch embroidery. Most have images embroidered in borders, and a much smaller number have additional figures stitched in their fields; normally, a single iconographic type repeats on a textile. My discussion will start with an examination of border images and will continue with a longer analysis of field figures.

Border Imagery

A Paracas Necrópolis embroidered textile comprises two main visual parts, a field and borders. The range of garments with borders includes mantles, headcloths, ponchos, tunics, skirts, and loincloths. Borders are usually worked directly on the ground cloth of these items of ritual attire, with the exception of mantles.[3] Each garment type has a specific border format (or formats in the case of mantles) that remains remarkably consistent over time—so unchanging, in fact, that it is likely that border arrangements themselves encode symbolic information (Paul 2000a).

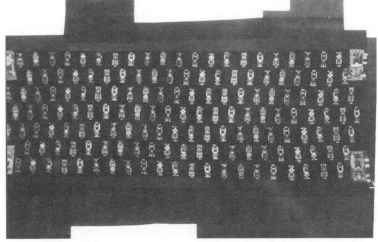

Figure 5.5 Mantle EMG 35.32.184, EIP 2, ca. A.D. 100–200. The symmetry pattern is D-PTPT (Figure 5.19). There are eight monocolor Z diagonals; the other three directions have eight alternating color blocks (8 mono.z, 1 octa.src; Paul 1997:Pattern 44).

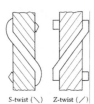

Figure 5.6 (a) Diagram showing the direction of twist in spun or twisted fiber element. The direction of twist is designated either S or Z according to the orientation of the slant of the twisted fibers. Reproduced from Emery (1966:11, Diagram 1), courtesy of The Textile Museum, Washington, DC.

S-twist (\ )　Z-twist (/)

Figure 5.6 (b) Drawing of border image on headcloth (MNAA 410-33a), EH 10, ca. 100 A.D.–0. The two strands depicted on the left half of the border have an S twist while those on the right have a Z twist.

Figure 5.6 (c) Drawing of the border in Figure 5.6b showing how the segments of an individual strand, instead of being stitched in a single color, appear in several colors.

Orientation

In another analysis of the borders on 543 Paracas Necrópolis woven garments, I explore the thesis that borders provide a symbolic, protective boundary on the weavings by partially "sealing" their edges with references to twisted or interlaced strands (Paul 2000c). My study relies on the pioneering work of Mary Frame (1986), who first pointed out the ubiquitous presence of visual images of fabric structures in ancient Andean textiles. Frame (1986) identified both explicit and implicit depictions of such structures—in particular twisted strands and oblique interlacing—in a wide range of stylistically diverse textiles.

While both of these fabric structures are common motifs on Paracas Necrópolis oblique interlaced headbands (see Frame 1991:Figures 4.1, 4.2, and 4.5 through 4.10), there are very few literal depictions of twisted strands, and none of oblique interlacing, on Paracas Necrópolis embroidered borders. One unmistakable representation has adjacent rows of two twisted strands, one pair with an S twist and the other with a Z twist (Figure 5.6). Other depictions of twisted strands use the outlines of the strands to frame linear-style feline and serpent images (Figure 5.7; see Paul 2000c a:Figure 3). In addition, there are occasional pictures of twisted strands in the borders of clothing depicted on the anthropomorphs

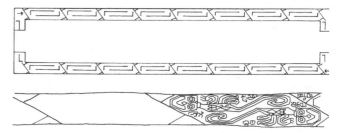

Figure 5.7 (a) Drawing of headcloth (MNAA 382-50a), EIP 1B, ca. A.D. 50–100. Feline figures in the borders are framed by an image of Z-twisted strands

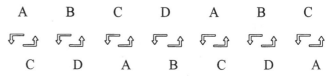

Figure 5.7 (b) Detail of the border symmetry pattern. The letters next to the arrows indicate the pattern of color block repetition; there are four different color blocks. The figures, depicted as arrows, repeat in bifold rotation.

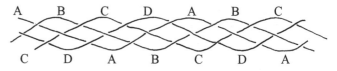

Figure 5.7 (c) Sketch showing that the positioning of color blocks in the borders is such that when like color blocks are joined with lines, it is possible envision an image of four-strand oblique interlacing.

embroidered on the textiles (Rickenbach 1999:Plate 44; Paul 2000c:Figure 4).

In addition to these relatively straightforward images of fabric structures, some images suggest the movement of twisting strands without actually depicting threads. For example, two snakes twist around each other (Rickenbach 1999:Plate 47) or adjacent double-headed snakes with threadlike bodies placed diagonally across the border width interlock heads so that they seem to entwine (Paul 1990a:Plate 19).

While snake imagery is obviously ideal for making visual analogies to strands, the same is not true for the other figural types on Paracas Necrópolis embroideries. How can a row of anthropomorphic figures, for example, evoke the image of a fabric structure? Paracas Necrópolis embroiderers apparently found a way to do so: they chose isometries in which the motions of symmetry used in the repetition of a design unit are comparable to the symmetry of fabric structures, a fact first recognized and demonstrated by Frame (1986 and 1991). These comparisons can

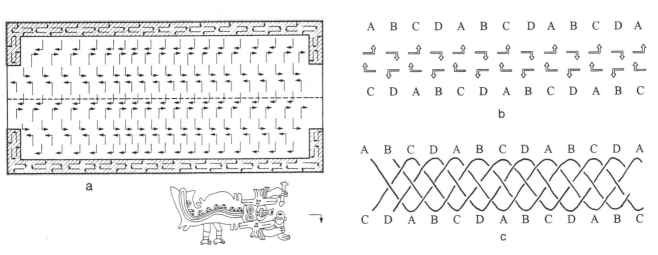

Figure 5.8 (a) Mantle and the figure that decorates its field and border (NMAA 89-16; reprinted from Paul 1991:Figure 5.7), EIP 1B/2, ca. A.D. 75–150. (b) Detail of the border symmetry pattern, showing two parallel rows of images repeating in glide reflection. The rows point in opposite directions. As in the headcloth in Figure 5.7, there are four different color blocks. (c) Sketch showing how the border color block pattern may invoke the image of four-strand oblique interlacing.

also be visualized in diagrams that plot figural orientation. For instance, the iconography in numerous borders comprises a motif that, when turned around a point midway between itself and another motif, is superimposed exactly on the other (Figure 5.7a). The symmetry operation employed in their repetition is bifold rotation, the same symmetry underlying twisted strands (Frame 1991:Figure 4.20).

Abstract references to another fabric structure, oblique interlacing, may be even more common in the border iconography, with glide reflection as the basis of the symmetry patterns of figural repeats (Figures 5.1–5.4, 5.8). In this symmetry operation there is a change in orientation as well as a shift in position: the motif glides up or down along the border as it simultaneously reverses itself as though it were reflecting in a mirror (two parallel rows of figures in the mantle are illustrated in Figures 5.3 and 5.8). In borders with this isometry, the repeating pattern of the embroidered images may be generated by the same axes of glide reflection that generate the structure of three-strand oblique interlacing (Frame 1991:Figure 4.22).

It is likely, then, that fabric structures are a meaningful aspect of the textile border iconography even when they are not explicitly represented, with "the underlying skeleton of fabric structure symmetry" determining the alternation pattern of the embroidered images (Frame 1986:54). Though she argues that the symmetry of fabric structures is at the core of the symmetry of figural

repeats, Frame cautions that the identification of a specific structure on the basis of symmetry is not always possible, or at least not always unambiguous (Frame 1986, n. 4). For one thing, more than one type of symmetry can be present in the repetition of a design unit (this is especially true in the field repeats to be discussed below). In such a case, which of the symmetries should be used to identify a specific structure? For another, "the symmetry of one fabric structure in a band can overlap with a different structure in a limited field repeat" (Frame 1986, n. 4). I view the band patterns and the two-dimensional field repeats as discrete design elements that occupy distinct areas of the cloth. While Frame's reservations are particularly pertinent to the field patterns, they are less so for borders: the sample examined in my study of Paracas Necrópolis borders (Paul 2000c) provides statistical and contextual data that support her thesis that fabric structures may have served as templates for figural repetition, at least along the perimeters of Paracas Necrópolis fabrics.

A Paracas Necrópolis design unit can be asymmetrical, bilaterally symmetrical, symmetrical on two axes, or possess point symmetry, and in a border it can be positioned so that its body axis is either parallel to, or at right angles to, the edge of the band.[4] These choices run across all styles of formal construction (i.e., linear, broad line, and block color; see Paul 1990a for descriptions of embroidery styles). Although mathematicians have enumerated seven different types of regular band

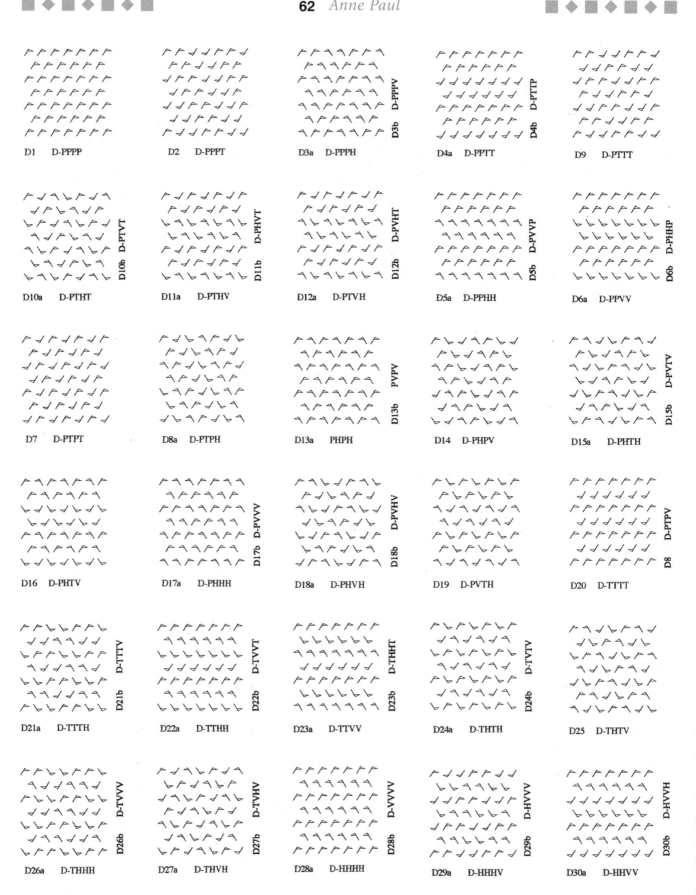

Figure 5.9 D-lattice egalitarian patterns, with serial numbers on the bottom left and the symbols of the symmetry schemes they represent on the bottom center of each pattern (after Grünbaum 1990:Figure 8; reproduced with the author's permission).

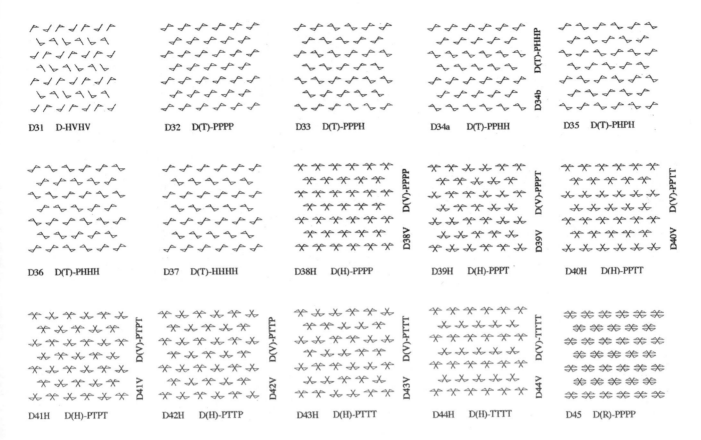

patterns (see Shepard 1948:218ff., Figure 2; Washburn and Crowe 1988:57–58, Figure 2.26), Paracas Necrópolis borders almost always employ just two: over 97 percent of the borders in a sample of 543 textiles have isometries that are either glide reflection or bifold rotation. Hence, though the range of iconographic types on Paracas Necrópolis textiles is large, the number of ways of arranging them in borders is severely limited—so restricted, in fact, that it is probable that symmetry type itself constitutes another level of iconography, underscoring the importance of manipulating threads in a culture whose people thought through fiber.

Color

Border patterns that are generated by bifold rotation have anywhere from two to eight differently colored figures (or color blocks, to be defined below) arranged in regular alternation. While it is tempting to suggest that the number of color blocks could allude to the number of strands twisting together—an interpretation that would superimpose the color design of figures on their structural symmetries—such a reading may be too facile, as the embroidered depiction of twisted strands

mentioned above makes clear (Figure 5.6c). In this representation, each individual strand changes color where it passes behind the second strand so that color does not work in tandem with structure.

Glide reflection patterns more clearly divorce color from the underlying symmetry type. Most of the borders in this class have four or more color blocks (only a few examples have three color blocks) so that the implied structure of three-strand oblique interlacing operates separately from the supposed number of "strands."

Though color may be used occasionally to invoke references to fabric structures, it seems to do so independently. For example, the borders on the headcloth illustrated in Figure 5.7 may have three discrete but overlaid references to fabric structures: first, segments of twisted strands frame pairs of felines (Figure 5.7b); second, the felines repeat in bifold rotation, mirroring the symmetry of twisted strands (Figure 5.7b); and third, the color blocks of these figures are staggered so that when like color blocks are joined by lines, the image of a four-strand braid is invoked (Figure 5.7c). Similarly, the symmetry and color arrangements on the mantle in Figure 5.8 may allude on two levels to

Figure 5.10 Drawings of an asymmetric arrow (top) and the four possible aspects of copies of the motif (bottom) on a fabric plane (adapted from Grünbaum 1990:Figure 5). With respect to the original, "P" is parallel, "H" is reflected horizontally, "V" is reflected vertically, and "T" is turned.

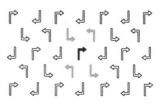

Figure 5.11 A fabric pattern in which motifs are disposed in a D lattice, producing the symmetry scheme D-HVHV (see text for explanation; adapted from Grünbaum 1990:Figure 6). This scheme is also depicted in Figure 5.23*a*.

oblique interlacing, with parallel rows of figures repeating in glide reflection (each row mirroring the symmetry of three-strand oblique interlacing; Figure 5.8b) a color block pattern like that in the headcloth described above (Figure 5.8c).

Field Imagery

The textiles produced by Paracas/Topará weavers are, structurally speaking, much less complex than many other ancient Andean fabrics. It seems, however, that the flexibility permitted by stitching images on cloth rather than weaving them into the structure of the cloth facilitated the creation of complexities of a different nature. It is hard to imagine that the range of orientation patterns present in the fields of Paracas Necrópolis–style weavings, or the number of different color patterns, could have been obtained in another structure (no other Andean culture adopted embroidery on plain weave to the extent of Paracas/Topará weavers).

Orientation

The two motions of symmetry that appear in borders are also present in the field patterns, but it is less clear to what extent these isometries replicate those of fabric structures. The number of textiles with field patterns is considerably smaller than those with border patterns, and the total number of symmetry schemes is larger. There are 165 textiles with embroidered field images in my sample, including 137 mantles, eleven ponchos, eight headcloths, seven skirts, and two tunics.[5] Iconographically alike[6] embroidered images are aligned in rows and columns on the plane of each fabric, almost always staggered to create a checkerboard effect, though in two cases unstaggered to form a compact arrangement. These field symmetries can be classified using a novel method devised by the mathematician B. Grünbaum (1990). In defining the fabric plane, the author notes that "the Euclidean plane is isotropic (all directions are mutually equivalent)" and

therefore not appropriate for the study of fabric planes, which "have directions that are special and not equivalent to all other directions" (Grünbaum 1990:45). These special directions—the horizontal and the vertical—echo the axes of the warp and weft elements of the medium. I will suggest below that diagonals also play a special role in the figure patterns. Finding the ornamentation of Peruvian fabrics complicated in ways that escape group theory analysis, Grünbaum searches for a classification system that could have been within the conceptual framework of the ancient weavers themselves. His solution is "a group-free approach to a classification that is appropriate for the kinds of patterns that occur on Peruvian fabrics" (Grünbaum 1990:50).

Disposing images in either a "diamond lattice" or a "rectangular lattice" (symbolized by the letters *D* and *R*), Grünbaum enumerates all of the egalitarian symmetry schemes possible on a fabric plane (Grünbaum 1990:47 and Figure 8; his D-lattice schemes are reproduced here in Figure 5.9).[7] After determining whether the motifs on a fabric are arranged according to a D lattice or an R lattice, he plots the ways the four nearest neighbors of a motif coincide with that motif. The copies of an asymmetric design unit have four possible aspects: they can be parallel to the original motif (P), reflected horizontally (H), reflected vertically (V), or turned (T) (Figure 5.10). To determine the symmetry scheme of a D-lattice pattern, we note the disposition of the two copies immediately above and the two copies immediately below a given motif. This procedure is illustrated in Figure 5.11, where the four gray copies adjacent to the black arrow have aspects (counterclockwise from upper right) H, V, H, V. Such patterns are said to be egalitarian because "for every copy of the motif, the disposition of the aspects of the motifs adjacent to it is the same" (Grünbaum 1990:51). The formal description of the symmetry scheme of this pattern is D-HVHV; its serial number (D-31) allows us to easily locate the pattern among Grünbaum's charts. In addition to the egalitarian patterns,

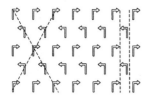

Figure 5.12 D-HHHH/D28a. The dashed lines are added to indicated axes of glide reflection between columns of asymmetric design units as well as along diagonals. For example of mantles with this pattern, see Figure 5.1 and 5.2. Sample: AMNH 41.2/8869; BM 34.1558, 34.1588; IMA 47.88/MR AAM 46-7-376; MBA accession number unknown (published in Mason 1961:27); MFAB 21.2556/NMNH 289614/ROM 916.7.3; MFAB 21.2563; MNAA 18-2, 38-15, 38-49, 243-4, 290-14; AIC 1970.293; MVMun 34-41-7; UM 39-11-1.

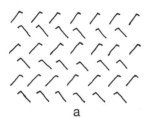
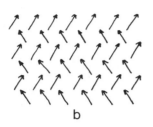
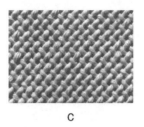

a   b   c

Figure 5.13 (a) Adjusted diagram of pattern layout in Figure 5.12, with arrows slanted. (b) Modified version of Figure 5.13a, showing arrows facing left and right by alternate rows (adapted from Frame 1991:Figure 4.23). (c) Photograph of oblique interlacing (Emery 1966:Figure 72), which has an underlying symmetry structure that is equivalent to those in (a) and (b).

Figure 5.14 D(H)-PPPP/D38H. This pattern comprises motifs that are bilaterally symmetrical. They repeat in glide reflection between vertical columns and along diagonals and have mirror reflection between images in horizontal rows. Sample: EMG 35.32.68; MNAA 382-36.

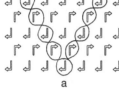
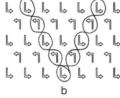

a   b

Figure 5.15 (a) D-TTTT/D20. This pattern has diagonal axes of bifold rotation, with S and Z diagonals "twisting" clockwise (following the direction that the arrows point). Sample DAM 1980.44; EMG 35.32.133, 35.32.188, 35.32.190, 35.32.191; MBA accession number unknown (published in Mason 1961:18); MNAA 89-13, 94-41, 254-5, 310-27; SM accession number unknown (published in Lumbreras 1974:Figure 102); UN SA 4604. (b) D-TTTT/D20. Here the S and Z diagonals "twist" counterclockwise. Sample: BM 34.1556; DMA 1972.4.MCD; EMG 35.32.182; MNAA 253-5, 378-2; ROM 931.12.11; Stafford (1941:Plate X).

Grünbaum includes the notations for those schemes that produce nonegalitarian patterns (Grünbaum 1990:59 and Table 2), some of which appear in the sample of Paracas Necrópolis textiles.

Paracas Necrópolis textile iconography is predominantly asymmetrical (135 cases among those in this sample), with a certain number of bilaterally symmetrical designs (nineteen in this study) and a few that have point symmetry or are symmetrical on two axes (six and five examples, respectively). Most patterns are D lattice (162 examples out of the 165). All of the known Paracas Necrópolis field patterns are illustrated in this chapter and described below and in the captions.

Egalitarian Patterns

The isometries present in the field patterns on Paracas Necrópolis fabrics are glide reflection, bifold rotation, mirror reflection, and translation, as noted by Grünbaum (1990:47). As on borders, bifold rotation and

glide reflection are the two symmetry operations that occur most frequently. In the diagrams that accompany this discussion, I have marked in and highlighted some of the paths of glide reflection and points of rotation to make these operations more visible as I discuss the symmetry patterns. All of the symmetry schemes present in the fields of 165 Paracas Necrópolis textiles are presented in these diagrams; the caption for each has the combinatorial symbol of the egalitarian pattern as worked out by Grünbaum (1990), followed by a slash and its serial number to facilitate finding the pattern among Grünbaum's charts.

One pattern that conceivably alludes to the symmetry of a specific fabric structure is generated by glide reflection along vertical and diagonal axes (illustrated in Figure 5.12). In addition, simple translation is the symmetry motion in rows and columns. Even though translation is present, however, patterns are generally described "by the other motions which clearly distinguish them. . . without

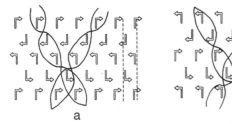

Figure 5.16 When tracks of bifold rotation are drawn along both diagonals to imitate the symmetry scheme in Figure 5.15, we can visualize the twining pairs of elements in double oblique twining (after Seiler Bladinger 1999:Figure 81a).

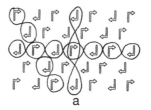

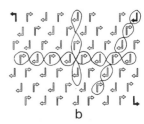

Figure 5.19 (a) D-PTPT/D7. This pattern is generated by bifold rotation on vertical and horizontal axes; bifold rotation is also present on S diagonals (see Figure 5.5). Sample: EMG 35.31.184. (b) D-PTPT/D7. Here the same scheme as in (a) has bifold rotation on Z diagonals. Sample: EMG 35.32.209.

Figure 5.17 (a) D-TTVV/D23a. Pairs of design units repeat in bifold rotation, with S and Z diagonals "twisting" clockwise. Images repeat in glide reflection within columns. Sample: BM 34.1581; MFAB 16.33; MNAA 89-14, 319-11; BM 34.1557; PM 32-30-30-45. (b) D-TTVV/D23a. In this pattern, the S and Z diagonals "twist" counterclockwise. Figures 5.3, 5.8, and 5.18 illustrate fabrics with this pattern. Sample: AMNH 41.0/1502, 41.0/1507, 41.0/1508; BM 34.1549, 34.1559, 34.1593; CMA 40.528; DO B-506.PT; MFAB 16.31, 31.501; MNAA 89-16, 217-3, 382-5, 382-6, 451-8; PC; PM 974-43-30/9413; ROM 916.8.1, 916.8.2; TM 91.113, 91.192.

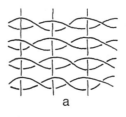 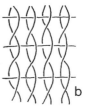

Figure 5.20. Sketches of fabric structures that possess the underlying symmetries that may be analogous to those in the symmetry scheme D-PTPT illustrated in Figure 5.19. Figures 5.20a, b, and c show, respectively, weft twining, warp twining, and oblique twining.

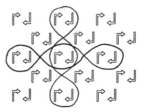

Figure 5.21 D-PPPP/D1, with bifold rotation on vertical and horizontal axes. Sample: BM 34.1560.

Figure 5.18 Detail of mantle with symmetry scheme D-TTVV (MNAA 382-6), EIP 1B, ca. A.D. 50–100.

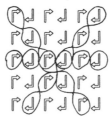

Figure 5.22 R-PTPT/R11c. The design motifs on this mantle, arranged in a rectangular lattice, repeat in bifold rotation on horizontal axes and on both diagonals. Sample: MNAA 378-8.

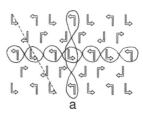

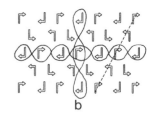

Figure 5.23 (a) D-HVHV/D31. Both of the schemes in Figure 5.23 have vertical and horizontal axes of bifold rotation, but Figure 5.23a has glide reflection on S diagonals while Figure 5.23b has glide reflection on Z diagonals. Sample: LM 093736; MNAA 318-5, 319-54, 319-55, 319-56. (b) D-HVHV/D31. The mantle in Figure 5.24 has this pattern. Sample MNAA 318-6, 318-7, 318-8, 318-9, 319-7, 319-57; UN SA 4603.

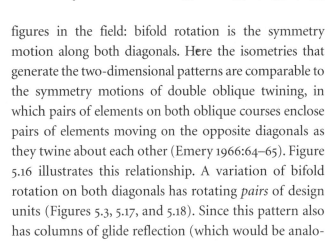

Figure 5.24 Detail of mantle with symmetry scheme D-HVHV (MNAA 318-7), EIP 2, ca. A.D. 100–200.

explicit mention of the translations which are present, by definition, in all repeated patterns" (Washburn and Crowe 1988:94). Frame (1991:138–139; Figure 4.23) was the first to suggest that orientation patterns of the type in Figure 5.12 have the same underlying symmetry as that of an extended oblique-interlaced fabric. Figure 5.13 shows how this textile pattern layout compares to plain oblique interlacing; fabrics with this symmetry type are illustrated in Figures 5.1 and 5.2.

The pattern illustrated in Figure 5.14 comprises bilaterally symmetrical images that also repeat in glide reflection in both vertical and diagonal directions. This diagram could be described as having the same symetry structure as that in Figure 5.12, although this identification is by no means unequivocal since this pattern also has mirror reflection between figures in rows.

Figure 5.15 illustrates another way of arranging

figures in the field: bifold rotation is the symmetry motion along both diagonals. Here the isometries that generate the two-dimensional patterns are comparable to the symmetry motions of double oblique twining, in which pairs of elements on both oblique courses enclose pairs of elements moving on the opposite diagonals as they twine about each other (Emery 1966:64–65). Figure 5.16 illustrates this relationship. A variation of bifold rotation on both diagonals has rotating *pairs* of design units (Figures 5.3, 5.17, and 5.18). Since this pattern also has columns of glide reflection (which would be analogous in terms of its symmetry to parallel bands of three-strand oblique interlacing), it is not possible to identify a single underlying fabric structure on textiles with this figural orientation.

Other schemes have bifold rotation in more than one direction. The diagram in Figure 5.19, for example, with bifold rotation in rows, columns, and one diagonal, could be seen as referring to the symmetry structure of either weft twining, warp twining, or oblique twining (compare the diagrams of the field patterns to sketches of the fabric structures in Figure 5.20a, b, and c). The mantle pictured in Figure 5.5 has this layout. Figure 5.21 has bifold rotation in columns and rows and hence an underlying symmetry structure that could be seen as being analogous to either warp twining or weft twining, and Figure 5.22 has the same isometry in both diagonal directions and in rows. Figure 5.23 also has bifold rotation on vertical and horizontal axes but with the glide reflection of oblique interlacing on S or Z diagonals (see Figure 5.24 for a fabric with this pattern). Fabrics with imagery that possesses point symmetry produce patterns employing bifold rotation on the vertical, horizontal, and S and Z diagonal axes (Figure 5.25). These patterns share symmetries with warp twining, weft twining, and oblique twining.

Other field patterns also have symmetries comparable to the symmetries of more than one fabric structure. Point symmetrical images (Figure 5.26) repeat in glide reflection between columns and along diagonals (perhaps replicating the symmetrical structure underlying oblique interlacing) and in bifold rotation along rows and within columns (comparable to weft twining and warp twining). Field images that are symmetrical on two axes (Figures 5.27 and 5.28) have all possible paths

Figure 5.25 (a) D(T)-PPPP/D32. Images with point symmetry are oriented so that their main axes are vertical. Axes of bifold rotation are present in the horizontal, vertical, and diagonal directions. Sample: MNAA 310-26, 421-84. (b) D(T)-PPPP/D32. Images with point symmetry are oriented so that their main axes are horizontal. Sample: MNAA 421-110, 421-133. (c) D(T)-PPPP/D32. Images with point symmetry are oriented so that their main axes are horizontal but with a reversal of the vertical orientation of crooks relative to Figure 5.25b. Sample MNAA accession number unknown (published in Izumi 1964:Plate 131).

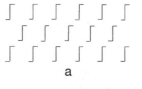
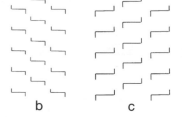

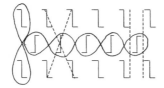

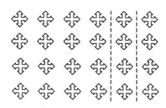

Figure 5.26 D(T)-HHHH/D37, with bifold rotation within rows and columns and glide reflection between columns and within diagonals. Sample: EMG 35.32.134.

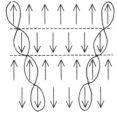

Figure 5.27 D(H)-PPPP/D45. Design units that are symmetrical on two axes are arranged in a diamond lattice pattern. Sample: MNAA 310-42, 318-3, 378-17, 378-20.

Figure 5.28 R(H)-PPPP/R71. Images appear in a compact arrangement to form a rectangular lattice. Sample: EMG 35.32.118.

Figure 5.29 D(H)-TTTT/D44H. Bilaterally symmetrical images create this pattern, seen on the textile in Figure 5.30. The symmetry scheme has glide reflection between horizontal rows and bifold rotation in both diagonal directions. Sample: AIC 1958:295; AMNH 41.0/1501, 41.2/632, 41.2/8735a, 41.2/8934; Anton 1984:Plate 13; CMA 46.226, 46.227; EMG 35.32.58; PC (one fragment, present location unknown, published in d'Harcourt 1924: Plate 14 and another in Brinckerhoff 1999:cover, Cat. No. 15); MNAA 94-8, 157-19, 157-26, 410-201; MVMun 833 33-27/MVBer VA63321; SM 0792 "U" 2274; UM SA 4602.

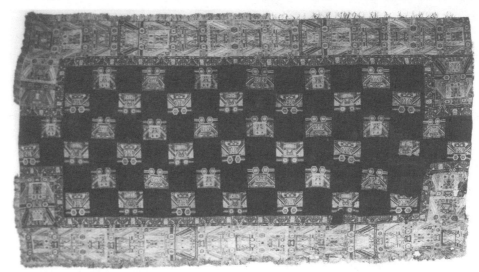

Figure 5.30 Skirt with symmetry scheme D(H)-TTTT (MNAA 157/410-201), EH 10B, ca. 50 B.C.–0.

Figure 5.31 D-VVVV/D28b. This pattern has glide reflection between horizontal rows. For an illustration of a garment with this symmetry scheme, see Figure 5.33. Sample: AIC 1958. 292; EMG 35.32.185, 35.32.186, 35.32.187, 35.32.206, 35.32.207; MNAA 190-7, 254-8, 310-?, 382-37; MVBer VA63327; MVMun 34-41-18, 34-41-26; TM 91.159, 91.337a

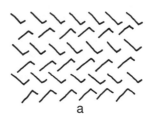
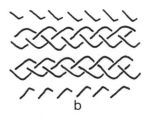

Figure 5.32 (a) Modified version of diagram in Figure 5.31 and (b) diagram of three-strand oblique interlacing.

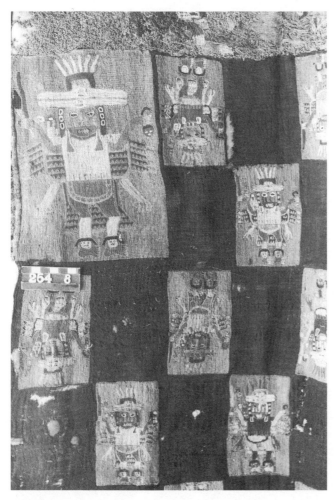

Figure 5.33 Detail of mantle with symmetry scheme D-VVVV (MNAA 254-8), EIP 1B, ca. A.D. 50–100.

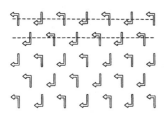

Figure 5.34 D-PVPV/D13b, with glide reflection within rows. Sample: AMNH 41.2/8870; EMG 35.32.208; MNAA 217-10, 382-7.

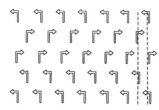

Figure 5.35 D-PPHH/D5a. This symmetry structure is generated by glide reflection within vertical axes. Sample: BM 34.1553; MNAA 290-15, 290-16.

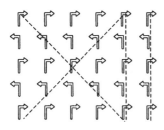

Figure 5.36 R-HPHP/R31r. Here images are disposed in a rectangular lattice and repeated in glide reflection within columns as well as within diagonals. Sample: MNAA 378-27.

of both bifold rotation and glide reflection, conceivably referencing several structures simultaneously. In Figure 5.29, glide reflection between rows and bifold rotation on both diagonals are the motions that generate, respectively, oblique interlacing and oblique twining (see Figure 5.30 for a photo of a skirt with this symmetry scheme).

The textiles presented up to this point have field symmetry patterns that can be compared to the two-dimensional planar symmetry of actual fabric structures, specifically oblique interlacing, single and double oblique twining, and warp or weft twining.[8] The remainder of the patterns cannot be correlated with these two-dimensional structures, though all employ the rigid motions already familiar to us. For instance, one scheme has glide reflection between horizontal rows (Figure 5.31). This symmetry pattern is comparable to that of parallel bands of oblique interlacing, as the pattern layout and sketch of the fabric structure in Figure 5.32 illustrate. The mantle in Figure 5.33 has this symmetry scheme. Another has glide reflection within horizontal rows (Figure 5.34) and one within columns (Figure 5.35). Two schemes have this isometry on vertical axes as well as along one diagonal (Figures 5.36 and 5.37). Other patterns combine glide reflection on one or more axes with bifold rotation in one or more directions (Figures 5.38–5.42), perhaps embedding simultaneous references to three-strand oblique interlacing and twisting strands. One EIP 2

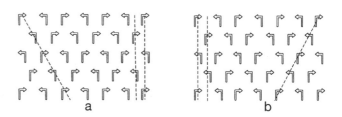

Figure 5.37 (a) D-PHPH/D13a. Figure 5.37a and 5.37b have axes of glide reflection within columns. The first also has glide reflection on S diagonals while the second has glide reflection on Z diagonals. Sample: AMNH 41.0/1500, SM 0643 "U" 2125; SM 659. (b) D-PHPH/D13a. Sample: AMNH 41.0/1505.

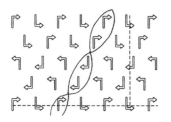

Figure 5.38 D-PVTH/D19. Horizontal and vertical isometries are glide reflection, with bifold rotation of pairs on Z diagonals. Sample: MNAA 1-20, 157-9.

Figure 5.39 D-PVHT/D12b. Horizontal axes have glide reflection, while vertical axes and Z diagonals have bifold rotation. The pattern is broken in a few places. Sample: MNAA 38-.

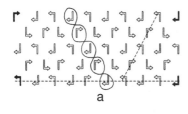

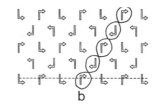

a   b

Figure 5.40 (a) D-THTH/D24a. Single design units repeat in glide reflection on horizontal axes and in bifold rotation on S diagonals. Two figures are oriented out of sequence in this example. Sample: MNAA 319-9. (b) D-THTH/D24a. Single design units repeat in bifold rotation on Z diagonals and in glide reflection on horizontal axes, as seen on the mantle in Figure 5.41. Sample: MNAA 382-29.

Figure 5.41 Detail of mantle with symmetry scheme D-THTH (MNAA 382-29), EIP 1B, ca. A.D. 50–100.

embroidery introduces something new: Figure 5.43 shows an egalitarian scheme in which bifold rotation is the symmetry operation that links iconographic units alternately on S and Z diagonals to create a zigzag movement. I will come back to this zigzag "image" shortly (Figure 5.44 shows the mantle that carries this pattern).

The only egalitarian pattern in the sample that does not employ either glide reflection or bifold rotation as the basis of field repeats is illustrated in Figure 5.45, where images repeat by translation alone.

What egalitarian patterns were *not* chosen by the Paracas/Topará embroiderers, and is anything to be learned from these omissions? Among Grünbaum's symmetry schemes for asymmetrical images in a diamond lattice (1990:Figure 8; Figure 4: serial numbers

1–31), fourteen are not present in the sample of textiles (those with serial numbers D2, D3, D6, D8, D9, D10, D14, D16, D17, D21, D22, D25, D26, and D29; see Figure 4). Of these fourteen "absent" all-over planar patterns, nine have patterns on rows, columns, or diagonals that are staggered. That is, the points of rotation or the lines of reflection do not align horizontally or vertically on the plane, thereby violating the underlying symmetry of a fabric structure (Figure 5.46).[9] Examination of the fabric and diagram illustrated in Figures 5.13 and 5.16 helps to clarify how these particular "staggered" symmetry schemes deviate from the symmetry structures of fabrics: in oblique interlacing (Figure 5.13) the points of passage of elements under (or over) other elements align on the horizontal and vertical axes, as do the

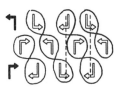

Figure 5.42 D-TVTV/D24b. In this symmetry scheme, S diagonals have bifold rotation and vertical columns have glide reflection. Sample: MNAA 310-1

Figure 5.43 D-THHT/D23b. The orientation of the images on this EIP 2 mantle creates a symmetry pattern that differs from those illustrated up to this point: bifold rotation alternates in segments of S and Z diagonals to produce a zigzag design. A detail of the mantle is shown in Figure 5.44. Sample: MNAA 253-6.

Figure 5.44 Detail of mantle with symmetry scheme D-THHT (MNAA 253-6), EIP 2, ca. A.D. 100–200.

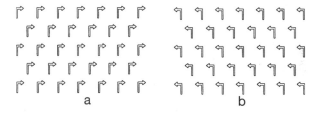

Figure 5.45 (a) D-PPPP/D1, with design units repeating by translation and pointing right. Sample: MFAB 16.34a, TM 91.280. (b) D-PPPP/D1, with design units pointing left. Sample: AMNH 41.0/1506; MFAB 31.502; MNAA 38-48; TM 91.279.

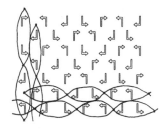

Figure 5.46 D-THTV/D25. This symmetry scheme is not present among Paracas Necrópolis textile field designs. The points of bifold rotation do not align on vertical and horizontal axes.

points in oblique twining (Figure 5.16) where twining pairs enclose one or more elements. It is conceivable that certain schemes (numbers D2, D3, D9, D10, D14, D25, D26, and D29) were deemed inappropriate due to the absence of these alignments.

Two other patterns that do not appear in the sample are D17 and D21. The first has isometries in rows and the second in columns in which mirror reflection between two design units alternates with translation between two images. This is not a symmetry choice found in any of the Paracas Necrópolis textiles with egalitarian patterns, and I tentatively suggest that it is because the isometry seems to discourage regular, fluid visual movement across the plane (contrast these with the horizontal axes in Figures 5.37 and 5.42 and the vertical axes in Figure 5.40, all of which have mirror reflection between every design unit so that the movement is regular and continuous).

One of the missing patterns (D6) has no axes of bifold rotation nor of glide reflection, a symmetry choice that might be considered undesirable since the movements of threads are not alluded to (although the scheme in Figure 5.45, which shares this trait, *was* used). Finally, a single pattern (D22) does have axes of bifold rotation by pairs on both the S and Z diagonals, and another (D16) has bifold rotation by pairs on the S diagonals; both of these therefore qualify as patterns that should have been acceptable to the ancient embroiderers.

To summarize, eighteen of the thirty-one diamond lattice patterns with asymmetrical images registered by Grünbaum are suitable for the creation of symmetry schemes if the underlying principle is to replicate either

the symmetry of fabric structures or the regular alignment of the fiber elements that comprise the fabric plane. Sixteen of these are present as patterns on the Paracas Necrópolis textiles in this sample (along with the pattern in Figure 5.45, which is not analogous to a fabric structure symmetry). It seems possible that a combinatorial logic was at work in the selection process of symmetry patterns and that over time, embroiderers tried to use as many different patterns as possible among those that embedded the appropriate references. This is not the only evidence that Paracas/Topará weavers used this type of logic, a point to be taken up below in the section on color.

Numerous diamond lattice patterns utilize either images with point symmetry or bilaterally symmetrical

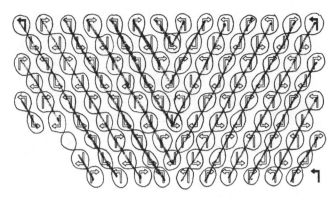

Figure 5.47 Nonegalitarian pattern in which paths of bifold rotation create a "hidden" chevron pattern. Sample: BM 34.1548.

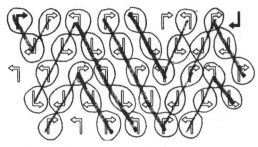

Figure 5.49 Nonegalitarian pattern with zigzag pattern incorporated into its symmetry structure through diagonals of bifold rotation. Sample: MNAA 319-47.

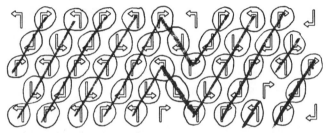

Figure 5.50 Nonegalitarian pattern with zigzag pattern "hidden" in arrangement of S and Z diagonals of bifold rotation. The orientation of one figure on the right side does not work with the rest of the pattern. Sample: MUC 27-5.

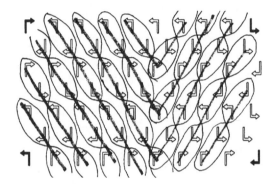

Figure 5.48 Nonegalitarian pattern with a chevron pattern created by bifold rotation of pairs of images on S diagonals (left) and Z diagonals (right). Sample: MFAB 16.32.

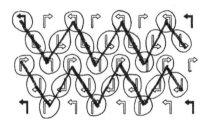

Figure 5.51 Nonegalitarian pattern with zigzag pattern. Sample: RISD 40.190.

images, including those with serial numbers D32-D37 and D38-D44 in Grünbaum (1990:Figure 8; Figure 4). Of those with point symmetry design units, two out of a possible six patterns are present. Two of the missing have irregular patterns in the sense described above (D33 and D36), while two have patterns with acceptable symmetries (D34 and D35). There are seven patterns conceivable for those with bilaterally symmetrical figures, two of which appear among the textiles studied. Three of the missing five do not "work" because they are irregular, but two do (D40 and D41). Hence, the maximum number of acceptable patterns is not obtained for textiles whose imagery is point symmetrical or bilaterally symmetrical. There is a single diamond lattice pattern possible when an image is symmetrical on two axes (D45), and this is present in the sample.

Nonegalitarian Patterns

In a sizable group of mostly very late (EIP 2) Paracas Necrópolis textiles different symmetry schemes are combined within a single textile to create nonegalitarian patterns, each unique to a single embroidery. The schemata in Figures 5.47 through 5.57 show how an ingenious use of bifold rotation on the S and Z diagonals, sometimes combined with mirror reflection and glide reflection on the other axes, can create chevron or zigzag designs across the cloth (see also Figure 5.43). It is surely not coincidental that chevrons and zigzags are occasionally embedded in field color patterns (Paul 1997:120–121; diagrams 11, 23, 26, 27, 45, and 47), though not on any of the particular examples with these orientation patterns. In addition, depictions of chevrons and zigzags appear in Paracas Necrópolis headbands (see

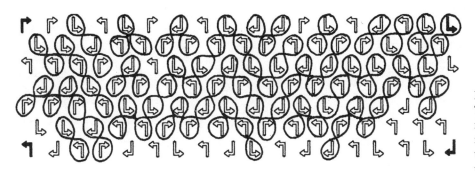

a

Figure 5.52 (a, b) Nonegalitarian pattern. The symmetry scheme in the field of this mantle may try to incorporate zigzag movements into the pattern, although if this is the case, it is not worked out perfectly (b). Sample: MNAA 38-5.

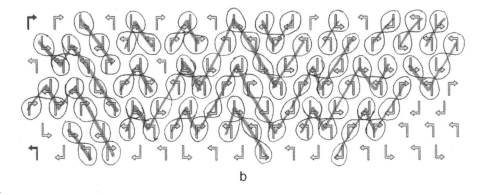

b

Figure 5.53 Nonegalitarian pattern in which the design echoes a zigzag image, except that at the points where the lines change directions, they are disconnected. Sample: MNAA 258-5.

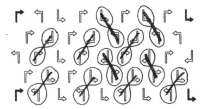

Figure 5.54 Nonegalitarian pattern that seems to be related to the pattern illustrated in Figure 5.53. Sample: MNAA 38-14.

Figure 5.55 Nonegalitarian pattern from textile fragment; the symmetry scheme may be related to the type of pattern illustrated in Figures 5.53 and 5.54. Sample: MC 0898.

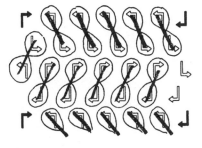

Figure 5.56 Nonegalitarian pattern in which the turning points of the zigzag lines are disconnected. Sample: MNAA 451-6.

Frame 1991:127–132), including several that were in the same late bundles as some of the woven garments discussed here (bundles 38, 253, 319, and 451). Frame tentatively relates these headband images to techniques of decorative wrapping, in which "the continuous spiral of a wrapping element might be visualized and depicted as a zigzag in two dimensions, showing both the front and back passage of the spiraling element" (Frame 1991:127). Whatever their significance, chevrons and zigzags are associated most strongly (though not exclusively) with late Paracas Necrópolis material.

Finally, six maverick textiles remain to be described. Except for the fact that all have nonegalitarian patterns, they are not alike. Figure 5.58 shows the patterns on two mantles that are too fragmentary to permit hypothetical readings of the figural orientations. Four other garments,

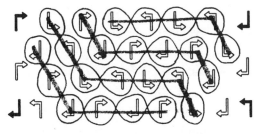

Figure 5.57 Nonegalitarian pattern with figures repeating in bifold rotation along rows and diagonals; when extended, the pattern can be read as a wider-angle zigzag (see Figure 5.4 for an illustration of the mantle that carries this scheme). Sample: MNAA 382-9.

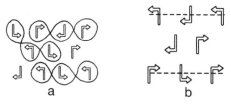

Figure 5.58 (a) Nonegalitarian pattern on textile fragment. Sample: MVMun 34-41.13. (b) Nonegalitarian pattern on textile fragment. Sample: MVMun 34-41-14.

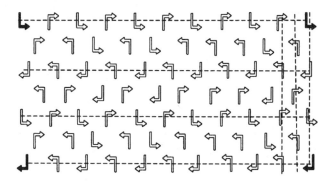

Figure 5.59 Nonegalitarian pattern. Sample: MMFA 1947.Ad.19.

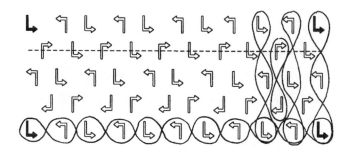

Figure 5.60 Nonegalitarian pattern. Sample: MNAA 319-10.

Figure 5.61 Nonegalitarian pattern. Sample: BM 34.1587.

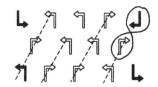

Figure 5.62 This mantle has no regular symmetry pattern in its field. Sample: MNAA 451-4.

in contrast, are complete specimens. A mantle dating to EIP 1 has bands of figures that repeat in glide reflection on the vertical axes, alternating up/down directions every two columns (Figure 5.59). The horizontal axes have glide reflection in every other row. Figures 5.60, 5.61, and 5.62 illustrate the patterns on three EIP 2 mantles. The mantle in Figure 5.60 can be described in the following manner if the pattern is extended beyond the five rows actually present on the mantle: horizontal axes have a regular repeat of three rows of bifold rotation alternating with a single row of glide reflection within rows; vertical axes have a regular repeat of three columns of bifold rotation alternating with a column of mirror reflection. The pattern in Figure 5.61 is regular in certain sections (the left-hand quarter, an area to the left of center, and an area a little to the right of center) but utilizes two different symmetry schemes. The last mantle (Figure 5.62) not only has no regular pattern, but also has fewer and larger design units than on most other Paracas Necrópolis embroidered garments.

The appearance at the end of the Paracas/Topará cultural tradition of embroideries with nonegalitarian patterns that introduce surface designs that do not reference the horizontal/vertical axes, or warp/weft structure, of a fabric—or seem to have no regular

pattern at all—may reflect a gradual unraveling of the system that determined the underlying organization of figural orientation on Paracas Necrópolis fabrics. Washburn (1999:555), in her study of how the Hopi encode cultural principles in the symmetrical structure of the patterns on their ceramics, notes that the design layouts of the decorated ceramics of Hopi ancestors were *not* based on the same isometries as those adopted by later Puebloans. "Rather," she says, "they appear to be a mixture of many different structural principles, suggestive of different kinds of organizational concepts coalescing from a number of different sources" (Washburn 1999:555). Among the woven garments placed in the last six bundles buried in the Necrópolis of Wari Kayan are a few that indicate a similar process but in reverse: transformations in the functions, structures, border formats, iconography, figural orientations, and color patterns typical of Paracas Necrópolis-style textiles signal the beginnings of the end of this textile style (see Paul 1999 for a discussion of these changes).

Color

One of the remarkable and beautiful aspects of Paracas Necrópolis–style textiles is their color. The ancient weavers were master dyers. They not only developed the technology to color camelid and cotton fibers, but perfected it to the point that they were able to produce the same colors over and over—a difficult feat when using natural dyestuffs (see Paul 1990b). Some Paracas/Topará artisans also experimented with dyes, dyeing recipes, and dyeing processes in order to produce new hues, a fact that is especially evident in one EIP 1B bundle (Paul 1990b:10–12). Preferences for particular colors are evident in the woven contents of certain bundles, suggesting that the personal taste of the individual buried in that bundle (or of the persons who made the garments) played a role in color design.

Apart from pure visual pleasure, color had a more esoteric function: through color, a particular kind of logic was encoded in cloth. To begin with, each of the images embroidered on a garment is filled in with colored threads according to a master plan that specifies the color of the iconographic details of that image. For example, in Figure 5.1, each figure has a specific combination of colors such that if the body is stitched in dark blue, the feather headdress must be stitched in light blue and the tunic in red. Every detail has its designated, correct color. This combination of colors is called a *color block,* and as we will see shortly, different color blocks can be employed on a single embroidery. The majority of Paracas Necrópolis textiles follow their particular color block plans to the letter, so that the entirety of an iconographic unit conforms to a particular color configuration. However, there are over twenty embroideries in which only a few of the constituent parts of an image may define a color block; the use of these partially defined color blocks occurs primarily on EIP 2 weavings, produced at the end of the sequence when the Paracas/Topará cultural tradition was experiencing major changes.

Even though its strict definition was modified over time, the concept of a color block as a way of ordering the color design runs throughout the Paracas/Topará cultural sequence. The number of color blocks per garment varies (Paul 1997, 2000b), and this number determines what kinds of repetition are possible in the field of the garment. Three, four, and five different color blocks per garment are the numbers of sets of colors most frequently employed on the textiles, although

some garments use many more; eleven textiles have twenty-eight color blocks each and another has fifty-nine. Like the design units in the field patterns, color blocks are aligned to create regular patterns along horizontal rows, vertical columns, and the S and Z diagonals, with the diagonals dominating in importance. There are, for example, patterns of sequentially alternating monocolor diagonals (Figure 5.5). Other patterns have bicolor diagonals, with different versions generated simply by varying the number of color blocks per row and the relative positions of the color blocks in subsequent rows (Figures 5.1 and 5.2). There are also arrangements with tricolor diagonals and others with tetracolor diagonals (the counterparts of bicolor diagonals). Color patterns with pentacolor diagonals (Figure 5.3) include variations that employ wild card color blocks. A final type of configuration has no repeating color sequences among diagonals facing the same direction (Figure 5.4). In summary, as I have noted elsewhere, the "weavers/embroiderers attempted to combine color blocks in as many different color configurations as possible within the limitations of certain compositional constraints; following these rules, most of the possible patterns of alternation were tried among the 153 specimens in my sample" (Paul 1997:124). In other words, a combinatorial logic was the cornerstone of field color design. Just as most of what I think were the acceptable symmetry patterns were tried at least once on the textiles, so were the ways of organizing color blocks.

With few exceptions, the color designs in the fields of Paracas Necrópolis textiles are not consistent with their structural symmetries. Among the 146 fabrics for which I have data on both the orientation and color patterns, four utilize a single color block, so that the structural symmetry is "uncolored." Of the remaining 142, only three have color block patterns that operate in conjunction with the underlying two-dimensional symmetry. One of these is a mantle discussed by Washburn (1986:771–773) in which color design is perfectly superimposed on the underlying symmetry: "The most unusual aspect of this pattern is that the addition of colors results in a perfectly colored *pg[3]$_1$* pattern. Such examples, where the coloring actually results in a colored symmetry consistent with the structural symmetry, are unusual on Paracas textiles; most have colorings which are not symmetrical or which have no relation to the underlying symmetry" (Washburn 1986:772).

The other two mantles (MNAA 382–6 and CMA 40.528) each have some irregularities in their color patterns, but major portions of the fields use three color blocks to color a D-TTVV symmetry scheme. All other embroideries in my sample have color patterns and symmetry schemes that function independently of each other. While some would consider this fact to reflect a failure in creative potential on the part of the Paracas/Topará weavers (see Makovicky 1986:951–952), others (including myself) view it as a positive attribute that "greatly increas[es] the number of possible overall effects" (Grünbaum 1990:66).

Conclusions

Paracas Necrópolis embroidered garments—in particular, those with images in their fields—functioned symbolically on multiple levels. The most apparent of these overlapping layers of meaning are iconography, symmetry structure, and color patterning. At the time of creation, the embroiderers' initial decisions included the selection of style of formal construction, motif, symmetry pattern, and color pattern. When embroiderers sat down to begin work on a textile, the first stitches of the chosen motif could not be taken before a global vision of the symmetry pattern was in mind. In the block color style of embroidery, the figures were stitched in outline form over the entire field before they were filled in with color, and in the linear style the image emerged as a negative form as the background was worked; broad line images were worked using both of these methods (for descriptions of these procedures, see Paul 1990a:65–74). In all cases, the underlying symmetry structure of the field was laid out in stitches before the images were filled in with differently colored embroidery threads.

Among the 165 Paracas Necrópolis textiles in my sample with embroidered figures in their fields, 148 have egalitarian symmetry patterns that can be classified following Grünbaum's symmetry schemes. Of these, 108 may share structures with the underlying two-dimensional planar symmetry structures of certain fabrics. Thirty-three have repetitive one-dimensional

patterns generated by glide reflection or bifold rotation on horizontal or vertical axes; although these regular band patterns do not allude to two-dimensional structures, they nevertheless rely on the types of symmetry motions that are at the core of fabric-making procedures: spinning, plying, twining, and interlacing. The same can be said for the textile with an egalitarian pattern that produces a zigzag design and the seventeen examples with nonegalitarian patterns, most of which use bifold rotation to create special diagonal designs.

It is probable that other features of the symmetry patterns on Paracas Necrópolis textiles are the result of deliberate choices that carry meaning. One such element is rotational direction. The diagrams in Figure 5.15, for example, have the same symmetry scheme, but variations in the left-right orientations of the figures result in a clockwise "twist" of the diagonals in Figure 5.15a and a counterclockwise "twist" of those in Figure 5.15b. The same opposition appears in Figures 5.17a and 5.17b. Furthermore, certain schemes are realized in two ways, one favoring S diagonals and the other Z diagonals. For example, the textiles schematized in Figures 5.37a and 5.37b share symmetries, but shifts in the alignments of rows of figures results in S diagonals of glide reflection in Figure 5.37a and Z diagonals of glide reflection in Figure 5.37b (see Figures 5.23a and 5.23b for the same type of opposition). Similarly, the diagrams in Figures 5.19a and 5.19b incorporate opposing diagonal patterns of bifold rotation. Thus, while the horizontal, vertical, and diagonal axes may have isometries that relate to the activity of making fabrics, some diagonals might encode references to directional concerns, such as the twist of fiber elements.

Once the underlying symmetry structure of the field was laid out in stitches, the figures were filled in with differently colored embroidery threads. Even though the imagery that encodes symmetry patterns is the same imagery that uses color to construct a combinatorial language on cloth, the two systems of organization are like diaphanous layers that, though congruent, function independently. Even so, S and Z directional issues resonate in the color patterns as well. For example, most of the configurations that have regularly alternating monocolor diagonals on one slant have a complementary pattern on the diagonal of the opposite

Figure 5.63 Photograph of stem-stitch embroidery stitches, showing that the way the thread is carried produces either an S slant (a) or a Z slant (b); the reverse side of the stitches in (a) and (b) appears in (c) (after Emery 1966:Figure 361). Courtesy of The Textile Museum, Washington, DC.

slant. Likewise, like patterns with two alternating bicolor diagonals exist on both the S and Z slants. In some cases two such complementary patterns appear in sets of clothing. Such sets, comprising different garment types with matching iconography and color blocks, were among the contents of numerous bundles, and some have embroidered field iconography. A matching mantle and skirt, for instance, share a color block pattern, except that on one piece the two bicolor diagonals are S, while on the other they are Z.[10] The garments in other sets share monocolor diagonal patterns but with the monocolors on diagonals of opposite slants.[11]

It is likely that other allusions to weaving and working with fiber are embedded in the structural and design elements of these textiles. To begin with, the checkerboard layout of field images is suggestive of the structure of plain-weave cloth, in which each weft yarn passes alternatively over and under the successive warp yarns, an observation first made by R. Carrión Cachot (1931:77). This analogy is especially apparent when images are either embroidered in blocks of narrow threadlike embroidered bands (Banco de Crédito 1983:45) or when they are "framed" by embroidered rectangles (Figures 5.18, 5.24, 5.33, and 5.44; see also Paul 2000b:Figures 9, 10, 11, 14, and 15). The equally spaced and sized embroidered figures and rectangular areas of ground cloth echo the image of balanced plain weave in which the warp and weft are "equal in size, spacing, and count" (Emery 1966:Figure 85). In addition, the textile structure itself—embroidery on plain weave—is suggestive of the over/under movement of yarns, with the embroidery literally "over" the underlying ground. This structural choice is culturally specific to the

Paracas/Topará tradition and, as W. Conklin (1996:325) points out, "produces an image that . . . is not coplanar with the underlying woven surface; instead the image is slightly above it—an image not 'of' the textile but one 'on' the textile."

Even the stitching itself reinforces some of the ideas presented here. The word *embroidery* describes a variety of needle-worked accessory stitches (Emery 1966:232–248). Emery (1966:234) notes that "one stitch is distinguished from another, structurally, by the particular relationship of one portion of the element to another and to the fabric into which it is worked" and that there is a wide range of simple stitch structures. The type of embroidery stitch most frequently used on the Paracas Necrópolis weavings is stem stitch; the overlapping stitches in a line of stem-stitch sewing on the face of a fabric resemble twisted strands (Figure 5.63). Furthermore, there is a difference in the form and effect of the stitch on the face of the textile depending on which way the thread is carried (either above the needle or below it), producing a "visible distinction . . . in the slant of the stitch, which, if viewed vertically (as a cord would be in determining the direction of twist), will in the first instance be in the Z direction, and in the second, S" (Emory 1966:239).

Finally, references to fiber may also be embedded in certain border formats: the exterior border arrangement on ponchos seems to be an abstracted image of a segment of two twisting strands (Paul 2000a, b). The majority of ponchos have a format that corresponds to S-spun strands, but there are also examples with a Z format. Furthermore, the images embroidered in these outer borders usually establish a clockwise orientation around the perimeter of the garment, while the orientation in the inner, neck border on the same garments is usually counterclockwise. I have speculated elsewhere (Paul 2000a, b) that these imaginary circuits allude to opposing spin and ply directions of threads (clockwise spinning produces an S twist, while counterclockwise plying produces a Z twist; the threads utilized in Paracas Necrópolis textiles are Z spun/S plied).

When viewed collectively, all of the design elements mentioned above underscore the importance of fabric-making processes in a culture that directed massive amounts of energy towards the creation of textiles. The images stitched on cloth convey information about the worldview of the society and about the social roles of high-status individuals, and the coloring of these images encodes a specific system of logic on cloth (Paul 2001). However, the keystone of textile design—the aspect that transmits the most fundamental cultural principles—is the way the images are arranged on the cloth. The specific symmetries favored by Paracas/Topará embroiderers silently bespeak the vital role of weaving in their culture, a fact made abundantly clear by the glorious results that we study here. ■

Acknowledgments

I would like to thank Dorothy Washburn, Carrie Brezine, and Sophie Desrosiers for having offered their critical comments during the preparation of this chapter. ■

Notes

1. Museum abbreviations: Anton, published in Anton 1984:Plate 13, at which time the textile was in the Edward Merrin Gallery, New York; AIC, Art Institute of Chicago; AMNH, American Museum of Natural History, New York; BM, Brooklyn Museum; CMA, The Cleveland Museum of Art; DAM, Denver Art Museum; DMA, Dallas Museum of Art; DO, Dumbarton Oaks Research Library and Collection; EMG, Etnografiska Museet, Göteborg; IMA, Indianapolis Museum of Art; LM, Linden-Museum, Stuttgart; MBA, Museo de Bellas Artes, Lima; MC, Museo Chileno de Arte Precolombino, Santiago; MFAB, Museum of Fine Arts, Boston; MMFA, Montreal Museum of Fine Arts; MNAA, Museo Nacional de Antropología, Arqueología, y Historia del Perú, Lima; MR, Musées Royaux, Brussels; MUC, Museo e Instituto Arqueológico de la Universidad Nacional de San Antonio Abad del Cuzco, Cuzco; MVBer, Museum für Völkerkunde, Berlin; MVMun, Museum für Völkerkunde, Munich; NMNH, National Museum of Natural History, Smithsonian Institution, Washington, DC; PC, private collection; PM, Peabody Museum, Cambridge, MA; RISD, Rhode Island School of Design, Providence; ROM, Royal Ontario Museum, Toronto; SM, Museo de la Universidad de San Marcos, Lima; Stafford, published in Stafford 1941:Plate X, location unknown; TM, The Textile Museum, Washington, DC; UM, University Museum, Philadelphia.

2. The chronological framework used here includes major time units called horizons or periods; the details that define these units have been filled in by numerous scholars, including D. Menzel et al. (1964), who established a ceramic sequence in which the beginning of each unit is marked by a change in the pottery styles of the south coast Ica Valley. Thus, the Early Horizon—an arbitrary block of time comprising numerous epochs—begins with the appearance of resin-painted pottery in the Ica Valley and ends with the introduction of slip painting on pottery. The sequence of this valley is used as the master sequence to which other objects are assigned on evidence of their contemporaneity with one of its phases. The absolute dates of the Paracas/Topará objects assigned to this system of relative chronology and mentioned in this chapter are Early Horizon epoch 10 (ca. 100 B.C. to 0), Early Intermediate Period epoch 1 (ca. A.D. 0 to 100), and Early Intermediate Period epoch 2 (ca. A.D. 100 to 200). These time units will be abbreviated elsewhere in the text as EH and EIP.

3. Mantles are large rectangular fabrics that often have a pair of separately woven embroidered bands attached to the two lengths of the field, with additional border "brackets" embroidered directly in each corner of the garment's field (see Figures 5.1–5.4). While the bracket parts of these U-shaped borders are physically in the field, I consider them to relate conceptually to the longitudinal borders (see Paul 1992, n. 5), a fact that must be taken into account when plotting the orientation and color patterns of field images: for charting purposes, the four figures in the field corners usually "belong" to the borders.

4. B. Grünbaum (1990:Figure 9) identifies the symmetry schemes for each of the possible types of band patterns; those that appear on Paracas Necrópolis borders include his S-PP, S-TT, S-VV, S(T)-PP, S(H)-PP, S(H)-TT, S(R)-PP, and R-VHV. Grünbaum's (1990) method of classifying the planar symmetries on Peruvian fabrics will be presented below.

5. This number does not include fabrics with vertical bands of embroidered images in their fields; for a mantle with this type of field design, see Paul 1990b:Figure 7.

6. Allan Hanson (Chapter 8, this volume) notes that "the defining feature of symmetry is that the same design figure or motif is repeated. That repetition constitutes the redundancy, which gives the composition a measure of predictability and therefore intelligibility." There are four specimens in my sample in which the field figures are not identical, but for purposes of plotting orientation patterns, I treat them here as if they were.

7. Grünbaum (1990:49) defines an egalitarian pattern as one "that has the following property: though there may be several transitivity classes of copies of the motif, all the transitivity classes play the same role in the pattern."

8. Paracas Necrópolis fabrics include many oblique interlaced headbands as well as a few wide headbands that use, among other structures, oblique twining. To my knowledge there are no examples of warp twining or weft twining among the fabrics originating from the Paracas Necrópolis bundles, although weft twining is present among earlier Paracas fabrics (see King 1965:208–211). Oblique twining was also used by the earlier artisans.

9. The pattern in Figure 5.31 also has diagonal axes of bifold rotation (with pairs of design units rotating) that are staggered so that the points of rotation do not align, but here I think that it is the zigzag reference that is meant to be "read."

10. For the textiles see Stone-Miller (1992:Plate 11 and Figure 192), and for the color patterns see Paul (1997:Nos. 19 and 20).

11. These include a headcloth, poncho, and mantle (EMG 35.32.185, 35.32.186, and 35.32.187) in the Ethnographic Museum in Göteborg with color patterns 17 and 18 in Paul (1997); a poncho and headcloth (EMG 35.32.188 and 35.32.190) in Göteborg with color patterns 43 and 44 in Paul (1997); and a mantle, poncho, skirt, and headcloth (BM 34.1557, 34.1581, 34.1593, and 34.1587) in the Brooklyn Museum with color patterns 39 and 40 in Paul (1997).

References Cited

Anton, Ferdinand
1984　*Altindianische Textilkunst aus Perú.* List Verlag, Leipzig, Germany.

Banco de Crédito
1983　*Culturas precolombinas: Paracas. Colección Arte y Tesoros del Perú, creada y dirigida por José Antonio de Lavalle y Werner Lange.* Banco de Crédito del Perú en la Cultura, Lima.

Brinckerhoff, Deborah
1999　*Weaving for the Gods: Textiles of the Ancient Andes.* Bruce Museum of Arts and Sciences, Greenwich, CT.

Carrión Cachot, Rebeca
1931　*La indumentaria en la antigua cultura de Paracas.* Wira Kocha: Revista Peruana de Estudios Antropológicos 1(1):37–86.

Conklin, William J.
1996　Structure as Meaning in Ancient Andean Textiles. In *Andean Art at Dumbarton Oaks,* edited by Elizabeth Boone, Vol. 2, pp. 321–328. Dumbarton Oaks, Washington, DC.

Emery, Irene
1966　*The Primary Structures of Fabrics: An Illustrated Classification.* The Textile Museum, Washington, DC.

Frame, Mary
1986　The Visual Images of Fabric Structures in Ancient Peruvian Art. In *The Junius B. Bird Conference on Andean Textiles, April 7th and 8th, 1984,* edited by Ann Pollard Rowe, pp. 47–80. The Textile Museum, Washington, DC.
1991　Structure, Image, and Abstraction: Paracas Necrópolis Headbands as System Templates. In *Paracas Art and Architecture: Object and Context in South Coastal Peru,* edited by Anne Paul, pp. 110–171. University of Iowa Press, Iowa City.

Grünbaum, Branko
1990　Periodic Ornamentation of the Fabric Plane: Lessons from Peruvian Fabrics. *Symmetry* 1(1):45–68.

d'Harcourt, R. and M.
1924　*Los Tejidos Indios del Antiguo Perú.* Ediciones Albert Morancé, Paris.

Izumi, Seiichi
1964　*Treasures of the Pre-Inca Cultures.* San-ichi Tokyo, Tokyo.

King, Mary Elizabeth
1965　*Textiles and Basketry of the Paracas Period, Ica Valley, Peru.* Ph.D. dissertation, University of Arizona, Tucson. University Microfilms, Ann Arbor.

Lumbreras, Luis G.
1974　*The Peoples and Cultures of Ancient Peru.* Translated by Betty J. Meggers. Smithsonian Institution Press, Washington, DC.

Makovicky, Emil
1986　Symmetrology of Art: Coloured and Generalized Symmetries. *Comp. & Maths. with Appls.* 12B(3/4):949–980.

Mason, Alden
1961   *Introducción al arte textil peruano (Brief Guide to the Peruvian Textiles).* Translated by Horacio Vera Portocarrero. Tipografía Peruana, Lima, Peru.

Menzel, Dorothy, John H. Rowe, and Lawrence E. Dawson
1964   *The Paracas Pottery of Ica: A Study in Style and Time.* University of California Publications in American Archaeology and Ethnology 50. University of California Press, Berkeley and Los Angeles.

Paul, Anne
1990a   *Paracas Ritual Attire: Symbols of Authority in Ancient Peru.* University of Oklahoma Press, Norman.
1990b   The Use of Color in Paracas Necropolis Fabrics: What Does It Reveal about the Organization of Dyeing, Designing, and Society? *National Geographic Research* 6(1):7–21.
1991   Paracas Necrópolis Bundle 89: A Description and Discussion of Its Contents. In *Paracas Art and Architecture: Object and Context in South Coastal Peru,* edited by Anne Paul, pp. 172–221. University of Iowa Press, Iowa City.
1992   Procedures, Patterns, and Deviations in Paracas Embroidered Textiles: Traces of the Creative Process. In *To Weave for the Sun: Andean Textiles in the Museum of Fine Arts, Boston,* edited by Rebecca Stone-Miller, pp. 25–33. Museum of Fine Arts, Boston.
1997   Color Patterns on Paracas Necrópolis Weavings: A Combinatorial Language on Ancient Cloth. *Techniques et culture* (janvier–juin) 29:113–153. Editions de la Maison des Sciences de l'Homme, Paris.
1999   Alte Textilien aus den Anden als Spiegel der kulturellen Entwicklung. In *Nasca: Geheimnisvolle Zeichen im Alten Peru,* edited by Judith Rickenbach, pp. 17–47. Museum Rietberg, Zurich.
2000a   The Configuration and Iconography of Borders on Paracas Necrópolis Ponchos. In *Lisières & Bordures,* edited by F. Cousin, S. Desrosiers, D. Geirnaert, and N. Pellegrin, pp. 101–115. Editions Les Gorgones, Poitiers.
2000b   Rank & File: Colour Block Patterning on Paracas Necropolis Textiles. *Hali* 109:112–120.
2000c   Protective Perimeters: The Symbolism of Borders on Paracas Textiles. *RES* 38 Autumn 2000.
2001   The Multiple Layers of Meaning in a Paracas Necrópolis Textile. In *Approaching Textiles, Varying Viewpoints, Proceedings of the 7th biennial meeting of the Textile Society of America,* September 2000, pp. 210–220. Textile Society of America, Earleville, MD.

Rickenbach, Judith (editor)
1999   *Nasca: Geheimnisvolle Zeichen im Alten Peru.* Museum Rietberg, Zurich.

Seiler-Baldinger, Annemarie
1999   *Textiles. A Classification of Techniques.* Smithsonian Institution Press, Washington, DC.

Shepard, Anna O.
1948   The Symmetry of Abstract Design with Special Reference to Ceramic Decoration. *Contributions to American Anthropology and History,* no. 47, pp. 210–292. Pub. 574, Carnegie Institution of Washington, Washington, DC.

Stafford, Cora
1941   *Paracas Embroideries: A Study of Repeated Patterns.* J. J. Augustin Publisher, New York.

Stone-Miller, Rebecca (editor)
1992   *To Weave for the Sun: Andean Textiles in the Museum of Fine Arts, Boston.* Museum of Fine Arts, Boston.

Washburn, Dorothy K.
1986   Pattern Symmetry and Colored Repetition in Cultural Contexts. *Comp. & Maths. with Appls.* 12B(3/4):767–781.
1999   Perceptual Anthropology: The Cultural Saliency of Symmetry. *American Anthropologist* 101(3):547–562.

Washburn, Dorothy K., and Donald W. Crowe
1988   *Symmetries of Culture: Theory and Practice of Plane Pattern Analysis.* University of Washington Press, Seattle and London.

CHAPTER SIX

Jazz

An Andean Sense of Symmetry

Ed Franquemont

BENITA GUITERREZ MADE A WARP WITH ME to begin my very first *llijlla* (woman's shawl) and constructed the pattern sections of *k'eswa* and *loraypu* designs. When the day came for me to actually begin the weaving, I was forced to confess that although I felt in complete control of the loraypu design, I had never woven k'eswa since I had been guilty of rushing my education through the *hakima* (ties) and *chumpi* (belts) stages of learning. Benita stared at me a moment and then broke into a broad smile. "You mean you know loraypu but not k'eswa?" she asked, and began to call neighbors and passersby to share the joke. Soon I was surrounded by a half dozen or so laughing women who took delight while Benita's finger traced the k'eswa that is within the loraypu. Then she made a small hakima warp of k'eswa pattern for me to teach myself what I already knew.

That sunny afternoon in 1977 was not the first nor the last of the good-natured ridicule I found as an adult North American man learning to weave in the Andean village of Chinchero, but it was definitely a defining moment in the growth of my understanding of the intellect of the Andean weaver. During my years as a weaver of traditional New England cloth, I had of course become accustomed to ways of representing weaving through drafts on paper that abstract the threadings and treadlings used to make patterns. These drafts generally show a "repeat block" of the pattern, a series of steps that can be repeated over again in the same order to create more iterations of the design as translations of the original block. That afternoon I began to realize that Andean weavers conceived of their designs as composed of much smaller units that repeated by many more rules than just translation and

that even their most complicated designs could be understood as a simple motif and a series of replication rules. In that courtyard, my Andean friends taught me to see symmetry and over the next eight years led me through a discovery of the rules they use to create pattern. This chapter is an exploration of an Andean sense of symmetry and results from the delight and the patience they had training my fumbling fingers and uncomprehending eyes.

The contemporary Inca weavers of the Cuzco area are heirs to a mighty textile tradition at least 5,000 years old that is enshrined within their culture in ways unique in human history (Murra 1962). The European invaders who reached Peru in the sixteenth century found a land that was certainly the richest, probably the best organized, and possibly the largest society on earth. The Inca command of engineering, mathematics, and human organization still reverberates to us through impressive monuments and institutions, yet the Inca accomplishment brings more questions and mysteries than answers and wisdoms. Andean culture reached its zenith without benefit of any of the foundations of European civilization such as the arch, the wheel, codified mathematics, and, most importantly, without written language. How could this have happened? It has become increasingly clear over the past forty years that the answer lies in cloth.

Few Andean scholars today doubt the pivotal role played by textiles in the development of Andean civilization, but in truth, we have had a difficult time demonstrating precisely how cloth can be so profound a medium. Much of the difficulty results from representing the richness of textile activity in more comfortable Western graphic media. Due to the demands of publishing, we find it necessary to represent textiles as pictures or drawings on paper, in effect reducing their fundamental character as fiber to an ersatz kind of painting. No wonder we tend to see those aspects of Andean cloth that most resemble the decorative and fashion arts that are the prime target of textile artists from European traditions! In so doing we focus on elements of design and layout that were probably never the principal intent of the Andean weaver nor of the society that produced and used this art. The perspective my Andean friends have on their cloth today is profoundly different from anything we might suppose.

Once I showed my friend Benita a book that contained a photograph of a piece of cloth she had woven. She looked at the book politely but nervously and handed it back with no comment. I persisted and finally had to tell her that this was a picture of her cloth.

"This is cloth?" she asked in disbelief, running her fingers over the shiny slick page. "My cloth?"

On another day, Benita was making a warp with a ball of hand-spun yarn that I had purchased in the Cuzco market. It had crimps and twists that betrayed the fact that it had been unraveled from another finished cloth. She slowed for a moment, examining a length of yarn. "*Ch'aska* pattern," she said, identifying by those crimps the pattern of the cloth from which the yarn had been unraveled.

Benita understood cloth more as a series of motions of yarn than as the visual image that resulted. It is as if she were a dancer who concentrated on her steps and inadvertently left behind a pattern of footprints for us to study. This is a great lesson for us. The ancient Andes developed a society that was like no other on earth and like no other that survives today. The people were highly textile literate, so nuance of construction and technique that are difficult to explain by any means to modern Western people were common currency in the Andes. For this audience, it was not just the medium that was the message, but the structure of the medium itself. It is as if we computer users today were all keenly aware of the codes and engineering behind the screen on which we construct text. This is a level of sophistication with basic media that has not been part of Western perception for centuries.

It is important here to recognize how differently Andean people perceive their work because for many years, the visual designs decorating the textiles of pre-Columbian Andean civilizations have been fertile ground for investigation of symmetrical patterning (see, e.g., Grünbaum 1990; Grünbaum and Shephard 1987; Stevens 1984, among others). The arrays found on finished cloth offer clear evidence that Andean people followed formatted rules to build complex surface designs from smaller units. And because it is possible to represent these surfaces on printed pages, most scholars have made little distinction between Andean textile patterns and those made by printing, tiling, or other media (Grünbaum's concept of the "fabric plane" is a

notable exception). Furthermore, group theory has led analysis to see larger Andean textile designs as "wallpaper" patterns that repeat motifs in two dimensions to cover theoretically infinite space. In this chapter I want to discuss the special qualities of weaving and its implications for construction of design and present ethnographic evidence to argue that the way contemporary Andean weavers see and make "wallpaper" patterns is both different than we might suppose and consistent with other cultural practices from the Andes.

The Andean Fabric Plane

In "Periodic Ornamentation of the Fabric Plane," Branko Grünbaum (1990) introduced the idea of a fabric plane differing from a Euclidean plane by having two preferred directions set perpendicular to each other. This device would appear to derive from the most common weaving procedures involving the interlacement of a fixed set of warp yarns with a set of weft yarns inserted perpendicularly to them, but curiously, Grünbaum proceeded to analyze embroidered fabrics that theoretically were not constrained in any way by these two directions. The embroidery yarns were inserted to embellish previously constructed fabrics and could have followed any plan to fill space regardless of direction, just as a drawing on paper might. However, embroideries actually represent only a very small part of the Andean textile tradition, and for virtually all other techniques, the construction of a textile is not like filling a blank fabric or piece of paper with printed design. The act of making the pattern also creates the physical space for design, requiring the weaver to integrate design choices with the engineering necessary to make functional cloth. As a result, the weaver works with a "fabric plane" that does have the two perpendicular preferred directions established by Grünbaum but also has a number of other properties, including thickness, an inescapable inverse, and a quantum nature.

The Andean fabric plane necessarily has a third dimension of thickness because it is constructed of yarn rather than applied to a surface. To hold the fabric together, the yarns that make patterns must be held down occasionally, and this requires somewhere for the yarns to go. If we imagine a Euclidean plane as relentlessly two dimensional like the frontier between a still body of water and the air, the Andean idea of the plane is more like a layer of ice upon that water: thin and of variable thickness but never without any dimension at all. Mary Frame (personal communication) calls this a "thick plane." The need to hold down yarns to make fabric also produces the inescapable inverse because in most cases when a yarn is not making pattern on the front side of the cloth, it necessarily appears on the back side of the fabric. Depending on whether the cloth is warp faced or weft faced, the back side can be a horizontally reflected copy of the pattern in reverse color scheme or a reflection of the pattern in the same color. We might say then that for Peruvians, the fabric plane has an intrinsic reversing quality.

Unlike painting, printing, stamping, or drawing, all weaving patterns are based on the quanta represented by the individual threads. It is possible to expand or shrink a warp to add or subtract iterations of pattern but only in whole-thread units. For instance, a nine-thread pattern can be doubled but cannot be accurately halved. Andean patterns are built of small units of meaning like pixels, except they can continue infinitely in each of the preferred directions; we shall call them *texels*. While a texel can and often does consist of more than one thread, it cannot be any smaller than a single thread. Figure 6.1a shows a band of *chhili* pattern made from eighteen dark/light contrasting pairs of warp yarns; that is, there are eighteen light threads each matched with a dark thread. This is a warp-faced complementary warp weave, which means the dark and light threads of any pair move in opposite directions and the weft yarn that holds them together is completely covered. When a dark thread is on the surface facing us, the light partner is on reverse side of the cloth, creating a reflected copy of the surface pattern in opposite color. While our weaving nomenclature calls this a complementary warp weave, a better name from an Andean point of view would be reciprocal weave.

Figure 6.1a and the bottom part of Figure 6.1b show the 18 threads of the warp organized into the nine texels needed to make the chhili pattern. Since the black/white pairs are always handled in groups of two that occupy one design place, we can call these two-thread texels. In the center of Figure 6.1b, the band shifts to one-thread texels, where each black/white pair is handled independently. Now there are eighteen texels in the same

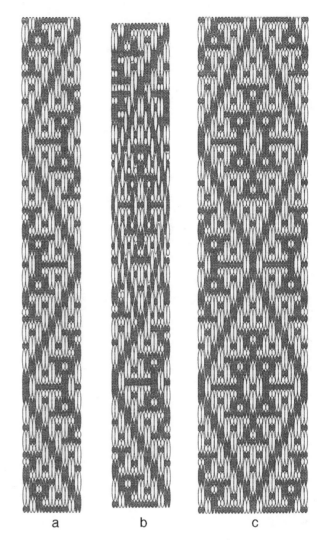

a	b	c

Figure 6.1 Patterns based on chhili: (a) chhili in nine two-thread texels, (b) chhili in two-thread texels with chongo chhili in one-thread texels, (c) chongo chhili in two-thread texels.

eighteen-thread warp, allowing two iterations of the same pattern reflected to create bilateral symmetry (at the top of Figure 6.1b, the pattern returns to two-thread texels and escapes from bilaterality). Should we choose to begin with twenty-seven black/white pairs and three-thread texels, the original pattern would work well, but the bilateral center section would not be possible. Figure 6.1c shows two reflected iterations of the chhili pattern done with two thread texels on a warp containing 34 black/white pairs.

Andean weavers past and present have exploited the quantum nature of the texels in their meaning system to create exciting and surprising visual effects, perhaps none so dramatic as the tunics of the Middle Horizon Huari culture (ca. A.D. 700–1100). Figure 6.2a is adapted

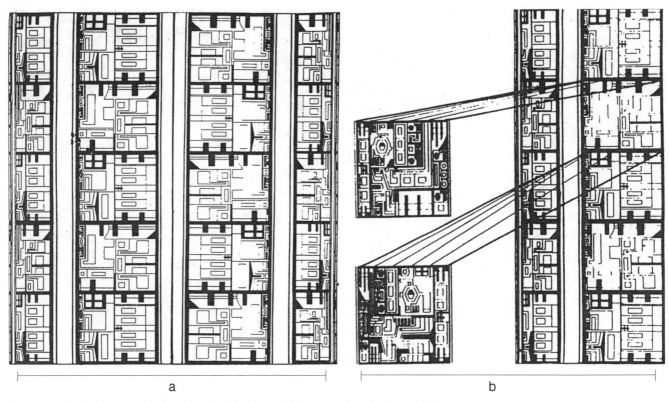

Figure 6.2 (a) Huari tapestry design from Conklin (1986), (b) design explanation by Conklin.

from a publication by William Conklin (1986:Figure 12) and shows a tapestry weaver's cartoon of one side of a Huari tunic. In each band, the number of threads in each texel of the design expands over the previous texel as the pattern moves toward the center of the garment. The result is a distortion that renders the pattern almost unintelligible to the uninitiated eye. A graphic explanation of this stylistic convention and the underlying motif on which it is acted is shown in Figure 6.2b, also adapted from Conklin (1986:Figure 13). While texels are the reality of Andean pattern thinking and changes in the size of texels is a significant way they achieve symmetrical and other mathematical variants of patterns, the rest of this chapter will use the words *thread* and *texel* interchangeably.

Stamping, tiling, and printing all depend upon the construction of basic design that is then applied repeatedly to a surface, thereby guaranteeing that all iterations of this basic unit are fundamentally identical. This is not true for Andean weavers, who construct their pattern as they construct their space. The basic unit for repeat exists only in their minds, and they must create each iteration independent of any other. In this regard, Andean weavers are more like musicians in that they can and do alter aspects

of the original unit with each iteration. For these weavers, the rules of the repeat scheme are more important than the exact details of the basic unit. They are able to embellish and improvise on their basic units so long as qualities that define the repeat scheme are preserved. In their system, rules of symmetry are guides, not rulers, and the notion that every point from one motif must map onto other iterations is not perfectly true.

Lessons from Little Girls

While the plane with which Chinchero weavers work is much different than that of Euclidean analysis and their textile process provides a level of freedom from the identities of design mathematicians seek, it is clear that the same rules of symmetry inform their understanding of how pattern is constructed. These rules are learned throughout youth in a system of age grades that each focus on a different textile activity or fabric type (Franquemont and Franquemont 1988). Girls begin this textile education by learning to spin at about age four, when they encounter the idea of two mirrored directions, one of which is proper while the other is magical (Franquemont 1986; Goodell 1969).

Between the years of about eight and twelve, girls become shepherds who form small groups away from the town center and teach each other to weave small warp-faced bands called hakimas. This learning is similar to the way North American children now teach each other to work knotted "friendship bracelets." Hakimas are one-quarter to one-half inch wide by about four feet long and are used as ties throughout the village. While very small in scale and stripped down to just pattern, hakima weaving teaches all the fundamental ideas of the textile system and much of the technology. It also allows the girls to explore basic blocks of pattern from which the design vocabulary of Chinchero is constructed. Figure 6.3 shows some basic hakima patterns that clearly show band symmetry and allows us to understand some of the thinking of these young girls. *Tanka choro* (Figure 6.3a) is the first weaving pattern any child learns. We might think of tanka choro as generated by a mirror placed down the center of the warp for horizontal reflection and another at the points marked with an *m*. In fact, the word *tanka* means "forked"; Andean girls see this design as built of Y-shaped or forked elements that repeat by translation and color shift followed by a color-preserving vertical reflection. The translation and color shift nest the tail of one Y nicely into the crotch of another.

The hakima pattern *mayo k'enko* (Figure 6.3b) provided me with my first glimpse of symmetrical thinking long before I knew what I was seeing. The first few months of my textile study in 1977 were spent working with shepherd girls in an effort to learn the essential set of understandings gained at this stage. One day, eleven-year-old Sabina Choque asked me to teach her mayo k'enko, which is dominated by a line that zigzags across the design field. We made a warp, and I began by reading the configuration of the finished design from one side as I had been taught other patterns by these girls. "One dark, two lights, two darks, two lights, one dark" read the first row. We proceeded in this way with her accurately following my instructions until we reached the place where the diagonal line passed the center of the warp. I continued to read from the same side, while she began to do the pickup from the opposite side. This brought the meandering line back in the direction from which it came rather than continue across the warp, causing the pattern to fail. Surprised, I asked her why she had reversed direction.

"*Chaupi hina,*" she said. "It felt like a center."

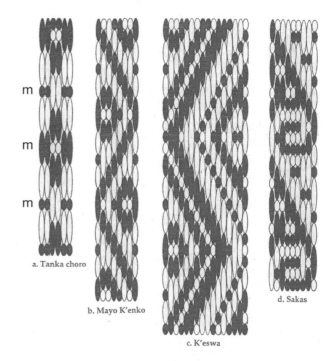

Figure 6.3 Some hakima patterns: (a) tanka choro, (b) mayo k'enko, (c) k'eswa, (d) sakas.

I had continued to read the pattern from one side to another following a literate model, while my young friend intuitively recognized a rotation point in the midst of a pattern she had never woven before. Later, I would come to learn that advanced weavers often do not pick up pattern from one side to the other but rather from significant places in a pattern. These places are usually lines of reflection and points of rotation and are sometimes marked by color stripes in the warp.

Sabina demonstrated that not only does the visual pattern reverse front to back and side for side at a rotation point, but the weaver herself changes the way she works, bringing the power of symmetrical thinking from design to action. We can see more of this in the way advanced weavers think about mayo k'enko pattern. In Figure 6.4a, I have drawn the pattern again and then broken it into (b) and (c), which respectively show the odd picks and even picks of the pattern. The odd picks shown in Figure 6.4b are "pebble rows," a widely used device in Andean patterns that always starts and ends with a single thread followed by alternating pairs of contrasting colors. Each pebble row reverses color from the one before. The even picks in Figure 6.4c are more complex but equally systematic. The row is always composed of four threads of one

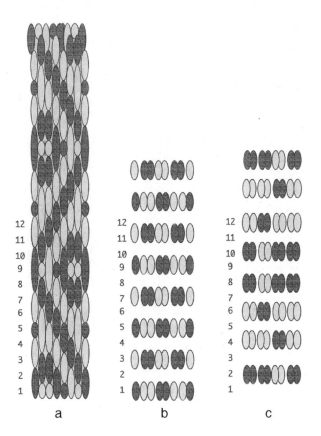

12
11
10
9
8
7
6
5
4
3
2
1

a   b   c

Figure 6.4 Deconstruction of mayo k'enko: (a) mayo k'enko pattern, (b) odd picks, (c) even picks.

color, two of the contrasting, and two of the original. This configuration repeats, reversing color, then reflects side for side. To accomplish this, the weaver does just what she had before but works from the opposite side of the warp. The next even pick the four/two/two sequence repeats, reversing color again, and then whole sequence is repeated in inverse order. The weaver knows where she is in this sequence by following the meandering line. When it crosses the center of the warp, the weaver reverses the direction of the work; when it is at the edge of the warp, the weaver works back the way she came, creating a vertical reflection. While I have shown here the odd picks separate from the even picks purely for illustrative purposes, there is ample evidence that some classes of Andean weaves are made precisely this way. "Dual lease" techniques are semi–loom controlled, with the pebble rows held on heddles and only the intervening pattern rows manipulated by the weaver (DesRosier 1986; Franquemont 1991).

In fact, Chinchero weavers think what they are doing at both reversal points of the warp is a kind of reversal. We call the sequence between picks four and six to be a

rotation because it reverses side for side and picks eight and ten a reflection because left-right orientation is preserved. However, the weaver does not think of the finished visual design as she works as much as the configuration of operations that gets her there. We might say Andean weavers see time where we see space. She makes pick four, a pebble row, and then repeats but starts from the opposite side; she does pick eight, a pebble row, and then repeats without changing directions. For her the difference is that picks four through six are balanced, or reciprocal, while picks eight through ten are not.

Among the other patterns learned by young girls during the hakima stage of life are k'eswa (Figure 6.3c) and *sakas* (Figure 6.3d). Sakas is a lovely pattern built of rotations and color shifts. It is difficult for young weavers to learn because the color shifts result in a pattern where the "pebble" rows are discontinuous. That is, a pebble row is never worked all the way across the web because the picks of pattern that have two-thread tie downs in the white areas do not have them in the black areas. K'eswa is the pattern that had escaped me at the warping of my first llijlla. The particular set of young girls with whom I worked as hakima weavers did not control k'eswa because the reversals and color shifts are quite complex. Instead of one diagonal meandering across the field like mayo k'enko, this pattern has two in alternating color, and each of these lines is complex in construction. No line ever reaches from one side to the other, making it difficult to find the centers for reversal of work. The point of reciprocal reversal (rotation) is marked not by a centered line, but by the point when the boundary between the two fields of diagonal lines is in the center of the warp, and the result is not just a reversal of sides for subsequent picks, but a reversal of color as well. Overall, k'eswa represents a considerable challenge to the intellect of these subteen girls.

Lessons from Teens
Armed with an understanding of how the system works and some basic building blocks of design, teenage girls explore larger bands called *chumpis*, or belts. These bands are two to six inches wide and usually are dominated by a massive central design flanked by stripes of plain color framing. These central designs are built by symmetrical rules from the blocks and ideas learned in hakima bands. To learn pattern expansion principles of chumpi weaving,

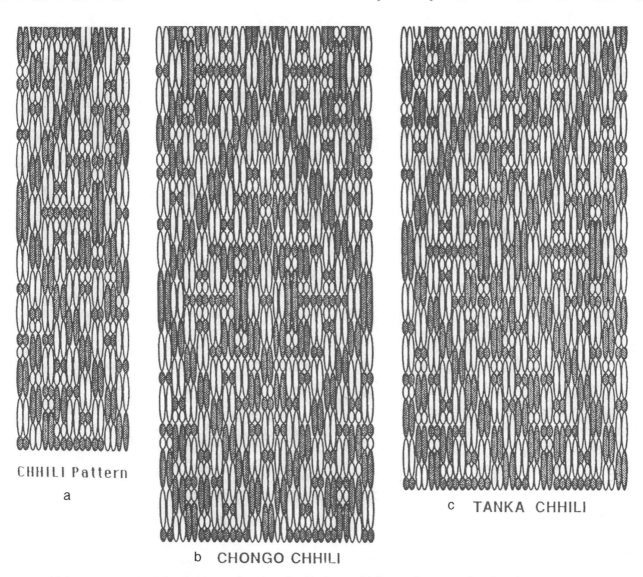

CHHILI Pattern

a

b   CHONGO CHHILI

c   TANKA CHHILI

Figure 6.5 Chhili expansion: (a) chhili on nine two-thread texels, (b) chongo chhili on eighteen two-thread texels, (c) tanka chhili on eighteen two-thread texels.

teens form tight friendship groups of two or three friends who actively solicit instruction from adults in the courtyards of the town (Franquemont and Franquemont 1988).

Some chumpi patterns are direct descendants of hakima patterns. The nine-texel chhili band shown in Figure 6.1, for instance, is similar to mayo k'enko in the course of the diagonal line that helps frame a design built of reciprocal reverses and nonreciprocal reverses. However, more often weavers at this stage learn to use symmetrical operations as a principle to guide pattern expansion. In the middle section of the chhili band shown in Figure 6.1b, we see the pattern doubled by vertical reflection by shifting to one-thread texels. The pattern could also be doubled on a different warp by doubling the number of threads, as shown in Figure 6.1c

and Figure 6.5b. The process of doubling by vertical reflection is called *chongo* in the Quechua language of these Inca descendants. When asked to describe the idea of chongo, virtually all people questioned thought a bit and then clapped to symbolize the meeting of reflected halves. The same chhili pattern can be doubled by the different principle of *tanka*, or forking, which we would see as the translation in Figure 6.5c. When asked to describe tanka, some people made a V of their fingers, while others searched the brush for a forked branch. One of my very wisest friends just shook his head with a knowing smile. He said, "*Mana runa tankayta atinchu*" ("People just can't do tanka"). This is because of the bilateral symmetry of the human body.

The expansion of chhili by chongo and tanka

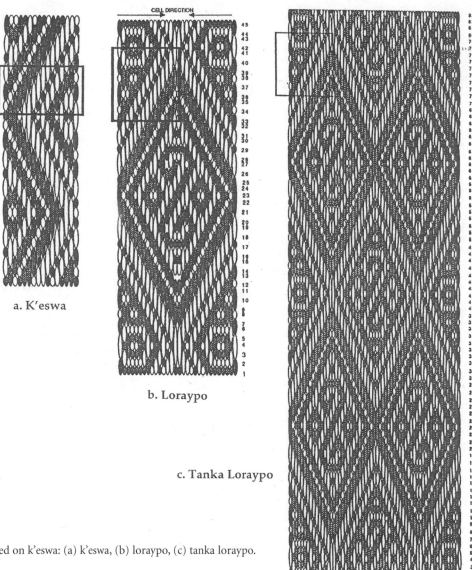

a. K'eswa

b. Loraypo

c. Tanka Loraypo

Figure 6.6 Patterns based on k'eswa: (a) k'eswa, (b) loraypo, (c) tanka loraypo.

reveals another aspect of the Chinchero sense of symmetrical space. Weavers construct the original chhili band as one-dimensional symmetry using principles we recognize as reflection and rotation. However, once constructed, the entire band becomes the unit for symmetrical action. Chongo or tanka chhili could be expanded to cover a great deal of design space, but these weavers never conceive of the process as taking a single motif and repeating it in two dimensions. Chinchero weavers move from one dimension to two dimensions not by using a grid, but rather by replicating whole bands by symmetrical rules to fill space. They "nest" symmetrical operations by working at one level to create bands and then use the product of that level as the unit for work at the next level. Their point of view is

hardly surprising since to add more space for horizontal expansion of the pattern, the weaver must add more warps. The number of warps must allow the number of texels she will need to complete her pattern, so as she winds warp, she is counting in numbers of band iterations.

Following a few patterns from hakima scale to larger design allows us to see the Inca weaver at work composing symmetrical space from her repertoire of design and principles. She uses symmetrical rules as a guide but not a limit and is willing to add or subtract threads as needed to achieve a more pleasing visual design. These are "accidentals," similar to the musician who adds or modifies notes outside of the proper key to accomplish effects. In adding more iterations of her original pattern, the weaver also discovers new design potential created by fields that overlap lines of reflection and translation. Here she is free to embellish however she can imagine, a rare opportunity for improvisation and individual expression within a highly formatted art style.

Figure 6.6 begins with the sixteen-thread k'eswa pattern as learned by advanced hakima weavers and shown in detail in Figure 6.3c. Here the band is doubled by reflection into a thirty-thread pattern called loraypo (Figure 6.6b) and then doubled again by translation into a sixty-thread pattern called *tanka loraypo* (Figure 6.6c). It was my failure to understand the doubling of k'eswa into loraypo that had so amused Benita during our warping of my first llijlla, and in truth, few scholars of symmetry would agree with my Andean friends that this indeed is a symmetrical operation. To begin with, a doubling from sixteen to thirty drops two threads we should expect, and even worse, the entire system of lines is shifted five places toward the edges of the design to accommodate a larger design potential in the center. For the Andean weaver the essential issues remain: two sets of complex lines in opposite colors that meander across the pattern field to create triangles of opposed color. With the shift of this system toward the edges of the pattern, these triangles are enlarged to allow a different kind of "eye" in the design triangles at the sides of the weave. In the center of the pattern where two triangles are joined across the line of reflection, the shift of the lines creates a diamond with far more design potential. This area "on the mirror" does not affect the motion of the lines defining the symmetry, and therefore the weaver is free to embellish the space as she might choose. Systems of "eyes," concentric diamonds, and other motifs are often used, but in contemporary Chinchero the S shape shown in Figure 6.6b is most popular. The motif has an internal rotation and must be constructed in space that comes from both halves of the loraypo pattern. In a sense, the doubling of k'eswa to loraypo now has the synergistic effect of creating new design potential in the center of the field.

The synergies that result from symmetrical doubling are even more profound when loraypo becomes tanka loraypo through a translation (Figure 6.6c). Once again, two expanded triangles meet at the centerline to create an expanded field that can be filled with a central S-shape motif, which due to color shifts is in reverse color. But let's think about this: doubling the loraypo band by translation has created three iterations of the diamond and S pattern, clear proof that at least sometimes one plus one equals three! That the third iteration is in reverse color, or reciprocal space, is of even greater interest to Andean people.

A series based on the nine-thread hakima pattern sakas offers an even more elaborate example of the power of symmetrical doubling of bands to provide color-reversing synergies (Figure 6.7). The original sakas band is built from a hooked triangle motif through rotation and color shift. When it is doubled by either rotation or reflection and slide, two threads are usually omitted to compress the pattern to sixteen texels. The effect preserves the integrity of the dark version of the hooked motif but transforms the light into a sinuous hooked line. In the glide reflected version (Figure 6.7a2), the hooks of the line all face up but are mirror imaged; this is unidirectional with respect to the vertical direction. The rotated version (Figure 6.7a1) shows the hooks of the white line reversed both in the top/bottom and left/right orientation; this is bidirectional with respect to the warp. Both of these whole bands can be doubled again by reflection, translation, or rotation. The reflected version is made without reduction in threads and is dominated by a heart-shaped motif flanked by sinuous hooked lines; in one case the heart points up, (Figure 6.7b2) while in the other the heart points down (Figure 6.7b1). If the second doubling is translation instead of reflection, thread compression is in place to make a thirty-thread design from two sixteen-thread halves. The result is that the central dark hooked motifs are collapsed into a sinuous hooked line like the white, once again giving the impression that a simple doubling can yield three iterations, including one iteration in reciprocal space (Figure 6.7c1). In the unidirectional world of Figure 6.7c2, the reciprocity of the design is especially evident because the hooks of the dark sinuous line are in reverse direction from those of the white lines. Finally, if we choose to do the second doubling by rotation and use thread compression, a bidirectional black sinuous line is introduced between two unidirectional white lines (Figure 6.7d2), and a unidirectional black line appears

Figure 6.7 Patterns based on sakas.

between bidirectional white lines. In each of these cases, repeated doubling produces greater design potential than might be expected.

Discussion

There is no doubt Chinchero weavers are playing fast and loose with the construction and size of motifs in expanding their patterns from the initial cells they learn as young girls, and this flexibility will give many mathematicians pause in thinking of these as symmetrical operations. Yet the narrow hakima patterns of the young girls conform closely to mathematical notions of how symmetry works. During their teen years, girls learn to expand these basic patterns and to improvise within the system in ways that use the ideas of symmetry but do not follow rules exactly.

This is "jazz," similar to the way jazz musicians in our culture use key, chord progression, rhythmic structure, and melody of a song. These are fundamental formats that allow the artist to embellish within certain parameters, and indeed, the formats challenge the artist to more creative ways of seeing. For the jazz musician and the Chinchero weaver, the format is a structural device that allows the artist to know what to do next based on what has been done before, rather than an overall plan by which an entire piece is first composed and then executed. This way of thinking is much more consistent with Grünbaum's idea of "symmetry schemes" (Grünbaum 1990) than with more accepted group theory analysis. This is reasonable, since aliterate Andean weavers do not work from drawn overall plans but must regenerate each new iteration of the design according to a process plan held in the mind.

The formatting rules used by teenage weavers to expand their patterns are highly specialized and do not function on the basis of motifs. Rather, once symmetrical processes have created a band from a motif, this whole band is doubled repeatedly to create a more complex pattern. Using the product of one operation as the starting point for the next is unusual in most weaving traditions but widely employed in the Andes (Franquemont 1991). Andean society in general is very interested in doubling and halving processes. Before the European invasion of the sixteenth century, the Inca Empire was divided into two moiety halves called *hanan* and *hurin,* or upper and lower, divisions that persist to this day in Andean communities. In Chinchero, these divisions affect social and economic relations and influence issues such as where tombs are located in the cemetery or displays are erected for the town festival. Anthropologists and ethnohistorians have always assumed these moiety halves are mirror images of each other, but textile evidence suggests that Andean people have a more complex understanding of relationships between two halves and that translated or rotational patterning may be equally valid as a model. I suspect relationships are dynamic and may be conceived as reflected, rotated, or translated, depending on circumstances and the perspective of the viewer. To think of social relations as rotated or translated as opposed to reflected may be difficult for Western researchers but worth the price. Evidence from dance (Platt 1976) as well as textiles demonstrates Andean society has an expanded sense of symmetrical patterning, and this sense may well underlie explanations for the structure by which the Inca could manage an empire the size of Rome without any written records.

The Andean fabric plane is space composed according to rules of the physical world seen through a culturally relevant filter. The Euclidean plane of Western geometry is not actually encountered anywhere in the real world but for two millennia has served mathematicians well as a vehicle for exploration of relationships of space and shape. The Andean fabric plane is precisely the opposite: it is an attempt to represent the real world in an artificially constructed flattened space. In a sense, these textiles give us a parallel to the point perspective

used by Western art to represent three-dimensional space on a flat plane. William Conklin (1986) suggests texel-based distortions of the huari shirts (Figure 6.2) are a representation of foreshortening produced as objects move father from us toward a distant horizon. Mary Frame (personal communication) has argued that color shifts of certain Paracas embroideries can be best explained as three-dimensional symmetries compressed into a two-dimensional space and these conventions are in use to indicate when the viewer should understand that elements are moving in a third dimension unavailable in the flat world of fabric surface. The k'eswa pattern we have been following provides a modern analog. The word *k'eswa* refers to elements that intertwine, or twist; a common example is a three-strand rope where the elements continually wrap around each other. The fabric pattern represents this rope through the banks of diagonal lines. The lines move first up the warp and to the left, and then return up and to the right. Where we see zigzagging diagonal lines, the Andean eye sees plies of rope moving to the left and then returning to the right on the back side of the rope, almost an x-ray vision. Here a spiraling movement has been represented as flattened onto the two dimensions of the front of the fabric.

The inescapably reversing quality of the Andean fabric plane has great power for Andean thought. As a weaver constructs a pattern on the surface facing her, she cannot help but create a reverse image on the opposite side of the cloth. It is as if every creative act in one domain has an equal but opposite consequence in the opposite domain. This process resonates with the deep-seated Andean sense of reciprocity that balances opposed pairs. In textiles, all yarns are two ply because everything needs its mate, and all ponchos and shawls are made of two identical halves joined in bifold rotation. In social and economic relations, men work in groups organized by principles of reciprocal labor exchange called *ayni*. A man owes a day's labor to each of the men who form the group that works on his fields, and there is no greater social stigma than that which falls to the few who fail to respond to the strict but never spoken accounting of ayni obligations. As a landless man in Chinchero who worked regularly in neighbors' fields, I presented a great challenge to the system. Many men were clearly nervous about their inability to find

Figure 6.8 Fragment, textile, pre-Columbian Peru. (Los Angeles County Museum olf Natural History, # L.2100.A.13.63.438) Reproduced from Washburn and Crowe (1988:15.75)

ways to discharge the ayni obligations they felt because of my work in their fields. Toward the end of my stay in Chinchero, I found myself creating work projects to provide opportunities to balance the skewed reciprocal relationships I had created in the town. Similar reciprocal relationships govern the behavior between scattered parts of villages.

The weavers of contemporary Inca villages in the Cuzco area are separated by great gulfs of time and culture from the people who made most of the cloth found in the museums, but it is interesting to apply some of their perspectives to see how they differ from our own. Washburn and Crowe (1988:170, here shown as Figure 6.8) illustrate an ancient Peruvian textile fragment as an example of symmetry group *p'b1*. To arrive at this conclusion, they assign the half of the motifs that are gray to the role of background and examine the motions that will map the remaining black-and-white versions of the motif onto each other. An Andean weaver would consider nothing background and foreground. Rather, she would note the design was built of step-and-hook motifs that form a horizontal one-dimensional symmetry through rotation and color shift. Rather than a simple color shift, however, this band shows gray as opposed to an alternation of white and black. That is, odd-numbered rotations of the motif always produce gray, while even-numbered rotations produce white or black in alternation. Once this band has been formed, it is then doubled by reflection and glide; this unit is then doubled again by reflection and glide and then once again by reflection and glide to fill the entire span of the fragment. One rule produces the band, and another fills the cloth. Of course, we cannot be certain ancient Andean people employed the same principle as contemporary weavers of Chinchero, and in fact it still remains to be demonstrated that the Chinchero perspective actually is in general use in other weaving cultures of the Andes.

Conclusions

The opportunity to see non-Western people at work using symmetrical thinking to construct space is both rare and instructive. Evidence from Chinchero demonstrates that symmetrical thinking is learned early and effectively by weavers in the contemporary Andes and that their approach to the problem of repeating design

differs from our analytical constructs in significant ways. Some of these differences result from use of a "fabric plane" that is not Euclidean in that it has thickness, preferred directions, two faces in reverse orientation, and a quantum nature based both on threads and on units of meaning I have called texels. While some of these qualities are intrinsic to any weaving process, others are distinctly Andean.

One distinctly Andean characteristic to their symmetrical thinking is the use of "nested" operations that use the product from one level of work as the unit of the next. The way girls learn in age grades associated with distinct fabric types encourages nested thinking since two-dimensional symmetrical operations are only introduced after years of studying one-dimensional symmetries of the hakimas. It is an easy and natural transition for the girls to separate construction of bands from the rules by which they can be replicated to fill larger spaces since that is the way they learn. Nested operations mean the motif for symmetrical operations in one dimension is not the same as the unit of symmetrical operation in the other; rather, whole bands of design become units for action.

In the process of building bands into two-dimensional space, Andean weavers can and do alter the configurations of motifs and space to produce visual designs consistent with their intent. They use the rules of symmetry as a guide to work rather than as a limit on what they are allowed to do, and they produce "jazz" by altering the number of threads from the expected or filling extra space with personally chosen designs. Since weavers do not plan their projects on paper before beginning work, the rules of symmetry provide a strong general map that allows them to know what to do next based on what they have already completed. This use of symmetry rules as a working guide conforms more closely to the notion of symmetry schemes than group theory analysis. While the patterns that result may not qualify as periodic in a strictly mathematical sense, it would be difficult to deny that the same rules of symmetry discovered by Western analysis also inform their work, especially with the discovery of words for the operations of reflection and translation. No word for rotation has been identified, but since the word *tanka* means "forked" and is applied to translations of

pattern, we can be sure the Andean notion of translation is not precisely the same as ours. These Andean concepts of symmetry may bring clues to a better understanding of the principles by which the Inca organized and ruled their vast empire without benefit of written language.

Contemporary Chinchero weavers use doubling by reflection, rotation, and translation with or without glides as a primary means of filling space from basic bands. In this process, they take special delight in finding iterations of basic design that appear in contrasting color. Since reversals of color on the back side of the cloth is an inescapable consequence of the type of weaving in use in the town, it is useful to consider contrasting color motifs as an example of the kind of reciprocity that dominates many of the fundamental institutions of Inca life. Viewed this way, the weaver prefers to create designs that "balance" the color schemes of the two sides of the cloth and is willing to compromise mathematics to achieve her goal. ■

References Cited

Conklin, W.

1986   The Mythic Geometry of the Ancient Southern Sierra. In
        The Junius B. Bird Conference on Andean Textiles, edited by
        A. P. Rowe. The Textile Museum, Washington, DC.

DesRosier, S.

1986   An Interpretation of Technical Weaving Data Found in an
        Early 17th Century Chronicle. In *The Junius B. Bird
        Conference on Andean Textiles,* edited by A. P. Rowe. The
        Textile Museum, Washington, DC.

Franquemont, C., and E. Franquemont

1988   Learning to Weave in Chinchero. *Textile Museum Journal*
        vol. 26, Washington, DC.

Franquemont, E.

1986   Cloth Production Rates in Chinchero, Peru. In *The Junius
        B. Bird Conference on Andean Textiles,* edited by A. P. Rowe.
        The Textile Museum, Washington, DC.

1991   Dual Lease Weaving. In *Textile Traditions of Mesoamerica
        and the Andes,* edited by M. Schevill, J. C. Berlo, and E. B.
        Dwyer. Garland Publishing, New York.

Goodell, G.

1969   A Study of Andean Spinning in the Cuzco Region. *Textile
        Museum Journal* 2(3):2–8.

Grünbaum, B.

1990   Periodic Ornamentation of the Fabric Plane: Lessons from
        Peruvian Fabrics. *Symmetry* 1(1):45–68.

Grünbaum, B., and G. C. Shephard

1987   *Tilings and Patterns.* Freeman, New York.

Murra, J.

1962   Cloth and Its Function in the Inca State. *American
        Anthropologist* 64(4):710–728.

Platt, T.

1976   *Espejos y Maiz Cuadernos de Investigacion.* CIPA No. 10,
        C.I.P.C.A. La Paz.

Stevens, P. S.

1984   *Handbook of Regular Patterns.* MIT Press, Cambridge, MA.

Washburn, D. K., and Donald W. Crowe

1988   *Symmetries of Culture.* University of Washington Press,
        Seattle.

CHAPTER SEVEN

The Ghost in the Machine
Symmetry and Representation
in Ancient Antillean Art

Peter G. Roe

THE CARIBBEAN EXPERIENCED a far-flung migration that still stirs archaeological debate. One or two migrations have been proposed for its horticultural settlement. Formal analysis of symmetry patterns in the ceramic designs of these two complexes (*Saladoid* versus *Huecoid*) reveals the close Saladoid affinities of both design systems despite differences in technique (polychrome painting vis-à-vis incision and zoned crusting). These are separate styles (Cedrosan and Huecan) within the same Saladoid series. The hidden grammar of symmetry belies the surface differences of technique, demonstrating cultural continuity, not discontinuity. This approach, "aesthetic syntactics," also shows the hidden representational aspects in the geometric art of the last Saladoid descendants, the Chican Ostionoid of the protohistoric Taíno who Columbus encountered, as well as its Saladoid affinities.

In this chapter I look at Insular Arawak (Classic Taíno and their antecedents and descendants) geometric and stylized depictions in multi- and cross-media contexts over a 2,000-year trajectory. This absurdly ambitious enterprise encompasses what I have learned in some twenty-two years of excavation, field documentation, and collection study in the Greater Antilles (particularly in the first of the Greater Antilles, Puerto Rico [see Figure 7.1], starting in 1978 and still continuing). It ranges widely from the arrival of the first Saladoid ceramic-using tribal horticulturalists, circa 500 B.C., to the emergence of "Complex Tribes" or "Incipient Chiefdoms" in the pre-Taíno period A.D. 800 to 1200. Then it progresses to the rise of the Complex Chiefdoms of the Classic Taíno, A.D. 1300–1400 (Figure 7.2). The chapter ends with the initial "cultural hybrid vigor" response of the Taíno

immediately after the arrival of Columbus in 1492–93, the persistence of this fertile collaboration of Western raw materials and Amerindian sensibilities in syncretistic elite "transculturative" artifacts that fluoresced until circa A.D. 1550. That ending date was the terminus of the native sequence with the "cultural extinction" of the Taíno and their replacement by West African slave labor. Recent "neo-Taíno" art (Vega de Boyrie 1987) represents the archaistic revival of a much altered style but with some of the same roots as its Amerindian antecedent. Indeed, it is a "roots-building" activity itself (Salazar 1990).

Divining the Messages in Ancient Antillean Art
Abundant lowland terra firma ethnography shows that these crafts are not "trivial" domains of culture for the people who once executed them (Guss 1989; Roe 1990, 1995a, 1996). Because many mainland groups, especially those of the Guianas, are culturally related to the ancient migrants who left northeastern South America for the Antilles starting at about 500 B.C. (Roe 1989a), the direct historical approach utilizing ethnographic analogy is appropriate to understanding ancient Greater Antillean craft.

We are exceptionally fortunate in Puerto Rico (and in neighboring Hispañola) in the existence of a work of precocious ethnology, the first since Tacitus circa A.D. 75! Unlike his earlier *Germania*, this was a study produced by true problem-oriented fieldwork coupled with local linguistic competence. It is the small but seminal work written about 1498 by the humble Catalán friar Ramón Pané (Bourne 1906; see Pané 1974, 1992, 1999). Commissioned by Columbus himself on his second voyage, its practical goal was making the Spanish missionization of the Taíno easier by teaching the Spanish missionaries something about the Taínos' religion. This short volume, which predates the chronicler works on the religions of the Aztecs and Incas, offers an exceptional opportunity, which many Puerto Rican and Dominican scholars have used with great success (Alegría 1978; Arrom 1986; Deive 1976; Jiménez Lambertus 1983; López-Baralt 1977; Stevens-Arroyo 1988, etc.).

The impact of this "Rosetta Stone" for Greater Antillean aesthetic artifact decoding has been hampered by the fact that it appeared only in modern editions in Catalan (Pané 1992) and in Spanish (Pané 1974), but not

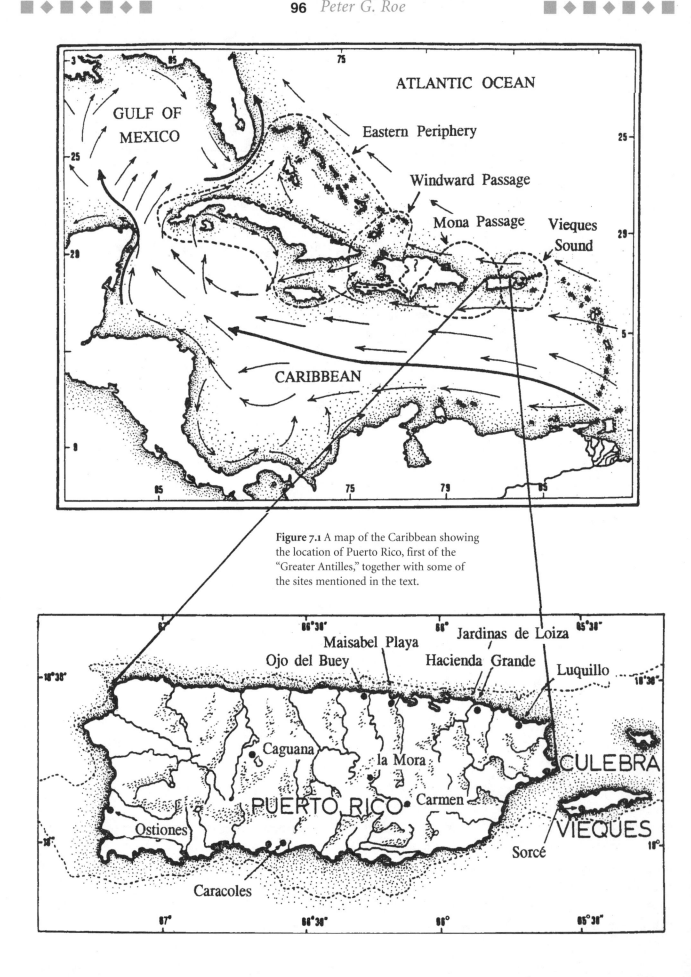

Figure 7.1 A map of the Caribbean showing the location of Puerto Rico, first of the "Greater Antilles," together with some of the sites mentioned in the text.

Figure 7.2 A regional chronological chart adapted from Rouse (1992:Figures 14 and 15), showing the cultural series and subseries (phases) referred to in the text.

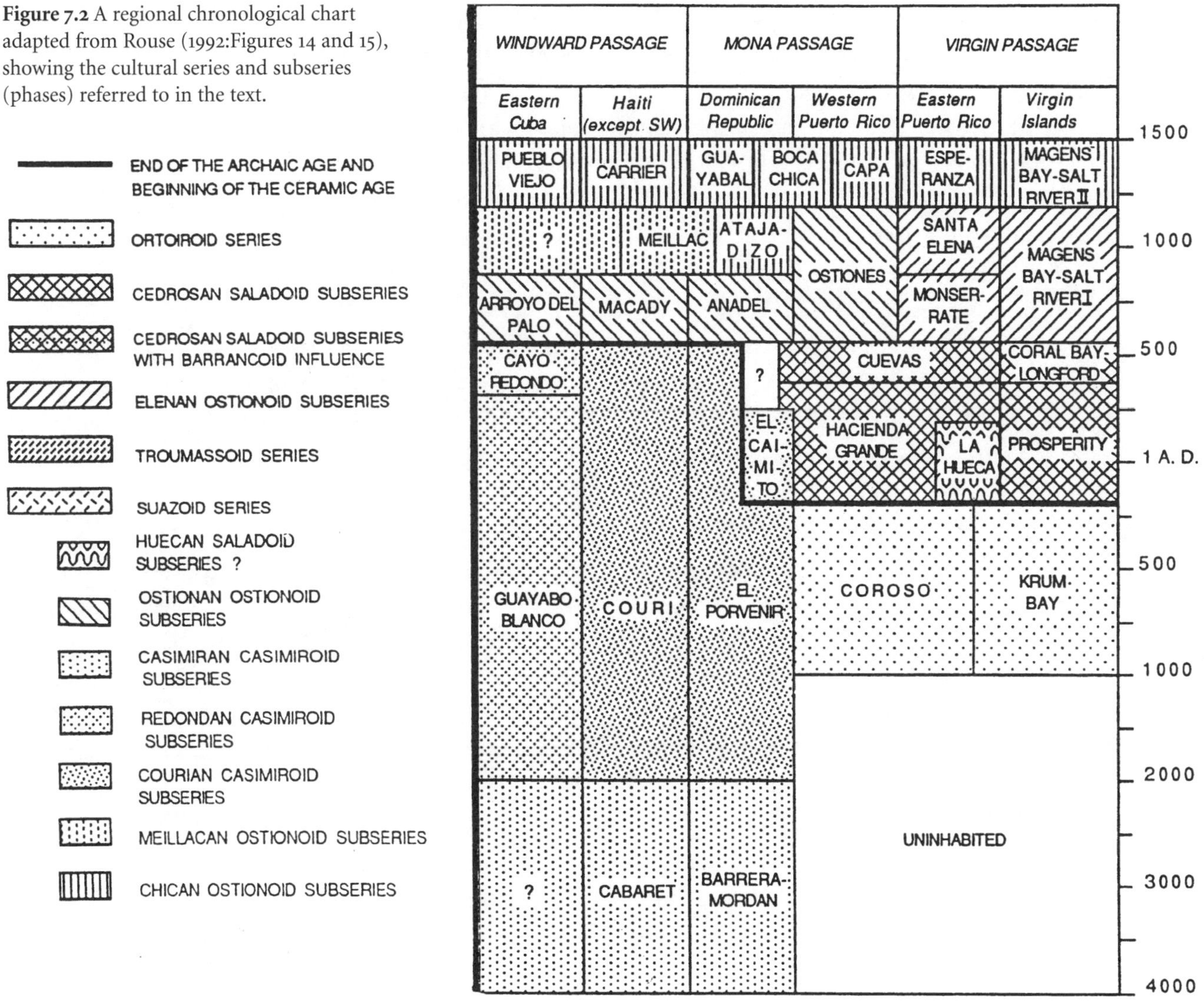

Legend:

- END OF THE ARCHAIC AGE AND BEGINNING OF THE CERAMIC AGE
- ORTOIROID SERIES
- CEDROSAN SALADOID SUBSERIES
- CEDROSAN SALADOID SUBSERIES WITH BARRANCOID INFLUENCE
- ELENAN OSTIONOID SUBSERIES
- TROUMASSOID SERIES
- SUAZOID SERIES
- HUECAN SALADOID SUBSERIES ?
- OSTIONAN OSTIONOID SUBSERIES
- CASIMIRAN CASIMIROID SUBSERIES
- REDONDAN CASIMIROID SUBSERIES
- COURIAN CASIMIROID SUBSERIES
- MEILLACAN OSTIONOID SUBSERIES
- CHICAN OSTIONOID SUBSERIES

	WINDWARD PASSAGE		MONA PASSAGE		VIRGIN PASSAGE		
	Eastern Cuba	Haiti (except SW)	Dominican Republic	Western Puerto Rico	Eastern Puerto Rico	Virgin Islands	(time)
	PUEBLO VIEJO	CARRIER	GUA-YABAL	BOCA CHICA / CAPA	ESPERANZA	MAGENS BAY-SALT RIVER II	1500
	?	MEILLAC	ATAJA-DIZO	OSTIONES	SANTA ELENA	MAGENS BAY-SALT RIVER I	1000
	ARROYO DEL PALO	MACADY	ANADEL		MONSER-RATE		
	CAYO REDONDO		?	CUEVAS		CORAL BAY-LONGFORD	500
			EL-CAI-MI-TO	HACIENDA GRANDE	LA HUECA	PROSPERITY	1 A.D.
	GUAYABO BLANCO	COURI	EL PORVENIR	COROSO	KRUM BAY		500
							1000
				UNINHABITED			2000
	?	CABARET	BARRERA-MORDAN				3000
							4000

English. That limitation was answered in 1999 by the appearance of an English translation by the noted ethno-historian Juan José Arrom (Pané 1992). I have used Pané over a number of years (1982, 1993) and do so again here.

However, while invaluable, Pané is not without his problems, such as the garbling of individual myths, the collapsing of several myths into one, and the literary conflation of the whole corpus (the tendency of literate Westerners to combine distinct oral myths into a linear written story line). This means that one can best approach Pané's fifteenth-century fragments via the lens of complete mythic cycles derived from modern lowland ethnography (Roe et al. 1997).

In addition to utilizing Pané, I employ my own ethnographic data from fieldwork on the meanings hidden behind geometric designs among related lowland South Amerindians. Utilizing archaeology, ethnography, ethnoastronomy, and ethnoarchaeology. Then, for comparative purposes, I conducted ethnographic work among the much less numerous interfluvial Waiwai "foot Indians" of the northeastern quadrant in the Guianas. They are equally famous for their own elaborate feather art and patterned twill-weave basketry. The Waiwai are distantly related to the ancient Taíno of Puerto Rico via centuries-long interaction with the local Arawaks (the Lokono). The latter are descendants of the mainland relatives of the early Antillean migrants. I have also pursued this matter archaeologically among their dead ancestors, both in the Peruvian montaña (Cumancaya), the sierra and the coast (Chavín), and in the Greater Antilles (the Dominican Republic and Puerto Rico—studying all the *agro-alfarero* [ceramic-using horticultural] styles). Obviously, for me archaeology is not "artifact physics" so much as it is the "ethnology of dead informants" via a study of their artifacts (Roe 1994a). It is in that spirit that I will conduct the following "material séance" into the cultural meaning and machinery of *Borinquen* = Puerto Rican Insular Arawak symmetry.

Since my first fieldwork in 1969 in South America, I have repeatedly been alternatively intrigued and baffled by the rich semantic content lurking behind the apparently purely decorative facade of geometric designs. In an effort to penetrate that facade, I also have investigated the oral traditions of the same ethnographic and ethnohistorical populations, from living Shipibo and Waiwai informants in the jungles of South America (Roe 1982, 1985) to the protohistoric Taíno as recorded in the *Relación* of Fray Ramón Pané (1974) in the Caribbean. What struck me there too was not only that behind every design lay a myth, but also that underneath every "arbitrary" symbol hid a breathing, pulsating natural icon (in the Peircian sense). The logical deduction, then, is that behind every "arbitrary" geometric shape, as symbol, lies the nonarbitrary iconology of the plants, reptiles, mammals, and birds that, in an analogical sense, gave their natural patterning to humankind for its cultural adornments. With the circular logic of the Lévi-Straussian "Savage Mind" these artifacts stand as "mythic empirical" evidence that the sacred stories believed to be true are correct. Objects "call up" their sacred etiology in myth by their usage and "annotate" the myths when the latter are recited in "myth/material cultural mutual referentiality" (Roe 1995a).

The "Ghost" in the "Machine":
The Beings Behind Symmetry

Thus, if we seriously want to penetrate alien cultures to reveal their internal complexity and coherence in an emic sense, we must leave the ethnocentric labels ("geometric"/"representational") behind. Or at the very least, we must restrict them to the purely etic ethnological level of comparison.

My thesis, the "ghost" in the machine, is the recognition of icons (the ghost) within the intricate "machinery" of ancient Antillean symbolic geometric designs. I maintain that behind every "decorative" layout lies the

hidden visage of a breathing icon giving life (animation) to the design. Proof of this is that both representational and geometric designs behave according to the *same rules of symmetry* because the "representations" are really planar stylized depictions characterized by the same "arbitrary rearrangement of parts" that Boas (1955 [1927]), Holm (1965), and Lévi-Strauss (1967) recognized in cognate North Amerindian styles.

The Problem of Geometry, Stylization, and Representation

Symmetry analysis remains a somewhat arcane field. Even the mathematicians, ethnologists, and archaeologists who do it tend to limit the styles they study to those composed of geometric, "nonrepresentational" designs, generally in two-dimensional media such as face and body painting, textiles, tile work, or banded ceramic incision and painting. Such arrays are easier to deal with since the semantic domain can be avoided in favor of the "plumber's delight" of the formal symmetry operations themselves. However, such circumscription also means that this powerful new method of analysis has been restricted to a trivial domain, what the Western tradition has disparagingly called the "decorative arts."

Another unfortunate by-product stemming from this selection of media is the cultural expectation of a limited semantic content of the sample or, even worse, none at all. Perhaps this explains the current emphasis on cultural syntax or grammars rather than the decoding of iconography and symbolism. Shouldn't we try to escape this mental prison of our own ethnotaxonomy of form (fine versus decorative arts, art versus craft) in the hopes of achieving a better view of someone else's? Meaning often lurks where we expect it least. Hence we need to pursue the "archaeology of signification," even in symmetry. Otherwise symmetry analysis becomes mere formalism, clever, theoretically interesting, but of limited cultural significance (although rich, I hasten to add, in phylogenetic import; cf. Humphrey this volume).

How can we build a bridge from the abstractions of geometry to the semantics of representation? In this chapter, I suggest that we can do so by looking at Amerindian planar stylized sculpture. This media is a masculine pursuit within the sexual division of labor of lowland South Amerindians and the ancient Caribbean

Indians derived from them. It is the result of a simple tool-using technology that utilizes men's greater upper-body strength to exert controlled force in a deconstructive manner, that is, by "killing" the natural donor (a tree, a mollusk, an animal, even a rock—all of whom are regarded as having "souls" or in-dwelling spirits). Such industrial activities are conceived as happening in the same manner as men hunt and kill animals or pursue enemy warriors on a raid. As beings who are iconically "hard" and "solid" in their own ethnotaxonomy of the sexes, Amerindian males work in obdurate (resisting) media by removing material, whether from shell, bone, stone, or wood, to produce artifacts that are often weapons or, at least, prevailingly linear and pointed in form. Thus, these "elongated, cut down" objects reflect both men's own body image and body processes, materially less than the original raw material but aesthetically more than the sum of their parts (Roe 1989b).

In contrast, the opposed-yet-complementary feminine crafts of ceramics and textiles tend to be additive and gestational in the sense that they are built up out of smaller constituent elements and manipulate soft raw materials (coils of clay, cotton string) to yield round and hollow objects that also reflect women's body image and processes. Thus, a "gendered technology and art" results (Roe 1990) that appears singularly natural and satisfying for the members of these harmonious societies.

Masculine planar sculpture is easier to relate to strictly two-dimensional techniques such as the incision and painting of the women's craft, pottery, than is three-dimensional true sculpture from Europe, Asia, or Africa. This is because most of the sculpture in the New World has a decidedly two-dimensional aspect even when executed in the round. This may be partially attributed to the paucity of metal tools until relatively late in the Amerindian sequences. Perforce, much carving in unyielding materials had to be done with relatively ineffective instruments, from shell gouges and ground-and-polished axes and adzes to hafted rodent incisor engravers and peccary mandibles. The result is sculpture that is formed by incision and/or excision, hence bas-relief. Thus, it is two-dimensional in appearance even though three-dimensional artifacts were carved or decorated. Because of technological conservatism this remained the case, even in regions such as the lowlands,

long after iron and steel tools became available due to trade with Europeans (or, earlier still, in the Andes when arsenical copper and bronze tools came in).

I introduce the symmetry analysis of planar sculpture in this chapter because it may ameliorate the aforementioned biases in the Western symmetry analysis of Amerindian material culture. Such analysis since Haddon (1884) has been hobbled by implicit ethnocentrism rooted in our own hierarchy of art (Anderson 1990). (1) Fine art, the highest category, is an elite possession of explicitly useless objects save for their aesthetic appreciation, such as an oil painting or a bronze statue. Such art with a capital A comes with an implicit or explicit message and so carries both symbolism and iconography. (2) Applied or decorative art is a lesser form that combines aesthetic elements with practical utility such as fine cutlery or bedspreads and is bereft of any message save the delight of decorated or well-designed objects. (3) Craft is a combination of utility with handmade aesthetic functions, such as jewelry or stoneware pottery, and is traditionally of rustic or artisanal affiliation. Amerindian culture made no such distinctions; all their production may be termed *craft*.

The bulk of Western fine art sculpture (whether realistic or abstract), for example, is highly volumetric, emphasizing mass and void, while much of our decorative art traditionally bore painted or inlaid decoration, often with geometric or stylized floral adornment with little semantic "weight." If even Amerindian sculpture looks decorative, that is, two-dimensional due to the carving technology alluded to above, especially since the bulk of its ornamentation, especially among tribal and chiefdom societies, is also geometric embellishment (and embellishment is ethnocentrically regarded as ideologically "trivial"), then the symbolic and iconic content of its decoration will tend to be ignored by Western students. This is especially the case if a completely different set of graphic conventions exists among this Amerindian "patterning" that is difficult for Western observers to penetrate.

My thesis here is that such decoration isn't, in the strict sense of the term, mere embellishment at all. This is because among Amerindians, it usually carries weighty cultural meaning and may even be considered representational by those who execute it. Further, just as their two-dimensional surface patterning on pottery, textiles, or wood carving is governed by symmetrical principles, so too will the designs that beautify the surfaces of their "representational sculpture" be governed by symmetry principles since it is often equally planar and carries the same kind of abstract patterning, frequently with isometries that are accommodated to its asymmetrical forms or surfaces. In other words, Amerindian sculpture has symmetry too, and meaning may be mined from it.

If form derives, in part, from the enabling technology, it also is steeped in the divergent cultural epistemologies of distinct societies. For example, we in the West labored, until the Impressionist and Cubist revolution of the late-nineteenth/early-twentieth centuries, under the weight of a tradition that gave pride of place to a rational worldview based on the primacy of macroscopic empirical reality. To represent that world of appearances, we adopted "camera-eye" realism long before the camera was invented for reasons that are rooted in this pervasive materialism. Even in this present age of "abstract" art, we as audiences and artists are still trained in all the Boasian (Boas 1955 [1927]) illusionistic devices that it has taken Western art some 800 years to master: single vanishing-point perspective, line overlap, density gradients, equal clarity, and relative size. Thus our cultural epistemology, Cartesian long before Descartes, gives priority to the macroscopic material world as "real."

That "reality," as we will soon see, withers during altered states of consciousness, the avenue of perception in South Amerindian society. For their part, native South Americans produce a highly contrastive set of their own illusionistic devices, all forms of "pictorial dualism" that derive, quite explicitly, from the ingestion of a powerful hallucinogenic snuff, *Cohoba (Anadenanthera peregrina)*, and other hallucinogens, and the central role these psychotropic plants played in shamanic rituals and ceremonies.

From a similar rational perspective derived from the waking states perception of the natural world, we divide images into "realistic" and "abstract" categories. Realism means that from a naive perspective, any observer can make an analogical linkage to a representation as standing for something in empirical reality by the verisimilitude of its depiction: a realistic painting of

a rabbit means that even to an untutored observer, it looks like a rabbit in the real world of the senses. In contrast, an "abstract" image is one that a naive perceiver cannot make a confident linkage to anything other than an irregular shape or color or perhaps a geometric form. Thus "geometric" and "abstract" frequently function as synonyms. A "stylized" portrayal is the overlap category between "realistic" and "abstract" in that the tutored viewer can recognize, with effort and/or instruction, the referent in an otherwise "geometricized" depiction, now schematic or simplified, such as the cartoon image of the "Playboy Bunny" as representing a rabbit's head. Most of the images in this chapter will fall under the "stylized" rubric.

Such stylized images combine decorative geometric detail with representational images that are, nevertheless, seldom realistic. As schematicized images, they have, themselves, been subjected to the same tyranny of geometry as the apparently "abstract" (but never really nonrepresentational) designs that embellish the artifacts that people make, use, and discard/destroy. They show us that "realism" and "abstraction" are merely opposite poles of the same cultural continuum of meaning; they are both "representations." Any symmetry analysis worthy of the name should attack the realistic or stylized images with as much vigor as it investigates the abstract geometric designs. Indeed, one of the findings of this chapter will be that "geometric" designs are resolutely "representational" for South and Caribbean Amerindians; they carry meaning.

But one cross-cultural generalization from the Western investigation of non-Western art does appear to have some validity as a "trend or tendency statement," à la Kaplan (1964), not a universal generalization, Linton's equation that *men:realistic & stylized art::women:geometric art* (Gjessing 1969). This pattern, in turn, correlates with the equation *men:asymmetrical designs::women:symmetrical designs* for a whole host of reasons, some of them perhaps psychodevelopmental. Certainly the economic and social relations of men and women in preindustrial society cohere with such patterns. Men tend to be the specialists in dealing with the "outside world" of figural alien humans (war, politics) and spirits (religion and magic), as well as animal and avian prey. All these beings, physical and spiritual, exist as representations, that is, as images. Women, in contrast, tend to be associated with the "internal world" of the family and kin group, the concrete, not the conceptual. They manipulate media whose tyranny of warp and weft tends to geometricize images as Boasian "resultant forms." Such highly gridded media as weaving and basketry will be more amenable to bilateral symmetry. Diachronic studies of current South Amerindian styles (Roe 2000a) tend to agree with such patterns, and there is every indication that the same logic held for the ancient Taíno and their pre-Taíno and Saladoid forebearers.

If every culture has its own cultural categories of "reality" and "abstraction," then they also have unique standards of "doneness." That is the condition reached when one stops messing with the material world and calls the resultant artifact "done" (Link 1975). Increasingly, in the West we consider something done when mere functionality is achieved, embellishment being considered optional. Even worse, in modernist terms, aesthetic embellishment must be defiantly "useless" to be art, leaving technology as an efficient undecorated residual category of "pure instrumental form" (Maquet 1971); "if it cuts cheese, it can't be art" (Blake 1964)!

Alas, this cultural baggage has nothing to do with either the world or "worlds" South Amerindians and their Caribbean relatives lived in (and, in some cases, continue to inhabit), nor with their actions, stylistic devices, or resultant artifacts. Their cultural epistemology specifically denies the paramouncy of this macroscopic, empirical world. Instead, many Amerindian groups view it as a sham, a lie, in favor of (in our terms) a "non-ordinary spiritual world" (Guss 1989) where all the gifts of culture emerge from Animal Cultural Custodians in Dawn Time, including the form and decoration of all artifacts. This thorough-going "Primitive Platonism" (which the West long ago rejected in favor of Aristotlean empiricism) is rooted in the hallucinogenic visions of shamanism. No wonder Western civilization remains, despite illegal recreational drug usage, resolutely drugophobic and South Amerindian society firmly drugophillic. Thus, as the few ethnographers who have bothered to look have noted, *no Amerindian artifact is considered "done" until the decoration goes on or is "embodied" in form* (Gregor 1977). Moreover, very little of the decoration annotates purely naturalistic biological beings, although observa-

tion of nature is, in fact, very keen.

Hence, rather than our static museum specimens, even the form of artifacts comes alive in Amerindians' playful recombinations of kinetic usage. This is an animistic technology and craft. These, after all, are cultures that invented the liquid-circulating stirrup-spout jar, the equally dynamic spout-and-representational bridge bottle, the whistling pot, the rattle base, the *paccha* water rim, etc. Artists within these traditions turned nearly every vessel into an effigy—a little portable "utilitarian sculpture" (Roe 1999). Thus, while in the West pottery equals functional containers, witness the humble red terra-cotta flowerpot, with or without the optional painted-on stereotyped silk-screened flower, in Amerindia (and one can treat the whole of the New World, from the Aleutians to Tierra del Fuego, as a single-style province in this regard); pots are miniature utilitarian sculpture. They are usually decorated, just like stools, sword-clubs, huts, or temples, and are, like them, all craft items. They indivisibly combine embellishment with functionality. Indeed, to escape the Maquetian (1971) Western Cartesian dualism of utilitarian technology and nonutilitarian art, we would do better to call all Amerindian forms the functional embellishment of craft items.

Thus, in contrast with our Western ethnotaxonomy of form and decoration, the first thing one discovers in working with modern South Amerindians or their ancient Caribbean ancestors is that "geometric" and "representational" or "realistic" do not exist as isolatable entities. They are *our* categories, not theirs. All "geometry" *is* "representation," all "representation," "geometry."

The Reason for the "Double Vision": Primitive Platonism

My further thesis is that Antillean stylistic conventions themselves spring from something deeper, a form of "ethnoepistemology" radically different from Western theories of knowledge. In domains as disparate as ethnoastronomy (Roe 1983a) and ethnoaesthetics, South Amerindians show that the purely geometric is invariably realistic in emic ethnographic contexts. The quatrefoil spots of the yellow jaguar *are* the Saint Andrew's cross *and* the Southern Cross, the quadrants of the world itself. The triangle or diamond, or even step fret, *are* the patterned scales of the anaconda *and* the undulations of the Milky Way, the very "pulse" of that world on diurnal/nocturnal (daily) and larger scales of time and movement in space (really a noncommutable, or "sacred," space-time). Any "pure" design is merely appropriated, stolen, by humans or given to them, from stingy or generous animal or avian "proto-cultural custodians" in Dawn Time. That roundel or undulating line is thus, for the artists who executed them, emblematic of the ceaseless transformation from Culture to Nature and vice versa via the paired dynamic liminal categories of Proto-Culture and Super-Nature. These liminal categories lie between, and connect, the static Culture/Nature dichotomies of the Western Cartesian worldview (Roe 1989b).

These designs, whether stylized or geometric, are thus part of a larger issue, a true "cultural ethnoepistemology" that I have called "Dual Triadic Dualism." This dynamic view can be accessed by the very holism that has always been central to anthropological methodology—by studying everything from ethnoastronomy (Roe 1983a) and ethnomedicine to material culture (Roe 1980), from kinship to religion and mythology (Roe 1982). Only cross-media and cross-dimensional isomorphisms, similarities in selection and form within and between cultural domains, can reveal these seldom articulated "Central Cultural Metaphors" (CCM) in thought and their "cultural scenarios" (Schieffelin 1976) in behavior. The CCM for South Amerindians and their Antillean cousins is a form of what I have called "Primitive Platonism."

Unlike the modern Western world, where we believe that the physical, empirical world is the ultimate reality (e.g., Boswell's Dr. Johnson kicking the proverbial rock to prove the reality of the empirical world in refutation of Bishop Berkeley's idealism), the first ceramic-using horticultural Indians to reach Vieques and eastern Puerto Rico, the Huecan Saladoids, evidently believed, as many of their living relatives in the lowlands of South America still do, that this world is a trick, an illusion. Like Plato, their artifacts reveal that they held "real" reality to be invisible, hidden in the sacred realm of the supernatural. This "non-ordinary" reality is a spiritual dimension populated by ethereal beings, without real flesh and blood but of quasi-normal, often inverted appearance. Because the descendants of the Saladoids

still occupied the islands when Columbus arrived in 1492–94, and he commissioned the very ethnography of the New World, that of Pané (1974) of circa A.D. 1498, we know more than we ought to about the cosmology and mythology of these now extinct Antillean islanders. I will make reference to that document, as illuminated by my own investigations into the cognate oral traditions of living South Amerindians, in an effort to attempt what is seldom embarked upon, to give semantic content to arid geometric symmetrical patterning.

The spirits of the dead, the Taíno *Opía*, for example, could only be communicated with by shamans, religious practitioners who directly spoke with the supernatural via altered states of consciousness. In the jungle (whether mainland or insular), the ultimate pharmacopoeia, this meant using hallucinogenic plants. Again, in contrast to modern society, drugs were seldom taken recreatively. Perhaps because of the respect people felt for these powerful vegetative compounds, such communication was only established to cure the sick and simultaneously bewitch one's enemies.

North of the Amazon and in the Caribbean, such altered states were achieved in visions, induced by the taking of a snuff made from a plant of South American origin, *Anadenanthera peregrina*. This powerful hallucinogen is better known in the Antilles by its Taíno name, Cohoba. Cohoba is a small tree that yields a seedpod high in very powerful alkaloids: 5-MeO-DMT and bufotenine. They produce serotonin receptor (LSD-like) Technicolor visions so vivid that many Indians faced death at the hands of the Inquisition rather than deny their validity.

The reason we know about this spiritual world lies in two things: (1) the survival of ancient religious rites in the lowlands of South America, such as among the Yanomamö Indians of southern Venezuela and northwestern Brazil (who use a related *Virola* sp. snuff), and similar culture-geographic regions from where the ancient Huecan Saladoid populations departed in the sixth or fifth centuries B.C. for the Antilles, and (2) the Caribbean archaeological evidence itself. The latter begins with the presence of fragments of very curious vessels with two projecting spouts, all incised with sinuous lines filled in with white (kaolin), yellow (limonite) powder, or red ochre (hematite), applied as a postfired crusting. These vessels are characteristic of the early "Huecan

Saladoids" in Vieques and eastern Puerto Rico (Chanlatte Baik 1981, 1994).

Such vessels are both small and highly decorated (Figure 7.3). They literally drip with designs that meander like snakes all over their upper surfaces (Figure 7.3a), giving the vessels a very "psychedelic" aspect. Such geometric designs are similar to what psychologists call "phosphenes," which are the concentric and wavy points of light that appear after you rub your eyes hard. They also arise during the first phases of a hallucinogenic "trip" as the firing of the rods and cones of the eyes. These auto-induced images soon are replaced by colorful ophidian or phytomorphic, ever-changing kaleidoscopes of vibrating entoptic patterns. Eventually, these geometric images fade and are replaced by visions of terrifying animals such as the jaguar and big snakes such as the anaconda that bear such "naturfact" designs. They approach the worshiper menacingly and seem to devour his body, which floats high above the jungle toward the sun. Such, at any rate, are the visions that modern mainland Indians have recalled, with fear and awe, for me on both sides of the Amazon.

Living Indians paint such designs on the vessels they use to consume hallucinogens as teas or inhaled powders, and certainly the ancient Puerto Rican vessels seem similarly and "otherworldly" decorated and bear the visual stigmata of inhaling spouts. Tellingly, such vessels are "effigies," that is, little spirit beings that combine human and animal forms into "monstrous," were-creature images, just as living shamans say they can change into animals at will and speak their languages under the spell of the drugs. The two spouts fit exactly into the nostrils (the Taíno descendants of the makers of this vessel used simple double-spouted inhaling sticks for the same purposes), while the squat little body contained the powder itself.

When one grasped the vessel in one's hand (and it fits in the palm nicely), one sees a humanoid face staring up at one, the round vessel body, its "belly," and the two projecting spouts, its lower "legs." Then, grabbing the figure's "nose" (Figure 7.3b), a handle *adorno* (a modeled, incised, and punctated figural element) that projects over its head (now broken off but reconstructable), one places the spouts to one's nose and inhales deeply. The nasal passages and sinuses are rich in blood vessels, and as

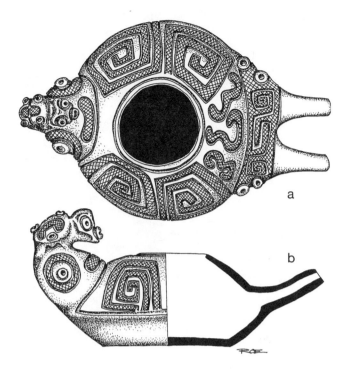

Figure 7.3 A reconstructed drawing, in two views, of a Huecan Saladoid effigy snuffing pot. (a) A top view. Note the "roundel" fillet appliqué nubbins marking the hip joints and other points of articulation. (b) A side view showing the "alter ego" nose handle, a dog effigy as psychopomp. This "pictorial dualism" (*humanoid:main figure::theriomorph:alter ego*) pervades all the island Arawak cultures until contact (collection, University of Puerto Rico [UPR], Centro de Investigaciones Arqueológicas.

Europeans snuffing with another Indian drug, tobacco, quickly realized, the active chemicals are soon drawn into the blood vessels, where it is but a short trip to the brain. Powerful visions ensue.

Unfortunately, the first effort of the body is to protect itself from the intrusion of such an irritant. The mucus membranes go into overtime, and copious streams of snot drip from the nose, dyed a tasteful green by the hallucinogenic snuff. The snuff taker, enraptured in his visions, does not notice, but these two strings of drug-impregnated mucus are the hallmarks of this vision quest. As they fall and dry on his chest, they are not washed off, as they are the tracks of the spirits who have entered his body (Lizot 1985). These strings of mucus are depicted hanging from the noses of transforming were-creatures in stone sculpture as early as 1,000 B.C. in the ancient Chavín culture of South America (Roe 2000b), a jungle-inspired "regional cult" that was to become the "cultural matrix" of most succeeding Peruvian civilizations.

Figure 7.4 A white-on-red (WOR) painted and modeled Cedrosan Saladoid unrestricted waisted jar with vertical "D"-shaped handles ending in opposed anthropomorphic adornos, or figurative lugs. (a) A profile view; the pot to the left of the diagonal line is reconstructed. (b) The "invertible," or anatropic, skeletal "ocular being." Note that after a 180-degree rotation from his original upside-down depiction in (a), his headdress is revealed as his mouth band, a form of "pictorial dualism." (c) A three-quarter view of this same vessel, showing the "false negative" positive white-on-red overpainting on the shoulder band (collection, UPR).

Characteristic of these visions is a dualistic worldview where the images from the nonordinary realm are like mirror images of the ordinary, profane world, yet inverted and alien. The early Spanish *cronistas* (chroniclers) such as Pietro Martire d'Anghiera actually recorded that the drug made beings appear inverted, walking about on their heads, and backwards. We will see abundant evidence for that inversion and reversal in the objects studied herein. Note that above the main vessel's humanoid figure's face is a "nose" that is another image, an "alter ego." This pot therefore reveals two beings, not one. What was human becomes animal, what was ordinary transforms into the sacred. Characteristic of this "double vision" derived from shamanism is the search for one's "power animal" or "familiar," much like the black cat of Western witches. For Antillean Amerindians, without access to big cats due to the impoverished island fauna, that spirit famil-

iar was the domestic dog, a creature blessed with keen hearing and nocturnal vision. It was in close touch with the spirits of the night and hence a guide to the souls of the dead, a psychopomp (Roe 1995d), rather like its role in ancient Egyptian and Greek mythology. The dog was the only domestic animal (apart from tamed "pets" such as baby peccary, or wild pig, and macaws) brought with these Indians into the Caribbean. Indeed, it functioned as a miniature "domesticated jaguar."

No wonder that the little zoomorphic handle used to grasp the snuffing pot is, in fact, a small dog adorno! Here too it helps the drug taker on his trip to the other world to commune with the spirits of the dead, with the animals that have captured the souls of his patients (and hence have fallen ill), from whom he must wrest them back and affect a cure. All this and more can be inferred from this ancient Huecan Saladoid vessel and those like it, a journey of "otherworldly" discovery that their

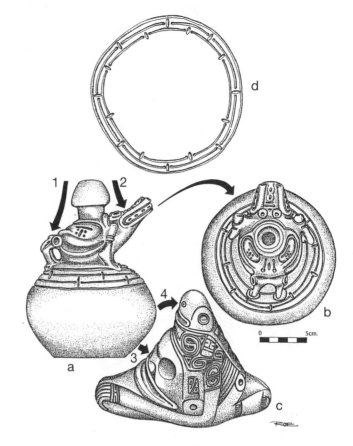

Figure 7.5 A portion of the life-size petroglyphs incised on a huge riverbed boulder at Pueblito Carmen, Guayama, south-central highlands of Puerto Rico. (a) One inverted "Wrapped Ancestor" next to (b) a right-side-up (180-degree rotation) analogous figure. This is a case of "bifold rotation" for whole representational figures rather than just geometric motifs. (c) An "alter ego" face on top of the major wrapped figure, another variety of pictorial dualism. (d) A partial "simple face." (e) A portion of another wrapped figure effaced by the incised depiction below it, somewhat later in time. (f) Yet another dual depiction. Here a wrapped figure has another visage "incisted" within it, a belly-button "simple face"! (g) Another parial simple face. (h) A complete simple face. (i) A partly "goggled" set of enclosed eyes.

Figure 7.6 "Double vision" in multimedia in Classic Taíno material culture (a) A profile view of a frog effigy spouted vessel at the Museo del Hombre Dominicano, Santo Domingo. Note that the back of the frog also forms a humanoid effigy (1), while the front of the vessel has the frog's head forequarters (2). (b) The top view of this vessel shows both heads looking Janus-like in opposite directions (*humanoid:rear::theriomorph:front*). The rear legs of the frog emerge from the humanoid's nostrils (which are also the frog's appliqué roundel hip joints) as strings of mucus impregnated (literally!—see Pané 1974, 1992, 1999) with hallucinogenic *Cohoba* snuff. The frog's back markings become the "eyes" of the hallucinating humanoid, close but open in ecstasy. (c) A Classic Taíno carved stone three pointer from Hispañola. It represents (3) Deminán Caracaracol, a mythical progenitor who was, although male, impregnated by that same magical snot from his maternal uncle's phallic nose. He grew a painful hunchback, represented by face (4), that acted like a "dorsal womb," filled with infants, one of whom peeks forward in the "alter ego" visage at the tip of the main figure's hunchback. Later he gave birth, as an inverted masculine "Wooden Bride," by having his hard swelling chopped open by men with stone axes; out of the hunchback emerged his offspring in an equally inverted sacred "cesarian section." This is a classic case of the masculine symbolic appropriation of the female's capacity to give birth. (d) The full roll out of this late Cichan Ostionoid bottle's subeffigy's incised design layout (of a and b), a design composed of horizontal dashes separated by short vertical tick marks in two lines marked by glide reflection, dates all the way to Huecan Saladoid designs of the fifth century B.C., yet another powerful argument for the in situ evolution of Taíno culture over two millennia.

descendants, the Taíno, were to continue up to and past their "encounter" with Europeans and their more human God some twenty centuries later.

This "artifactual dualism" or "dual-view" perspective begins in Cedrosan Saladoid (Roe 1989a) with "anatropic" representation (where images can be inverted 180 degrees to reveal other images that share features such as mouths (Figure 7.4). It is further elaborated in pre-Taíno Elenan times and eventually reaches a crescendo of figural complexity in Chican Ostionoid pottery of the Taíno protohistoric period (Roe 1995c, 1997a, 1999, 2000c). The same anatropic imagery is found in Elenan (Figure 7.5) and Chican rock art (Roe and Rivera Meléndez 1999) and portable stonework (Figure 7.6). Both media betray this same "cognitive style" unique to South Amerindian culture and its derivatives, past and present.

Such a kinetic view of "manifest" and "hidden" reality, where the perceiver has to work to see shifting

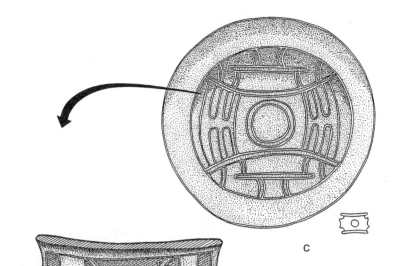

Figure 7.7 A "nested" open bowl depicting a rectangular tray incised within itself, another form of pictorial dualism. (a) The central design is a rectangular open effigy tray of a manta ray, another typical Saladoid vessel shape, seen here in plan view. (b) A tilted profile view of this tray with modeled and incised "eyes." (c) A slightly later Tibes-style open carinated bowl (plan view), showing the internal incised rectangular tray motif (collection, UPR).

c

a

b

0 5 10cm.

images (unlike the equal clarity of traditional Western art, where a passive perceiver can comprehend all the imagery from a single viewing position), was shared by both men and women, though men were largely the ones to engage in it as shamans and priests. Yet the women's art of pottery provided a parallel expression of this artifactual dualism to the men's wood, bone, and shell carving. It also gave them an important outlet for the aesthetic imperative by building in multiple views within the same artifact, thus turning one representation into another as the observer's view shifted from profile-to-end, or inner-to-outer (Figure 7.7), or up-to-down via offering and consuming food and drink.

This "double-view" figural dualism is nowhere better expressed than on a little Elenan hemispherical bowl (Figure 7.8a). Here the classic "monkey" head that peers up at the rim (Figure 7.8c, d) transforms into an anthropomorphic mask on its back (Figure 7.8a)! Even more tellingly, the act of transitioning between the two as the vessel is tipped reveals a *third* image, the monkey head

being "eaten" (or at least emerging from) in the gaping mouth of an anatropic dorsal humanoid face (Figure 7.8e)!

In the little D-shaped handle of another Elenan Ostionoid bowl in Figure 7.8f, a top view from the rim of the vessel to which it was attached yields a staring squid, the vertical channel incision forming tentacles and the appliqué pellets becoming eyes. An end perspective generated by a 45-degree rotation of the handle (Figure 7.8g) and a profile view (Figure 7.8h) generates, in contrast, a fish with staring pellet-appliqué eyes and a gaping wide-lipped mouth. Perhaps the aquatic fauna that adorn this vessel alluded to its function as the container of liquid.

Such artifactual dualism utilizes the same "figure/ground" shift seen in the perceptual ambiguity of positive-negative ceramic designs. In the otherworldly art of the Antilles, everything has a double meaning, both on the level of *perception* and on the level of *execution*. Yet the executions of the designs are all variations on common bilateral, concentric, and diagonal symmetry rules.

In sum, central to the Antillean Amerindian use of symmetry is this "perceptual dualism," or visual ambiguity. It is the ability to perceive figure-as-ground or ground-as-figure. This mental "changing of gears" is a common skill of artists the world over but was uniquely elaborated in South America and the Caribbean (and indeed in all of the New World). It may be executed in two ways: positive painting or negative-resist decoration. Thus a Punnet square of perception and execution is formed. On one axis is positive perception and negative perception, on the other is positive execution and negative-resist execution.

Of the resulting four cells, the steadfastly empirical West has used primarily positive perception (figure-as-ground) and positive execution (painting the figure), as in coloring books and indeed all of Western painting down to modern silk-screened T-shirts. This is a mundane world of "what you see is what you get" (WYSIWYG), to use the computer metaphor. Even our constellations on the largest canvas of them all, the night sky, form just another class of "connect-the-dots" designs. These are positive star-to-star groupings that form the outlines of fantastic figures like Orion and his Belt.

The much more intensely spiritual ethos of Amerindian culture regards what you don't see (or don't see easily) as even more important than what the waking eyes can grasp. Hence, Amerindians have elaborated a whole battery of techniques untried in the West until recently in ceramics (negative-resist), in textiles (*ikat* and tie-dye), in metals (depletion gilding), and in painting (false-negative overpainting). Most tellingly, in addition to the positive star-to-star constellations (like the Western ones), South and Antillean Amerindians have a whole series of "Dark Cloud" negative constellations that are absent from the Western cosmos, both in the highlands and in the lowlands (Roe 1983a). We will look more closely at false-negative positive painting in our survey of symmetry during Saladoid times.

In moving from perception and execution to what is being executed, the *image*, this Amerindian "double vision" takes its most common form in ceramic vessels via *opposition*, mutually confronting dual adornos, each staring at the other as "twins" (like the Magical Twins of their mythology), forming two identical figurative handles. The vessel's interior becomes their shared belly (Figure 7.4a, c). Or one may have ceremonial axes with carved heads that are exact *inversions* of each other, mounted vertically, the "life" visage right-side up and the "dead" face below it upside down (Roe 1997a:Figure 122). Or, going from face to full body depictions, we find pre-Taíno carved petroglyphic wrapped ancestral figures (the dead were wrapped in the net of their own hammocks) that were incised both "right-side up" and "upside down" right next to each other on the same river boulder (Figure 7.5a, b)!

Another logical possibility, also instantiated in the ancient Antilles, was to have the inverted images (again,

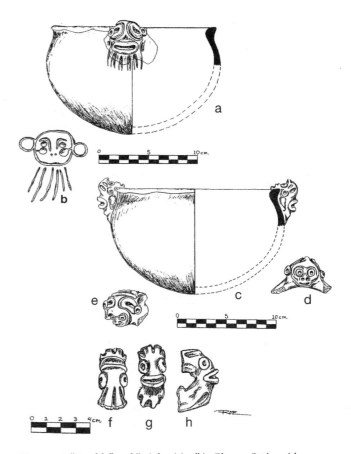

Figure 7.8 "Double" and "triple vision" in Elenan Ostionoid ceramics and petroglyphs. (a) A small restricted bowl from the Jardinas de Loiza site in northeastern coastal Puerto Rico. This end view reveals a dorsal image of the appliquéd vertical "D"-shaped handle with a modeled and incised humanoid visage sporting large earplugs. The "beard" below his face is the vertical channel incision on the wide flange of the very handle the figural adorno sits on. (b) An Elenan Ostionoid period petroglyphic "rayed" face with an identical pictorial structure: large ear spools and a necklace with vertical beaded rays (the "rays" or "beard"—the latter a misnomer lodged in the literature) from the Barrio Cibuco site in the east-central highlands (Roe 2000a:Figure 19). (c) A profile view of the same pot as (a) showing the dual opposed adornos that also bear the anthropomorphic rayed face on their backs. (d) A frontal view of one of the two inward-facing theriomorphic "monkey head" adornos, also afforded humanoid ear spools. The anthropomorphic visage on the monkey's back appears when this visage is rotated 90 degrees. (e) In a half rotation of 45 degrees yet another scene is revealed. The inner "monkey" is being consumed by a monster (or, alternatively, is emerging from the monster's mouth) that is formed by the anatropic eyes of the outer anthropomorphic visage! (f) Another modeled and incised effigy "D"-shaped handle from a similar vessel, from the Jardinas de Loiza site. It shows a squid, complete with roundel punctated appliquéd eyes and tentacles below. This "dual-view" water creature emerges when the upper part of the figurative handle is half rotated 45 degrees. (g) With another half rotation of 45 degrees an additional sea creature emerges, a frontal fish whose wide gaping mouth is the forehead band of the "squid" above it. (h) This "fish" visage in profile depicts its bulging lips, the "forehead bands" of the squid!

"life/death") looking *away* from each other on the same figure rather than *at* each other. Thus in post-Contact times, we have Janus-headed depictions with dual "life/death" faces that look in opposite directions (Roe 1997b:Figures 127–128).

Yet another dualistic possibility is to have a double-headed Janus depiction but now with the heads "siamesed" in back like the Polish or Russian double heraldic eagles (Wilson 1997:Figure 34). Such a portrayal is easily mistaken for two separate heads.

An additional form of artifactual dualism is to have two visages but staring in the same direction, stacked one on top of each other. Thus Taíno artists carved three-pointers (unique triangular stones which are sculptural skeuomorphs of the tip of a columella of a conch) with dual stacked "alter ego" depictions (Figure 7.6c). In this case the lower visage (Figure 7.6c3) is both larger and "humanoid," while the upper (Figure 7.6c4) is smaller and theriomorphic. Note that the upright large petroglyphic "Wrapped Ancestor" of Figure 7.5b also possesses a smaller "alter ego" face (Figure 7.5c) above its visage, so one sees this device in multimedia: petroglyphs and portable stone sculpture. Later, we will also come across it in ceramic-modeled adornos, or figural lugs.

A cleverer example of dualism is so subtle that it can only be recognized by cognoscenti. It is a symmetry device, the nesting of one image inside of another, a form of concentric symmetry. Beings may be nested, one inside another, and viewable as a shaman sees them, via x-ray vision, revealing souls within the transparent shells of their bodies. Or they may be concentrically arranged artifacts in clever visual puns, one upon the other. In this latter case an image of one kind of ceramic vessel, a rectangular manta ray effigy tray (Figure 7.7a-b), is incised inside of another, an unrestricted circular bowl (Figure 7.7c)! One image lies within another.

In this mélange of double vision we have already seen yet another symmetrical device, "biview rotation," or "anatropic imagery," as it is known in cognate South Amerindian archaeological traditions like Chavín (Roe 1974, 2000b). This perceptual shifting dates back to Saladoid times, where below the dual-facing modeled adornos (Figure 7.4a) a curiously invertible agnathic skeletal face (Figure 7.4b) is painted in white-on-red.

A related mechanism continues in the reversible imagery of pre-Taíno and Taíno ceramic lugs, where the face of one visage hides another image on the top of its head or back and is seen at a 90-degree angle of observation (Figure 7.8a). In that case, the inner image is theriomorphic (Figure 7.8d) and the upper is anthropomorphic (Figure 7.8a).

But this persistent "double vision" is *not* the static dualism of Western thought, which pits mutually exclusive dyads against each other (Good/Bad, Man/Woman, Life/Death, God/Devil). Ancient Antillean Amerindians were as interested in the conceptual "bridges" (the gray areas) between dyads as they were in the (black-and-white) "poles," the opposed concepts, themselves (see Crocker 1983 for the lowland equation of "bridges" to liminal overlap concepts). The "processual" view of ancient and modern Amerindians allowed them to traverse the cognitive landscape between "life" and "death" from either direction and back again via intermediary overlap categories. Skeletons sport erect phalli and consort sexually with nubile women from the ancient Moche culture on the coast of Peru to the proto-historic Taíno of the Greater Antilles (Roe 1997b:Figure 3) and continue to so cavort on modern Mexican folk art based on ancient Aztec paradigms. Death is not the end of life, merely its beginning in an endless cycle between "ordinary" and "non-ordinary" reality. Art thus adopts the symmetry of life-death itself. Only the Western world, with its irreversibly linear timeline, from Creation to End of Times, denies death and strives to remain forever young.

It is at the contrasting locus of "death-in-life" that we see the modal transformation of "representational" into "geometric" designs in lowland and Antillean contexts. Thus we have "rotatable" Taíno images of dead ancestress/goddesses in petroglyphs, whose "belly roundels" can be transformed into common subrim-banded geometric symmetrical designs on pottery (Figure 7.9h-i), just as one can see the "inside" on the "outside" (x-ray depiction) in her ribs seen through her chest. Or those same "decorative" designs can be rotated to produce stylized herons (Figure 7.10a-d). We find similar "reversible" images carved into stone collars that must be inverted to reveal contrasting images (Walker 1997:Figure 1a). In this way supposedly "static" images come alive as true kinetic sculpture via the simple act of

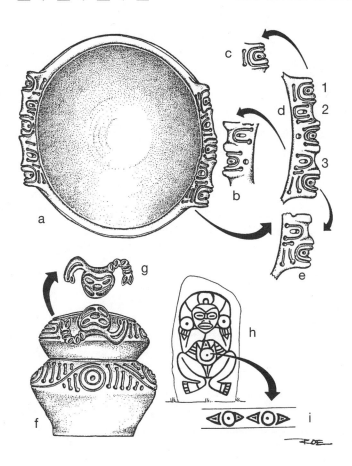

Figure 7.9 Cross-media "double vision" in Classic Taíno (Chican Ostionoid) incised and modeled ceramics and petroglyphs. (a) A vertical, plan view of a small open bowl with horizontal tab handles from the Museo del Hombre Dominicano in Santo Domingo, Dominican Republic. Each of the perforated tabs (paired and opposed discontinuous labial flanges), appear, at first inspection, to consist of abstract "geometric" "U"-shaped incisions, bifold rotated, and some perforations. This "nonrepresentational" design layout, is, in fact, a series of "invertible" stylized human profile faces! (b) An inverted profile face (no. 1). (c) This image-within-an-image is "encisted" in the larger flange faces. The eyes of these small faces "kenn," or present a visible "stock" or "frozen metaphor" for the tongue of which it is a part. (d) These flange faces present two "siamesed" profile heads joined at the forehead by horizontal reflection (Nos. 1 = [b] and 2). Each becomes recognizable as the pot is held vertically. Incised roundels, centering on the perforations, become their "eyes," complete with concentric incised "eyebrow" and "eye-bag" lines. (e) The last, or "stacked" profile face 3, is isolated. The half-circle incised mouth of these faces, together with the bracketing incised "grimace lines" at their corners, hold the simplified "eye faces" of (c). (f) A small biglobular vessel from the Fundación García-Arévalo, Santo Domingo, Dominican Republic. The vessel shape itself is yet another form of "artifactual dualism" generated by stacking similar sections, one on top of the other, like the "platter worlds" of their cosmology. (g) A modeled and appliquéd adorno in the form of an anatropic (reversible) were-crab. Note within this generally bilaterally symmetrical figure the asymmetrical pincer treatment. The crab's face is reversible in the other (vertical) direction. By having four pits surrounding a central nose pit, the "nose" does double duty by forming both an upright face (f) and, via vertical reflection, another face (g)! Thus, no matter if one looked at the vessel from the outside or from the inside, as in drinking, one always sees the same crab's face! (h) The famous "menhir" petroglyph of the Classic Taíno Earth Goddess, Attabeira, at the ceremonial ballpark of Caguana, Utuado. (i) The central roundel of her belly button, the intermammary triangle on her chest, and her vulva triangle below, form when rotated 90 degrees, a common incised design on the subrim band of Chican Ostionoid ceramics, the female-made pottery contemporary with this male-created rock art.

changing the angle of perception.

This perceptual ambiguity allows each artifact to condense several different meanings polysemically, enabling the "thing made" (the artifact) and the "thing told" (the myth) to mutually reinforce each other via "myth-material cultural mutual referentiality" (Roe 1995a). The myth provides the sacred etiology of the artifact, explaining the history of its origin while at the same time using the object tautologically as "mythic empirical" (tangible) proof that the sacred-story-believed-to-be-true (the myth) is real. Simultaneously, the artifact "calls up" the myth it instantiates as informants narrate the tale as they make or handle the artifact. As Walker (1997:85) suggests, the artifact thus becomes animated; as it is "read" in shifting perspectives, the story it represents is told, both object and myth unfolding in time as "embodied narration" in a very "material" sense. Cultures, especially harmonious South Amerindian ones, are but "machines" of vast semiotic redundancy.

The dynamic dualism evident in this repetition means that the focus of interest, perceptually and cognitively, is as much on the "bridge" of the "shifts between,"

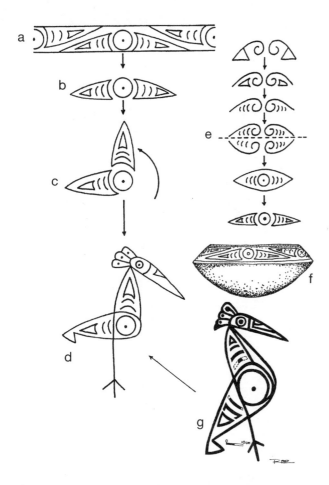

Figure 7.10 A derivational chain of one of the menhir petroglyphs at the side of the Frog Lady, Attabeira, is the Great Blue Heron whose "hard and pointed large phallic beak" broke her hymen in cognate South Amerindian myths whence this petroglyphic frieze in the Greater Antilles derives. (a) A common Classic Taíno band design layout. (b) It is composed of vertically reflected and bifold-rotated "design modules" consisting of two opposed triangles with internal triangles and curved short sides that fit around a central roundel. (c) By rotating one of these triangular "wings" upward 90 degrees, the body and neck of the avian figure are generated (the head is yet another triangle). (d) The resulting profile heron, a "geometric" design again turning into a stylized "representational" design (e) In turn, this protohistoric design derives from a layout of vertically reflected Cedrosan Saladoid step scrolls that date to the fourth century B.C.! We are back to (a) again, the subrim design on Taíno *cazuelas* (restricted, carinated bowls). (g) This generates the design in the Earth Goddess's chest (Figure 7.9i) as well as the body of her avian consort, the actual Great Blue Heron menhir.

the liminal overlaps, as it is on the figures or symbols (the polar categories) themselves. Death is not the end of life, but a step in its re-creation. That is why half the depictions are of "life" faces while the other half stare with the vacant orbits of "death." Carved or painted ancestors (sacred efficacy still "inside" society although "beyond" it) thus "procreate" new life in descendants; by being dead they are the most "alive," the donors of life force = fecundity. Similarly, current spirits (sacred well outside of society), like the *Taíno Opía,* Spirits of the Dead, harm via seduction (Roe 1997a, b). Improper sex (between mortal and spirit) leads to mental illness just as proper sex (between mortals and within the prescriptive marriage rules) produces life.

The Culture Historical Context of Symmetry in an Island World

The ancient Caribbean was the locus of far-flung migrations that still stir archaeological debate. The first migrations formed a "pincer's movement" from Belize, lower Central America, and the Orinoco Delta in South America respectively. Beginning around 4,000 B.C., they met at the "Mona Passage," so named for the small island between western Puerto Rico and eastern Hispañola by 3,000 B.C. This journey was undertaken by "Paleoindians" and "Meso-Indians," first Big Game and then Archaic groups of hunters and gatherers, who initially discovered this insular paradise (excepting Jamaica, which they bypassed, unaware of its existence). They arrived during a time of lower eustatic levels in pursuit of giant ground sloths and the abundant molluscan and marine resources of the ancient Caribbean.

The second set of migrations began around 500 B.C., this time departing only from the southeast, near the Delta of the Orinoco. They too followed the "stepping stones" of the Lesser Antilles until they established a frontier with the indigenous, numerous, and bellicose Archaic Indians centered again on the Mona Passage (Rouse 1992). It will be this later migration and the fate of its descendants, the classic Taíno Indians of Hispañola and Puerto Rico, the people (together with their "sub-Taíno" relatives in the Bahamas) who had the misfortune to be the first Amerindians to meet Columbus in his first two voyages to the New World, that will form the cultural context for this chapter.

Irving Rouse, the veritable "father" of northern South American and Caribbean archaeology, argued for the Amazonian origins of the later waves of horticultural populations (Rouse 1952). Hence he called them members of the "Saladoid" series from the type site of El Saladero on the Orinoco River of Venezuela. He has continued to update and refine his chronology; its most recent articulation (Rouse 1992) forms the framework I employ here. Indeed, the type of symmetry analysis that I apply to Saladoid-Ostionoid material culture is itself a distant progeny of Rouse's modal analysis precociously dating to his Fort Liberté study of 1941.

Recently, based on a typology of vessel shape and decoration, Luís Chanlatte Baik, a Dominican archaeologist long resident in Puerto Rico and director of the Centro de Investigaciones Arqueológicas of the University of Puerto Rico, Río Piedras, San Juan, has argued that another migration of non-Saladoid (Huecoid) populations, with origins in the Venezuelan Andes, preceded the Saladoid movement. He sees this "Huecoid" pottery from the type site La Hueca on Sorcé, Vieques, the island to the east of Puerto Rico and the last of the Lesser Antilles (Figure 7.1), as being very different from the Saladoid series and unrelated to it. At first sight, these two pottery assemblages look very different. "Huecoid" pottery is of indifferent craftsmanship, unpainted, and decorated with sloppy incised lines filled with equally haphazard cross-hachured fine-line engraving. The incisions themselves are highlighted with either white or red postfire powdered pigment crusting, and modeled adornos, or lugs (Figures 7.3 and 7.11a), are attached to the vessel's rims. In contrast, "Saladoid" pottery (Figures 7.4, 7.11b) is of jewel-like thinness and precision, elaborately decorated with both polychrome prefire white-on-red slip painting and postfire interior smudging, as well as finely executed cross-hachured incision and modeling. In Chanlatte's view about the only thing these two assemblages have in common is cross-hachured incision, and even then, "Huecoid" incision tends to be sloppy and irregular while "Saladoid" incision is regular and machinelike in its symmetrical execution.

Rouse and others, like myself, prefer to note the similarities in vessel shape categories and surface decoration modes of the "Huecoid" pottery to the Saladoid series while admitting that the "Huecoids" did, in fact,

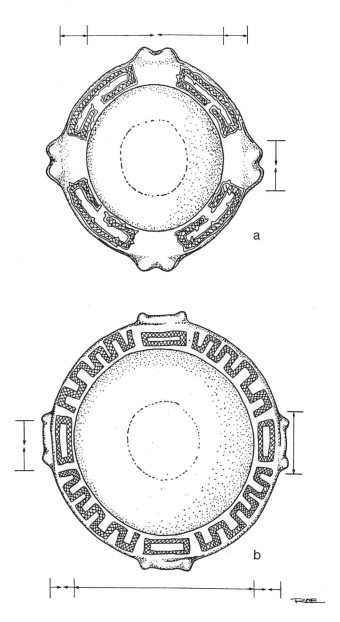

Figure 7.11 A plan view of two cognate early Saladoid pedestal-based open bowls with labial flanges from the collections of the Center for Archaeological Investigations of the University of Puerto Rico, Río Piedras, San Juan. (a) Note the concentric banded design field and the cross-hatchured and incised "C" motifs that occupy the earlier form's upper surfaces. This "Huecan Saladoid" bowl's flange is a part of the body wall, simply canted out at a 45-degree angle from the upper vessel body wall (redrawn from Chanlatte Baik 1994). These simple designs have sloppy cross-hachuring, and the vessel itself is both smaller and more crudely fabricated than (b). (b) A later and larger "Cedrosan Saladoid" bowl of similar shape except that its flanges are appliquéd onto the upper body wall, projecting out at a 90-degree angle from a much better made pot with more regular and complex cross-hachured designs. The Cedrosans replaced the Huecan subseries on both Vieques and Puerto Rico.

arrive first in the Greater Antilles, although by apparently only a few years. Can symmetry analysis help solve this cultural historical debate? Was "Huecoid" similar enough in style to "Saladoid" to be included within the Saladoid series as a sub-series ("Huecan Saladoid"), as Rouse or I would classify them? Or, are the two styles so different that they must belong to two separate series: "Huecoid" versus "Saladoid," as Chanlatte sees it?

Here is one example of the productivity of a grammatical approach to symmetry and of the explanatory power of symmetry analysis itself. The typological approach used by Chanlatte simply designates a design as "geometric" with "cross-hachured" incision. This is of minimal use other than as a simple presence or absence Peircian "index" on a trait list. It is possible to do much more. One can make design structure, of which symmetry operations are an integral part, an independent measure of cultural comparison along with other indexes commonly used in archaeology such as settlement pattern, funerary rites, lithic technology, and dietary patterns. Then a sharing of common modes (structured and systematic selections from among known alternatives) across multiple cultural dimensions (institutions and fields of cultural knowledge, major constructional decision pathways of artifacts) can lead one to infer that (1) two assemblages are "cognate" in an ethnohistorical sense, (2) minimally have enjoyed sustained mutual interaction and intensive and/or selective diffusion, or (3) are truly alien in historical background, any mutual similarities being the product of parallel development.

To help decide among these options, one can use symmetry as another index of style. The student can break geometric designs down into their primitive formal elements, as well as the rules that manipulate them to produce "intelligible" designs. One thus enters into a more internal or "emic" understanding of the alien or ancient tradition, rather than an external or "etic" perspective. Any resultant similarities between styles are more likely to be a product of a shared history and a culturally genetic relationship rather than independent development or chance diffusion.

This generative grammatical approach derives from studying a whole corpus of artifacts and isolating a specific design that appears on them to function as a

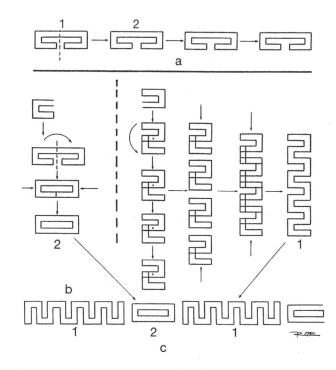

Figure 7.12 My grammatical analysis of the shared design grammar that produced *both* types of Saladoid labial flange cross-hachured designs. (a) The simpler and older Huecan Saladoid moves vertically reflected (1) to form the translated "C" motifs (2) as in Figure 7.11a (b) The later and more evolved design layouts of the Cedrosan Saladoid subseries, as found in Figure 7.11b; a "combined" layout with a "C"-based meander based on bifold rotation and fused "C"s based on reflection (2). (c) The resultant layout after the application of an alternation rule between "b1" and "b2."

"kernel statement" within the style. For example, one such motif is the vertically reflected "C" of the Huecan system. A number of these continually vertically reflected "C's" produces a series of translated "U's," such as in Figures 7.11a and 7.12a. Such a layout is a simple presentation of the rules and elements of the style in its most basic form. These "kernel statements" are design layouts that can serve as points of departure for more elaborate designs. Then one can search for other layouts that seem to be related to the kernel and hypothesize rule changes that will connect the two. Then one arranges these designs into a linked series of derivations, each separated from the last by, minimally, the addition of one new rule, such as a "union" rule that closes the "U" into a rectangle, as in Figure 7.12b2.

Some of these designs will have to be intercalated (Figure 7.12b) between two designs (Figures 7.12a and 7.12c) that have actually been recovered from artifacts.

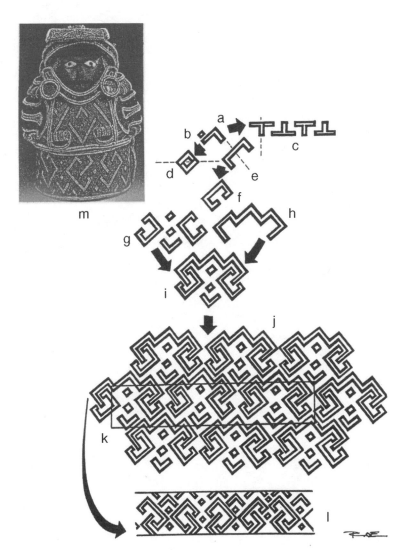

Figure 7.13 My "derivational chain" generating the late Chican Ostionoid (Classic Taíno) beaded designs on the transcultural "Bead Baby" reliquary of the Pigorini Museum, Italy, from Huecan Saladoid antecedents some 2,000 years earlier in a process of in situ evolution coupled with the borrowing of alien raw materials after contact. (a) The key alteration simply tilts the Huecan "L" constituent of the original "T" motifs 45 degrees. (b) A "dot" motif. (c) The antecedent Huecan Saladoid "T" layout generated by vertical reflection and bifold rotation. (d) The "L" motif, now a "V," rotated to form a diamond. (e) The diagonal mirror reflection of the same "L" to produce a diagonal "C" motif. (f) Two "C"s vertically reflected to generate a "hooked C" motif. (g) Design module #1, composed of two vertically reflected "hooked C"s and two medial stacked diagonal dots and "V" motifs. (h) The other basic design module, #2, composed by linking two opposed "hooked C"s with an interstitial inverted "V" motif. (i) The resultant "super-module" with "g" nested within "h." (j) The translation of the multimodule to generate an overall "invisible" (conceptual) and infinitely extendable diagonal array. (k) That diagonal "background" array is "truncated" and thereby transformed into the visible "foreground," by a movable horizontal "design field" window. (l) These ideal world "invisible" machinations produce a "this world" (visible) horizontal panel of diagonal design layouts, the beadwork on the lower body design field register of the "Bead Baby (m)."

Such hypothetical intercalations stand as "graphic predictions" that can be confirmed or disconfirmed once the corpus increases in size or intactness via additional excavations or collections study. In other words, such connecting designs either will be discovered or not, and when they are not, their principles can be called into question and perhaps discarded in further, and more refined, iterations of the constantly evolving grammar.

The result of such a process (Figure 7.12b) is a "derivational chain" (Figure 7.13a-j) of linked designs that represents one formal vector of possibility within the infinite possibilities of any complex style. In turn, many linked vectors can be explored, each diverging at a different angle to extend the multiple potentialities inherent in any systemic selection of elements and rules. Some vectors will be explored early, some later, and some not at all. Certain of these vectors will become popular—defining constellations for the style itself—while others will be

rare and deceptively aberrant. As always, the larger the corpus and the more repeated and sensitive its exploration, the better these vectors will be mapped and the more completely the style will be understood.

For the first time such devices allow the investigator to predict what is likely to turn up as artists work out the logical possibilities of a styles. The construction of such chains also permits the investigator to become a real participant in the fullest sense of the term in regard to the design tradition being investigated. He or she can now interact with other artists (even the "dead" ones of a "closed" archaeological corpus) rather than having to depend on fortuitous chance that his/her sample will happen to include such steps. The analyst can also fine-tune the questions he/she asks of native artists by presenting them with real alternatives, some conservative and others fantastic, to probe the limits of the style as well as its established canons (Raymond et

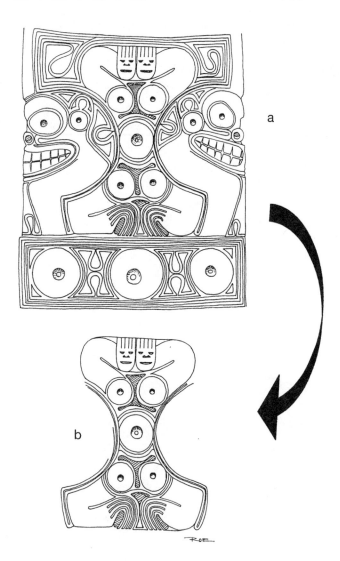

Figure 7.14 The design panel from a high-backed *duho,* or ceremonial seat of a cacique, or chief, in Classic Taíno chiefdoms. This example (Ostapkowicz 1997:Figures 45–46) comes from the Museo del Hombre Dominicano in Santo Domingo, Dominican Republic. (a) It depicts a quadrupedal animal that still retains the carved manatee bone "dentures" in the animal seat's grinning mouth. (b) The "interstitial" and "reversible" anatropic human torso "encisted" within the siamesed figural layout is another example of concentric symmetry and tessellation in Taíno art. In one vertical view, the "head" is now composed of the two sole heads of the bottoms of the feet, giving the appearance that the hands are folded behind this double head. The roundels become the kneeling figure's high joints/buttocks, the central one its navel, the upper two its breasts and/or shoulder joints. Another vertical, and reversible, view generates a monster with wide roundel-staring eyes above a navel-mouth, the double feet its "hair." Lastly, the image can also be reversed to form a figure standing on its hands, the taloned curved "toes" becoming the hands, the "buttock" roundels now the eyes, the belly button roundel seen in x-ray depiction through the back, and the upraised visaged feet held by bent legs against the upper roundels, now the buttocks, not the breasts of the vertical image.

al. 1975).

The last advantage of derivational chains is that they allow ethnoaesthetic criteria to be investigated. Which are puerile designs and which are interesting ones? How can one tell good artists from bad? Who has "insight" in a tradition? Field tests have proven that very good artists will pick "upper hierarchy solutions" (Figure 7.13j) rather than "lower" ones (Figure 7.13c). That is, while journeymen will stick close to the kernels, seldom venturing beyond them, very capable artists will incorporate so many rule changes into their work that it will be nearly impossible to derive their designs back down to the original kernel. The observer is convinced it can be done due to the overall pattern of stylistic similarities between the derived design and the kernel. Such very evolved "upper-hierarchy solutions," and their ethnographic evaluations, have shown that women and men who can achieve them are regarded with awe and emulation by those with less insight into the style. They have a regional reputation and tend to be emulated by lesser artists (Roe 2000a, 2004).

Another not inconsequential advantage of generative grammatical approaches is that they simply provide a logical way of arranging and cataloging designs. By specifying the steps between two designs that may otherwise look very unrelated, this method can also unite disparate layouts within larger logical groupings. By simply counting steps and rules employed ("links" in the chains), one can also quantify exactly how much more "complex" or "simple" one style is from another (as in "Huecan" from "Cedrosan" Saladoid) or one statement within a style from its contrasting array (Figure 7.12a from 7.12c), by the same or different artist, or, indeed, by artists within cognate traditions. Heretofore all such labels have been purely subjective in aesthetic analysis.

If the grammar behind these chains is the "design structure," then such logical working out of the grammar's possibilities is the style's "design organization." Even more illustrative of the flux of organization compared to structure is the case of what happens when artists have to accommodate such "logical" geometric arrays to the exigencies of figural elements ("representational" ones) within the same design field. After all, such "realistic" elements constitute an irregular, or asymmetric, "obstacle" (Figures 7.14 and 7.15) to the execution of rigidly symmetrical designs (Figure 7.15c).

This struggle between regularity and the requirements of realism is the principle "machine" behind stylization as the representation becomes bent and curved (in the Island Arawak tradition) into the volutes of the geometric background (Figure 7.14b). Both icons and symbolic tracery can thus flow together to form a coherent design layout within a culturally codified design field. In other words, the human or animal figure is treated *as if* it was geometry and in so doing becomes distorted and its elements spread about in an "arbitrary" fashion (but only "arbitrary" from the point of anatomy, *not* of design structure within coherent design fields). This process of artful accommodation culminated, in the skilled hands of Classic Taíno full-time artisans, in the high-backed *duho,* or elite stool, shown in Figures 7.14 and 7.15.

Precocity and Tardiness:
Symmetry Analysis in the Antilles

The study of the material culture of the peoples of the ancient Caribbean encompasses a contradictory picture of both great precocity and appalling tardiness in the utilization of symmetry analysis. An awareness of symmetry analysis begins, ironically enough, in 1939. In response to the economic and social impact of the depression, and in hopes of fostering the local textile industry, two Puerto Ricans, Matilde Pérez de Silva, a home economist, and the famous island archaeologist Adolfo de Hostos, published in Philadelphia a precocious pattern book of mostly Taíno Indian pottery designs. This work, *Industrial Applications of Indian Decorative Motifs of Puerto Rico* (1939), presages modern concerns with art grammars in trying to decipher, reproduce, and appreciate the complex indigenous art of the Taíno. While few such designs found their way into the local textile industry, they ultimately produced a large economic impact in providing endless designs for island *artesanos.*

It was in Hispañola, although this time in Haiti, that the next major step in the analysis of geometrical symmetry occurred with the publication in 1941 by Rouse of his prehistory of the Fort Liberté region. He presented a new and precocious method of analyzing material culture called "modal analysis" since it broke pottery down into the patterns of decisions, or "modes"

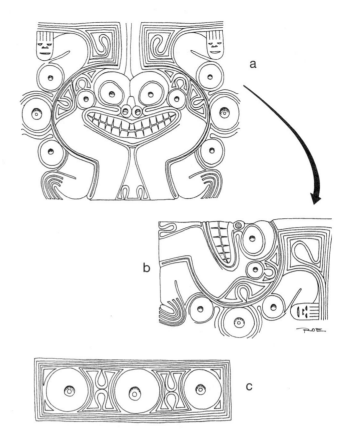

Figure 7.15 The upper-back panel from figure 7.14, but now instead of a "siamesed" portrayal, where the main figures are split from the forehead, spread out, and doubled over, I have redrawn it as a "split presentation" with isolatable "frontal" depiction. (a) In this conjoined full-frontal portrayal, the main visages are attached by being split from the crown of the head backward to the neck and laid out flat as in a map projection or a "flayed pelt" (Roe 1974). Both halves of the creature are split also, with taloned claws below and "visaged" feet above or behind, the *planometric projection* in 2-D of the 3-D quadruped carved below, that is, in the stool's effigy form itself. (b) One can isolate one of the split figures, which are vertically reflected, to form a *frontal* view of the froglike limbs splayed reptilianlike, the head twisted up and viewed in profile, in "twisted" perspective to the frontal body (Roe 2000b). (c) The "geometric" design that may be the "abstract" symbol of the animal icon itself. The roundels are like the earplugs of the split and/or siamesed creature, the inverted "U" elements the same as the ones above the earplug, representing the "ear" itself. Seen alone, this design would be regarded as completely "nonrepresentational" by everyone except the Taíno Indians who commissioned, carved, and sat in this elegant stool.

of execution, of every stage in the manufacture of a ceramic vessel, including its decoration. Although in principle modal analysis could account for design structure as well as vessel form, Rouse preferred to just categorize techniques and describe the fragments of designs present on potsherds ("rectilinear incision") rather than go on to the next step of hypothesizing design layouts and the rules and elements that might underlie them (e.g., "a rectangular incised step fret characterized by bifold rotation produces a layout").

This next step toward "artifact grammars" came when his student, Donald W. Lathrap, added the category of "dimension" to Rouse's modes (Lathrap 1970). A "dimension" is an area of formal variability in an artifact's production, such as a rim or a base that serves to organize the modes (i.e., base modes = flat base, annular base, etc.). These were arranged in the order that an artisan made pottery, from the paste recipe to the first base coils and ultimately to the rim and lip treatment, surface decoration, and firing styles.

Then in the mid-1970s, Lathrap's students, such as J. Scott Raymond of the University of Calgary and myself (Raymond et al. 1975), added the notion of "rules and elements" that could manipulate the modes in each dimension from start to finish, including geometric symmetric design structure and organization. The results were "decision programs" inferred from a corpus of artifacts that broke material culture down into the normative decisions that went into each stage of their manufacture.

While this was happening using South Amerindian data (Shipibo-Conibo pottery) and South American archaeology (the Cumancaya Tradition of the ninth century A.D.), an independent exploration of "grammar" in symmetry analysis occurred simultaneously in the Dominican Republic. Abelardo Jiménez, a physician and physical anthropologist, arranged classic Taíno symmetrically incised designs into a series of linked derivations that presaged my own "derivational chains." Although his work was unattributed in the original article, it appeared in a work by the Dominican journalist-turned-archaeologist Marcio Veloz Maggiolo (see esp. Jiménez Lambertus 1972).

Starting from the cognate formalist system of French structuralism, a number of Caribbean archaeologists of the Lesser Antilles (Duprat 1974; Mattioni 1968), principal

among them Henri Petitjean Roget (1976a, b, 1978) discovered the homologies between "geometric" designs and representations of "real" animals from the impoverished island faunas (principally bats and frogs). This revelation has now spread to the Dutch, who have discovered that the apparently "geometric" outline of postmolds in Cedrosan Saladoid communal circular huts in St. Eustatius (the Golden Rock site) are actually accurate maps of the joints, limbs, and shells of the giant sea turtle, the carey (*Chelonia mydas*), complete with "flipper effigy" windscreens (Versteeg 1992). Intentional turtle burials (as with intentional dog burials unique to the Antilles) and a regular class of rectangular turtle effigy trays (Roe 1989a) all imply that this large aquatic reptile played a disproportionate role in the art and ideology of these insular populations. Thus, in everything from incised designs on pots and stools to the hut plans of communal residences, "geometry" yielded "representation" in Island Arawak culture.

After I began doing fieldwork in Puerto Rico, I became fascinated with the elaborate petroglyphs found on the island. In the process of discovering and documenting a new type of petroglyph, the "beach" petroglyph (Roe 1991a), I did a componential analysis of anthropomorphic petroglyphs on the island, with an eye to isolating the elements of their depictions and the rules, including symmetry rules, that produced such observed images. Many of my master's degree candidates at the Centro de Estudios Avanzados de Puerto Rico y el Caribe in Old San Juan, where I taught in the summers and winters, began to apply this grammatical method (Cosme 1983; Hernández Rivera 1983; Maíz López 1983; Ortíz Montañez 1993; Pons de Alegría 1983, 1993; Rivera Fontán 1983). In 1989, I published (Roe 1989a) the first grammatical analysis of early Saladoid pottery at the other end of the culture historical spectrum in Puerto Rico. In the same study, I also applied the "derivational chain" method to a whole series of Cedrosan Saladoid vessel shapes, thus showing that vessel form obeys the same symmetry constraints as surface decoration.

This chapter developed out of these earlier efforts and extends the analysis into the succeeding period of the Elenan (and Ostionan) Ostionoid cultures. It also links them to the last phase of Classic Taíno designs (of the Chican Ostionoid) with which I began my Antillean odyssey some twenty-two years ago.

Are the Earliest Ceramic Styles Related?
The Fruit of Symmetry Analysis

The formal analysis of symmetry patterns in the ceramic designs of the first two Saladoid complexes resolves the issue of whether the earliest pottery to be found in Vieques and Puerto Rico, the Huecan and Cedrosan Saladoid ceramics, is related. That they were closely cognate traditions within the same Saladoid series was revealed by the intimate Saladoid affinities of both design systems, despite differences in decoration technique (polychrome painting versus incision and zoned crusting). The revised schema for both corpi places them as separate "styles," or subseries (Cedrosan Saladoid and Huecan Saladoid), within the same Saladoid series (Rouse 1992:83). The hidden grammar of symmetry thus belies the surface differences of technique to demonstrate cultural continuity, not discontinuity (see Figure 7.11).

Similar "aesthetic syntactics" shows occult representational aspects in the geometric art of the last Saladoid descendants, the Chican Ostionoid of the protohistoric Taíno Indians "discovered" by Columbus. Thus, symmetry analysis can also address the issue of in situ development versus a separate migration as has been suggested by other authorities such as Ricardo E. Alegría. The continuities recorded here through the middle "Ostionoid" period settle the question in favor of local development, as Rouse has argued for years based on other criteria.

Symmetry isomorphisms also unite otherwise disparate media in cross-media isomorphisms, from rock art to pottery. In addition, symmetry analysis effectively attributes artifacts of disputed African or Amerindian transcultural artifacts to their correct tradition. The beaded zemí illustrated in Figure 7.13m, because it incorporated Italian glass beads and mirrors as well as rhino horn, was thought to be African, not Antillean, in origin! Yet a symmetry analysis of the piece (Figure 7.13a-l), demonstrates the uniquely Amerindian Taíno "platonic" graphic device of a "moving design window" to create visible design panels out of a continuous invisible design background based on cognate derivative Saladoid

motifs. In short, it is a "transcultural" syncretic artifact that embodies Amerindian symmetry concepts with foreign raw materials in a work of "cultural hybrid vigor" characteristic of the first several decades of European occupation before the indigenous cultural collapse (Roe 1997b). Lastly, symmetry analysis can be extremely useful in telling modern "neo-Taíno" forgeries from the original artifacts since there is now a thriving local industry in the Dominican Republic fabricating fake Taíno artifacts for the collector market. The technology of these ancient artifacts can be duplicated with skill, but the symmetric order of their intricate designs frequently eludes modern replicators. Formal symmetry study thus proves to be a powerful analytical tool for a whole range of archaeological problems.

What Happens in the Middle?
The Paradox of Continuity and Devolution

The period of the initial migration of ceramic-using horticulturalists to the Greater Antilles, the Saladoid migrations from 500 B.C. to A.D. 500, is beginning to be better understood, partly through the findings of symmetry analysis itself. However, there is still a little-known period in Greater Antillean prehistory, the pre-Taíno period of the Elenan Ostionoid occupation of eastern Puerto Rico (from A.D. 600 to 1200). This is an era of transition, a phase of relative "ceramic devolution" sandwiched between two epochs of ceramic complexity on the island: the early Saladoid apogee of polychrome, complex-silhouette pottery and the late Taíno period of A.D. 1200–1492 of intricate, yet unpainted modeled and incised pottery. Comparatively little is known about the Elenan phase of ceramic simplicity. Not many whole pots have survived, and even fewer still have been accurately studied or drawn.

One of the major aims of my work with the ceramic assemblage at the small Jardines de Loiza site on the northeastern coast of Puerto Rico (excavated by my student Juan González Colón) is to make accurate reconstructed drawings of the diagnostic pieces recovered with a view to understanding the modes of decoration, including the symmetrical operations, characteristic of this period. Beyond that, the study of this collection affords possible explanations for the enigmatic period of ceramic "devolution." The explanatory models I have developed combine both the artistic consequences of changing gender roles and the patterns of residential and craft specialization within the overarching context of increasing local social complexity.

Based on the unique assemblage of artifacts and features at this site and their similarities with other neighboring "satellite" hamlets vis-à-vis the large "central place" villages of Loiza, such as Vacia Talega and Hacienda Grande, I have also hypothesized a specific function for this small residential site (Roe 2000c). It may have acted as a specialized ceramic production hamlet, a "satellite" locked in the exchange of pottery for foodstuffs (both processed shellfish and prepared bitter manioc cakes) with the larger "central place" villages.

Gender enters the picture as a possible variable since we know from analogous South America ethnography that bitter manioc cake production, the staple of pre-Taíno society, requires heavy labor from coordinated work parties of women (Gregor 1977). We also know that feasting was becoming increasingly important as Elenan "Big Men" sought to build authority via egalitarian redistribution (the size of cook pots skyrockets to some of the largest terra-cotta vessels ever built in the Antilles). An explosion of sites, the emergence of site hierarchies, and the huge size and material complexity of the largest central place sites all argue (as does the emergence of monumental public art in the form of ballparks and petroglyphs) for the appearance of "complex tribes" or "incipient chiefdoms" out of the egalitarian predecessor Saladoid society. Since the labor of women was essential to the carbohydrate staple of the feasts, the manioc cakes and the fermented beer made from that same tuber, perhaps men urged them toward ceramic production and food preparation to make ever larger and more frequent feasts possible as part of their social and political aggrandizement strategies. The unique existence of features best understood as multiple teepee-firing platforms for production of these large vessels at subsidiary sites like Jardinas de Loíza suggest a pattern of trade of pottery for subsistence goods and hence site complementarity. All this time and effort locked up in feast preparation may have come at the expense of craft training and instruction in complex symmetry rules. The pottery does in fact become cruder and the symmetry usage radically simplifies during this

time, a period when vessel shape is growing larger, thicker, and more utilitarian. These factors form a suite of variables, including that of a changing aesthetic of material culture to be argued below, that conspire to explain the radical "devolution" of pottery technology and craft during this transitional time.

At a higher level of generality within the culture history of the Greater Antilles, this study also makes possible the sketching of the strings of connection that Elenan pottery retained with both the earlier antecedent Saladoid as well as the subsequent descendant Taíno (Chican Ostionoid) series. Once again, Rouse's thesis of in situ evolution is supported.

The Elenan Ostionoids diverged from the Ostionan pattern during Rouse's period IIIa (A.D. 600–900) and solidified as a style in period IIIb (A.D. 900–1200), the dating of the material at the Jardines de Loiza site. The phase then lost its cultural integrity during the Chican Ostionoid expansion of period IVa (A.D. 1200–1492), evolving into the latter.

The anomaly of the Elenan/Ostionan phase was that instead of becoming even more complex than the precursor Saladoid ceramics in the expectable pattern of regional ceramic evolution, the pre-Taíno pottery reflected a paradoxical ceramic "devolution," although that devolutionary process is less evident in central sites such as Vacia Talega than on its periphery (Rodríguez López, personal communication, 2000). That is, Ostionoid ceramics got progressively simpler than the Saladoid heritage, losing the intricate painted designs and the complex carinated and restricted battery of numerous Saladoid vessel shapes. Only an occasionally inflected vessel shape (a gentle carination, or vessel corner point) and slip baths remained (brown for the Elenan, red for the Ostionan), as well as simple spirals painted in red slip paint on a plain surface of the earliest Elenan materials (once classified apart as first "Collores," then "Monserratean"; cf. Roe et al. 1990; Rouse 1992:Figure 32d). The surface decoration retreated to plastic treatments: vestiginal appliqué handles, some open but most reduced to skeuomorphic "C"-shaped solid appliqué filets with vertical incised lines between them or on top of the blind faux handles (which then functioned as tab handles; Figure 7.16b).

Instead of the realistic and stylized bird and animal

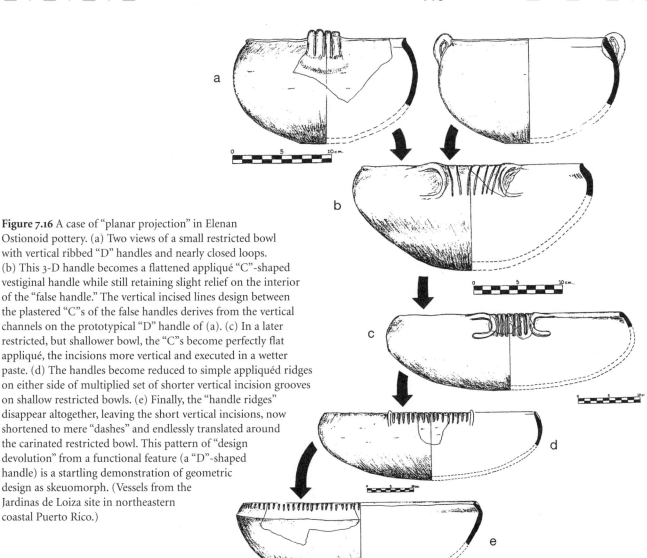

Figure 7.16 A case of "planar projection" in Elenan Ostionoid pottery. (a) Two views of a small restricted bowl with vertical ribbed "D" handles and nearly closed loops. (b) This 3-D handle becomes a flattened appliqué "C"-shaped vestiginal handle while still retaining slight relief on the interior of the "false handle." The vertical incised lines design between the plastered "C"s of the false handles derives from the vertical channels on the prototypical "D" handle of (a). (c) In a later restricted, but shallower bowl, the "C"s become perfectly flat appliqué, the incisions more vertical and executed in a wetter paste. (d) The handles become reduced to simple appliquéd ridges on either side of multiplied set of shorter vertical incision grooves on shallow restricted bowls. (e) Finally, the "handle ridges" disappear altogether, leaving the short vertical incisions, now shortened to mere "dashes" and endlessly translated around the carinated restricted bowl. This pattern of "design devolution" from a functional feature (a "D"-shaped handle) is a startling demonstration of geometric design as skeuomorph. (Vessels from the Jardinas de Loiza site in northeastern coastal Puerto Rico.)

zoomorphic adorno handles, often identifiable down to specific species of the Saladoid period (Roe 1989a), the Ostionoid retained dual-facing adornos, but they morphed into just "generic beasties" (Figure 7.8d). Highly variable and fantastic, they were no longer recognizable as to species, remaining just stylized "bat" (Ortíz Montañez 1993:134, Foto 37; Rouse 1992:Figure 32b), "monkey," "frog," or "lizard" paired representations. Their relative simplicity explains why few people have collected or studied this type of pottery beyond a handful of *saque-adores* ("pot hunters") who wire Elenan *caritas* ("little figural head lugs") to plywood display boards.

Indeed, so different does this "middle" pottery appear that many early authorities, like Alegría, hypothesized that the Ostionoids represented a separate migration into the Antilles. Even today, Chanlatte Baik (1981) maintains that the Ostionoid pottery is a direct development out of his "Huecoid" culture with the acculturation of the resident Archaic (non-ceramic-using) Indians. In contrast, Rouse and I view it as a "devolution" out of antecedent Cedrosan Saladoid pottery after the latter had assimilated some Huecan plastic decorative modes such as cross-hachured design. I suspect that assimilation was due to the wife capture of Huecan female potters as the Cedrosans competitively excluded their ancient rivals. The Archaic Indians may also have been involved as another source for captured women since they too became extinct as a cultural group on the island of Puerto Rico during this time period.

The most common shape in this Elenan pottery, taking up the highest percentage of the form vocabulary and coming in the greatest range of sizes, is a shallow bowl with a slight "inflection" at the shoulder, which then angles inward above its widest point to produce a restricted orifice (Figure 7.16b). This *cazuela* form is "primitive sphericity" à la Linné (1925) incarnate. The comparatively weak paste of this phase cannot sustain sharp breaks in the orientation of the vessel wall, thus constraining potters to adopt smoothly rounded shapes. They also lacked the technology to continue to execute salient appliqué such as labial flanges and annular bases like those of the Saladoid ancestral forms (Figure 7.11). Therefore most of the subtle changes in direction at the shoulder of these vessels are really rounded "inflections" rather than true carinations (for a partial exception see Figure 7.16e). These trends represent a significant technical "devolution" from Saladoid levels. The soft, thick sherds of the Elenan period that tend to break along coil lines contrast with the thin and hard Saladoid pottery.

Symmetry Doesn't Just Apply to Designs: Elenan "False" Handles

One can apply symmetry concepts to structural features of pots, like handles, if they too become "decorative" devices, as is frequently the case in Amerindian ceramics. For example, based on a detailed examination of the handles in the Jardines de Loiza, Ojo del Buey, and El Bronce Elenan assemblages I have studied, it is even possible to construct a hypothetical path of evolution from functionality to pure decoration that also includes the typical vertically translated channel incision. One starts the derivational chain (Figure 7.4a) with the elevated "D"-shaped handles of the Saladoid tradition, truly functional since they are characterized by an ample space between the handles and the vessel for inserting the index finger. Frequently they carry a "button" atop them or even an actual modeled and incised (and sometimes painted) figural head lug.

By Elenan Ostionoid times, these freestanding functional handles could no longer be made due to the weakness of the paste. They would have simply broken off in the fingers if they had been grasped! Instead a set of three

to four coils was molded vertically into the interior of the vessel below the rim, thus forming a reinforcing bulge at the point of maximum stress. Nevertheless, the rims break precisely at either side of this reinforcement, proving that the strengthening was not effective. Then the coils were laid over the rim and welded to the outer upper vessel body wall below the exterior lip. Originally the handles were arched, or at least elevated, leaving a small space within the "D" handle that was irregular and never finished simply because fingers could not penetrate the space. One could not in fact grasp the appendages as true handles (Figure 7.16a). Instead, the plastered handles functioned as mere vertical "tabs."

Eventually the vertical coils were merely laid on the exterior of the direct rim, projecting above it less than 1 to 6 mm as a decorative lug, the pinch molding from the fingers still visible (unsmoothed) on the outer lateral surfaces of the coils (Roe 2000c). The spaces between the coils looked like vertical channel incisions, and that is exactly what they became. From this stage it was a short step to space the vertical, broad "U"-shaped channel incisions farther apart, producing a small set of decorative incisions that end above the vessel inflection at precisely the same point the original handle would have terminated (Figure 7.16b, c). Thence, it was a logical extension to multiply these translated vertical incisions all the way around the pot as mere decoration (Figure 7.16d) and then to reduce these long incisions to just short vestigial vertical "jabs," totally encircling the pot on its upper design field (Figure 7.16e).

These sets of vertical incisions are more frequently bounded by two vestigial handles on either side of a vessel, producing two paneled design fields (Figure 7.16c) rather than just one encircling field. In this case, the handles go through an additional process of morphological "devolution." Again they start as vertical "D"-shaped handles of separate coils, then mutate into plain or effigy handles with three or four obligatory channel incisions down their lower exterior. These mimic the original bundled vertical coils. Since the representational adorno heads are actually transmuted handles, they too bear deep vertical channel incisions (three or four) that also recall the vertical bundled coils (Figure 7.8a). If these adorno faces sit at the top of a "D"-shaped handle, again with a vestigial space within the "D," then the exterior of the dual faces will have four wide channel incisions below it, again evoking the original bundles of vertical coils that composed the prototypical handle.

Since handles substitute vertical incisions for vertical coil bundles, the wider the handle, the more incisions will fill its outer surface. As the handle becomes fused into the upper body wall, no longer with an internal void, the former space at the side of the handle will remain concave (Figure 7.16b) as a vestigial skeuomorph. Such solid handles continue to project, however, some 2 cm from the rim (Figure 7.16c)!

As they are plastered even farther into the upper vessel body wall below the rim to become mere decorative relief, these vestigial handles morph into the characteristic "C"-shaped appliqué faux handles that border a panel of incision. Here we need to invoke the dualism that is embedded in the "multiple-view" adornos that can decorate some of the original "D"-shaped handle prototypes. In Amerindian art, one can always change one's perspective to obtain a different view, thus bringing an object alive by adding a kinetic aspect to perception. The ancestral Saladoid potters would invert the "Saladoid anthropomorphic being" around a top-of-the-head mouth to reveal a different anatropic image (Figure 7.4a, b). Their Elenan descendants reversed their view from the top of an adorno (an upward and inward-staring "monkey" face) to its back (frontal-dorsal dualism). In the process, they would reveal an outward-staring humanoid face (Figure 7.8a versus 7.8d).

The last and by far the subtlest form of perceptual dualism (a species of "visual ambiguity," like shifting figure-and-ground) is to show both profile and end views at once, right next to each other. This is "profile-plane view dualism" (Roe 2000b), what is happening with the two vertically reflected "C"-shaped faux handles bordering a panel of translated vertical incisions (Figure 7.16c). The two "C" shaped handles are, in fact, one. They are the profile views of each side of a vertical "D"-shaped handle. Each has been splayed outward like "split representation" (see Figure 7.15a) and laid flat. The paneled vertical incision between them is, in reality, the vertical incision on the outer surface of the prototypical "D"-shaped handle (Figure 7.16a)! Ultimately the "C"-shaped handle profiles are elongated and welded into the upper vessel body wall to produce "negative" internal rectangular horizontal spaces of deep relief, like "windows" into the pot (Roe 2000c).

Another possibility for the adorno on the top of the "D"-shaped handle is for it to lose the handle altogether and become a "tab" lug all by itself. This is the case with the beautiful "bat" adorno illustrated by Ortíz Montañez (1993:Foto 37, Carita #530) from the Elenan site of Ojo del Buey in Dorado, far to the west of LO-26. Like the "D"-shaped "monkey" adornos of this site, it looked inward into the orifice of a vessel (there unrestricted, in the Jardines de Loiza instance restricted), thus turning the whole vessel into an effigy and the concavity of the pot into the bat's or monkey's belly.

A last possibility with regard to appendages is also illustrated at the Jardinas de Loiza, LO-26, site. It takes only a single vertical coil, often oriented slightly toward the center of the pot, and pairs it with another to produce two projections marginally above the rim on either side of the vessel (Figure 7.16d). These are then decorated with vertically aligned punctations. In the Ojo del Buey assemblage (Ortíz Montañez 1993:Foto 35, Tiesto #379) and in the LO-26 (Jardines de Loiza) assemblage as well, these upright coil projections can border a central panel of vertically translated channel incisions, thus proving that they too are the outer vertical coils in the original bundled prototypical "D"-shaped handle. To continue this proof, such single vertical coil projection can itself carry three parallel vertical channel incisions below its punctated "head" (Figure 7.8a)!

Thus handles, once a functional "D"-shaped bundle of vertical coils bent over a rim and fused to it, become, by separate-but-linked derivational chains, paired profile-frontal "C"-shaped appliqué faux handles flanking a central panel of vertically translated channel incisions. Or in the other chain, paired, punctated vertical projections flanking a central panel border the same vertical incisions. Evolving style and declining technology conspire to turn the functional into the decorative in the dimension of Elenan Ostionoid handles, tabs, and incisions.

The Complexity of Symmetry Traditions Responds to Social Processes

How does the intermediary pre-Taíno period of the Elenan occupation of sites such as LO-26 relate to the two ends of the Greater Antillean continuum (Saladoid-Chican Ostionoid)? More pertinently, why did the complex Saladoid pattern of symmetrical designs decay into vestigial Elenan translated vertical dashes? One notices the increasing simplification of the pottery as well as the schematization of the designs as they devolved from Saladoid prototypes. Yet connections abound that both reflect the "last gasp" of the antecedent Saladoid series and "foretell" the elaborations of the succeeding Chican Ostionoid series on several "linear incised" sherds (Roe 2000c) that would not even be included within the "Elenan" series if they had been found out of context, despite their evident Elenan paste and color. They bear fine-line linear incision that was characteristic of the last stages of the preceding Saladoid series, such as the Cuevas and Tibes styles. Moreover, such vessels reveal their open orientation by the presence of a horizontal fine-line incised line on the interior of the rim only a few centimeters from the lip. This is yet another Saladoid pattern.

Other vessel shapes within this Elenan assemblage also look back toward the epi-Saladoid period and thus connect this transitional series to the one before it. While most of the LO-26 vessels have just a subtle "inflection" at the shoulder, changing direction gradually to produce a curved maximum vessel diameter, some retain the Cuevan pattern of a true sharp carination. In these vessels, the lower vessel body wall departs at a distinct angle from the subrim neck (Figure 7.16e). The sharp bevel of the flat lip (although the rim form it is associated with varies dramatically within the same vessel) on such pots also harks back to the precision of Cuevas and Tibes forms.

The last gasp of the appliquéd Saladoid labial flange is the now-reduced internally thickened rim with internal bevel and externally projecting rounded lip. This rim form (called an "undecorated ridge inside a rim") is typically Elenan (Rouse 1992:Figure 32a). A study of the vessel wall shows that it was appended to the upper body as true appliqué, like the ancestral much-lengthened Cedrosan Saladoid labial flanges. Such rims appear on shallow open bowls.

If there are traits that look backward to the Saladoid, the LO-26 assemblage also reveals examples that look forward to the very late Elenan or early Esperanzan of the Chican Ostionoid series. The typically Elenan reptilian critters that peer from either side into the restricted orifice of the inflected bowls while gripping the rim with splayed fingers reveal a limb treatment that shows

up as appliquéd and impressed fillets that encircle very early Esperanzan Ostionan Ostionoid vessels, such as the one pictured in Ortíz Montañez (1993:Appendix C:22). A LO-26 house lizard (Roe 2000a), skillfully modeled and incised as appliqué, has two outward and upwardly curved limbs that bear deep impressions. They were executed when the appliqué was very wet and plastic. The impressions cause the arms to splay outward in a "nodal" wavy pattern identical to the nonfigural appliquéd semicircular fillets of the Esperanzan vessel of similar restricted shape. This type of upward-reaching figure persists in the very late Elenan component at the Aguilita site on the south coast (Juana Díaz), although this time with punctate anatropic eyes. Similar appliquéd figures with impressed upward-reaching "U"-shaped arms continue into the Classic Taíno Chican Ostionoid pottery in analogous subrim positions (Figure 7.9g), also revealing local development throughout this intermediate Elenan phase.

All of these modeled, incised, and appliquéd figures lack the precision of execution and the fealty toward identifiable fauna that characterized antecedent Saladoid representational lugs (Roe 1989a). They also lack the paint of the earlier adornos, thus representing, despite their inventiveness and arresting appearance, a continuous process of ceramic devolution in surface decoration.

Most tellingly, ceramic stamps of the sort discovered by Ortíz Montañez (1993: Fotos 13–14), with their simple concentric incised pattern, suggest that even the skills to do intricate freehand body painting had disappeared. Why had the level of art and ceramic development fallen so low from such an early apogee as the Insular Saladoid?

Paradoxically, the very simplification of this pottery may reflect the increasing subsistence and social success of the population that produced it. If the early Saladoid peoples, with their utilization of the land crab, looked more toward terrestrial resources (although recent faunal studies have shown that the Saladoid diet was not just composed of land crab), the Elenan Ostionoids, as a "shellfish culture," looked more toward the ocean. This is really where the protein is in the Antilles when one considers the insular impoverished terrestrial fauna. The utilization of shellfish, coupled with fishing (both of freshwater fish via weirs such as at the coastal Elenan site of Maisabel Playa [Roe 1991a] and the pursuit of saltwater

fish, reptiles, and mammals), indicated a true insular adaptation on the part of the Ostionoid cultures. This was inherently a more productive strategy than that of the imported terra firma orientation of the Saladoid pioneers.

This localized adaptation (people slowly realizing they were, indeed, on islands) and the apparent vanquishing or acculturation of the indigenous archaic peoples, at least on Puerto Rico, allowed a demographic explosion that permitted the Amerindians to expand inland up the river drainages into the interior. There was some terminal Saladoid (Cuevas) penetration of the highlands, but that was limited. In coastal valleys where we have adequate site survey data, such as Valle del Toa of the Río La Plata far to the west of Loiza, the home valley of the Santa Elena type site, we can pick up a "bipolar" movement (Roe 1989a) both toward the modern shoreline on the one hand (Saladoid sites are always some distance back from the coast on high ground) and up the river valleys with their fertile floodplains of easily cultivated and well-drained new alluvium on the other. The type site of Santa Elena itself is one such inland location while loci such as Ojo del Buey, Punta Corozo, and Punta Mameyes are examples of the coastal ones. It is tempting to map this double-pronged movement onto inland horticultural and coastal fishing and shellfish-collecting stations respectively.

Not only do the sites become much more numerous, but the linear space between them contracts. In contrast, the preceding Saladoid sites were huge but far between, as befitted pioneering settlements. In addition to this multiplication of sites and bipolar movement of sites during the Ostionoid period, the first appearance of a site hierarchy occurs. Big sites tend to be surrounded by smaller, satellite sites (Ortíz Montañez 1993:40). This factor in turn hints, as does the spatial movement pattern, at a social division of labor between sites locked together in a densely populated landscape of mutually supportive settlements. Coastal sites produced maritime protein resources and traded them inland as inland sites generated cultivated foods rich in carbohydrates and sent them seaward, a pattern of exchange that apparently was to continue into the Taíno period. Perhaps it is this division of labor that explains both the small size of the Jardines de Loiza site and the apparent absence of shellfish remains associated with it (and also the scarcity of griddles for bitter manioc cake production). Perhaps this

small site was engaged in some local resource extraction or task specialization. Indeed, I have reconstructed the enigmatic piles of limestone boulders that dot a downwind sector of the site as open-air teepee firing loci since they are associated with large sherds that could have acted as wedges to level the largest vessels, mouth downward, that were apparently fired at the site (Roe 2000c). Thus it may have been a specialized ceramic-producing site, both ephemeral and dependent on larger regional sites such as Hacienda Grande and Vacia Talega only a couple of kilometers away. Rodríguez López (personal communication, 2000) has also excavated several sites in the vicinity of the Jardines de Loiza site that seem to mirror its small size and "incomplete" material cultural assemblage. As peripheral and dependent sites, they may have produced goods such as pottery for the Big Men in the central places, who could have sent them in turn processed shellfish and manioc cakes. All this regional exchange supported an intensifying "fiesta" complex as a means of building alliances between villages within the context of increasing stratification. This was to make the Elenan period a time of "Complex Tribes" or a series of "Incipient Chiefdoms" antecedent to the fully developed chiefdoms of the succeeding Classic Taíno protohistoric period. Thus, a picture of "central places" and their supporting "hinterland" of smaller surrounding and apparently dependent sites has begun to emerge on the northeast and north-central coasts of Puerto Rico during late Elenan times.

Perhaps the intermediate environmental and social circumscription (à la Carneiro 1974) of insular settings led to the first indications of social stratification in Elenan Ostionoid times. The Greater Antilles, being part of a closely spaced archipelago, achieved "medial" geographic isolation because the large islands were, perforce, surrounded by water. Yet due to their proximity to other landmasses such as the Virgin Islands, that isolation was nothing that could not, with effort, be circumvented because of the ease of inter-island travel. Therefore a medium form of stratification, the chiefdom, developed (truly isolated islands such as Hawaii saw the emergence of veritable mini-states). I have already made an argument, based on a qualitative seriation rooted in the Elenan sites of Maisabel Playa, Pueblito Carmen, and El Bronce, that petroglyphs and pictographs emerged for the first time during Elenan Ostionoid times as the initial expression of the large-scale art of incipient public power although still couched in the visual language of ancestral worship (Roe 1995a). It is not a coincidence that these "frontal," long-distance-visible monumental forms also appear at the same time as the first, albeit small and relatively simple, ballparks and their side-marker petroglyphs in such early sites as Tibes (González Colón 1989).

Then by later Elenan Ostionoid times at sites such as El Bronce (Robinson et al. 1985), a shift occurs from the generalized visage to that face's accoutrements, such as feathered crowns, ear plugs, and pendant necklace elements (the so-called bearded or, more appropriately, "rayed" faces as in Figure 7.8b). After all, the unadorned human face cannot express social hierarchy, but the festooned visage, surrounded by sumptuary adornments, can. This differential embellishment hints at increasing social complexity as certain descent groups took precedence over others, glorified their leaders, and marshaled labor to make public statements of nascent power (Roe et al. 1997).

We also know that when a style begins to express the same stylistic conventions across the natural propensities of divergent media, thus overriding the "inherent perfectibility of form" (Link 1975) of each raw material in fealty to projecting minimally altered aspects of ideology, such a style expresses very important central cultural concepts. If not, each media "goes its own way" and media-based separate substyles emerge, such as a substyle for rock art and another for pottery decoration. I have already argued that such cross-media isomorphisms permeate the late classic Chican Ostionoid art, seemingly "abstract" geometric designs from ceramic incision being nested within "representational" arrays (Roe 1997a). With the same logic other "nonrepresentational" ceramic designs actually generate "stylized" representations in Chican stone art (Roe 1993).

If Elenan Ostionoid is evolving toward Chican Ostionoid forms and Elenan culture already has the incipient expressions of the social hierarchy evident in Chican culture, then it comes as no surprise that we can begin to pick up "cross-media isomorphisms" in symmetry within the divergent domains of Elenan material culture. These distinct media are linked by the process of incision. Thus, in Figure 7.8a we find little hemispherical bowls with representational "dual imagery" "D"-shaped handles, which are in themselves continuations of ancestral Saladoid practice. Their ceramic incised and modeled motifs also recall petroglyphic incised motifs of the period in a way that presages the complexities of Chican elite art. Thus the little classic "monkey" faces that cling below and peer upward toward the pot's orifice on the inner portions of the "D"-shaped handles' upper registers (Figure 7.8d) have on their dorsal surfaces another "reversible" humanoid face. Note the equation *inner face:zoomorphic representation::outer face: anthropomorphic representation.* Perhaps the notion of animal spiritual "doubles," or *naguales,* was being represented. In any event, the ear plugs and subfacial "rays," both indications of visual hierarchy, are mirrored in an Elenan petroglyph from the Barrio Cibuco in the east-central highlands of the island (Figure 7.8b). Thus, the "rays" below the petroglyph face may have originated in the ubiquitous vertical channel incisions on the outer surfaces of the "D"-shaped handles retained in Elenan pottery. Both in turn are probably representations in different media of pendant necklace elements tied to a single neck cord, as is the case in lowland South Amerindian body art (Roe 1995b). Yet the Elenan incised and modeled anthropomorphic and theriomorphic lugs are themselves simplified descendants of the modeled, incised, and painted Saladoid effigy handles.

Thus, the fact that simplification occurs in the pottery (the old egalitarian tribal "Personal Presentation" material culture) to one of monumental stonework (the first elements of the material culture of "Public Power") indicates that Elenan Ostionoid society was beginning to be ranked. Hence, it qualifies as an "Incipient Chiefdom" and/or a series of "Complex Tribes." The replacement of simple faces with whole torso figures, human and animal (the shark petroglyph of El Bronce), or the complex functional distinction between the central polychrome cult images of pictographs and the peripheral guardian figures of simpler petroglyphs at Cueva de la Mora in Comerío in late Elenan times (Roe et al. 1997) hint at greater skill and effort expended on monumental *arte rupestre* ("rock art") as a by-product of social complexification. In effect, the social locus of art was shifting from pottery to larger-scale stonework and architecture with the inevitable simplification of the former as mere craft.

Comparative evidence from other world areas supports this argument by showing how it is difficult to make status-affirming statements based on simple earthenware alone since everyone must have utilized pots (Miller 1985). Only those media accessible to the socially powerful, via command or commissioning, such as monumental stonework and public architecture, can both express and validate increasing social stratification.

Cross-Media Isomorphisms: Taíno Geometry and Representation

Only later, at the climax of the native tradition in Chican Ostionoid times, did the pottery once again become complex, but never to the level of its Saladoid precursors. Judging from the vessels themselves, one can surmise that full-time female specialists directed by men produced this complex and subtle art in great quantity. Meanwhile the bulk of the women became simple pottery consumers, not producers. It is a common pattern in South America that with increasing stratification, masculine artisans usurp or "appropriate" part of the feminine pottery-producing role. Comparative evidence suggests that this was especially the case with the most "sculptural" class of Taíno ceramics: the creation of the representational hollow human effigy jars (Roe 1997a:Figures 100, 104, 105, 108), the iconographic apogee of Taíno ceramics.

Yet the same "cross-media isomorphisms," or similarities across media, that we have found in regard to Elenan Ostionoid ceramics and petroglyphs also exist in the Chican Ostionoid period. That was the succeeding phase associated with the Classic Taíno complex chiefdoms that Columbus encountered. I discovered incised design layouts of the sort frequently found on Chican ceramics "encised" within specific design fields of "stele" or "menhir" petroglyphs (large, freestanding boulders with incised depictions on their front faces) of the western bordering stone alignment in the largest ballpark, Plaza A, of the site of Caguana (Capá), Utuado (Figure 7.9h-i). This important late ceremonial-residential site in the central highlands of Puerto Rico is associated with both Ostiones (Ostionan Ostionoid, the western contemporary of Elenan Ostionoid) and Chican Ostionoid (Capá) ceramics (Alegría 1983:78). It has been identified, at the latter end of its occupation, as the seat of the Taíno chief Guarionex (Rouse 1952:478, following Mason). Among the important monuments of the site is the largest and most impressive of the west alignment stele (only the boulders on the side of the setting sun have petroglyphs, perhaps as markers of the western Land of the Dead). It bears a full-body stylized female figure incised into its face, the oft-illustrated Diosa de Caguana (Figure 7.9h) as Alegría (1978) has called her. She has been identified by Stevens-Arroyo (1988:162) with Attabeira, the Earth Goddess. I will utilize the cataloging system proposed by Oliver (1992:Figure 5, 1998) for the west alignment glyphs and characterize her as Petroglyph 9. Flanking her, to her right, and separated by two large menhirs, one of them decorated with a heart-shaped face (Petroglyph 8), is another large boulder with a long-beaked heronlike bird incised on its face (Petroglyph 7, Figure 7.10g). Together they appear to constitute parts of a lithographic "scene" that visually annotates a Guianan myth. This is an important tale of creation about the origin of women as a Fish-Frog (Aquatic) Woman Seductress armed with a *vagina dentata* (Roe 1982) and the Phallic-Beaked Bird who "breaks her teeth" to convert her into the first marriageable woman and the ancestress of people.

"Hidden" within the design fields of the major component body parts of the lithographic (anthropomorphic and zoomorphic) depictions is classic Boca Chica pottery and wood-carving designs. Specifically, the wing element of the "heron" (Petroglyph 7) depicted to the right of the Goddess (the "Frog Lady," Petroglyph 9) is treated as an analogous design field to the subrim, above-carination field of the most common form of restricted Chicoid (Chican Ostionoid) bowls (see Figure 7.10a, b). In turn, that design is a direct derivative of an ancient Cedrosan Saladoid horizontally and vertically reflected step-scroll layout (Figure 7.10e). Both fields are filled with similar triangle and roundel design layouts: the wing is one triangle and the neck another, while the beak is yet a third. To create the ceramic designs, the neck is simply rotated 90 degrees vertically (Figure 7.10c) to form a roundel (at the wing-base joint, polysemic with an "eye"). It is flanked by two triangles that have become concave on their short sides via a conformational rule. In essence they are vertically reflected on either side of the roundel and appear on the subrim neckband of Chican Ostionoid cazuelas, or restricted vessels with a pronounced shoulder or carination and a round-to-flat base (Figure 7.10f).

Note that both in the Attabeira Menhir and, starting at the very beginning of the sequence with the Huecan Saladoid snuffing vessel pictured here (Figure 7.3a), the navel of humanoid figures, like the major joints of the shoulder or the hip, becomes a roundel. Here is where the "ghost" meets the "machine" (literally!).

Studying how an Amerindian butchers a carcass helps to understand art style and its symmetries. One "gets into" a carcass by dismembering it, cutting apart the limbs at the joints. Thus, points of articulation "open up" the body. The torso, whether animal or human, is thought of like a "hut" or some other "container," especially in the shamanism of the sort present today in the lowlands and documented in ethnohistoric times in the Greater Antilles. Within that hollow and protective shell lives the ethereal soul or souls (Indians often have multiple souls, each with a different function, aspect and "half-life"). One emic explanation of illness (in addition to soul capture) comes from spirit intrusion within the "hut," contaminating or binding up (obscuring) the soul with the *asymmetry* of contagion (Roe 2004).

In this curing/bewitching context, it is interesting to note that *spiritual contagion:asymmetry::health:symmetry* in current lowland South Amerindian shamanism (Roe 2004). For example, the Shipibo of the Peruvian montaña regard the malignant spiritual intrusion as a wriggling "worm," a swirling cloud of black formless clouds or winds (*nihuë*) or old, black, tattered spiderwebs—all images of chaos and disorder and by definition asymmetric. In contrast, their lattice-based body and face painting is rigidly bilaterally symmetrical and constitutes a "design armor" that protects the body from invasion. Perhaps the intricate bilaterally symmetrical body and face painting of the Classic Taíno, as evidenced by their pottery effigies and wood-bone-stone carving, acted as similar protection: maybe the roundels and the triangles really did "close the door" of the body's natural orifices and joints to spirit intrusion.

From this metaphysical diagnosis comes the famous Amerindian "sucking cure" to extract the spiritual pathogen and the equally well-known, and related,

"blowing curse" (called *Taling* in the Guianas, where the concept is still alive). The sucked-out pathogen is "blown" from the mouth of the shaman and thus sent on its way like some primitive missile to infect the souls of enemies (and thereby find a secure home far enough away from oneself or one's relatives to prevent the possibility of reinfection—what better "home" for an errant pathogen than the body of one's foe?).

Like the circular opening of a cave (where much of the rock art is found), the joints become circles (like the round ball-and-socket joints of the femur and hip, for example, an exact analogical "fit" as well as an anatomical one). Moreover, while the bones or skull have just single round or oval holes, the fleshy coverings of the skin invariably add concentric folds surrounding that hole (lips for the mouth, eyelids for the orbits, ears for the ear canal, etc.), hence the concentric circles of the roundel with the central dot indicating the orifice.

In an act of what Lévi-Strauss (1967) would call "mythic deduction," the roundel joints (like the circular orbits as portals into the hollow skull) form "doors" or "portals" of light into the darkness of the body's "hollow" interior. They are the entry and exit points of soul energy; both marked (hence their delineation in art as an incised or painted roundel or an appliqué nubbin) and defended against soul intrusion or capture. That is why the belly button, centrally located in the torso, is invariably so highlighted as the medial portal. In the early Huecan Saladoid effigy snuffing pot (Figure 7.3a) note that it has "opened wide" to become the expanded circular orifice, still surrounded by a circular incision to form the roundel. Through that orifice the hallucinogenic powder is poured into the pot's body, just as intrusive soul stuff enters the corporeal body. It leaves the vessel by snuffing (sucking with the nose rather than the mouth, but the same shamanic act nevertheless) out the effigy's leg tubes. That is why, at the end of the sequence in Classic Menhir petroglyphs of the Caguana ballpark, the belly roundel of Attabeira, the Earth Goddess as South Amerindian–derived Frog Woman, transforms into a roundel with flanking triangles (Figure 7.9h) that, with a 90-degree act of rotation and horizontal reflection, becomes a standard subrim design layout on restricted Capá (Classic Taíno) ceramic pots (Figure 7.9i). It is likely, then, that even when seen alone, as in a design

band centered around roundels (Figure 7.15c), the roundel still stood for ear, eye, navel, doorway, and soul entrance/exit to observers of that majestic carving. Attabeira was still, even in death (note her closed "goggle" eyes), the "House of Souls" as ceramic pots were little "portable wombs" filled with the water of parturition and grown by the coiling technique, the coils themselves perhaps metonymically recalling the umbilicus!

All of this may seem like the machinery of overinterpretation were it not for one seminal observation made by the humble Catalán friar Ramón Pané (1974). He noted that the Taíno spoke of their Spirits of the Dead with trepidation. They were the fruit-eating *Opía,* batlike creatures, pale nocturnal seducers and erratically flying ancestral "souls." Abundant iconographic isomorphisms exist between bats, Opía, and owls (García Arévalo 1997), all negative creatures that were both nocturnal and carnivorous-cannibalistic. The vampire bat figures in South Amerindian lowland mythology as a deadly seducer (Roe 1994b) as well as in its Caribbean extension. The most common bat in Hispañola and Puerto Rico (the denizen of the caves where the rock art is found) is, however, not a vampire but a harmless frugivore, *Artibeus jamaicensis,* whose favorite food is the same guava fruit (*Psidium guajava*) beloved of the similarly nocturnal Opía (Petitjean Roget 1976b). Yet the sharp teeth of this frugivore still carried the fearsome connotations of the mainland vampire as "Species Master."

All throughout South America and the Caribbean, thanks to Lévi-Strauss's "culinary metaphor," we know that sweet fruits are seductive. As one of the few substances in nature (in addition to the equally delectable, hence seductive and dangerous, honey) that can be eaten "raw," they are therefore aligned with Nature rather than the "cooked" substances of Culture. There is no more "natural" a phenomenon than death itself, just as the archive of transmitted knowledge in Culture given to new generations is evocative of life eternal. Hence the symbolic grid that overlies the icons should predict that eating sweet fruits is tantamount to seduction and seduction equivalent to madness or death (even today, in the lowlands an orgasm is called "a little death"). To be led astray from cultural duties into the jungle of animalistic desires is the essence of Nature, as Stevens-Arroyo, the author of a structuralist treatment

of Taíno mythology and cosmology (1988), based on Pané's texts, asserts. He points out that this notion survives even today in Puerto Rican popular culture and language. *Jobos* are the sweet fruit, *"a comer Jobos,"* "to eat Jobos," means to forget one's social obligations and descend into asocial narcissism and inaction. Hence what one would predict, Pané's ancient text describes. If one succumbed to the charms of the beautiful and handsome Opía (for as the Dead they came in both sexes), being accosted at night on a moonlit path, one would go crazy (and, I add on comparative grounds, fall into a coma filled with deadly erotic dreams, waste away, and die).

Moreover, the Opía left their Land of the Dead in the West at night (which could also be Underworld caves) and, like bats, visited the groves of Jobos near people's huts to eat the delectable fruit and seduce errant humans. They, like all Spirits of the Dead in South America, were lonely and desired company. The living (especially their surviving relatives) were "company." Therefore they would seduce them into coming along. The result, again to extrapolate from lowland South Amerindian concepts, was that the human would die and join the Spirits of the Dead in the west.

Thus, if the Wrapped Ancestors (Figure 7.5a, b, f) were the "quiet dead," benevolent in their care for their descendants, the Opía acted as the "unquiet dead," a constant danger to them. Perhaps via some delict in life such as incest or stinginess, they did not depart but hung around the hut and underwent an act of "sacred devolution" to become were-bats. These creatures, frequent effigies in the pottery (Figure 7.18c), mirrored, as drab and nocturnal structural inversions, the colorful and diurnal "solar" birds soaring high in the Upper Heavens far above the mountain (Roe 1997a).

The key element that anchors this exercise in ethnosemantics and design structure in paleoethnography is that Pané (1974) informs us that the only way the attractive but malevolent Opía could be told from living humans (apart, one surmises, from their pallor and coldness, two traits universally ascribed to the dead by South Amerindians) was that the Opía *had no navel!* Of course not! If they were already dead, their ethereal bodies contained no souls; they were the souls themselves, hence they needed no "portal" for soul passage and thus sported

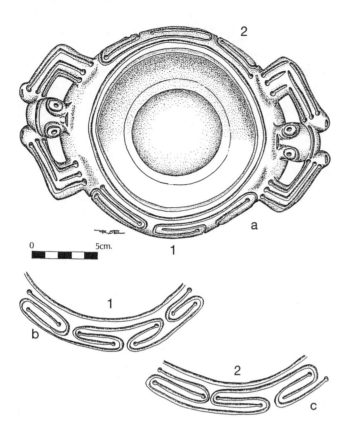

0   5cm.

Figure 7.17 (a) A Chican Ostionoid effigy bowl with figurative handles that always appear in *pairs* on either side of an open or mildly restricted bowl. The open orifice and round internal base turn the "shared" belly of these twins into a belly roundel with central belly button, a motif shared with Taíno petroglyphs. (b) Between the figurative elements on side 1 appears a geometric design composed of horizontally reflected "C" motifs, which are bifold rotated and then nested to yield a series of interlocked scrolls. (c) On panel 2, the same layout appears. See Figure 7.25d for its derivation. (Collection, Museo del Hombre Dominicano, Santo Domingo, Dominican Republic.)

no navel. The encircling geometric bands of roundels that girdle women's ceramic vessels or march in ordered bands across the backs of men's duhos are therefore protective talismans, the armor of art (as geometric art functions in South America today). The roundels "close the door" and keep contagion and evil soul intrusion, or equally vile soul-kidnapping spirits, at bay! No wonder roundels are ubiquitous as the central Taíno motif.

One also notes that each incised line in classic Taíno (Capá) designs ends in a "dot finial" (Figure 7.17). This is one of the defining attributes that Rouse first used to isolate the Classic Taíno style and distinguish it from provincial versions such as Esperanza in Puerto Rico. I suggest that these little circular punctations that terminate a line are like the central punctations in the middle of roundels. They *are* miniature roundels. After all, what are lines other than "open-ended" invitations, or pathways, to spirit intrusion? One way to convert the straight line into a circle, and thus afford spiritual protection, is to fold it back upon itself (Figure 7.17b, c) in endless meandering curves (evocative, perhaps, of the folded umbilicus itself). The artist could "split" circles by vertically reflecting "C," then end such loops with circular punctations. Thus, the Taíno artisans terminated their lines in "closed doorways" to keep contagion out so that it would wander ceaselessly lost in the maze of their interlocking designs and never enter the body = hut of the person using the ceramic vessel or sitting on the stool.

Perhaps the best design array that encapsulates everything I argue for in this chapter is the high-backed duho from the Museo del Hombre Dominicano (Ostapkowicz 1997:Plates 45, 46), from which I have redrawn the two design layouts here as Figures 7.14 and 7.15. This stool for a high-ranking *cacique* demonstrates peerless workmanship and depicts a quadrupedal animal with carved shell "dentures" that project a menacing aspect. Big cats do not exist in the Caribbean, but the high back that carries the designs certainly gives the appearance of a tail (perhaps it is the feline substitute, the dog?). The design layout above (Figure 7.15a) is representational while the layout below it (Figure 7.15c) is geometric. This stool is all about hierarchy, and part of that was gender hierarchy. This is social information that the properties of symmetry subconsciously transmit. High-ranking noblemen sat on stools, and their women sat below them on ground mats. The few female cacicas recorded for the contact period, like Luisa (Loiza) herself, were artifacts of Spanish conquistadors' political ambitions. Since the titles were transmitted matrilineally, the Spanish thought, erroneously, that by marrying such a princess they could accede to the native titles (in a matrilineal system, of course, husbands do *not* assume their wife's titles; the brothers of the wives do). In any case such high-ranking females became "honorary males" and could also sit on duhos as South Amerindian chiefly analogs suggest.

On the high back of this stool the *lower* geometric array is like the geometric designs women incised on the necks of their ceramic vessels, whereas the upper figurative design, that is, *above it,* looks like the animal visages men carved into other obdurate materials such as bone and shell. Therefore, the symbolically connected dual equation, *men:upper::women: lower,* and *men:figurative designs::women:geometric designs,* confirmed cross-culturally, holds here as well. However, gender and the spatial code are not all that are at issue in this extraordinary carving.

Note that the mouths on the upper figures are hollow, ready to have the same shell denture inlays inserted as on the lower carved seat. But unlike the lower theriomorphic seat figure, these upper seat-back figures seem to be anthropomorphic, at least in one visual reading. That is the conundrum. There are at least two ways of looking at this figure. First, like a "split representation," it has an image that has been split apart and laid flat like a map projection (Figure 7.15a). But unlike a split representation, which is parted from the crown of the head down the back of the skull and the skin folded out to produce a flattened face with deep negative "V" in the forehead (classic "split representation"), this figure has the *dissected or siamesed* representation. It has been split from the forehead down the face to the neck and the flesh spread outward, stretched, and folded back. The result is two half faces and attached bodies that are still "siamesed" by a shared navel roundel (Figure 7.14a).

In this view, the respective forearms extend forward from the half faces with gaping mouths. As usual, the shoulder joint is indicated by a roundel and the arm, bent inward, ends in long "claws." The siamesed figures sport huge vacant orbits that would have been filled with a gold

or white shell disc with a central punctation for the pupil (all of the other central roundel punctations would have been similarly adorned with incrustations). Each nostril has been drilled through, as have the central spaces between the hip and shoulder roundels, giving the intricate work an airy cutout effect (remember that all this carving was done *before* metal tools, with fire, sand abrasives, shell, and animal teeth—one still sees the abrasion lines that formed the outer lips of the split main figure!), a real tour de force of controlled power.

Next to the eye is the ear as an inverted "U" ending in a large ear spool roundel. Note that the geometric design below (Figure 7.15b) has the same "ear" motifs, vertically reflected, spacing large ear-spool roundels within a "nested" multiply outlined rectangular panel. Perhaps the lower "geometric" design is nothing but a schematic paraphrase of the "representational" design above!

The biwinged motifs below the ears and on either side of the shared belly button roundel are probably headdress elements moved by "arbitrary relocation," due to space constraints, from their normal position above the figure's heads (the headdress is a semicircular diadem like the Frog Lady's [see Figure 7.9h], only here it gives a "hunchbacked" appearance to the twins—perhaps Deminán Caracaracol). Above, near the top of the stool back, are the split rear legs ending in two feet, twisted and sole up. The soles reveal twin faces with five toe strands of hair (Figure 7.14b)! It is common in South Amerindian villages for villagers to recognize a man by his unique footprint, an impression that "calls up" his face (Gregor 1977), so naturally one wears faces on one's soles! The hip joints out of which the flexed legs emerge are roundels, as is the convention. Then, in the space where a tail should be, a dense nested square coil of ropelike lines that enmesh the entire bellies of these figures appears. When viewed full face after a 90-degree rotation, their highly flexed limbs give the impression of a frog (Figure 7.15b), the belly button roundel in correct "ventral" position and the head cocked to the side. Note that this meandering looped "rope" centers on the belly button itself (Figure 7.15a); hence my interpretation of it as the umbilical cord. Perhaps these "siamesed" figures are twins (and twin figures riddle Caribbean mythology as they do lowland South American tales), united by a shared umbilicus.

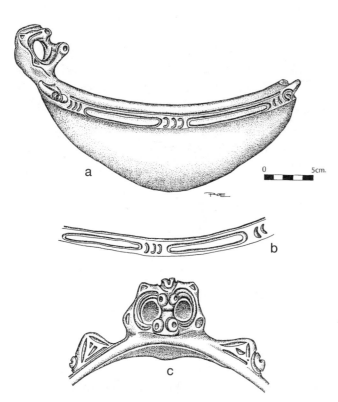

Figure 7.18 A Chican Ostionoid bat effigy bowl from the Dominican Republic. (a) The profile view ("tail" element broken off). (b) The above-carination/subrim design field of (a) with a band of geometric designs composed of elongated ovals alternating with "C" triple elements that are themselves translated thrice. See Figure 7.25e for its derivation. (c) An enlarged plan view of the bat's head—note the large oval "owl" eyes framed in appliqué "C" motifs to create ocular roundels and how they are flanked by miniature "wing" tabs with internal triangular incised motifs.

Thus, via the manipulation of symmetry operations (rotation, reflection) and nesting, we have a dense image indeed! (1) Using rotational imagery, we have two "frogs" joined at the navel (Figure 7.15b), one a vertically reflected mirror of the other (Figure 7.14a). (2) When we put the two "siamesed" visages and linked bodies together into a classic "split-representation," yet another dual representation emerges, a crawling quadruped not unlike the four-footed animal that supports the stool's seat, although with somewhat twisted limbs (Figure 7.15a). Last, (3) we have the most interesting representation (Figure 7.14b), a visually ambiguous *nested* kneeling human figure with a curious double head, arms upraised and hands held behind the dual head. The nipples of that figure are the upper roundels with the middle one his belly button roundel. Below that, symmetrically, the body sports two pelvic/buttock roundels and outspread legs, yoga style. The curious sole double head may signal a decapitated body since the foot soles could represent the palms of the upraised hands of a headless figure.

Alternatively, via anatropic imagery, one sees an inverted handstanding figure with bent elbows and long, theriomorphic claws, framing a staring frontal face, the lower two roundels its "eyes." Above, via x-ray depiction, one sees his belly roundel and then the twin roundels of his buttocks, his bent legs ending in twin foot soles that become bicephalic small heads.

There is even a third depiction "excavatable" within this medial figure. It is another reversible face composed of the large belly roundel as the "mouth" and the buttock roundels above its "eyes," with the upraised sole faces its "hair." These multiple central figures are perforated (here coded by diagonal lines), hence rendered "ethereal" via the passage of light, perhaps indicating that it is a ghost of a dead person. The Greater Antillean Taíno were already fighting the invading Caribs, and their own ancestors had taken heads (Roe 1991b), so perhaps this high-backed duho on which a victorious chief sat represented the soul of his defeated enemy? Being able to "lift" this central image right out of the nested peripheral images (what I have called a "background transformation" when it appears in geometric symmetry in cognate lowland styles [cf. Roe 1980]) is not only another case of concentric symmetry in figural designs but also an additional form of "visual dualism," cognate with all the other techniques investigated in this chapter. One artifact yields three, or possibly even five images, a dense visual "text" indeed!

If elite artifacts such as duhos as the cult objects carved in obdurate materials by men, are full of multiple images, women were no less capable of portraying complex imagery in their "gestational," additive medium of pottery. The pot itself is an animistic entity, coiled from the soft, pliable body of the serpent, hissing, in fermentation vessels, with the serpent's breath and capable of coiling and uncoiling when the Culture Heroes such as the Magical Twins need cooking vessels (Roe 1991b:93, on the cognate Guianan Waiwai). Hence "effigy vessels" abound, their orifices becoming the mouths or bellies of anthropomorphic (Figure 7.17a) and zoomorphic (Figure 7.18a) beings. Nor are these static creatures. They are but frozen as they slither around the pot, some with head twisted upward (Figure 7.24, for a lizard), or as an owl encircles in flight, in the same upper register of the carinated faintly ovoid, boat-shaped bowls that serve as the major form and design field for Chican Ostionoid pottery (Figures 7.19 and 7.20). Asymmetrical features, such as opposed dual handles placed diagonally at opposite corners of the vessels (Figure 7.19c), add a further rotational "kinetic effect" to these lively depictions.

Such vessels and the incised and modeled designs they bore are shadows on clay, as in Plato's Cave, of Species Paragons (the "Ideal Types" of each species lodged in Heaven), the natural symbols of myth. This World/Other World, Solar Bird/Lunar Bird, Male/Female, and other dyadic oppositions of this dualistic "cognitive style" confront and overlap categories to produce not only a preference for dual images, as in opposing adorno heads (Figure 7.4) or bodies, but also biglobular vessels that stack dual body segments (Figures 7.21 and 7.22), in the same way as the cosmos in which the artist lives superimposes platter or domelike worlds that hover, one above another, from Underworld to Earth and Sky World (Roe 1982:Figure 3). In emulation of this cosmic pattern, the encircling bands of the pot's design fields stack one above another in a material recapitulation of the macrocosm via the bi-globular ceramic "microcosm" (Figure 7.9f). Spirits (Crab Exemplars) hover in the upper band (Figure 7.9g) while

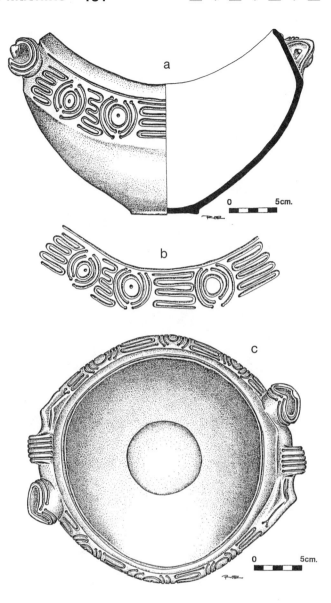

Figure 7.19 A Chican Ostionoid owl effigy bowl. (a) A split profile rendering. Since roundels indicate hip and shoulder joints in Taíno wood carving and ceramics, this effigy could be encoding complementary anatomical information with regard to the bird's jointed wings. The modeled, incised, and appliquéd head lug is to the left, and the incised, modeled, and appliquéd "rib cage" vertical "D"-shaped handle to the right. (b) Its above-carination incised design layout with a "geometric" array composed of roundels nested in concentric "C" motifs alternating with vertically compressed and laterally elongated meanders. See Figure 7.20c for its derivation. (c) The plan view of the same pot from the Fundación García-Arévalo in Santo Domingo, Dominican Republic. Bilateral symmetry is reserved for the body "rib cage" vertical incised "D"-shaped handles, as befits their technical function.

Figure 7.20 A frontal view of the owl effigy bowl in Figure 7.19 with the generation of its "abstract" and "geometric" incised designs of the above-carination design field, as a schematicized anatomy of the flying skeletal (hence ancestral) owl as "Herald of the Dead." (a) The "stylized" representational incised, modeled, and appliquéd "head" lug of the owl has huge staring eyes formed by nested "C" motifs delineating its characteristic goggled eyes. The vertically incised appliquéd "D"-shaped handle becomes the owl's rib cage while the appliquéd and modeled fillets behind the rib cage transform into the owl's dangling and trailing legs, the bones and taloned feet of which are denoted by medial incisions. The owl is flying, twisted on its side to fit into the space defined by the parallel bands of the above-carination field, with one wing forward and the other behind and trailing. (b) One owl redrawn to clarify its schematic union. (c) The dual derivational chains of roundels and meanders that together form the wing joints and primaries of the owls. (1) The "C"-shaped motif (2) bifold rotates in a vertical register (3) to generate a series of "C"s that partially internest. (4) They are translated. (5) They also alternate with paired vertical lines from yet another chain to form a design layout in Figure 7.22f. (6) Via the applications of a "merging rule" the respective upper and lower lines of proximate "C"s from step 2 (7) fuse into a single vertical meander. Then, by an "lateral elongation" and a "vertical compression" rule, a horizontally expanded and vertically compressed meander forms (8). It is then translated (9). As part of another (but related) chain, the "owl," the typical dual roundel (eye-orifice-joint indicator/ cover, (10 from Figure 7.9i is then subjected to a "nesting" rule yielding an additional enclosing circle (11). Then a "vertical and medial break" rule disarticulated the two encircling outer lines to produce a "split roundel" (12). Last, via a recursive application of the "alter-nation" rule, the end products from both derivational chains (the "split roundels" and the "compressed and expanded vertical meanders") combine to yield the "wing" elements (wing joints and wing primaries respectively) of the owl (b). Note that the bowl's carination line itself forms the lower edge of the wings while the upper incised subrim band produces the upper edge of the outstretched wings. Thus vessel form and surface decoration combine to yield stylized depictions of elegant simplicity and vigor.

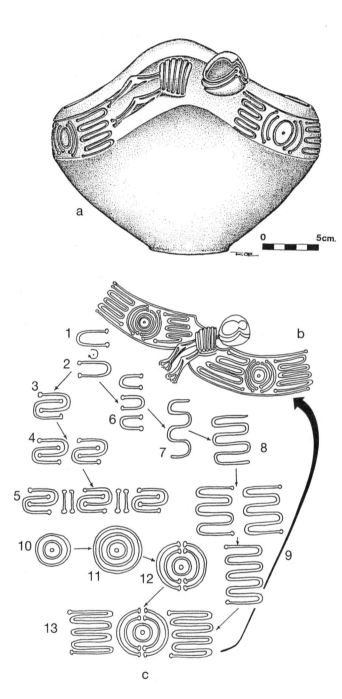

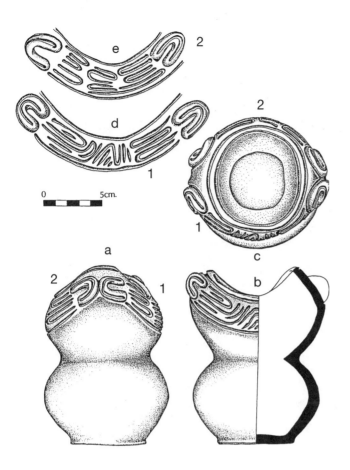

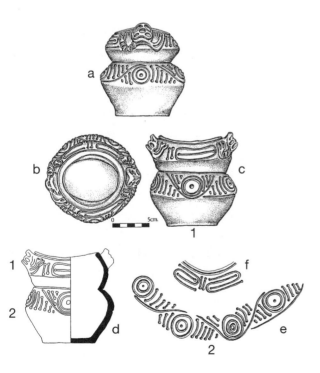

Figure 7.21 A small biglobular (dualistically stacked) Chican Ostionoid jar from La Cuchama (San Pedro de Macorís) in the Fundación García-Arévalo, Santo Domingo, Dominican Republic. It has vestiginal "C"-shaped handles that are the "split-representationally" derived transformations of the original Saladoid "D"-shaped handles that developed in the intermediary Elenan Ostionoid period (Figure 7.16). Here they appear again in the terminal Classic Taíno phase, tying the whole sequence together as an in situ development. (a) An end view of the vessel, showing the two vertically reflected "C"s of the vestigial appliquéd and modeled handle tabs as well as the two design panels, 1 and 2. (b) A cut-profile view of the biglobular pot. (c) A vertical (plan-view) perspective of the little vessel. (d) Design panel 1. (e) Design panel 2. Note that both are *not* identical and incorporate some asymmetric details. Nevertheless, these incised design layouts are derivations from the interdigitated chains depicted in Figure 7.20c13 with the "C"-shaped appliqué vestiginal handles acting like one side of the "split roundels" of the other vessel!

Figure 7.22 A detailed drawing of Figure 7.9f, showing all design fields and layouts. (a) And end view of this little biglobular vessel showing the anatropic were-crab adorno with its asymmetrical arms within an overall pattern of bilateral symmetry (life and dynamism within stasis). (b) A top view of the vessel. (c) A profile view of the pot; note how the vertical "pincers" of the were-crabs act as the framings "I"s of the upper register's elongated roundel with a medial horizontal line. (d) A vertical cross-sectional view of the vessel, *lower design filed:geometric::upper design field:representational*. (e) The lower design field with its roundel-and-flanking-triangle design layout. (f) The design layout panel from one side of the upper design field on one side of the jar. The design layout on the other side is different; the elongated roundel is visible in d-1. Thus, constant design innovation in linked derivation rules provide maximum visual stimulation and creativity.

their geometric stigmata undulate below them in the lower register. Tellingly, those same spirits with anatropically reversible heads only *appear* to be bilaterally symmetrical: their contrasting pincers (single/double) hint at the asymmetry (overlap) within the symmetrical (opposition) depiction. Thus, the dualism of these miniature ceramic worlds is not static, but dynamic and transformative just like the imagery of ritual or the symbolism of the verbal texts they annotated.

As this brief excursion shows, and contrary to the expectations of most students, the ancient ceramic and other arts of the Caribbean are *not* transparent to modern Western analysis. Images such as Figure 7.9a are easily misunderstood. Rather than displaying, as it does, a series of reversible faces, this elongated discontinuous labial flange appears to most viewers to be adorned with incised "geometric" decoration. Perhaps we are too used to dealing with styles like ours that portray positivists' paradises, where structure is obvious and analysis easy. Amerindians did not live in such sterile worlds or depict them in their art. A radically different worldview is reflected in these effigy pots, one of "Primitive Platonism," whereby visible reality is most emphatically *not* real and only the ideal world of the hallucinogenic vision (our "illusion") is "real." To quote a Yanomamö shaman from Venezuela, "The toucans of this world are distressingly ugly; only the others [of the Spirit World] are magnificent—they are as red as the blood in our veins and their breasts are covered with down" (Lizot 1985:104).

This ethereal world of the Spirit Masters-Mistresses is hidden and occult, accessible only to those brave enough to use hallucinogens. Psychotropic drugs are the shaman's path to these Spiritual Paragons, and the medicine man must be learned enough to penetrate their mysteries once he has arrived, bedraggled and afire, at these animal spirits' otherworldly homes. These are cultures, after all, in which, to quote a Jívaro (Achuar) example, infants must be introduced to the "true" world once they have proved themselves biologically viable by partaking in a small amount of the hallucinogen! The profane world of the senses is *not* the "real" world for Amerindians. This "radical dualism" informs everything in lowland and Antillean cultures, from the stylistic conventions and subject matter of Amerindian pictorial art to their oral mythology and even the basic details of

ecological interaction (Descola 1996). The chronicler as well as iconographic evidence in the Caribbean demonstrate that shamans there also used a hallucinogen, a snuff, *Anadenanthera peregrina,* Cohoba, similar to the *ebene* of the Yanomamö. Thus, the Taíno shared in this invisible but realer-than-real worldview.

If we as prehistorians pretend to approximate a truly "cultural archaeology" (rather than exclusively pursuing the "artifact physics" of merely counting and weighing potsherds), we must also make an effort to address the cognitive patterns of the ancient populations we study, no matter how difficult they are to access. We must start by treating Amerindian cognition as *une idée problématique,* not as a presupposition. We should expect to find these cognitive strategies expressed in radically different material constructions than those of our experience. After all, this was also a world (on the mainland of both Central and South America) where temples hid, via encasing, earlier temples, or where their facades were divided into *two* colors of stone, not just one, or where pots are adorned with two facing heads, not one. Something unique is going on, as profoundly dualistic as the verbal art of modern groups and protohistoric Antillean mythology but modeled and incised in clay or engraved into wood-bone-shell-stone.

The advantage of such a realization is that it reveals hidden aspects in ancient monuments or artifacts that everybody has been staring at for decades without ever really seeing, from unrecognized stylistic conventions, to misunderstood motifs, to iconographic figures misinterpreted, or not even seen, and to whole levels of imagery just not discussed. Archaeologists should not despair, however: the same myopia has afflicted ethnology, where even a great student like Lévi-Strauss (1981) saw one mytheme where nearly every major South Amerindian animal symbol really possesses two (Roe 1983b). That is, every mytheme (not just a selected set) is a "binary operator," projecting two overlapping aspects that oppose each other within each symbol. At the same time, each binary symbol overlaps with other apparently "contrasting" symbols on each end of their respective semantic ranges. Thus, the Owl we have discussed is *both* a wise shaman of the night and a fearsome herald of the Dead.

Anatropic imagery endures in bicephalic Saladoid-Ostionoid adornos by treating the mouth and the head crest in isomorphic ways, via encircling incision (Roe 1989a:Figure 19a). This simultaneously turns the head crest, once the lug is inverted, into another "mouth" of a second face. By Chican Ostionoid times, this "double punning" ran rampant on incised-and-modeled rim lugs. Again, there is no better illustration of this pattern than the small open bowl with horizontal tab handles (discontinuous labial flanges) drawn in Figure 7.9a. Each of the perforated tabs presents a veritable battery of dualistic pictorial devices and a "crowd" of jostling subjects, including "siamesed heads," whereby two profile heads are joined at the forehead by horizontal reflection. Thus, on both the exterior and interior of the tab handle two profile faces (Figure 7.9d2, 3) look outward in the same direction. They become recognizable once the pot is held vertically (the "kinetic" function again). Incised roundels, centering on the perforations, become their "eyes," complete with concentric incised "eyebrow" and "eye-bag" lines (Figure 7.9e). The half-circle incised mouths, with their bracketing incised "grimace lines" at their corners, hold simplified "faces" (Figure 7.9c). This image-within-an-image is another form of dualism. The eyes of the small encised faces "kenn," or present a visible "stock" or "frozen metaphor," for the tongue of the larger face of which it is a part. Lastly, a third (medial) simplified face (Figure 7.9d1) allows the whole image to be inverted 180 degrees to straddle two siamesed faces, thereby "transitively" generating a third face (Figure 7.9b). There is no better argument for treating the symmetry operations utilized in geometric and "planometric" representational images as one and the same than this involuted vessel.

Another dualistic device evident in this pottery is "terminal transformation," whereby each end of the same depiction turns into two different beings. For example, in Figure 7.6a, the rear quarters of the frog transform into a humanoid face (Figure 7.6a1), with incised lines forming the eyes and bridge of the nose). The roundel hip joints become this second being's nostrils, and the frog's back legs turn into the strings of hallucinogen-impregnated (and "impregnating" à la Deminán Caracaracol) snot hanging from the nostrils of this hallucinating spirit (Figure 7.6b).

Double "twin" figures share a belly roundel orifice in open Chican Ostionoid effigy bowls (Figure 7.17a). Meanwhile, on the subrim design field another expression of symmetrical dualism occurs. It is "interlocking," whereby design elements fit into each other in an open-ended syntax (Figure 7.17b, c).

Conversely, higher-order rules of "vertical" and "horizontal compression" and/or "horizontal expansion" deform these primitive "C" motifs into elongated oval "roundels," closed by deleting the protective dot finials and merging their shafts (Figure 7.18b). Representation and abstraction fuse where the large staring eyes of the bat (Figure 7.18a) become roundels framed by "C" motifs executed in appliqué, while its pointed "wings" turn into triangular motifs incised on flanking tabular lugs (7.18c). Thus, the modeled effigy recalls the two-dimensional incised central roundel and flanking triangles of a common geometric Classic Taíno layout (Figure 7.10a).

If these ceramic creatures are dualistic and multivalent, they are also "alive," frozen in movement around the design registers of the pots they inhabit. To decipher this kinetic aspect, one must take another lesson from related living lowland Guianan Indians such as the Cariban Waiwai. Myths of the origins of designs affirm that what looks like simple geometric figures in twill-weave Waiwai baskets (mere "decorative pattern" to Western eyes) are actually highly "representational" copies of the skin markings on the "reluctant donor" of all designs, the *Urufiri* Dragon (a composite anaconda form of the "feathered serpent" spanning Central and South America; Roe 1989b).

The same "representational core" of geometric patterning appears relevant for ceramic incisions in the ancient Antilles. Roundels, as I have argued above, frequently indicate hip and shoulder joints in Chican Ostionoid wood carving and ceramics (Figure 7.14b). Polysemically, they may also indicate eyes, since in Guiana joints are the "eyes" of the body (to repeat, one "enters," that is, disarticulates, a body via its joints; therefore they are portals = eyes of the torso). If so, the vertical compressed and elongated meanders of a Chican Ostionoid owl effigy pot (Figure 7.19a) are seen as feathers (wing primaries) extending out of wing joints, represented as concentric circle joint eyes (Figure 7.19b).

Thus, kinetic features and pictorial dualism combine as *two* owls "fly" around the above-carination design field (Figure 7.20a). The projecting head lugs are

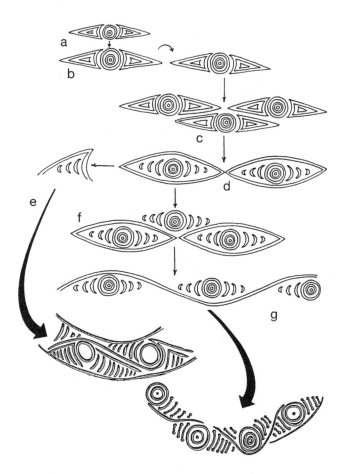

Figure 7.23 A series of derivational chains that explore the "roundel and flanking triangles" kernel statement of the Chican Ostionoid (Taíno) style of incision. (a) The kernel itself, from Figure 7.9h, the "belly button and interbreast and pubic triangle" design of the Frog Lady. (b) The kernel is vertically reflected to produce the layout in Figure 7.9i. (c) Then the kernel is bifold-rotated to yield the staggered design layout shown in Figure 7.10a. Next, a "deletional" rule is applied to the ends of the projecting "horns" of the concave-faced flanking triangles, thus opening the lines for a "merging rule" that connects them into a lozenge-shaped surround for the now-nested central roundel (d). Meanwhile, another deletion rule removes the angled lines in the flanking triangles, leaving the concave "C"s in diminishing sizes, now floating "free inside the lozenge cartouche. (e) Another design "vector," or line of formal possibility, wherein the floating "c"s and angled surround become a triangle, essentially by deleting the lower line of the cartouche. This the design layout of Figure 7.24a. (f) The roundel designs are bifold-rotated. (g) The middle lozenge lines are then fused via a deletion and merging rule to produce an undulating design (the layout of Figure 7.22E2) and another deletion rule removes the central dot of the roundel, thus generating the final layout in Figure 7.24a, b.

not located horizontally across from each other (surmounting their "rib-cage" bodies that are represented as vertically incised "D"-shaped handles, which must occupy opposite sides due to their technical function). Rather, they are oriented at 45-degree angles at some distance from those handles, giving a distinct kinetic effect to the pot when viewed from above (Figure 7.19c). They provide the clockwise flight path of the nocturnal raptors whose calls herald the arrival of death spirits at night. As *malagueros,* they must be chased off by even modern rural people in the Greater Antilles.

The right wing of these circling owls is stretched out in a trailing fashion (Figure 7.20b) behind its dangling legs; talons end in Y-shaped incisions with dot finials. The fluted handle of the pot becomes the owl's rib cage while above it the owl's head is the projecting lug, with eye-ear feather roundels indicated by a binocular concavity and its beak by concave incised lines. Ahead, the owl's left wing extends outward, the meanders again forming its flight feathers and the concentric roundel-eye its wing joint. The paired owls circle ceaselessly around the vessel, animating and imbuing it with power. Everywhere in the lowlands, the owl was a spiritual bird and, due to its nocturnal eyesight, one of the shaman's wisest and most powerful doubles.

All of the "geometric" two-dimensional incised designs on this owl effigy pot complement the three-dimensional modeled "representational" elements and derive from them. The "C" motifs of the owl's concentric facial feathers merge into compressed meanders, which now morph into the bird's wing primaries, by symmetry rules (Figure 7.20c1–13), while nesting of the same elements produces the wing "joints" themselves, as "split roundels" (Figure 7.20c12). The two separate ends of both related derivational chains, roundels and meanders, are then combined via an alternation rule to yield the "decorative" subrim design layout, which really sketches the owl's stylized wings projecting outward from its modeled body and head.

In sum, this two- and three-dimensional "decoration" obeys the same rules of symmetry as "functional" elements such as handles did in the preceding Elenan Ostionoid period (Figure 7.16). The "D"-shaped handles of the Saladoid become the "C"-shaped vestiginal tab handles of the Elenan and Chican Ostionoid (Figure

7.16a-c) via the symmetry operation of "split representation." Elsewhere, that device applies to "representational" designs, just as does its inverse, "siamesing" (Figures 7.14 and 7.15). Then these "sculptural" elements act the part of incised "C" motifs bordering purely planar incised designs that again represent compressed meanders produced by "C" motif fusion (Figure 7.21d-e).

Significantly, these permutations appear on dual-segment pots whose stacked body components metaphorically recall the superimposed platter worlds that the owl and bat fly through. These biglobular vessel designs (Figures 7.21 and 7.22) split the pot vertically just as the symmetrical/asymmetrical appliquéd adornos that occupy their upper registers split the vessel dualistically into horizontal halves (Figure 7.22a). Moreover, syntax is operative here that always gives priority to the vertical "heavenly" realms over the lower "terrestrial and subaquatic" realms just as it does in the cosmology. Note that *upper register:stylized representational designs::lower register:geometric abstract designs* (Figure 7.22c).

The planar incised designs (Figure 7.22e, f) are derived from a grammar (Figure 7.23) that yields an undulating line punctuated by roundels (Figure 7.23a–d) and triangles (Figure 7.23e) filled with conformationally nested "C" motifs that are, themselves, transforms of the same "C" designs that once originated in the eye and joint roundels of the "critters" they embellish.

Thus, the undulating incised "abstract" line becomes the slithering appliquéd body of a stylized lizard that snakes around the same register of another effigy bowl (Figure 7.24a). Its two-dimensional designs alternate triangles and roundels as recombinatorial substitutes for each other just as their grammatical derivations independently confirm. The "D"-shaped handles, earlier mounted singly and vertically to indicate an effigy's rib cage, are now paired and oriented horizontally to represent the lizard's hind legs (Figure 7.24b1–2).

Alternation, as in the interdigitation of "C" elements in the "O" geometric designs (Figure 7.25e), represents the same dualism as the stacking of two pottery vessel segments or the pairing of two adornos. It may be combined with both "interlocking" (Figure 7.25d) and "nesting" (Figure 7.25l) as well as the more

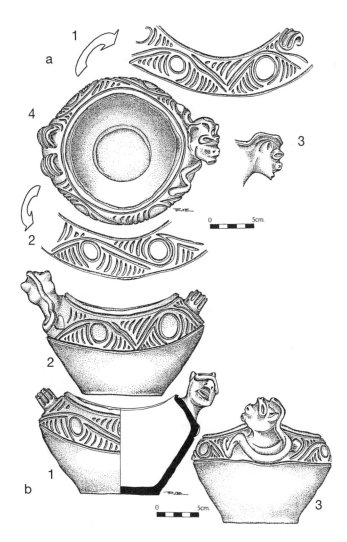

Figure 7.24 A small Chican Ostionoid crested lizard effigy vessel from the Museo del Hombre Dominicano in Santo Domingo, Dominican Republic. (a) A plan view of the lizard, whose belly roundel is now the open orifice of the bowl, marked, as always, by an encircling outside line. The head of the lizard is modeled and the sinuous body is appliquéd. The horizontal appliquéd and incised "D"-shaped handles become the lizard's rear feet. (1) The above-carination, subrim design field roundel and flanking triangle design layout from one side of the vessel. (2) The geometric layout from the other side of the vessel. (3) A profile view of the lizard's head. Again, note that the designs are *not* perfectly identical. These designs have lost their central roundel dot via a deletion rule. (b) Three more views of the lizard effigy vessel. (1) A vertical cross-section drawing of the vessel's "front." (2) The "back" of the vessel. (3) An end view of the pot centering on the lizard's head and front limbs and body.

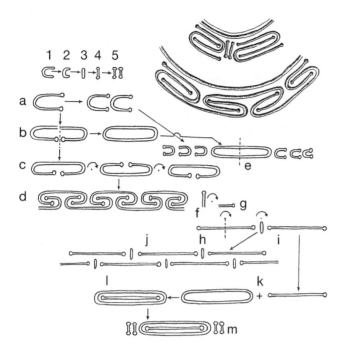

Figure 7.25 The ancient "C"-shaped motif derivational chains dating to the Huecan Saladoid initial invasion (Figure 7.11a and 7.12a) but now applied to the end of the sequence 2,000 years later. (a) The full elongated "C" with dot finials of the Chicoid terminus of this evolution. (1) The application of a deletion rule that removes the dot finials and shortens the "C"s. (2) A horizontal compression rule that further shortens the horizontal extensions of the "C." (3) Extreme horizontal compression that converts the vertical segment of the "C" into an "I" via the deletion of the forward-projecting "arms" of the initial "C." (4) The addition of the dot finial to the "I." (5) Translation of this motif produces a set of two "I"s. (b) The original elongated "C" with dot finials can be translated to yield a series of directional "C"s. (c) The "C"s may also be bifold rotated to create an enclosed elongated roundel via both merging and deletion rules, (d) and then interlocked, producing the layout of Figure 7.17c. (e) In yet another aligned vector we can combine, via the alternation rule, the translated "C"s and the elongated oval to produce the design layout in Figure 7.18b. (f) To pursue yet another vector, we can take the "I" and rotate it 90 degrees (g). Then, via alternation, we can insert a single vertical "I" to yield an alternating horizontal "dash" and vertical "dot" design layout. By applying a "glide-reflection" rule, we can produce the two-registered layout of Figure 7.6d. Or we can take the same "I" and, via another nesting rule, place it inside a horizontally elongated roundel (l), and with a last alternation rule (m), we can interdigitate it with the paired vertical "I"s to generate the design layout in Figure 7.22c.

dynamic motifs placed in "glide reflection" (Figure 7.25j) to animate the surface of these little portable and utilitarian sculptures. Writ small and in a plastic medium and executed by women, these pots share the same designs and symbolism as the large immobile sculpture and petroglyphs produced by men in the obdurate materials of stone-bone-wood-shell.

It is significant that these most elaborate symmetrical images appear at the end of this 2,000-year saga of in situ political and social evolution. Such multiple images-in-one could only have been decoded by a cognoscenti audience that would have rivaled that of the small kingdoms on the mainland. These objects represent the pinnacle of craftsmanship and artistry in the Caribbean, authored by and for the elites of a complex chiefdom that was, perhaps, on its way to state status had not the Caribs and the Spanish interfered.

The Ghost in the Machine: Conclusions

I hope this chapter, in its 2,000-year romp through Greater Antillean prehistory, has shown, what to etic-oriented Euro-American analysts may look like contentless "geometric" designs are as full of both mythic and cosmic meanings as the "representational" designs that tend to be ignored in symmetry analysis. Not only do the same morphological and syntactical rules govern both classes of designs, but one can derive the geometric from the representational or the representational from the geometric. Moreover, symmetry is not even restricted to designs: the components of vessel shape in ceramics can also go through similar derivational chains and interact with either stylized or abstract designs (by providing bordering lines) just as representational elements can take the place of geometric elements within abstract layouts (arms acting like vertical alternating "I" motifs) on those vessels.

Similarly, the "structural" and "functional" parts of pots (handles and tabs) not only morph into representational effigy adornos, but also go through the same transformational operations as surface decoration (split representation, siamesing). Thus, these pots are not simple Western "containers," but little pieces of "functional sculpture." They are living beings that consume liquids and solid foods via their mouths, hold them in their bellies, and dispense them, and hallucinogens, through their feet.

These artifacts and their symmetric embellishments are all surface representations of a deep structure of ideational dualism that has its roots firmly in shamanic animism and the ritual use of hallucinogens. Psychotropic plants are used to see the "other world" of perfect and eternal symmetry as well as the visible "imperfect" world of asymmetry, growth, and death.

Yet this dualism is not static Western binary opposition, but a dynamic and shape-shifting perspective where figure and ground, symmetry and asymmetry dance together in a beautiful ballet of form and meaning. Just as bilaterally symmetrical elements include asymmetric details (e.g., an appliqué were-crab adorno's contrasting "pincers"; Figure 7.9g), so too do dual versions of the same symmetric layout differ from one side of the vessel to the other. Lastly, what at first sight might look like sloppy renditions of symmetrical designs, producing local asymmetries, may not be unintentional "mistakes" (Figure 7.21d, e). Rather, they may be added to give life to inert vessels.

Even the incised images on large and ponderous river boulder petroglyphs or ballpark "menhir" petroglyphs are not static images, but living beings that come alive via inversion and rotation. They hide one design "encisted" within another just as they reveal, through x-ray depiction, their symmetric bones within the transparent shell of their stylized bodies (Figure 7.9h–i). Such figures participate in "cross-media isomorphism" with designs on humbler media such as pottery, incorporating symmetry into their bodies and faces. Thus, the "geometric" or "abstract" designs are but "shorthand" symbols for the stylized icons themselves. This means that geometric shapes are not simple forms. They stand for living and breathing, albeit ethereal, beings via the stigmata of their bones and skin.

Hence, in ancient Antillean art (as in cognate South Amerindian ethnoaesthetics) there is no "form" without "decoration," no "abstraction" without "representation," no "visibility" without "invisibility," no "symmetry" without "asymmetry." We must embrace the symmetrical principles held within "planar stylized" figures, the planometric overlap category between "geometric" and "realistic" designs. We must also study the symmetry operations evident in purely "geometric" or "nonrepresentational" designs if our reconstructions are to pretend to be any

approximation, no matter how crude and ethnocentric, of the alien world the earliest Europeans stumbled upon in 1492, which continues to elude their descendants down to the turning of this new millennium. ■

References Cited

Alegría, R. E.

1978   *Apuntes en torno a la mitología de los indios taínos de las Antillas Mayores y sus orígenes suramericanos.* Centro de Estudios Avanzados de Puerto Rico y el Caribe, San Juan.

1983   *Ball Courts and Ceremonial Plazas in the West Indies.* Yale University Publications in Anthropology No. 79. Department of Anthropology, Yale University, New Haven.

Anderson, R. L.

1990   *Calliope's Sisters: A Comparative Study of Philosophies of Art.* Prentice Hall, Englewood Cliffs, NJ.

Arrom, J. J.

1986   Fray Ramón Pané o el rescate de un mundo mítico. *La Revista del Centro de Estudios Avanzados de Puerto Rico y el Caribe* 3:2–8.

Blake, P.

1964   It May Be Art, but It Won't Cut Cheese. *New York Magazine* July:64–66.

Boas, F.

1955   [1927] *Primitive Art.* Dover, New York.

Bourne, E. G.

1906   Columbus, Ramón Pané and the Beginnings of American Anthropology. *Proceedings of the American Antiquarian Society,* n.s. 17:310–348.

Carneiro, R. L.

1974   Slash-and-Burn Cultivation among the Kuikuru and Its Implications for Cultural Development in the Amazon Basin. In *Native South Americans: Ethnology of the Least Known Continent,* edited by P. J. Lyon, pp. 73–91. Little, Brown, Boston.

Chanlatte Baik, L. A.

1981   La Hueca y Sorcé (Vieques, Puerto Rico): *Primeras migraciones agroalfareras Antillanas.* Santo Domingo, Puerto Rico.

1994   El inciso entrecruzado y las primeras migraciones agroalfareras antillanas. *Boletín del Museo del Hombre Dominicano* 20(26):41–55.

Cosme, R.

1983   *La cultura Huecoide.* Ms. on file, Department of Anthropology, University of Delaware, Newark, DL.

Crocker, W. H.

1983   Ultimate Reality and Meaning for the Ramkómekra-Canela, Eastern Timbira, Brazil: A Triadic Dualistic Cognitive Pattern. *Journal of Ultimate Reality and Meaning* 6(2):84–111.

Deive, C. E.

1976   Fray Ramón Pané y el nacimiento de la etnografía americana. *Boletín del Museo del Hombre Dominicano* 6:133–156.

Descola, P.

1996   *The Spears of Twilight: Life and Death in the Amazon Jungle.* Translated by J. Lloyd. New Press, New York.

Duprat, J. P.

1974   Les themes de décoration de la poterie Arawak. *Proceedings of the Fifth International Congress for the Study of Pre-Columbian Cultures of the Lesser Antilles,* pp. 72–81. Antigua, 1973.

García Arévalo, M. A.

1997   The Bat and the Owl: Nocturnal Images of Death. In *Taíno: Precolumbian Art and Culture from the Caribbean,* edited by F. Bercht et al., pp. 112–123. Monacelli Press, New York.

Gjessing, G.

1969   Comments on A. W. Wolfe, Social Structural Bases of Art. *Current Anthropology* 10:34–35.

González Colón, J.

1989   *Tibes: Un Centro Ceremonial Indígena.* Unpublished Master's thesis, Centro de Estudios Avanzados de Puerto Rico y el Caribe, Old San Juan, Puerto Rico.

Gregor, T.

1977   *Mehinaku: The Drama of Daily Life in a Brazilian Indian Village.* University of Chicago Press, Chicago.

Guss, D. M.

1989   *To Weave and to Sing: Art, Symbol, and Narrative in the South American Rain Forest.* University of California Press, Berkeley and Los Angeles.

Haddon, A. C.

1884   *The Decorative Art of British New Guinea.* Dublin, Ireland.

Hernández Rivera, V.

1983   *Analisis de diseños de la cerámica de la cultura Igneri (Saladoide) de Puerto Rico.* Ms. on file, Department of Anthropology, University of Delaware, Newark, DL.

Holm, B.

1965   *Northwest Coast Indian Art: An Analysis of Form.* University of Washington Press, Seattle and London.

Jiménez Lambertus, A.

1972   Design Analysis Section of Marcio Veloz Maggiolo's Resumen tipológico de los complejos relacionables con Santo Domingo—unattributed in the article. *Boletín del Museo del Hombre Dominicano* 1:47–56, Figures 1–10.

1983   Las dos partes de la relación acerca de las antigüedades de los indios, de Fray Ramón Pané. *Boletín del Museo del Hombre Dominicano* 11(18):141–146.

Kaplan, A.

1964   *The Conduct of Inquiry: Methodology for Behavioral Science.* Chandler, San Francisco.

Lathrap, D. W.

1970   A *Formal Analysis of Shipibo-Conibo Pottery and Its Implications for Studies of Panoan Prehistory.* Paper presented at the 35th Annual Meeting of the Society for American Archaeology, Mexico City, Mexico.

Lévi-Strauss, C.

1967   Split Representation in the Art of Asia and America. In *Structural Anthropology,* translated by C. Jacobson and B. Grundfest Schoepf, pp. 239–263. Doubleday, Anchor Books, Garden City, NJ.

1981   *The Naked Man: Introduction to a Science of Mythology 4.* Translated by J. and D. Weightman. Harper & Row, New York.

Link, C.

1975   *Japanese Cabinetmaking: A Dynamic System of Decisions and Interactions in a Technical Context.* Unpublished Ph.D. dissertation, Department of Anthropology, University of Illinois, Urbana-Champaign.

Linné, S.

1925   *The Techniques of South American Ceramics.* Vetenskapsoch Vitterhets-Samhälles, Handlingar, Fjärde Földjen, Band 29, No. 5., Göteborgs Kungl.

Lizot, J.

1985   *Tales of the Yanomamï: Daily Life in the Venezuelan Forest.* Translated by E. Simon. Cambridge University Press, New York.

López-Baralt, M.

1977   *El mito Taíno: raíz y proyecciones en la amazonía continental.* Ediciones Huracán, Río Piedras, San Juan, Puerto Rico.

Maquet, J.

1971   *Introduction to Aesthetic Anthropology.* A McCaleb Module in Anthropology, Addison-Wesley, Reading, PA.

Maíz López, E. J.

1983   *El análisis de la decoración incisa rellena con pintura y el 'Cross-Hatch' en el estilo Hacienda Grande de Puerto Rico.* Ms. on file, Department of Anthropology, University of Delaware, Newark, DL.

Mattioni, M.

1968   Symbolisme de la Decoration des Poteries Arawak. *Proceedings of the Second Congress of the International Association for Caribbean Archaeology,* pp. 69–80, Barbados, 1967.

Miller, D.

1985   *Artefacts as Categories: A Study of Ceramic Variability in Central India.* Cambridge University Press, Cambridge, UK.

Oliver, J. R.

1992   *The Caguana Ceremonial Center: A Cosmic Journey Through Taíno Spatial & Iconographic Symbolism.* Paper presented at the X Symposio Internacional, Asociación de Literaturas Indígenas Latinoamericanas (LAILA/AILA), Old San Juan, Puerto Rico.

1998   *El Centro Ceremonial del Caguana, Puerto Rico: Simbolismo, Iconografía, Cosmovisión y el Poderío Casiquil Taíno de Borinquen.* British Archaeological Reports (B.A.R.), International Series 727. Archaeopress, Oxford, UK.

Ortíz Montañez, H.

1993   *Razgos distintivos del estilo Santa Elena del sitio arqueológico "Ojo del Buey" Dorado, Puerto Rico.* Unpublished Master's thesis, Centro de Estudios Avanzados de Puerto Rico y el Caribe, Old San Juan, Puerto Rico.

Ostapkowicz, J. M.

1997   To Be Seated with "Great Courtesy and Veneration": Contextual Aspects of the Taíno Duho. In *Taíno: Precolumbian Art and Culture from the Caribbean,* edited by F. Bercht et al., pp. 56–67. Monacelli Press, New York.

Pané, Fray Ramón

1974   *Relación de acerca de las antigüedades de los indios.* Edited by J. J. Arrom, Siglo Veintiuno, México, DF.

1992   *Relació sobre les antiguitats dels indis.* Edited by J. J. Arrom, Generalitat de Catalunya, Comissió Amèrica i Catalunya, Barcelona.

1999   *An Account of the Antiquities of the Indians.* Edited by J. J. Arrom, translated by S. C. Griswold. Duke University Press, Durham, NC.

Pérez de Silva, M., and A. de Hostos

1981   [1939] *Aplicaciones industriales del diseño indígena de Puerto Rico/Industrial Applications of Indian Decorative Motifs of Puerto Rico.* Translated by I. M. de Gallardo. Instituto de Cultura Puertorriqueña, San Juan, Puerto Rico.

Petitjean Roget, H.

1976a   Note sur le motif de la grenouille dans l'art Arawak des Petites Antilles. *Proceedings of the Sixth International Congress for the Study of the Pre-columbian Cultures of the Lesser Antilles,* pp. 177–182. Pointe à Pitre, Guadeloupe, 1975.

1976b   Le theme de la Chauve-Souris Frugivore dans l'art Arawak des Petits Antilles. *Proceedings of the Sixth International Congress for the Study of the Pre-Columbian Cultures of the Lesser Antilles,* pp. 182–186. Pointe à Pitre, Guadeloupe, 1975.

1978   *L'art des Arawak et des Caraibes de la decoration des ceramiques.* Centre d'ètudes régionales Antilles-Guyane. Fort de France, Martinique.

Pons de Alegría, C. A.

1983   *Un análisis de los diseños saladoides.* Ms. on file, Department of Anthropology, University of Delaware, Newark, DL.

1993   *El diseño pintado de la cerámica saladoide de Puerto Rico.* Colección de Estudios Puertorriqueños, San Juan, Puerto Rico.

Raymond, J. S., W. R. DeBoer, and P. G. Roe

1975   *Cumancaya: A Peruvian Ceramic Tradition. Occasional Papers 2.* Department of Archaeology, University of Calgary, Canada.

Rivera Fontán, J. A.

1983   *Análisis de diseños geométricos en la cerámica saladoide de la colección del Instituto de Cultura Puertorriqueña.* Ms. on file, Department of Anthropology, University of Delaware, Newark, DL.

Robinson, L. S., E. R. Lundberg, and J. B. Walker

1985   *Archaeological Data Recovery at El Bronce, Puerto Rico: Final Report, Phase 2.* Submitted to the U.S. Army Corps of Engineers, Jacksonville District. Ms. on file, Office of the State Historic Preservation Officer, San Juan, Puerto Rico.

Roe, P. G.

1974   *A Further Exploration of the Rowe Chavín Seriation and Its Implications for North Central Coast Chronology.* Studies in Pre-Columbian Art and Archaeology Vol. 13. Dumbarton Oaks Research Library and Collections, Trustees for Harvard University, Washington, DC.

1980   Art and Residence among the Shipibo Indians of Peru: A Study in Microacculturation. *American Anthropologist* 82:42–71.

1982   *The Cosmic Zygote: Cosmology in the Amazon Basin.* Rutgers University Press, New Brunswick, NJ.

1983a   *Mythic Substitution and the Stars: Aspects of Shipibo and Quechua Etnoastronomy Compared.* Paper presented at the 1st International Conference on Ethnoastronomy, Washington, DC.

1983b   Review of *The Naked Man,* by C. Lévi-Strauss. *American Anthropologist* 85:686–687.

1985   *Fiwa's Tales: Waiwai Mythology in Comparative Perspective.* Ms. on file, Centro de Investigaciones Indígenas de Puerto Rico, San Juan, Puerto Rico.

1989a   A Grammatical Analysis of Cedrosan Saladoid Vessel Form Categories and Surface Decoration: Aesthetic and Technical Styles in Early Antillean Ceramics. In *Early Ceramic Population Lifeways and Adaptive Strategies in the Caribbean,* edited by P. E. Siegel, pp. 267–382. British Archaeological Reports International Series, Oxford, England.

1989b   Of Rainbow Dragons and the Origins of Designs: The Waiwai Urufiri and the Shipibo Ronin ëhua. *Latin American Indian Literatures Journal* 5(1):1–67.

1990   The Language of the Plumes: "Implicit Mythology" in Shipibo, Cashinahua and Waiwai Feather Adornments. In *L.A.I.L. Speaks! Selected Papers from the Seventh International Symposium, Albuquerque, 1989,* edited by M. H. Preuss, pp. 105–136, Plates A-F. Labyrinthos Press, Culver City, CA.

1991a   The Petroglyphs of Maisabel: A Study in Methodology. *Comptes Rendus des Communications du Douzième Congrès International d'Archeologie de la Caraïbe,* pp. 317–370. Cayenne, Guyane Française, 1987.

1991b   The Best Enemy Is a Killed, Drilled, and Decorative Enemy: Human Corporeal Art (Frontal Bone Pectorals, Belt Ornaments, Carved Humeri and Pierced Teeth) in Pre-Colombian Puerto Rico. *Proceedings of the 13ᵗʰ International Congress for Caribbean Archaeology,* Netherlands Antilles. Part 2, pp. 854–873. Reports of the Archaeological-Anthropological Institute of the Netherlands Antilles, No. 9, Curaçao, 1989.

1993   Cross-Media Isomorphisms in Taíno Ceramics and Petroglyphs from Puerto Rico. *Proceedings of the Fourteenth Congress of the International Association for Caribbean Archaeology,* pp. 637–671. St. Ann's Garrison, St. Michael, Barbados, 1991.

1994a   Ethnology and Archaeology: Symbolic and Systemic Disjunction or Continuity? In *A History of Latin American Archaeology,* edited by A. Oyuela-Caycedo, pp. 183–208. World Archaeology Series, Aldershot, Avebury, England.

1994b   Impossible Marriages: Animal Seduction Tales among the Shipibo Indians of the Peruvian Jungle. *Journal of Latin American Lore* 16(2): 131–173.

1995a   Style, Society, Myth and Structure. In *Style, Society, and Person,* edited by C. Carr and J. E. Neitzel, pp. 27–76. Plenum, New York.

1995b   *Arts of the Amazon,* edited by B. Braun. Thames & Hudson, London and New York.

1995c   Pictorial Dualism: Some Thoughts on the Iconography of Chavín, San Agustín and Chican Ostionoid. Paper presented at the 60th Annual Meeting of the Society for American Archaeology, Minneapolis.

1995d   Eternal Companions: Amerindian Dogs from Tierra Firma to the Antilles. *Actas del XV Congreso Internacional de Arqueología del Caribe, San Juan, Puerto Rico,* pp. 155–172. Centro de Estudios Avanzados de Puerto Rico y el Caribe, La Fundación Puertorriqueña de las Humanidades and la Universidad del Turabo, San Juan, Puerto Rico, 1993.

1996   Estilo artístico e identidad étnica entre los Shipibo y los mestizos de la montaña peruana. In *Tramas de la Identidad,* edited by J. J. Klor de Alba, G. H. Gossen, M. León Portilla, and M. Gutiérrez Estévez, pp. 343–408. De Palabra y Obra en el Nuevo Mundo Series, vol. 4. Siglo Veintiuno, Madrid and Mexico City, 1995.

1997a   Just Wasting Away: Taíno Shamanism and Concepts of Fertility. In *Taíno: Precolumbian Art and Culture from the Caribbean,* edited by F. Bercht, E. Brodsky, J. A. Farmer, and D. Taylor, pp. 124–157. Monacelli Press, New York.

1997b   The Museo Pigorini Zemí: The Face of Life/The Face of Death. In *Taíno: Precolumbian Art and Culture from the Caribbean,* edited by F. Bercht, E. Brodsky, J. A. Farmer, and D. Taylor, pp. 164–169. Monacelli Press, New York.

1999   Utilitarian Sculpture: Pictorial Kinesics and Dualism in Dominican Republic Chican Ostionoid Pottery. *Actes du XVI Congrés International D' Archeologie De La Caraïbe,* Basse Terre, Guadeloupe, pp. 272–291. Conseil Régional de la Guadeloupe, Mission Archéologique et du Patrimoine, 1995.

2000a   Miniature Worlds: Technology and Stylistic Innovation in Shipibo Pottery, the Peruvian Montaña. Paper presented at the 65th Annual Meeting of the Society for American Archaeology, Philadelphia.

2000b   The Tello Obelisk: A Lowland Pleiades Calendar for Highland Chavín. Paper presented at the Ancient Skywatchers Symposium, the Albert Einstein Planetarium, Air and Space Museum, Smithsonian Institution, Washington, DC.

2000c   *Jardines de Loiza: Analysis of the Ceramic Component.* Prepared for Ing. J. González Colón, Ponce, Puerto Rico.

2004   At Play in the Fields of Symmetry: Design Structure and Shamanic Therapy in the Upper Amazon. In *Symmetry Comes of Age,* edited by D. Washburn and D. W. Crowe. University of Washington Press, Seattle, pp 232–303.

Roe, P. G., A. G. Pantel, and M. B. Hamilton

1990   Monserrate Restudied: The 1978 Centro Field Season at Luquillo Beach: Excavation Overview, Lithics and Physical Anthropological Remains. *Actas del Unidécimo Congreso Internacional de Arqueología del Caribe, San Juan,* pp. 338–369. La Fundación Arqueológica, Antropológica e Histórica de Puerto Rico, La Universidad de Puerto Rico, U.S. Department of Agriculture, Forest Service, San Juan, 1985.

Roe, P. G., and J. Rivera Meléndez

1999   Recent Advances in Recording, Dating and Interpreting Puerto Rican Petroglyphs. *Actes du XVI Congrés International D' Archeologie De La Caraïbe,* Basse Terre, Guadeloupe, pp. 444–461. Conseil Régional de la Guadeloupe, Mission Archéologique et du Patrimoine, Basse Terre, 1995.

Roe, P. G., J. Rivera Meléndez, and P. DeScioli

1997   The Cueva de Mora (Comerío, PR) Pictographs and Petroglyphs: A Documentary Project. Paper presented at the 17th International Congress of Caribbean Archaeology, Nassau, Bahamas.

Rouse, I.

1941   *Culture of the Ft. Liberté Region, Haiti.* Publications in Anthropology 24. Yale University Press, New Haven.

1952   *Porto Rican Prehistory: Introduction; Excavations in the West and North.* Scientific Survey of Puerto Rico and the Virgin Islands, vol. 18, parts 3, 4. New York Academy of Science, New York.

1992   *The Taínos: The Rise and Fall of the People Who Greeted Columbus.* Yale University Press, New Haven and London.

Salazar, T.

1990   El diseño taíno y su integración en los proyectos artesanales. *Boletín del Museo del Hombre Dominicano* 17(23):129–140.

Schieffelin, E. L.

1976   *The Sorrow of the Lonely and the Burning of the Dancers.* St. Martin's Press, New York.

Stevens-Arroyo, A. M.

1988   *Cave of the Jagua: The Mythological World of the Taínos.* University of New Mexico Press, Albuquerque.

Vega de Boyrie, B.

1987   *Arte neotaíno.* Pamphlet. Fundación Cultural Dominicana, Santo Domingo, Dominican Republic.

Versteeg, A. H.

1992   Introduction. In *The Archaeology of St. Eustatius: The Golden Rock Site,* edited by A. H. Versteeg and K. Schinkel, pp. 3–13. St. Eustatius Historical Foundation No. 2; Foundation for Scientific Research in the Caribbean Region No. 131. St. Eustatius, Netherlands Antilles and Amsterdam.

Walker, J. B.

1997   Taíno Stone Collars, Elbow Stones, and Three-Pointers. In *Taíno: Precolumbian Art and Culture from the Caribbean,* edited by F. Bercht, E. Brodsky, J. A. Farmer, and D. Taylor, pp. 80–91. Monacelli Press, New York.

Wilson, S. M.

1997   The Taíno Social and Political Order. In *Taíno: Precolumbian Art and Culture from the Caribbean,* edited by F. Bercht, E. Brodsky, J. A. Farmer, and D. Taylor, pp. 46–55. Monacelli Press, New York.

CHAPTER EIGHT

Symmetry for Itself, for Culture, and for Practice

F. Allan Hanson

A PREMIERE CHALLENGE FACING THE anthropologist who addresses symmetry is how to interpret it. The problem can be approached in at least three ways. Symmetry can be analyzed in terms of, first, its universal properties and appeal, as aesthetic form in its own right; second, in terms of its cultural meaning in the particular art traditions that employ it; and third, in terms of its role in the ongoing praxis of cultural life, particularly the relation between culture as a system and the minds of the individuals who practice and reproduce it.

Symmetry Has Universal Aesthetic Appeal

By definition, representational art represents something and nonrepresentational art does not. Any analysis of representational objects includes identification of what they represent, but few analyses of representational art stop there. Other issues—virtuosity, use of color, perspective, symmetry, and other aspects of composition—also demand attention. Indeed, precisely these matters set representational art above mere cartoon. When the analysis moves to these other questions, the particular event or object that is represented diminishes in importance. As Susanne Langer has pointed out, for example, a painter wishing to represent perpendicular planes may do so by depicting a fence, a row of trees, or a column of soldiers. Frequently what is depicted is less significant than the fact that a particular spatial structure has been established (Langer 1953:Chapter 5).

With nonrepresentational art, the question of what is being represented is by definition out of order, and analysis focuses on the other issues mentioned above. Because it is so widespread, symmetry obviously must have some universal human significance and appeal. This is partly explicable in terms of the physiology and psychology of visual perception. As Dorothy Washburn

has recently reviewed this aspect of the issue (1999:550–553), I will not repeat it here. Instead, I will look at symmetrical patterns as messages and discuss their unique but universal capacity to establish familiarity, provoke interest, and stimulate aesthetic response. Doing this requires the application of some basic concepts from information theory.

In that theory, any message is composed of information, redundancy, and noise. The last refers to elements of the message that are unintended and interfere with its communication, such as static on the radio or snow on the television screen. Noise will not be considered further here. The information and redundancy in a message vary inversely, the former referring to its unpredictability and the latter to its predictability. For example, the message "Fine" sent in response to "How are you?" is highly predictable and hence high in redundancy. Our understanding of messages and what we learn from them are explicable in terms of redundancy and information. The example just given is so high in redundancy and low in information that, while we understand it instantly, we learn virtually nothing from it. The response "I have an earache" to the same question is less predictable than "Fine": it is higher in information, lower in redundancy. We still understand it readily enough, and we also learn something from it. "Thank God for Viagra" is higher still in information and lower in redundancy, and it takes slightly longer to understand it. However, if the same question elicits "Water boils at 100 degrees centigrade," that message is so high in information and low in redundancy that we do not understand what it means and thus learn nothing at all from it (beyond wondering if our question was properly heard or if our interlocutor is sane). Thus, the intelligibility of messages varies directly with their redundancy. Messages very high in redundancy are entirely intelligible but tend to be banal, those very high in information are unintelligible, and as those in between increase in information and decrease in redundancy, we learn more from them, but it takes longer to figure them out.

These concepts are readily applicable to art. Imagine a band composed of a series of figures. For the present purpose it does not matter whether the figures themselves are representational (say, pictures of animals) or nonrepresentational, for we are interested in

Figure 8.1 Maori rafter pattern with horizontal and vertical mirror reflection (from Hamilton 1901).

Figure 8.2 Rafter pattern with glide reflection (from Hamilton 1901).

Figure 8.3 Canoe prow bifold spiral (courtesy of the Auckland Institute and Museum).

the compositional structure of the entire band, the *relations between* the figures. If no figure was ever repeated and there was no order to the figures (such as reptiles first, then birds, then mammals), the composition would be like a string of random numbers: knowledge of what came before would provide no grounds for predicting what figure will come next. Such a composition would be high in information and therefore largely unintelligible. About the only thing that could be predicted from having seen part of it is that the next figure will depict an animal. A composition with more information and less intelligibility still would be a string of many disparate forms—numbers, depictions of animals and all sorts of other objects, letters from many different alphabets, pictograms, abstract shapes—all in random order. Here we would have no idea what might come next.

The defining feature of symmetry is that the same design figure or motif is repeated. That repetition constitutes redundancy, which gives the composition a measure of predictability and therefore intelligibility. Moreover, redundancy is found between symmetrical compositions as well as within them. That is, the same motifs and the same symmetrical arrangements are typically found on different kinds of objects and in different contexts. Among the New Zealand Maori, for example, a finite repertoire of motifs arranged in relatively few motions of symmetry ornament flax cloaks, many parts of houses and canoes, weapons, wooden boxes, and people's faces (by means of tattooing).

Symmetrical compositions have more or less redundancy depending on the type of symmetry involved. For

the most part, symmetry in Maori art uses the four motions of translation, mirror reflection, bifold rotation, and glide reflection. It seems fair to say that translation has the greatest amount of redundancy, followed closely by reflection, in the sense that in these forms of symmetry the viewer most readily grasps the relation between the repeated forms (Figure 8.1). Generally, it takes a bit longer to see how the forms map on each other when they are related by rotation, meaning that such compositions have somewhat less redundancy and more information. Glide reflection contains more information still, more concentration usually being required to grasp how the forms are related to each other (Figure 8.2). Maori artists also made frequent use of equable spirals. They are virtually always formed of double, interlocking spirals. Their symmetry can thus be analyzed as two spirals, related by rotation (Figure 8.3).

Of course, another important variable in determining the relative amount of redundancy and information in symmetrical compositions is the complexity of the constituent images or motifs. The simpler they are, the less information. Some Maori rafter patterns use very simple motifs and have a high degree of redundancy, while other motifs are much more complex and thus contain more information. I studied the barge boards of the carved house Te Hau ki Turanga in the National Museum in Wellington for at least half an hour (sitting in the audience in front of it during the opening ceremonies of the 1978 Pacific Art Congress) before I finally figured out that the motifs within each barge board are related by glide reflection and that the two barge boards taken as wholes are related to each other in the same way.

Another way to add information to symmetrical compositions is to use design features signaling that, of two possible ways of interpreting the symmetry, only one is correct. In Figure 8.4, for example, the motifs on first glance seem to be related both by reflection and bifold rotation, but the small, curled *koru* forms along the top and bottom of each repeat allow only rotation.

Information can also be increased by breaking the symmetry in more or less subtle ways. Then the task of the viewer becomes not only to identify the type of symmetry in play, but also to discover where and how the symmetry is broken. This is commonly used to add interest (information) to compositions that would otherwise be highly redundant and therefore banal. In the Maori case, symmetry tends to be broken most frequently in wood carving and male facial tattoos (Figure 8.5). It is not difficult to imagine that the interest of meeting new people was increased for Maoris as they tried to analyze the symmetry of a newcomer's tattoo and identify how it was broken. Since the breaks often occurred well back on the cheeks below the ears, both sides could not be seen simultaneously and the viewer would have to memorize intricate designs on one side of the face and compare them with the other side as the individual turned his head.

Symmetrical forms with a high degree of redundancy are perhaps most apt for conveying simplicity and stability. Readily understood on quick inspection, they are well suited for providing a context or frame for other art compositions or events. Symmetrical compositions high in information draw attention to themselves. The viewer must expend more effort to understand them and has, consequently, less time and energy to attend to other things.

Design motifs and ways of relating them symmetrically tend to be repeated on many different objects, again providing a redundancy of information. This in turn establishes a certain comfort level of intelligibility so that when individuals encounter an object for the first time, its size, shape, and surface decoration quickly establish it as belonging to the universe of familiar objects. Thus, they can view it or use it easily, almost automatically, without having to spend time and effort to classify it or figure out what it is. (As analysts, we use the same sort of

Figure 8.4 Rafter pattern (from Hamilton 1901).

Figure 8.5 Drawing by the Maori Te Pehi of his own facial tattoo (from Robley 1896).

redundancy to identify the provenance of objects we encounter: "This is a Maori carved box, this is a Desana basket," and so on.) The repetition of the same motifs and forms of symmetry also means that, when viewers choose to analyze an object, they know the rules for doing so. Certainly the Yekuana or Desana take pleasure in distinguishing which of a large repertory of motifs are used in particular woven baskets (Guss 1989; Reichel-Dolmatoff 1985), and Maoris enjoy examining wood carvings, tattoos, rafter patterns, and other decorated forms to determine the type of symmetry they contain.

Symmetry Conveys Cultural Meanings

Much more may be said about symmetry beyond the interest and pleasure that stem from its intrinsic aesthetic form. Symmetrical designs are associated with other expressions within the culture that produces them, and as anthropologists, we are particularly concerned with understanding what those associations are.

In a recent article, Dorothy Washburn (1999)

recommends that symmetry be understood as metaphorical. Metaphor, she argues,

> communicates some significant information and insight about the world. This information is not about specifics . . . but rather it embodies important truths and guiding principles about individuals and their place in the cultural and natural world. Because metaphors are about domains of objects/activities rather than about single objects, they can be multivocalic, speaking on many levels about a specific set of fundamental beliefs. . . . The role of visual metaphors on objects and in the practice of activities is fundamental to the preservation and communication of basic attitudes and ways of doing that embody deep-seated cultural concepts [Washburn 1999:553, 554].

In Washburn's analysis the interlocking design motifs on Puebloan pottery and their common symmetrical motion of bifold rotation are metaphorically related to the interdependent roles of husband and wife in reproduction and the cycles of the generations:

> The specific interlocking of two parts expresses the way the Hopi conceptualize the relationship of the married couple: two people have interlocked their lives to make new lives. . . . The Hopi thus see life and death as a continuous process of planting. . . . For every Hopi that passes on, another child is born and the cycle continues. In this way, bifold rotation symmetry visually replicates the quintessential essence of Pueblo life. This specific arrangement of pattern elements best visually depicts the Puebloan concept of two individuals' roles in the cycle of life and death [Washburn 1999:557].

This should not be taken to mean that bifold rotational symmetry signifies Hopi marriage and the succession of generations. Instead, pottery design, marriage, and the succession of generations *taken together* metaphorically represent more general and abstract Hopi attitudes and ways of doing. This is not a

trivial distinction. When analyzing metaphors, the task is to identify the signifiers and signifieds and to explain how they are related. If we conclude that the signified of symmetry in the art of a culture is some aspect of social structure, then once we have shown how that particular art form represents that part of social structure, our job is done. But if we imagine that symmetry in art and some aspect of social structure, taken together, metaphorically represent something else, then we still must identify what that other signified is and explain how the relationship works. In the process, we penetrate more deeply into the culture and come to grips with new questions. I will attempt to demonstrate how such an analysis might work with reference to art in New Zealand Maori culture.[1]

That certain sorts of symmetry are prevalent in Maori art has already been discussed. The question before us now is what, beyond their self-contained aesthetic value as the pure form, recurrent motifs and symmetrical patterns might mean in the particular context of Maori culture. Louise Hanson and I expended a great deal of time and effort trying to identify connections between the nonrepresentational art forms and other aspects of eighteenth- and nineteenth-century Maori culture. We worked especially hard on male facial tattoos (*moko*). David Simmons (1983:229) has suggested that the right to wear moko was limited to those of high hereditary status or of significant achievements in battle, leadership, or learning and that the lines around the mouth related to tribal affiliations. However, in the same article, he quotes authorities such as Richard Taylor, Louis Servant, and Elsdon Best to the effect that all classes had moko and that the designs did not carry any information about tribal or family identity (Simmons 1983:234, 236). Simmons does not explain just how lines around the mouth relate to the various tribes, and our own examination of the portraits of men from different tribes failed to turn up anything in their moko that indicated tribal affiliation. Our effort to ascertain if the tattooing applied to a certain part of the face signified a particular accomplishment or milestone passed by the individual (tattooing was done in sections, and the entire process could take months or years to complete) was also fruitless. We finally despaired of finding any systematic association between

moko motifs or symmetrical patterns and matters of identity or achievement.

Another candidate for specific significance was decorated meetinghouses. It has been suggested that the house itself represents the founding ancestor of a tribe. The front end of the ridgepole, often carved in the form of a face, is the head of the founder, and the barge boards on the front gable are his encompassing arms. The ridgepole is his spine and the rafters his ribs. Wall posts, carved in tiki (human) forms, represent other tribal ancestors. Hence, upon entering a meetinghouse one literally enters the body of the founding ancestor and is surrounded by representations of other famous ancestral figures. Perhaps this is so, although I have the impression it could as well be a post hoc example of a Maori being reminded of something when looking at a work of art instead of being the intention behind the original design of decorated houses. Again, a New Zealander analyst of Maori art suggested (in a personal communication) that the number of repeats in the symmetrical pattern on each rafter corresponds to the number of generations between the ancestor represented by the wall post and the founding ancestor of the tribe. However, we could find no collaborating evidence for this, and the fact that opposing rafters have the same number of repeats but connect to different ancestors on opposite walls of the house (who might have lived at different times) led us to doubt it.

Some wall posts in late-nineteenth and early-twentieth-century houses are carved with symbols indicative of particular ancestors. Thus in the decorated house Tama te Kapua at Ohinemutu, Rotorua, carved around the turn of the twentieth century, Tutanekai is depicted playing a flute and Hine Moa has gourds tied around her waist, representing events in their love story. However, the more common pattern was for the posts to be carved first and the ancestors they were to represent designated later, with nothing in the carving to identify the ancestor (McEwan 1966:415). In short, we could find precious little of a representational quality anywhere in Maori art and nothing at all that could be imagined to be specifically represented by one type or other of symmetrical composition.

Nevertheless, it was clear to us that the idea of symmetry pervades Maori culture in many ways in addition to visual art. Our book *Counterpoint in Maori Culture* (Hanson and Hanson 1983) is devoted to analyzing two dynamic or syntagmatic patterns related to symmetry that can be understood to inform a great many institutions, rituals, myths, and behavioral regularities in Maori culture.

The reciprocal syntagm[2] underlies dyadic interactions between two equivalent agents, such that what A does to or for B is similar to what B does to or for A. In its positive mode this is represented by the exchange of feasts between neighboring tribes or the exchange of specialized products, such as inland people giving coastal dwellers preserved birds, rats, and other forest products and receiving sea products in return. Its negative mode is represented by the Maori preoccupation with revenge and frequent warfare.

The complementary syntagm is more complicated. Here two different beings are attracted to each other, and from their union something new is created. But the union is confining to one, both, or to some other party associated with the relationship, and they separate. This condition is also unsatisfactory because it is sterile or unproductive. One or both of the original parties or their offspring then seek union, which again produces something new, and so the cycle continues. A vivid example of complementarity is the mythological creation saga of the god Tane. He and his brothers were born of the union of their sky father and earth mother, who were pressed closely together in a lovers' embrace. The sons found existence to be intolerable in such cramped quarters, and Tane finally succeeded in wrenching their parents apart. Although they were still able to look lovingly in each other's eyes, thus separated, they produced no more offspring. To this point, the myth has gone through one cycle of union, production, confinement, and separation with its attendant sterility.

The cycle picks up again when Tane began copulating with female beings. However, he was never satisfied and left each mistress for another. Each union produced offspring, and that is how many of the furnishings of the world (water, various species of insects, birds, and plants) came into being. Ultimately Tane formed the figure of a human female from the earth, breathed life into her nostrils, and got a daughter on her. However, he left her too, to take up with his daughter. From that

Figure 8.6 Maori war canoe (from the Hawkesworth edition of Cook's Voyages, III and reproduced in Best 1925, p. 154)

Figure 8.7 Portion of a canoe side strake (from Archey 1960).

union, humankind sprang. The entire myth is readily seen as a connected series of passages through the complementary syntagm of union, production, confinement, separation, union again, and so on.

The complementary syntagm also informs much of Maori ritual, one purpose of which is to bring humans into productive contact with the gods. This, a state called *tapu,* enables prowess in battle, creativity in art, and other productive activities. However, the tapu state is inconvenient and confining. Another class of rituals separates humans from godly influence, placing them in a more comfortable but unproductive condition called *noa.* Each individual passes between the states of tapu and noa innumerable times in the course of a lifetime. The cycle of human marriage, reproduction, divorce, and remarriage is, of course, another case of complementarity.

Both of the syntagms produce change. A relationship governed by the reciprocal syntagm may escalate. Exchanged feasts, potlatchlike, get bigger and bigger: in insults, revenge, and warfare one always tries to give better than one received. Reciprocity may also oscillate between positive and negative modes, as when an unintended affront transforms a cordial relationship into an adversarial one or an act of unexpected magnanimity toward a rival turns it the other way. The dynamic qual-

ity of the complementary syntagm is greater still, for it produces new beings and conditions that go on to engage in their own way in various reciprocal and complementary relationships, the latter producing still more new beings and conditions.

In the absence of evidence that symmetry in Maori art represents particular institutions or activities, it is tempting to think that different types of symmetry might metaphorically represent, at this considerably higher level of generalization, the reciprocal or complementary syntagms. It is possible to imagine that translation and especially reflection have a tit-for-tat or confrontational quality that fits with the reciprocal syntagm, while bifold rotation and glide reflection have a developmental quality that might be associated with the complementary syntagm. Certain objects can be invoked to support this hypothesis.

One of the most bellicose artifacts in Maori culture, and one of the most beautifully decorated, is the war canoe (Figure 8.6). Its purpose associates it with the reciprocal syntagm, and its decoration may do so as well. The side strakes of war canoes are typically carved with alternating tiki and *manaia* ("beaked") figures, all facing downward (Figure 8.7). The symmetry of each strake is translation of tiki/manaia pairs. Moreover, because all figures on both sides of the canoe are facing forward, the two strakes taken together demonstrate reflective symmetry. Similarly, the composition of the dominant style of male facial tattoo, probably the ideal image of the warrior, is reflection across a vertical axis down the middle of the face.

It is difficult to maintain this hypothesis for long, however, because there is too much counterevidence. As a prime example of the complementary syntagm, objects associated with rituals to establish and terminate the state of tapu ought, by the hypothesis, to feature bifold rotation and/or glide reflection. Very little art was explicitly associated with such rituals, but one form is the *taumata atua* (Figure 8.8). These are stone figures roughly carved in human form that gods are supposed to enter. They are placed in sweet potato gardens or other places where the influence of the gods is desired. They show nothing of the decorative virtuosity of most of the rest of Maori art, and they are not structured in symmetrical form at all. On the other hand, carved meetinghouses include a variety of art forms frequently executed with great virtuosity. As a memorial to tribal ancestors and a symbol of tribal unity, the significance of marriage and procreation over the generations represented by such houses might be supposed to link them with the complementary syntagm. Again, the hypothesis would lead us to expect bifold rotation and glide reflection in the art of such houses. And indeed it is there, particularly in painted rafter patterns. But translation and reflection are also present with at least as much frequency in the art of meetinghouses, for example in their carved facades, in the woven wall panels between the posts, and also in many rafter patterns.

The truth is that while some forms such as war canoe strakes and storehouse exteriors seem always to manifest translation, reflection, or both, no such generalization can be made for other art forms or symmetrical structures. In particular, bifold rotation and glide reflection are not the invariable decorative form for any kind of object. Glide reflection, indeed, seems to have been limited to painted rafter patterns, the form in which the Maori artist's fascination with symmetry of all sorts found its richest expression.

Thus, the analysis has reached this point: while it seems clear that the symmetrical forms in Maori art are structurally related to many other Maori cultural institutions such as mythology, ritual, social, and political relations, there is insufficient evidence to back any claim that a particular kind of artistic symmetry represents any particular concept or behavior pattern in other

sectors of the culture, even at the very general level of reciprocal and complementary syntagms. The relationship between symmetry in Maori art and other Maori institutions is indeed metaphorical, but not in the sense that art specifically signifies any of the other institutions. Rather, my contention is that art and the other institutions (even at the level of reciprocal and complementary syntagms) are all signifiers of something more general still: the premise that the objects, events, and conditions of the world relate to each other in terms of bilateral organization. What Clifford Geertz (citing Robert Goldwater) said of artworks in general is especially true of Maori symmetrical compositions: they are "primary documents; not illustrations of conceptions already in force, but conceptions themselves that seek— or for which people seek—a meaningful place in a repertoire of other documents, equally primary" (Geertz 1983:99–100).

From this perspective, art is one of the means by which culture imposes order on reality, and Maori art is one expression of a fundamental bilateral organization of form and relationship that pervades Maori culture. Having reached this point, I think we can pursue the analysis still further by exploring the role of symmetry in art in the actual practice of cultural life. Specifically, what is the relation between culturally defined order and individual minds? How do individuals assimilate the order their culture imposes on reality, and how do they perpetuate it?

Symmetry Participates in Cultural Praxis

Sherry Ortner concludes her well-known essay on the state of anthropological theory between the sixties and the eighties with a discussion of the theory of practice. Central to this issue is the relation between practice (the everyday activities of human beings) and the cultural system regulating that practice. Ortner asks the paired questions: "How does the system shape practice?" and "How does practice shape the system?" (Ortner 1984:152–154). It is the same relationship that Peter Berger and Thomas Luckmann were addressing when they said, "Society is a human product. . . . Man is a social product" (1967:61), or Clifford Geertz when he wrote that "culture patterns have an intrinsic double aspect: they give meaning, i.e., objective conceptual form, to social psychological reality, both by shaping themselves to it and by shaping it to themselves" (1973:92), or finally, Wilhelm Dilthey when he stated that the (cultural) world is both mind affected and mind affecting (1962:120). People mold and construct their lived reality in accordance with the cultural principles and expectations that they carry around in their minds. It is equally true that people learn or acquire those principles and expectations from daily experience of the lived reality. Maori artists learn what art is by observing the decorated objects all around them. When they produce art of their own, it takes a similar form to the art from which they have learned.

The fundamental question is, How does this reciprocal process work? It is not, I think, a simple back-and-forth relationship. The process whereby minds affect the world differs in important ways from the process by which the world affects minds. The difference resides in the distinction between what I will call consequential and semiotic relationships.

Consequential and Semiotic Relationships

Consequential relationships are those for which it is possible to distinguish independent and dependent variables, the latter being in some sense a result or consequence of the former. One variety of consequential relationships is causal. This occurs when the independent variable physically renders the dependent variable necessary or highly probable. A causal relationship in cultural life exists where, for example, in arid conditions such as the Kalahari or Central Australia a hunting-and-gathering technology taken as the independent variable may be said to cause the dependent variables of small group size and a nomadic way of life.

Another variety of consequential relationship may be termed derivational. Here the independent variable is a general concept or principle of some sort. The dependent variable is not physically caused by the independent variable, but is rather derived from it, as an example, instance, or application. Therefore, the belief that an excess of blood is a source of illness is an independent variable and the application of that belief in the use of leeches or bloodletting in therapy is the dependent variable.

Semiotic relations are those for which it is not possible to establish dependent and independent variables. In this case, one item is not a consequence of the other; instead, their relationship is one of signification. It may be that one member of the relationship signifies another, so that we may speak of signifier and signified (as in the relationship between a coat of arms and the family it represents). Two or more items may be related because they are signifiers of the same thing (as in the relationships among a coat of arms, a name, a hereditary title, and a hereditary estate, all of which may be signifiers of a family).

Again, it is convenient to divide semiotic relationships into two categories. This may be done on the basis of Hume's distinction between ideas associated by contiguity and resemblance. Semioticians have produced a number of variations and elaborations on this contrast, distinguishing between syntagm and association, syntagm and paradigm, syntagm and system, or metonymy and metaphor. Here, however, we will continue to use Hume's simpler terminology. Things are related by contiguity if they commonly appear together or if one is part of the other. Hence, the relationship mentioned above among a family, its coat of arms, its name, its title, and its estate are contiguous, as are the relationships between knives and forks or bread and butter. An example of a contiguous part-for-whole relationship (synecdoche) is the nickname of the jazz drummer Nesbert Hooper, known as "Sticks."

The other category of semiotic relationship is resemblance. Here things are related because of some kind of similarity between them. Depending on the context, it may be similarity of appearance, color, shape, odor, sound, use, and so on. Metaphors are relations of resemblance, such as Eliot's link between an evening and an etherized patient.

These distinctions are helpful in modeling the process whereby the world is both mind affected and mind affecting. Briefly, my claim is that minds affect the world by consequential (particularly derivational) relationships while the world affects minds via semiotic relationships.

How Minds Affect the World

Those parts of reality that are cultural products are related to general cultural principals by derivation. For example, religious symbols, objects, and practices are derived from general theological postulates; good manners are applications of canons of proper and graceful social interaction; conventional behavior patterns among various types of relatives, friends, acquaintances, and adversaries are examples of principles of social organization; musical compositions and performances, paintings, and sculpture are instances of canons of art and style.

The Maori artist who sets out to paint, weave, tattoo, or carve, knows that in certain cases, the design should be symmetrical and that, depending on the particular object at hand, there is a more or less wide range of choice of motifs and symmetrical movements to relate them. The resulting work of art becomes a part of experienced reality. It is part of the mind-affected world, its form deriving from the artist's application of general principles of design or rules for decorating objects of this sort. At the next higher level, the principles governing the use of symmetry in decorating such objects are themselves derivations from or applications of a still more general principle that dictates that symmetry in Maori art pairs motifs by the motions of translation, mirror reflection, rotation, and glide reflection.

I have argued that symmetry in art is a primary princple in Maori culture, having a meaningful place in a repertory of other equally primary principles. I have also suggested that two other such principles that incorporate symmetry in forms other than visual art are the reciprocal and complementary syntagms. Although in my mind art is clearly connected to them, I have been careful to avoid the notion that art represents or depicts these other cases of symmetry in Maori culture. It is possible to model the proper association between them by adding another level to the hierarchy of principles and derivations. Symmetry in art, the reciprocal syntagm, and the complementary syntagm are all derivations from a still more general principle of Maori culture: that reality takes the form of symmetrical interaction between pairs of entities. A simplified diagram of this hierarchy of consequential relationships is given in Figure 8.9.

The diagram models an important part of Maori culture that was internalized in Maori minds. (The question of individual Maori awareness of the model is taken up in the conclusion.) It was precisely by applying consequential relationships as described in the diagram that the Maoris were able to produce art, engage in

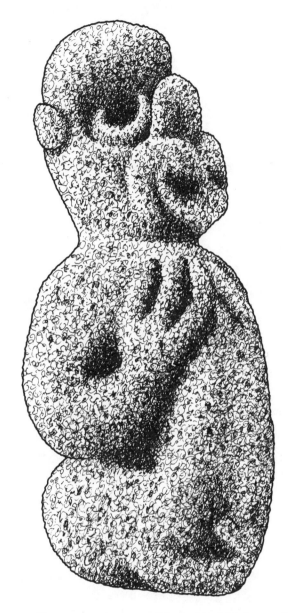

Figure 8.8 Taumata atua (courtesy of the Auckland Institute and Museum).

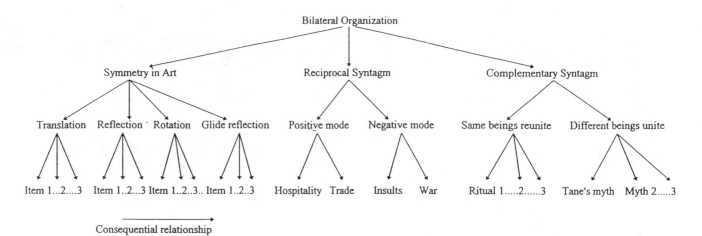

Figure 8.9 Diagram of the hierarchy of consequential relationships.

social relationships, conduct rituals, and retell and appreciate myths in their daily lives. By doing all these things, Maoris brought a large number of objects, situations, and events into experienced reality, and thus they created their mind-affected world.

How the World Affects Minds

If Maoris produced their mind-affected world as derivations or applications of general cultural principles, how did they acquire those principles in the first place? Obviously, they learned them. However, this learning process occurred without explicit instruction or verbal articulation. The higher-level cultural principles belong to the category that Bourdieu (1977:164–169) calls *doxa:* the underlying, taken-for-granted set of assumptions about the world in terms of which objects and events are organized and understood. Doxa "goes without saying," wrote Bourdieu (1977:167), "because it comes without saying." Instead of being formally taught, doxa is learned from the experience of living in a world that is (culturally) organized in a certain way, taking it for granted, and expecting that it will continue to be roughly the way it is.

It is critical to realize that this learning process cannot be explained by retracing the consequential relationships that pass from higher-level principles to lower-level applications. That is to say, the arrows in our diagram cannot be reversed. An individual cannot grasp a general concept or principle from being exposed to a single example of it. The Maori who had seen only one object decorated with

bifold rotation could develop no concept of bifold rotation as a type of design or, at a higher level, of symmetry in general. Having heard only that Tane and his brothers were born of the union of earth and sky, whom Tane then separated, that same Maori could form no sense of the complementary syntagm as an organizing principle for bilateral relationships.

The reason for this is that it is impossible to generalize upon a particular experience unless it is reinforced by other experiences of the same type. To call again upon the concepts of information theory, the similarity among a variety of experiences constitutes the redundancy necessary for them to be intelligible. Only upon seeing numerous instances of bifold rotation can the Maori develop the notion of bifold rotation as a design type that can be used in more than one way; only upon encountering numerous cases of pairs of entities joining, producing, experiencing confinement, and separating can the Maori begin to get a sense of the general class of relationships that I have termed complementary. The connection among these various instances is semiotic; in the examples I have used, resemblance. That semiotic relationship enables the mind to form a notion of (or, since this is a case of communication, to get the message about) what that principle is.

It will be recalled that instructive messages contain information—unpredictability as well as redundancy. If the Maori artist had been exposed only to several examples of the same motif organized in bifold rotation on

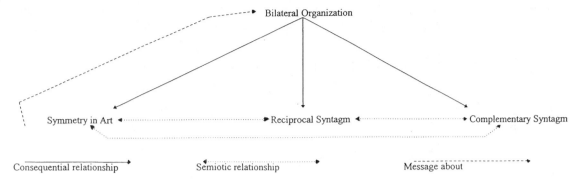

Figure 8.10 Diagram of the experience of semiotic relationships.

painted rafters, the general notion that would be conveyed is no more than that when a new rafter is to be painted: it should be with that particular motif organized in that particular way. The *difference* among the cases that the Maori actually does encounter—different motifs arranged in bifold rotation on rafter patterns, carved boxes, canoe prows and sterns—constitute the information in the message. This makes the message much more general: that a variety of motifs can be organized in bifold rotation to ornament a variety of objects. Similarly, the difference between examples of the complementary syntagm constitutes the information that allows people to form a sense of that syntagm as an organizational form for a variety of bilateral relationships between people, natural and supernatural beings, and so forth.

Now we are in a position to explain how, simultaneously, culture is a human product and humans are cultural products or how the world is both mind affected and mind affecting. Culture is a human product (the world is mind affected) because the things people make and do are consequences (primarily derivations) of general cultural principles that they have internalized. Humans are cultural products (the world is mind affecting) because people internalize general cultural principles through experience of semiotic relationships (primarily resemblance) among the things that their contemporaries and predecessors have made and done (Figure 8.10). Symmetry in art, demonstrated here for the Maori case but certainly equally significant in many other cultures, is an important participant in this general process.

This model can account not only for the perpetuation of culture but also for its change. Remaining with our example from Maori art, once they have grasped the message or principle about how bifold rotation might be applied, more creative artists might go on to expand that principle, applying it in ways that have enough redundancy with previous instances to be understood but enough difference from them (information) to make the new composition interesting and thought provoking. Those results deemed successful might inspire other artists to follow suit. Then their minds would affect the world in a new way as the set of instances of bifold rotation expands. That expanded set of instances would in turn affect the minds of the people who view them, resulting in a change in the Maori cultural principle concerning bifold rotation. Similar arguments, of course, could be made for all other cultural principles and their applications.

Conclusion

Two important criticisms are likely to be raised against the model and analysis I have proposed. The first is how to determine if hypothesized semiotic relationships and cultural principles have been correctly identified. Any mode of analysis that claims to be objective or scientific requires some means of corroborating or falsifying its hypotheses. The matter is relatively straightforward in the case of consequential relationships, where we can follow the procedures of natural science (which has traditionally also been concerned with consequential—specifically causal—relationships). One interferes with the independent variable and observes whether the dependent variable is affected in the predicted way (e.g., if the belief that an excess of blood causes disease is discredited, bloodletting in therapy will be discarded).

Of course, in social science such testing procedures may be difficult to carry out practically, due to ethical, political, and other constraints on experimentation with human subjects. This is why cross-cultural comparison and social change are of such methodological significance to social science: they often provide us with ready-made experimental conditions. However, whatever the practical complexities, at least the logic of testing hypotheses about consequential relationships is clear.

It is different in the case of semiotic relationships. Difficulties of verification are the primary reason why the impact of brilliantly creative interpretations of scholars such as Lévi-Strauss has diminished in recent years. This is a serious problem, particularly for studies that concentrate on worldview, because semiotic relationships are of primary importance in the establishment of cultural constructions of reality. They are, as we have seen, a major means whereby knowledge of the world as it is construed in a particular culture is communicated to the members of society.

If one examines the question of testing hypotheses about semiotic relationships from the perspective of the model developed above, it becomes less problematic. For one thing, that model specifies what semiotic relationships *do* in culture, and, for another, it shows how they do it in conjunction with consequential relationships. Both factors are relevant to testing procedures.

Consider again the postulation of a complementary syntagm that organizes a wide variety of stories and event sequences in Maori culture. Is there sufficient evidence that the complementary syntagm really exists as a Maori cultural principle built from the semiotic relationship among those stories and event sequences rather than having been hatched by Louise Hanson and me in a moment of fevered overanalysis? The model used here provides at least a way of thinking about that problem. Semiotic relationships can be understood as messages about the world communicated to members of society. To communicate successfully, the messages have to be intelligible, and their intelligibility is directly proportional to the redundancy they contain. Therefore, hypotheses about semiotic relationships can be tested by checking for redundancy. If little redundancy is found, it is unlikely that a semiotic relationship has in fact been discovered. As far as the Maori complementary syntagm

is concerned, redundancy can be measured by the frequency of the distinctive pattern of union, production, confinement, and separation in Maori stories and event sequences. Different analysts may have varying thresholds for how frequently the pattern should occur before acknowledging that a semiotic relationship and its attendant cultural principle are indeed present, but at least this is a method upon which they might agree for testing hypotheses.

Hypothesized semiotic relationships can also be tested by tracing through the communicative processes in which they participate. The investigator attempts to formulate the message communicated by the semiotic relationship and then searches for other cultural regularities that might also be seen as members of the set that communicates that message. Insofar as this investigation is a fruitful one, yielding insights and suggesting associations among cultural components that had not been previously perceived, confidence increases that a real semiotic relationship has been identified and its message correctly interpreted. But if the analysis leads to a dead end, it is likely that what was hypothesized to be a semiotic relationship was only a fortuitous and nonsignificant association or else that the interpretation of the message communicated by the relationship is faulty.

The other likely criticism has to do with the ontological status of cultural principles and native awareness of them. I have laid great stress on the notion of cultural principles. These have a determining effect on reality as experienced in that cultural institutions and actual behavior are logical consequences of them. Conversely, the messages communicated by semiotic relationships among those institutions and behaviors are messages about the cultural principles. Hence, it is important that we be clear about the nature of such principles.

One thing can be stated unequivocally at the outset: especially at the higher levels of generalization, cultural principles are rarely verbalized by members of the society under study. Informants cannot provide the anthropologist with a neat list of the axioms upon which their culture is predicated. These belong, as indicated above, to the foundational but unarticulated body of subjective knowledge. The anthropologist must infer them, and this is done by the same process that has been described for how the world affects people's minds. That is, the anthropologist observes or experiences patterns of institutionalized behavior, seeks semiotic relationships among them, and receives from those relationships intelligible messages about the cultural principles informing the patterns of behavior. The main difference between this and the native's experience of living in and learning about the culture is that the investigator makes the entire process explicit.

The inability of members of society to articulate the principles raises a serious question about their reality. Instead of claiming, as we have been, that they exist, one view is that they have no reality in the culture under study but are heuristic abstractions created by the investigator to assist in anthropological analysis (for the debate, see Caws 1974, 1976, 1977; Chaney 1978; Hanson 1976; Maquet 1964; Rossi 1977). If this were true, our model with its contention that cultural institutions and patterned behavior are logical consequences of such abstracted principles would be highly vulnerable to the criticism that it reifies abstractions and then considers those abstractions to have a determining influence over the very things from which they were originally abstracted (Bidney 1944:41–43).

My position, however, is that the principles are far more than just figments of the analyst's imagination. They are objective components of culture. One way to account for the fact that members of society cannot articulate them is to locate them in their unconscious minds, or "primary process." Gregory Bateson (1972:141–142) has explained this in terms of the economy of mental resources. The conscious mind has a finite capacity: there is a limit to the number of things one can think about, appreciate, plan, or decide in any given span of time. Habits contribute immensely to the economy of mind in that they make it possible to do certain things "automatically," allowing attention to be focused on other matters. For instance, one can think about what to eat for breakfast in a lecture while tying one's shoe because that operation has become so habitual that it no longer requires attention to accomplish it. That task, as Bateson would say, has been "sunk" in primary process. A child of four, on the other hand, has not yet accomplished this sinking and must devote the full resources of conscious mind to getting the shoe tied properly.

Only those procedures that are invariably the same

can be sunk in primary process. One can think about other things while tying one's shoe but not while selecting which of several pairs of shoes to wear. The latter task has variable outcomes, and so the flexibility of consciousness is required to deal with it. Hence, the mind approaches maximum economy and efficiency when those things that are unchanging and deemed to be permanently true are sunk in primary process (and so drop out of awareness), thus freeing consciousness to focus its attention on the contingent and variable elements of experience. People are not aware of their most basic cultural principles (subjective knowledge) because, as the firm foundations upon which their behavior is predicated, they are sunk in primary process.

This is a useful way to conceive of the nature of cultural principles as long as a pair of provisos is kept in mind. For one, it must not be taken as an implication of the terminology Bateson uses that all things that are sunk in primary process were originally on the surface, available to consciousness. Sometimes, indeed, they have been, as is the case with the example of learning to tie one's shoe. However, a great deal of culture is acquired from lived experience, with the principles never having been explicit. The rules governing gestures, facial expressions, body positioning in social interaction, and language are clear examples. To say that these are sunk in primary process does not entail that during the learning process they were conscious.

The second proviso is to resist the common assumption that the inhabitants of mind (conscious or unconscious) are first and foremost propositions. It is very easy to fall in with this idea. Bateson speaks of premises that may be sunk and conclusions that remain conscious; I have repeatedly used terms such as principles and rules, and all of these are conventionally stated in the form of propositions. A statement or description of something is not that thing; as Korzybski was careful to point out, the map is not the territory (1958:58, 498, 750–751). The unarticulated cultural principles that are sunk in native primary process are not a bunch of shadowy propositions that never quite get said. They belong more to the realm of action than to the realm of speech. Wittgenstein, who characterized cultural principles as rules that are simply accepted without grounds, wrote: "As if giving grounds did not come to an end sometime.

But the end is not an ungrounded presupposition: it is an ungrounded way of acting" (Wittgenstein 1972:Section 110).

In their own right, cultural principles provide the grounds for conventional behavior. The principles that appear in propositional form in our analyses are *statements of* those principles. While not identical with them, to the extent that they are accurate descriptions or maps, the analytic principles are vital tools for understanding the structure and working of human cultures. ■

Notes

1. The following discussion of Maori art and culture distills a general interpretation of it developed by Louise Hanson and myself over the last twenty-five years. More extended treatment of its various elements may be found in Hanson and Hanson (1983) and Hanson (1976, 1982, 1983a, 1983b, 1983c, 1983d, 1985, 1987, 1988, 1990).

2. In the book it is called symmetrical but because that term, used in a different sense, is so central to the present discussion, I have changed the name.

References Cited

Archey, Gilbert
1960   Sculpture and Design: An Outline of Maori Art. *Handbook of the Auckland War Memorial Museum,* Auckland, New Zealand.

Bateson, Gregory
1972   *Steps to an Ecology of Mind.* Ballantine, New York.

Berger, Peter, and Thomas Luckmann
1967   *The Social Construction of Reality.* Doubleday, Garden City, NY.

Best, Elsdon
1925   *Tuhoe: Children of the Mist, vol. 1,* Wellington: Polynesian Society Memoirs, vol. 6

Bidney, David
1944   On the Concept of Culture and Some Cultural Fallacies. *American* Anthropologist 46:41–43.

Bourdieu, Pierre
1977   *Outline of a Theory of Practice.* Cambridge University Press, Cambridge, UK.

Caws, Peter
1974   Operational, Representational, and Explanatory Models. *American Anthropologist* 76:1–10.
1976   The Ontology of Social Structure: A Reply to Hanson. *American Anthropologist* 78:325–327.
1977   More on the Ontology of Social Structure: A Reply to Rossi. *American Anthropologist* 79:914–916.

Chaney, Richard Paul
1978   Structures, Realities, and Blind Spots. *American Anthropologist* 80:589–596.

Dilthey, Wilhelm
1962   *Pattern and Meaning in History.* Harper & Row, New York.

Geertz, Clifford
1973   *The Interpretation of Cultures.* Basic Books, New York.
1983   Art as a Cultural System. In *Local Knowledge,* by Clifford Geertz, pp. 94–120. Basic Books, New York.

Guss, David M.
1989   *To Weave and Sing: Art, Symbol, and Narrative in the South American Rain Forest.* University of California Press, Berkeley.

Hamilton, Augustus
1901   *Maori Art.* New Zealand Institute, Wellington.

Hanson, F. Allan
1976   Models and Social Reality: An Alternative to Caws. *American Anthropologist* 78:323–325.
1982   Method in Semiotic Anthropology; or, How the Maori Latrine Means. In *Studies in Symbolism and Cultural Communication,* edited by F. Allan Hanson, pp. 74–89. University of Kansas Publications in Anthropology No. 14, Lawrence.

1983a   Syntagmatic Structures: How the Maoris Make Sense of History. *Semiotica* 46:287–307.

1983b   Dynamic Forms in the Maori Concept of Reality. *Ultimate Reality and Meaning* 6:180–204.

1983c   When the Map Is the Territory: Art in Maori Culture. In *Structure and Cognition in Art,* edited by Dorothy K. Washburn, pp. 74–89. Cambridge University Press, Cambridge, UK.

1983d   Art and the Maori Construction of Reality. In *Art and Artists of Oceania,* edited by Sidney M. Mead and Bernie Kernot, pp. 210–225. Dunmore Press, Palmerston North, New Zealand.

1985   From Symmetry to Anthropophagy: The Cultural Context of Maori Art. *Empirical Studies of the Arts* 3:47–62.

1987   Maori Religion. In *Encyclopedia of Religion,* edited by Mircea Eliade, Vol. 9, pp. 178–182. Macmillan, New York.

1988   Structure in Objective History: A Reply to Webster. *Journal of the Polynesian Society* 97:325–329.

1990   Deciphering the Language of Things: Aesthetics and the Cultural Process. In *The Language of Things,* edited by Pieter ter Keurs and Dirk Smidt, pp. 37–44. Leiden, Rijksmuseum voor Volkenkunde.

Hanson, F. Allan, and Louise M. Hanson
1983   *Counterpoint in Maori Culture.* Routledge & Kegan Paul, London, UK.

Korzybski, Alfred
1958   *Science and Sanity.* International Non-Aristotelian Library Publishing Co., Lakeville, CT.

Langer, Susanne K.
1953   *Feeling and Form.* Routledge & Kegan Paul, London.

Maquet, Jacques
1964   Some Epistemological Remarks on the Cultural Philosophies and Their Comparison. In *Cross-Cultural Understanding: Epistemology in Anthropology,* edited by F. S. C. Northrop and Helen H. Livingston, pp. 13–31. Harper & Row, New York.

McEwan, J. M.
1966   Maori Art. In *Encyclopedia of New Zealand,* edited by A. H. McLintock, 2:408-429.

Ortner, Sherry B.
1984   Theory in Anthropology since the Sixties. *Comparative Studies in Society and History* 26:126–166.

Reichel-Dolmatoff, Gerardo
1985   *Basketry as Metaphor: Arts and Crafts of the Desana Indians of the Northwest Amazon.* Occasional Papers of the Museum of Cultural History, University of California, Los Angeles, No. 5, Los Angeles.

Robley, H. G.
1896   *Moko; or Maori Tattooing.* Chapman and Hall, London, UK.

Rossi, Ino
1977   On the Notion of Social Structure: A Mental or Objective Reality? *American Anthropologist* 79:916.

Simmons, David
1983   Moko. In *Art and Artists of Oceania,* edited by Sidney M. Mead and Bernie Kernot, pp. 226–243. Dunmore Press, Palmerston North, New Zealand.

Washburn, Dorothy K.
1999   Perceptual Anthropology: The Cultural Salience of Symmetry. *American Anthropologist* 101:547–562.

Wittgenstein, Ludwig
1972   *On Certainty.* Harper & Row, New York.

Figure 9.1 A work group of women beating out bark cloth, Ekubu Village, Vatulele Island.

Figure 9.2 A typical ceremonial hanging, or screen, gatu vakaviti, made in Namuka, Lau, in 1985. In normal use it would be hung on a line across the interior of the house; here it is shown hung over clothesline in the yard, the two photographs showing its two halves. (a) Stenciled "face" half of the cloth, which in use would face out to the public, (b) the "back" half, predominantly figured by rubbing in the Tongan manner, which in use would be back toward the private (family) area of the house.

CHAPTER NINE

Symmetry and Semiotics
The Case of Fijian Barkcloth Figuration

Rod Ewins

WASHBURN AND CROWE (1988:268) set a challenge when they wrote that "even . . . nonrepresentational art has important cultural communicative value . . . and we must investigate the significance of different geometries in different cultural contexts." Wise counsel, but it must be followed with caution. Today at least, in many societies such art is made within parameters of traditional form and style, which the makers understand in very general or emotional ways rather than as carrying specific information. Therefore, rather than directly seeking to identify particular ideas or objects that such "geometries" might or might not signify, I propose here that we should look at the entire systems of meaning of which they are component parts and attempt to understand their sociocultural role in that totality.

The particular signifier I focus on in this chapter is Fijian barkcloth, today called *tapa* by most westerners but actually called *masi* in Standard Fijian.[1] To make it, Fijian women first beat the inner bark (bast) of the paper-mulberry plant (*Broussonetia papyrifera*) into thin sheets (Figure 9.1). These are then felted together with further beating to make rectangular units of strong, even-textured fabric that traditionally performed all the functions of both cloth and paper in Western society. Its use as clothing has long been supplanted by Western cloth except in the case of ritual dress. Most of its other utilitarian roles have been lost.

But quite separate from these, masi carries arguably the most diverse range of meanings of any Fijian artifact, and it is these that secure its ongoing importance to Fijians. Its "official valuable" status means that it is produced by certain designated areas/groups of people,

Figure 9.3 Group of women stenciling the design onto the gatu vakaviti illustrated in Figure 9.2, Namuka, Lau, 1985. They are working on the "face" of the cloth; the blank area to the left of the picture will be rubbed with weak, watery paint to produce the "tasina" area of the "back."

both as their principal item of ritual exchange as well as a commodity in nonritual trade between groups. The 1.8-by-0.5-meter pieces that result from the process of beating and felting are end- and/or edge-joined to make often huge pieces of ceremonial cloth for these ritual and trade purposes; for example, the typical size of ceremonial hanging cloths or screens (called *taunamu* or *gatu vakaviti*) is 5.5 by 3.7 meters (Figure 9.2). Some are as large as 7.5 by 5 meters. These are commonly figured[2] with nonrepresentational geometric designs arranged in symmetrical patterns (Figure 9.3).

My chosen task in this chapter is to establish that the symmetries that exist in the form and figuration of masi draw directly on the same sources of cognitive understanding, spiritual belief, and social knowledge that have generated the symmetries, reciprocities, and resonances that can be clearly seen to operate in Fijian social structures and processes. It would be difficult to sustain an argument that the cloth itself, its design,[3] or its abstract figuration *directly* symbolize, or are signs or metaphors for, any specific natural forms or social structures. However, I contend that masi in all of its particulars *does* signify, indeed stands as a tangible physical expression of, the overarching idea and organizing principles of symmetry. By corollary, therefore, it relates to, indeed in light of its role as a signifier may be regarded as at least an *indirect* symbol of, every other Fijian social and cultural expression of symmetry.

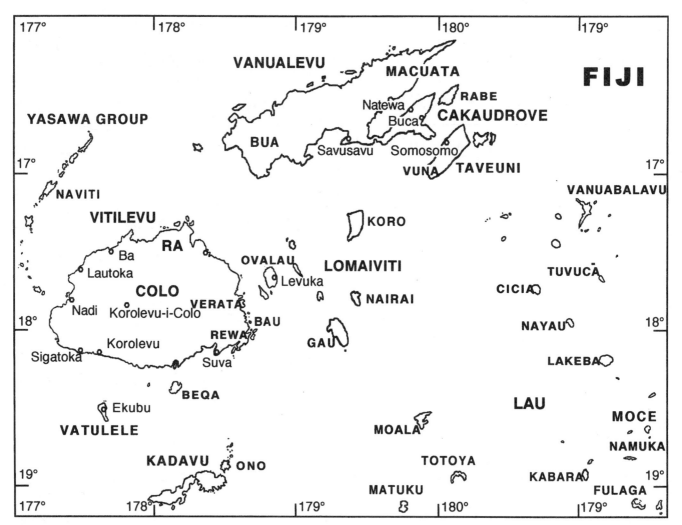

Figure 9.4 Fiji.

There is a long sociological precedent for postulating such connections between ideas, social structures, and significant objects. Eighteenth-century Scottish philosophers David Hume and Adam Smith held that human intelligence and sentiments derive from society (Shott 1976), and Emile Durkheim extended this to include the physical domain, suggesting that societies classify "things" on the same basis as they order their social structure and interpersonal relationships (Durkheim 1976 [1912]:esp. Chapter 3; Durkheim and Mauss 1963 [1903]:esp. Chapter 5). He recognized that all classification is based on an "ensemble of mental habits by virtue of which we conceive things and facts in the form of coordinated or hierarchized groups" (Durkheim and Mauss 1963 [1903]:88). What is relevant here is not how such "mental habits" may have initially been formed, but that for the people concerned they have effectively constituted a virtual lens through which

to view the world. The perception that results from this view is what the French philosopher Durand (1999 [1960]) terms an "imaginary" and is applied to not merely understanding, but also organizing both conceptually and physically virtually all aspects of existence. This conceptualization has resonances with Thomas Wynn's discussion of algorithmic thought in Chapter 3 of this volume.

Cultural and Social Symmetry

The "imaginary" relevant to the present discussion is one that is common to many cultures—the conceptualizing of everything as existing in pairs. Maybury-Lewis (1989:vii) writes that "the human predilection for binary systems . . . [is] a mode of thought and social organisation that has represented an attractive option throughout human history. . . . [For some societies it] involves their cosmologies, their ideas about time and aesthetics, their ways of dealing with age and gender, their structures for coping with power, hierarchy, competition and exchange, and a host of other factors." The concomitant human predilection for balance and stability means that the pairing is very commonly symmetrical.

Symmetry pervades the Fijian imagination in all of the ways Maybury-Lewis describes—spiritual, social, political, gendered, and aesthetic. An informant declared to the anthropologist A. M. Hocart that "all things go in pairs, or the sharks will bite" (Hocart 1952:57). The comment was neither whimsical nor theatrical, nor, I would argue, even metaphorical (cf. Toren 1998), but in the informant's view, a statement of literal fact, elegant in its simplicity. He was from northeastern Fiji (Figure 9.4), from a region called Cakaudrove (pronounced *thah-cow-n-draw-veh*), the art of which is discussed at some length in this chapter. The people there trace their descent from Dakuwaqa (pronounced *nda-coo-wah-ng-ga*), a powerful god who often takes physical form as a great shark. Through him, they possess immunity from attack by sharks, which are not viewed as totems, but literally as kin.

This man was, therefore, explaining his group's perception of the symmetries both between and within the earthly and cosmological orders, the disruption of any part of which would "inevitably result in natural calamities" (Maybury-Lewis 1989:4). It is common in Fiji to hear the remark that failure to observe some custom would "bring harm to my family," which of course extends conceptually to the entire clan, the phratry (group of clans), even the large geopolitical group within which the phratry operates. A Fijian from a different region would have chosen a different disaster to illustrate this point, but a belief in the continuities of symmetry in and between the natural and cosmic orders would hold good throughout Fiji, as would the perils of disrupting them at any level.

Symmetries in Ritual and Nonritual Social Practices

Reciprocity in Fijian society relates to kinship, gender, and the mutual obligation that exists between all members of groups and the kinship-based networks of ritual and nonritual exchange through which they simultaneously provision themselves with life's necessities, construct and define group identities, and maintain social interconnections and solidarity.

Bloch (1977:283–287) has pointed out that there are two cognitive systems, which he calls "ritual communication" and "nonritual communication," which societies use at different moments in the "long conversation" of social intercourse. They can compete for precedence and can merge at their boundary. Ritual communication mediates the relationship of past, present, and future and has generally been drawn on in positing "social structure," whereas nonritual communication, Bloch proposes, is a different cognitive system, which deals directly with the more worldly concerns of the present.

Because many anthropologists have seen social structure as their primary concern, they have tended to focus on the ritual interactions that epitomize and reinforce social structure. This has resulted in a failure to note coexistent systems of nonritual interaction or to see them merely as aspects of ritual systems. The corollary of this is that since the first formulations of Mauss (1969 [1925]), though direct observers regularly stressed the social roles of ritual "exchange" systems rather than economic roles, the reciprocities associated with ritual goods presentations have been persistently defined in terms of Western economic notions of direct exchange and debt.

In the language of symmetry, direct exchange is a mirror reflection,[4] a rarity in ritual exchange systems. There is often an apparent imbalance in a ritual "exchange," or a time lapse between a goods presentation in one direction and an answering presentation in the other direction. Both occur in Fijian rituals, and they have normally been analyzed in similarly economic terms of debt and obligation. Exchange theorists have therefore viewed transactions such as those of Fijian rituals as examples of "asymmetrical reciprocity." This too is misleading, since Fijians require that the reciprocity should actually be absolutely symmetrical, even though the element of time is built into it.

What occurs is a glide reflection—an action (normally with some form of response, but one that does not purport to mirror the initial action), a translation (passage of time in the ongoing relationship), and then a reaction, which is equivalent in meaning and social value. Meaning and social value are far more nuanced than purely economic value. The "glide" between action +

response and reaction + response ensures the continuity of the system through time. Indeed, perhaps the most important social utility of ritual is that it can mediate relationships between past, present, and future, whereas, as Bloch (1977) points out, nonritual interactions tend to primarily address the needs of the present.

In fact, the mirrored symmetrical interchange that theorists have tried to construct out of ritual goods transactions *does* exist, but not in ritual. It exists in the anthropologically neglected interactions of nonritual trade, or barter, through which societies such as Fiji's deal more directly (and far more extensively) with their worldly concerns. The economically balanced symmetry found here is actually much less demanding and sociopolitically sensitive than the symmetries of kinship and gender that are critical to ritual and thus facilitate the servicing of everyday needs with minimal strain. Through such trade, they also provision themselves with much of the wherewithal for their ritual encounters.

In Fijian ideal types, then, ritual interaction may be defined as a kinship-based system in which exchange takes place as a glide reflection and nonritual interaction as transgressing boundaries of kinship and taking place as a mirror reflection. In practice, however, the distinction is not always so clear-cut. It is often obscured by the fact that most, if not all, ritually sanctioned goods may, at some stage in their lives, be bartered nonritually (though of course there are also routinely bartered goods that are never involved in ritual). Further, the kinship-based networks of production and distribution through which ritual interaction occurs were virtually the only channels of social intercourse (other than war) in pre-Western Fiji, and therefore nonritual exchanges utilized these networks. Many observers, therefore, have found it difficult to know whether they were observing ritual exchanges or organized bartering and have tended to lump them together as ritual.

Further complicating the ideal types, mirroring is absent from perhaps the famous Fijian nonritual institution, called *kerekere,* in which people may solicit goods and services from those with whom they have social connections of almost any sort. Ritual is either totally absent or minimal, and no direct reciprocity is implied. However, an overall symmetry is notionally the ideal, and recipients accept an obligation to perpetuate the *system*

by being ready to give at some future time; their obligation is not necessarily to the original donor. Therefore, in kerekere there is not a specific exchange relationship between two individuals or two groups to provide a temporal band along which glide reflection occurs. Rather, the institution itself is symmetrical. What goes around comes around, with a pool of participants giving and receiving on an ad hoc basis as their relative need and affluence dictate. For the survival of the system, participants have to feel there will be a roughly equivalent return to them for their input, but there is never a final point at which "the books will be balanced."

Symmetries of Kinship and Gender

Pre-Christian Fijian religion was essentially ancestral, but kinship continues to pervade every aspect of Fijian social life. Gender symmetry is the overarching principle that organizes individual identity and social structure. Male and female "sides" determine every individual's relationships, responsibilities, and rights. Personal clan membership, land entitlement, and sustenance are mainly (though not absolutely) inherited patrilineally, while important aspects of assigned status and intra- and inter-group relationships are derived matrilineally.

The individual may be represented as the axis of the symmetry established between the social groups whose relationship, in terms of that individual, is configured as male and female. For a different individual, the two groups may reverse that gender "polarity" and thus their relationship to each other. This is important in determining the formal relationship of clans to one another in different situations and is critical to the perception an individual has of him/herself.

In many ways, one's most profound relationship exists with the oldest of one's mother's brothers, called *gadi* (pronounced *ngah-n-dee*), and one's cross-cousins, the children of maternal uncles or paternal aunts, called *veitavaleni* (prounced *vay-tah-vuh-lennie*). The gadi is mentor as one grows up. He organizes one's marriage and other critical life stages, finally making all of the arrangements for one's burial. Cross-cousins are predestined to be one's best friends and associates in all of life's projects if of the same sex, one's natural marriage partners if of the opposite sex. So integral is the concept of friendship with kinship that one's best friends will be referred to as

tavale—"cross-cousin." "Parallel" relationships (with siblings or parallel cousins who are regarded as siblings) are seldom as strong for same-sex members and are often subject to avoidance rules across sexes.

When groups engage in rituals, whether solely with members of their own group or with people from external groups, symmetries between male and female principles configure the action and determine the principal actors and the goods that change hands. Rituals are the traditional means Fijians have employed to gain power over forces that cannot be controlled by either might or logic, from those of the cosmos and the spirit world to temporal processes. In the latter, as "rites of passage," they mediate transitions and facilitate changes in social structure and process and so connect past, present, and future. Thus, though rituals are the means by which traditional social knowledge is sustained and reiterated, they are also always implicated in change concerning births, deaths, marriages, installations, and most other transitions and changes. Because they are the means by which the society maintains steerage of its identity and norms through times of change, they have been of particular significance in the unsettled recent history of Fiji (see my comment cited in Boissevain 1996:18).

Masi is one of the sanctioned goods that are indispensable to ritual, and here the meaning it carries is most completely expressed in its functions as both ritual dress and presentation wealth. Ritual goods are produced and distributed through a carefully regulated system of geographical, political, and social networks that both guarantee need (by exclusive "licensing" of certain places to produce items many other places require) and ensure supply (by obliging each area to always and only use its own "licensed" products in ritual exchange and/or barter). A further layer of symmetry exists in this arrangement insofar as all of these goods are gender specific, both in terms of who makes them and in terms of who controls them.

Masi is an exclusively female product and operates with other female products such as hand-woven pandanus mats, scented coconut oil, and Western "female" items such as soap and bedding. But no ritual is complete if it involves the passage of goods of only one gender, and these female goods "answer" (and are answered by) only male goods, including sperm whale teeth, carved wooden artifacts, plaited coconut fiber (sinnet), and today, drums of kerosene. Similarly, males and females control different components of the provision, preparation, and presentation of the food that is essential to such ritual exchanges, for both prestation and for consumption in shared feasting.

The manner in which Fijian ritual is implicated in gender symmetry (and vice versa) is clearly manifested in "lifting of mourning" rituals. This is the third set of rituals after death, following the funeral proper and the "hundred nights" rituals. In all three sets of rituals there are elaborate interchanges in which much masi and many mats change hands between maternal and paternal kin. These rituals first rehearse the connection that the individual's identity created between the two groups and then renegotiate their altered relationship following his/her death. In the first two ritual rounds the maternal uncle of the deceased dominates proceedings but not in the lifting of mourning. Here the two sides formally acknowledge the finality of the death and prepare to move on in life. In doing so, they first make manifest the symmetry that the deceased established between them and then ritually break it. In this way, they not only lift the mourning of those bereaved but facilitate their transition to the altered roles they must now play in relation to each other and to other groups.

In the central "act" of the ritual, there are obvious mirror symmetries. There is always the same number of mourning "lifters" as there are mourners. Second, although they are all women, these "lifters" are drawn equally from the male and female sides of the deceased. They sit directly facing the principal mourners (men and women) on the village sward (Figure 9.5). All wear barkcloth over street clothes (or if they do not have barkcloth, as in the photograph here, a plethora of Western cloth), and the principal mourners top off the whole with black overgarments. The mourners' herald (in the photograph, seated near the hurricane-destroyed building) then presents one whale tooth (the most weighty of male ritual objects) for each mourner and in return receives one from each of the "lifters," presented jointly by their herald. Then the mourners divest themselves of their black overgarments and their garments of barkcloth or Western cloth (female goods). Each one presents these to his or her designated "lifter,"

Figure 9.5 A *Luvabenu* (also called *vakataraisulu*) ritual, Ekubu Village, Vatulele, 1993. The "lifters of mourning" can be seen seated in a row, with their backs to the camera and facing the row of mourners.

who responds by taking off and presenting her masi or surplus Western cloth. Thus, everyone comes out even, but a total interchange has occurred.

The other exchanges are reciprocal but subject to competitiveness as each "side" attempts to outdo the other with the munificence of its gifts. Female goods relevant to their area are presented by both sides, at the beginning of the ritual by the mourners and near the end of the ritual by the women of the "lifter" clans. In each case, the goods are brought onto the ritual grounds with much ceremony and heaped up for later collection by their opposite numbers. The display at all stages is ostentatious. In the photograph, the mourners "supporting" women can be seen passing from hand to hand great lengths of bolting cloth. This is a surrogate for masi because these particular women came from a mat-weaving district that no longer makes or has ready access to masi. Although mats were essential at earlier funerary rituals, their mats are not an appropriate signifier at this particular ritual. Similarly, also at the beginning of the ritual, the mourner men place male goods (carved wooden objects, woven sinnet, and drums of kerosene) in a heap together with the female goods of their women. These are reciprocated by the men of the "lifter" groups as the last act of the ritual, when they present much sanctioned "special" food, cooked and uncooked, to the mourners, who take it away for future consumption. The

glide reflection, and an opportunity to reverse any competitive advantage either side may have achieved, will occur at a future ritual, arranged following another death or on some other pretext, in which today's mourners become tomorrow's hosts, today's hosts the guests. The process then starts again, the order reversed.

Meaning in Masi

The nature of the meaning *masi* carries for Fijians is generally difficult for them to elucidate and even more difficult for others to understand. Most modern Fijians, for example, would probably agree readily enough with the populist view expressed in a recent Fiji newspaper article that its designs are merely decorative (*Daily-Post* 2000). Yet they value their masi as a powerful, if not the principle, Fijian identity marker with which they distinguish themselves from Others and as a deeply spiritual sign, particularly in rituals such as those described above. They also make it very clear that the form of the cloth itself, and its figuration, determine both the purpose to which it can be put and the style to whom it belongs (Figures 9.6, 9.7). Clearly, a good deal more is going on than mere decoration, and meaning *is* being carried and transmitted both by the cloth itself and by its figuration. Equally clearly, the designs are not recognized as illustrations or even as symbols in any easily understood sense of "this-stands-for-that."

Figure 9.6 Three different garment cloths, Buca Village, Cakaudrove, 1984. Left: a "double width" (*matairua*) skirt or *i-sulu;* center: a "single-width" (*mataidua*) cummerbund or *i–oro,* and right: a single-bark noble's shoulder shah, or *wabale.* The picture shows how even within one place, differences in size, shape, figuration, and symmetry are all specific to the particular cloth type and the use to which it is put.

Bourdieu (1992) insisted that it is not possible to adequately comprehend the full meaning of art without an appropriate and specific knowledge of aesthetic context. Without that understanding, a work of art may be interpreted as having a totally contrary significance to that which would be perceived *with* it. As he summed up: "The aesthetic disposition . . . is . . . inseparable from specifically artistic competence" (Bourdieu 1992:50). It is part of the group's "cultural capital." Cultural capital, however, like economic capital, is far from being an immutable resource. It is subject to accumulation, to exchange, to inflation, to deflation, and to loss. Through any of these processes, meanings that would have been immediately apparent to a group member a century ago may well be obscure to group members today.

Such a process of change may result in the sort of distinction Chomsky (1977) draws for language between *grammatical competence*—understanding its rules, principles, and particular meanings—and *pragmatic competence*—having the ability to use it to achieve certain ends. Applying this distinction to masi, it may be said that pragmatic competence remains widespread, but few Fijians beyond the actual makers can demonstrate much grammatical competence in terms of design "correctness." In addition, after twenty years of working with makers and users all over Fiji, I have found *none* who can clarify the connection between the powerful

Figure 9.7 The three types of garment *masi* worn by the daughter of the *Ramasi,* or paramount chief of Moce Island, Lau, in 1985, who "modeled" her elder sister's bridal dress for this photograph. Moce's motifs and design layout can be seen to be regionally distinct from those of Cakaudrove. The chiefly sash is figured here but minimally, a style called *tutuki* and specific to sashes. The masi bow (*tekiteki*) in the model's hair is ornamental only.

emotion masi engenders in them and the embedded/transmitted meaning this implies. If we are to gain any understanding of this, therefore, we must seek other analytical tools than simple empiricism.

Sociosemiotic Analysis[5]

A sociosemiotic approach recommends itself, since as Barthes (1972:111) pointed out, semiotics "studies significations apart from their content." In other words, it permits a degree of detachment in teasing out the manner in which systems of social knowledge (including art) work. It offers the possibility of approaching some understanding of *what* things mean by analyzing *how* they transmit that meaning. In the case of highly evolved systems such as the social use of masi, there is in such an approach less temptation to use guesswork to fill in gaps that exist in our knowledge of which things or ideas were being encoded in which signifiers by the originators of the system, how those associations have changed over time, and how the signifiers have come to operate today.

Unfortunately, while semiotics may be simply enough defined as "the study of signs," there are many theoretical approaches to it, and the writing is too often "in a style that ranges from the obscure to the incomprehensible" (Lewis 1991:25). However, as Edmund Leach remarked, "Although the jargon is exasperating, the principles are simple" (1989:48). The simple principle he refers to is that signs work by association of two sorts, contiguity and similarity. In this volume, Allan Hanson (Chapter 8) reminds us that this was actually proposed long ago by David Hume, who wrote, "To me, there appear to be only three principles of connexion among ideas, namely, *Resemblance, Contiguity* in time or place, and *Cause or Effect* [or meaning]" (Hume 1986 [1777]). In his discussion of how Lévi-Strauss used this dichotomy, Leach distilled the perceptions of Roland Barthes and Roman Jakobson, both of whose work extended Saussure's.[6] As well as those authors, I will also draw on the work of Peirce. But to avoid semiotics' common malady of getting hopelessly bogged down in definitions, I will use as little of the "exasperating jargon" as possible or, where it is unavoidable, will limit it to that used by Saussure and Barthes.

Before going on, it should be noted that the semiotic analysis of signs and symbols has had mixed support in anthropology, ranging from rejection (e.g., Sperber 1975), through every stage of flirtation, to wholehearted embrace (e.g., Jules-Rosette 1984). The main disquiet has been semiotics' origins in linguistics, from which persist attitudes that do not sit well with nonlinguistic symbolism. For example, Douglas (1994:17) insists that if it is to be used, semiotics must disengage from the "authority of linguistics which too much dominates the analysis of the meaning of objects." She is highlighting what Gottdiener, a strong proponent of the sociosemiotic analysis of art, calls the "linguistic fallacy" of assuming that object-based systems such as art function exactly like spoken languages, with meanings that are specific, literal, or even constant. To account for this widespread fallacy, Gottdiener (1995:20, 66–67) suggests that it is because most of us rely on spoken language, which extensively employs the *specific* communication of *connotation*, whereas art depends heavily on the more *general* communication of *denotation* to transmit meaning.

In day-to-day speech, the terms *connotation* and *denotation* are frequently used as though they were synonymous, but in fact, they are subtly different. *Denotation* might be described as the "first order" of meaning of a sign—for example, the way a fur coat signifies warmth. *Connotation* would then be the second order of meaning, those associations that progressively become attached to the sign in a particular cultural milieu. In the fur coat example, in the West today these might include wealth, social status, fashionability, or increasingly, ecological insensitivity. Because denotation is broader and less culture specific, it is readily assimilated and crosses cultural boundaries easily, and often with greater emotional force, than specific connotation. Gottdiener's point is that nonlinguistic art tends to operate in this more general manner, which means that while it is more immediately and easily grasped and functions across cultures in ways that verbal language does not, it is less effective at communicating specific detail.

In fact, the more literally visual art sets out to convey specific connotations, the weaker its denotation often becomes—one of the key observable differences between advertising art and "fine" art. It is possible to see a connection between this proposition and that of the psychologist Paivio, who holds that images are

assimilated independently of words, in a cognitive process he calls "dual coding." He considers that images operate in synergy with words but speaks of "picture superiority" both in terms of the directness with which images communicate ideas and the recipient's recall capacity, which experimentally is twice as great for images as for words (Paivio 1986:esp. 159–161).

The Mythification of Meaning

Barthes (1972) provides a means of understanding that what appears to be a loss of "grammatical competence" in relation to masi may rather be read as a change in the way its meaning is now perceived. It was noted above that it is often difficult to be sure exactly what signifieds (things or ideas) may have originally been referred to by particular signifiers (words, motifs, or designs). Baudrillard (1981) has famously argued that (post)modern societies are content with "detached signifiers," which have often lost any relation to original signifieds or referents. He suggests, indeed, that they are now autonomous of their originating signifieds; others hold that this is not possible (e.g., Eco 1973, 1979). Actually, the process of attenuation between signifiers and their signifieds is far from a new phenomenon but is an inevitable part of the changing ways in which societies interpret their signs, as Peirce (1955) stressed.

Barthes (1972) shows that it is possible to see those changes in terms other than those of detached signifiers or lost signifieds. He explains that in the case of groups of particularly potent signifiers (both words and objects), their meanings can become conflated and generalized as *myths*, losing specificity but increasing their impact and the breadth of their applicability. As used by Barthes, a myth, by its incorporation of many signs, becomes in effect a single enlarged, composite, and multivalent sign, which conveys numerous important cultural ideas in a general, even ineffable manner. To those who insist that "myth" means a story, his extension of the term to include objects such as photographs may seem strange, as it may to those who impute to "myth" a sense of unreality or falsity. However, while Barthes's usage does not preclude either of these, they are merely two of the ways in which signs may be assembled to transmit the generalised meanings characteristic of myths. He points out that "every object in the world . . . [may be subject to] a type

of social *usage* which is added to pure matter . . . [and] by no means confined to oral speech. . . . Myth can be defined neither by its object nor by its material, for any material can be arbitrarily endowed with meaning" (Barthes 1972:109–110). Thus, despite his debt to his fellow structuralist Lévi-Strauss, Barthes's is a more encompassing conception of myth.

A shift of the sort Barthes describes is argued here to have occurred with masi. Specific connotations, even denotations, of designs and motifs have been progressively submerged in, and incorporated as component parts of, masi's myth, which is its widely perceptible, if somewhat vague, association with "Fijianness." Such a broad idea, embodying as it does ethnicity, cultural values, behavioral norms, geopolitical associations, and so on, needs to embody the meanings conveyed by the battery of signs that have over a long time come to be associated with masi. However, within the totality of the myth, not only do these no longer require separate decoding, they must actually operate *only* in concert, or the myth's immediate impact would be lost. Hence, their sublimation.

Such myths change and develop, just like the signs they incorporate. Groups that own myths progressively adjust their meanings in response to changing interests and needs. Those meanings can be redefined with little need to adjust the myths' constituent parts, since the autonomous meanings of those parts have become obscured. Therefore, they travel through time very successfully. Hagen (1986:117) noted this with her observation that a given style structure within the art of a culture tends to remain remarkably internally consistent across great spans of time. We have learned the folly of regarding any whole culture as immutable; nor, therefore, should we imagine that the meaning of the art Hagen saw remained static, though meaning change and stylistic change can occur at different rates.

That having been said, one must understand that the remarkable flexibility of myths does mean that even dramatic stylistic change need not be disruptive to the system of meaning. In the case of masi being discussed here, since its constituent signifiers (motifs, designs, and patterns) are making only small contributions to the meaning of the myth ("Fijianness"), there can be considerable change in these over time without diminishing its

Figure 9.8 A ceremonial cloth colored by rubbing in the Samoan/Tongan manner. The repeat pattern is a result of rubbing over the same plate many times. Photographed in Somosomo Village, Teveuni Island, Cakaudrove, in 1984, but the owner (seated with the cloth) was unsure whether this piece was made there or not since this type of cloth (here called *'umi*, elsewhere *kumi* or *gatu vakatoga*) has not been made there for many years.

force if those changes are consistent with any revised meanings of the myth and the relevant group "imaginary." To reiterate, for Fijians symmetry is the relevant "imaginary." Therefore, since symmetry is not merely a formal device, it must remain part of the structural template employed in making and figuring the cloth—though it is quite conceivable that the type of symmetry employed may also change.

To more easily conceptualize all that has been discussed above, meaning might be imagined as a nested structure, like Chinese boxes, Russian dolls, or the layers of an onion. In this imaginary model, myth, denotation, and then connotation are the outermost three layers. Myth is both the first encountered and the most readily grasped but communicates the least specific information, through emotional impact and general feelings. The most specific, esoteric meanings exist in the innermost layer. However elusive, it is only here that we may find clues about "lost signifieds" and an understanding of how the "sublimated" signifiers function in their revised role.

Barkcloth, Color Symbolism, and Symmetry

Perhaps the first place we should look for a simple relationship between masi as signifier and that which is signified by it (its perceived meaning) is in one of the oldest and most pervasive of human sign systems—color symbolism. Masi can be used as plain white cloth

(*masi vulavula*), or it may be stained a golden color with turmeric (*masi vakarerega*), smoked to a red-ocher color (*masi kuvui*), or rubbed on one surface with weak red dye (*kumi, masi vakatoga)* (Figure 9.8). In some places it may be rubbed over with black paint (*liti*), or, finally, it may be figured with geometric patterns in black and red paint (*masi kesa*).[7]

We do know that throughout Polynesia, white is the male color, associated with life, light, and day (Hanson and Hanson 1983:20). It is also described as the color of *tapu* (Barrow 1972:55), which is perhaps best defined as "the [divine] rules governing human conduct" (Hanson and Hanson 1983:49) and conveyed in Fijian by the word *lewa* (pronounced *leh-wah*). Unstained, unfigured masi is white to off-white in color, and this supplements the fact that in Fiji, as in a great diversity of other cultures across time and geographical boundaries, fabrics and/or textiles carry the denotation of spirituality (see Barber 1994; Ewins 1987; Gittinger 1989; Weiner and Schneider 1989).

Thus, whereas Peter Roe in this volume (Chapter 7) proposes that Antillean art was not considered complete until it had been decorated, that has never been the case for Fijian masi. Plain white masi is a potent sign in itself, particularly in religious applications. The early missionary Thomas Williams observed that in Fijian temples, "a long piece of white *masi*, fixed to the top, and carried down the angle of the roof so as to hang before the corner-post and lie on the floor, forms the path down which the god passes to enter the priest, and marks the holy place which few but he dare approach" (Williams and Calvert 1982 [1858]: 222–223).

Figuration, therefore, does not complete the masi, but rather adds further layers of meaning to it. These meanings may well originally have been both specifically and widely understood, though today all that we can do is to infer what they might have been from our broader cultural and historical knowledge. What *is* clear is that different types of figuration specify particular roles for the cloth, and thus to some extent they are restrictive rather than additive. In other words, while in its plain white state it can perform in virtually any situation where it is appropriate to use masi, as soon as figuration is added, its applicability is both directed and limited. The specificity starts with the very limited color palette used.

The main color of figuration is black, the color of death, of nature, and the earth, and of women, who are the guardians of all of these. In Vanualevu, mortuary-cave human remains that were investigated by the Fiji Museum in the 1980s were shrouded in masi that was principally black. Black remains the color of masi or bolting-cloth mourners wear right up to, and during, the lifting of mourning ceremonies described earlier in this chapter. I have also been told in Cakaudrove that traditionally, during the time women had to remain cloistered following giving birth, they were required to shroud themselves totally in black masi whenever they had to venture out of the house for calls of nature. The symbolism of female fecundity, birth, and death may be seen to interlock in these usages.

Apart from such completely black cloth, much masi was traditionally figured simply as black figures on a neutral white "ground." Sometimes the design is such that black-and-white forms work together simultaneously in counterpoint, a feature I have also noted in relation to patterns on mats (Ewins 1982b:16) that, in the literature of symmetry, is commonly referred to as "two-color" symmetry. Nowhere is it more evident than in Cakaudrove cloth. Western artists speak of such black-and-white forms as positive and negative (Figure 9.9).

The device of alternating and/or interlocking positive and negative was explored most famously and wittily in Western art by Maurice Escher. He relied on

Figure 9.9 Recombined symmetrical design components, with both positive and negative elements. (a) *Drali* (to knead or daub), (b) *Vetau* (species of tree), (c) *'Alo'alo* (star), (d) unnamed composite design, combining (b) and (c) in a variation on the theme of (a). #M499, Tasmanian Museum and Art Gallery (see Ewins 1982a:20), possibly from Yacata or Kanacea, Southern Cakaudrove.

the unexpected juxtaposition of recognizable depictions of people, animals, and objects. But in totally abstract Fijian art, the color symbolisms of black and white can be "unpacked" as denoting life and death, male and female, traditions and laws, nature and the land—the building blocks of Fijian identity.

As described above, the other colors that occur in masi figuration (and indeed in barkcloth throughout Polynesia) are those covered in Fijian by the word *damu*, broadly translated as "red" but actually spanning a broad segment of the spectrum from brown through red ocher to vermilion and even to the warm golden orange of some types of turmeric. Red is associated with Burotu, the spirit world of Fiji and Polynesia (Geraghty 1993:363–364), the gods, and chiefs who are gods-on-earth (Barrow 1972; Sayes 1982:5). Thus, when it is used,

Figure 9.10 Corner of the face of a taunamu ceremonial hanging/screen, Somosomo Village, Taveuni, Cakaudrove, 1981, showing the traditional Cakaudrove style of bold black-and-white two-color patterns, here including panels of the *ceva* and *drau ni niu ceva* motifs (see Figure 9.18 and 9.20). Red-ochre colored bands (here lighter gray) form a separate two-color pattern. The white inclusions in these red bands, of "Maltese crosses" and asterisks, bear the name *tu'i tu'i pu,* a nondialect name that may relate to the strong Samoan connections of this area and of these large ceremonial cloths.

red adds further cosmological and hierarchical connotations to the existing spiritual denotation of the cloth.

Red elements are always added last in the printing sequence, and are normally arranged in red-and-white bands or grids in such a way as to be contiguous with but separate from the black-and-white patterns (Figures 9.9, 9.10, 9.11). Thus, the three colors are organized as two discrete two-color patterns. In some rare museum examples, there are instances of genuine three-color patterns, in which black, red, and white have equal roles in the pattern, but instances of this level of design sophistication are extremely rare in masi today.

Today, barkcloth is seldom printed in black only but typically is figured with both black and red on white, and in such a piece, color interrelates the spiritual and temporal domains, life and death, male and female, human and natural laws. The simple device of using two colors on a white ground thus enables the embedding of a remarkable range of conceptual symmetries. Whether today's masi makers think consciously about all (or any) of this as they figure a piece of cloth, color symbolism is still a widespread part of Fijian cultural capital, and I propose that, in this way, the color signifiers contribute, even if only subliminally, to the impact of masi as myth.

Figuration and Meaning

While it is possible to speculate on a number of now-enigmatic denotations and connotations that might exist in the figuration on masi, one thing we do know with certainty is that, as mentioned above, it has traditionally functioned as a group identity marker. How it performed this role relates to its "visual semantics."

The kernel of our imaginary nested layers described above, the detailed mechanics of how form and content interact to convey meaning, takes us back to the earlier brief discussion of the "simple" semiotic principle emphasized by Leach (1989:48–50), that the meaning of signs is transmitted through two types of association, those of contiguity and those of similarity. It was schematized by Saussure (1974 [1916]) as functioning on two axes, defined as "associative," or *syntagmatic,* and *paradigmatic* (Adams 1996:134–141; Culler 1986:59–62, 102–103; Gottdiener 1995:6–7)[8]:

• The syntagmatic axis concerns juxtaposition, such as the way words occur in sentence chains or visual elements interrelate in a work of art.

• The paradigmatic axis concerns the recognition of similarity, analogy, or difference, such as linguistic similes and metaphors or art that references the natural world in some way.

Meaning always engages both axes, but which axis is preeminent in a particular instance or in a particular type of meaning transmission varies between different groups, times, and media. In the twentieth century, some Western visual artists realized that the art of Africa, Oceania, and the Americas was operating in a quite different way from Western art, which since the Renaissance had embraced pictorial illusionism and sculptural naturalism. They began to imitate or appropriate non-Western forms and restructure them in novel ways. Though some of the early examples of this in Fauvism, Cubism, and Expressionism may today seem ingenuous, they were attempting to shift the weight of meaning more toward the syntagmatic axis. None of the major twentieth-century art movements could have emerged without this axis shift, in particular Western abstraction. However, over the next half century this

Figure 9.11 The face of a ceremonial hanging/screen (*taunamu*), Buca Village, Cakaudrove. While the corners bear large drau ni niu motifs and the endemic red ochre panels have white tu'i tu'i pu Maltese crosses, the maker of this cloth has also borrowed many stencil motifs from Lau. These are also, however, invariably symmetrical, as is their placement within the overall design.

developed its own authority, and as Clifford (1988:192) has pointed out, its intentions, forms and meanings today bear little relation to those of non-Western art.

The insights that resulted from this focus on syntagm have contributed greatly to the understanding of symbol and meaning. Douglas (1973:11) asserted that a symbol "only has meaning from its relation to other symbols in a pattern. The pattern gives the meaning . . . no one item in the pattern can carry meaning by itself." Even Sperber, opposed as he was to a semiotic approach to meaning, acknowledged that "the interpretation [of symbols] bears not on the elements but on their configuration" (Sperber 1975:48).

Notwithstanding this, the fact that much ethnic art remains enigmatic to Westerners is at least partly because contextual (syntagmatic) meaning transmission in art still remains less widely understood or appreciated by nonartists than associative representation (paradigmatic). Rather ironically, this Western bias has, because of the inordinate weight of Western culture, actually provoked a shift away from traditional approaches and toward representation, illusion, and naturalism in much postcolonial art.

Syntagm, Paradigm, and Symmetry

As pointed out above, syntagmatic and paradigmatic axes invariably operate together. Not merely their relative

weight is variable, but also the *manner* in which they operate. Historically, Fijian two-dimensional art as seen on masi, mats and pots, plus sinnet lashings, female tattooing, and "decoration" on wooden artifacts has never been representational, let alone realistic.[9] Here paradigm operates not through imitative similarity of aspects of the natural world, but rather through something resembling the parallelism that Jakobson stressed for poetry (and which also exists in music)—similarity or contrast expressed internally through repetition of motifs and shared structural features (Kiparsky 1983). Symmetry, therefore, operates on both the syntagmatic and paradigmatic axes of masi figuration since *both* relate to the form of the art itself rather than referencing externals.

Masi figuration consists of geometric patterns of grids and panels with one- and two-dimensional symmetric arrangements of geometric elements, predominantly triangles. All four types of planar symmetry motions—translation, reflection, glide reflection, and rotation (Washburn and Crowe 1988:44–51)—are found in profusion in the overall organization of the figured/nonfigured sections of the cloth, the arrangement of motifs into patterns, and even the motifs themselves.

The overall design of the cloths varies according to type and has changed over time. However, symmetry is always the dominant rule of design. In the simplest types, such as the long narrow cloths worn as loincloths (*malo*), sashes (*wabale*), and cummerbunds (*i-oro*) and also the decorative friezes in houses (*i-uku-uku ni vale*), parallel bands of repeated motifs run the length of the cloth. With the development of wider "skirt lengths" (*i-sulu*) in the Christian era, the same design system was applied to them. At some stage, it became customary to make the bands mirror one another from the center outward, and the ends of the cloth were "closed" with a set of bands at right angles to the main direction (Figure 9.12). The larger cloths, bedspreads, or *solofua* (Figure 9.13 and 9.14) and the great ritual cloths that are in different parts of Fiji called *taunamu* or *gatu vakaviti* (Figure 9.15, and Figures 9.6, 9.9, 9.10, 9.11) and *kumi* or *gatu vakatoga* (Figure 9.7) measure many square meters and provide the greatest scope for spatial organization and for layer upon layer of design symmetries. Even large finite designs seldom "stand alone" but are combined "to stop

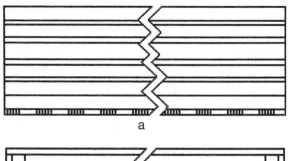

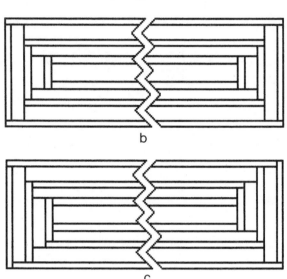

Figure 9.12 Different design layouts of "long" masi such as is worn or used for house decoration. (a) Simplest layout with translation symmetry. Still used in some places on ritual clothing and house decoration strips, though the striped bottom edge, once an absolute "marker" of Fijian cloth, is now seldom seen·(b) Layout used in almost all tourist tapa and some *i-oro, i-sulu,* and *solofua,* displaying translation and mirror symmetry, and (c) translation symmetry with layout rotation.

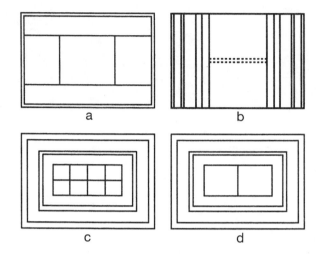

Figure 9.13 Typical solofua (bedcover) pattern layouts: (a) Moce, (b) Namuka, (c) Oneata, (d) Vatulele.

them feeling lonely," as one informant expressed it.

The geometric structuring in Fijian masi figuration produces the identity marker. Both the specificity of motifs to the group *and* how they are arranged spatially in the overall design play a part. As I pointed out nearly two decades ago, "Some areas which share virtually all [of] their motifs can still distinguish their *masi* by the actual placement of these" (Ewins 1982a:11). That insight was based on explanations provided in Natewa Village (Cakaudrove Province). There, within living memory at the time of my initial research in 1981, the three large clan groups or phratries (called *yavusa*) within the village could distinguish their masi from that of other areas by both the specificity of their motifs *and* the arrangement of these. However, each phratry, indeed each clan *within* each phratry, had been able to distinguish their masi by design arrangement alone. That level of detailed knowledge had been lost even at the time of my research, but the people of Natewa Village were still readily able to distinguish their masi from that of the village of Buca, within the same geopolitical grouping (*vanua*) and a few miles distant, though the

motifs used were largely the same in each village.

It is also in Cakaudrove that symmetry is most overwhelmingly obvious as the basis for overall design organization (see particularly Figure 9.10), a fact highlighted by Crowe and Nagy (Crowe and Nagy 1992; Crowe 1991; Nagy 1993). Symmetry in fact occurs consistently in the regionally distinct design systems of *all* of the masi-producing areas in Fiji, both within motifs and in their disposition in the overall design of the cloth.[10]

Names, Meanings, and Notations

Apparently contradicting the above assertion that Fijian masi figuration does not directly reference the natural world, the names that motifs and designs bear are often nouns for flora, fauna, or even ideas. These hint seductively at totemic or other socially significant meanings, and for decades Western students of Fijian art have been dutifully recording names and then hunting about in their lists for clues to the meaning of the art. Names such as "clothespin," "safety-razor blade," and "motorcar tire" have been recorded apparently unquestioningly, though to imagine that profound social significance

Figure 9.14 Putting finishing touches (highlighting figures in the "rubbed" area) on a solofua bedcover, Namuka Island, Lau, 1985. This has both continuities and differences in design with taunamu from the same island (Figures 9.2 and 9.3).

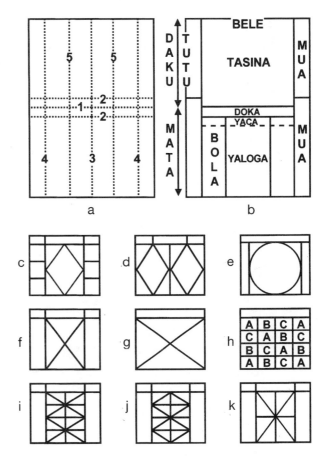

Figure 9.15 Some typical layouts for the great ritual cloths taunamu/gatu vakaviti. (a) Order of preliminary creasing of the cloth to determine layout. (b) Division and nomenclature for Vatulele taunamu: *daku* means "back," the "Tongan" rubbed half of the cloth, while *mata* means "face." Lauan layout is very similar, but the *yalogo* is called *i potu loma, tasina* is called *potu tasina, mua* is called *i potu sau,* and *bola* has no name. (c) to (h) Layouts used in Vatulele for patterns in the critical *yaloga* panel. In (d), (g), and (h) the bola are not discrete panels, the large patterns extending right to the mua. (h) A now virtually obsolete form, using four patterns in what is effectively a glide arrangement. (i) to (k) Typical layouts used in Lauan gatu vakaviti for the same panel, there called *potu i loma:* (i) Namuka, (j) Moce, and (k) Kabara.

attaches to any of these stretches credulity.

I have proposed elsewhere that these names were assigned after the motifs were developed by the artists, perhaps as "nicknames" to serve as aides mémoire to classify abstract forms (Ewins 1982b:16). This practice is familiar to Western abstract artists, who, without implying any literal representation, often give names to elements in their work, or to entire works of art, based on some likeness these are fancied to bear to things or ideas. However, to infer that the image and name in such cases are both signifiers relating back to a single "ultimate signified" is unnecessary and unjustified. Generally the more fanciful the name is, the more memorable. To recall again the work of Paivio, he has shown experimentally that recall of images is greatly enhanced by associating them with words, even unrelated words, through the "code additivity" or synergy of "dual coding" (Paivio 1986:160).

The names, then, function very much as Goodman (1976:128) proposed operates with systems of "notation," providing "authoritative identification" from one usage to the next. He rejected the use of such a system for fine art on the basis that it relies on the originality of its invention and thus requires a system of specific and/or explanatory naming for each unique piece. However, Fijian art does not operate in the manner of Western "fine art." In Goodman's terminology, it is "allographic" rather than "autographic," which means that the social value of the art lies in truth-to-type, not uniqueness.

A finite number of motifs are found within the totality of each group's masi (though over time they may be reduced or added to, as described above in the discussion of the signs within myths). They are used in specific sequences and combinations depending on the particular type of masi. This may be compared with music, where a finite number of sounds and structures

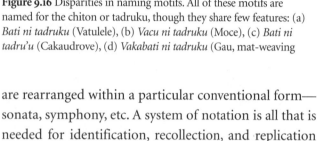

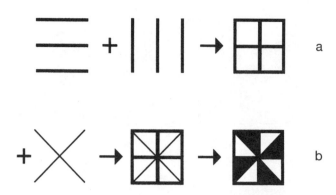

Figure 9.16 Disparities in naming motifs. All of these motifs are named for the chiton or tadruku, though they share few features: (a) *Bati ni tadruku* (Vatulele), (b) *Vacu ni tadruku* (Moce), (c) *Bati ni tadru'u* (Cakaudrove), (d) *Vakabati ni tadruku* (Gau, mat-weaving

Figure 9.17 The "box-frame" module. Top row: method of first using a stencil to create a *waqani matairua,* then restenciling at right angles to produce a box frame, in Lau called *kamiki.* Bottom row: this frame may be further divided by drawing diagonal pencil lines and finally filling alternate "vanes" to produce what is called either *bika ni kamiki* or *boko ni kamiki* (meaning either "divided" or "blocked" frame motif).

are rearranged within a particular conventional form—sonata, symphony, etc. A system of notation is all that is needed for identification, recollection, and replication of the motifs. In categorizing the symmetries that occur in other allographic art systems, Washburn and Crowe (1988) and other analysts use systems of notation with letters and numerals to identify the elements and organization of the patterns and designs they study.

Finally, in masi, just as I have pointed out previously in relation to mats (Ewins 1982b:16), the same motifs often have totally different names in different regions, or, conversely, quite different motifs may be named after the same object. For example, in Figure 9.16 are illustrated a group of motifs that are all called *tadruku* ("chiton"). Most of the names specifically refer to the distinctive serrated plates that make up the shell of this small limpet like reef dweller (a little like an armadillo's carapace). Certainly, their interest in it is purely formal—it is of no symbolic or economic significance to Fijians, and omnivorous though they usually are, they do not eat the chiton. The manner in which they depict its twofold repetition varies, perhaps coming closest to "illustration" in the Vatulele motif. The complex and totally nonillustrative little motif that is called "chiton" in Moce is also used in Vatulele but is called "in the style of Tuvuca," another island that actually does not use the motif!

Therefore, the value of the motif names is not that

they refer us to the objects named, but that they provide a notational system. The manner in which that system works in turn supports the argument that paradigm operates here through formal similarities rather than representation or facsimilation. The following "pattern system" may help clarify this. Throughout Fiji, there is a very simple masi pattern of a number of parallel lines, applied with a stencil of three to four short lines, printed end to end to achieve the desired length. The pattern is widely called *waqani* (pronounced *wah-ng-gah-nee*), a word that means a frame, boundary, or border and is today applied to window frames among other things. The pattern is designated as "double" (*matairua*), "triple" (*mataitolu*), or more, based on the number of *enclosed* spaces, not on the number of lines. It may be used end to end to create continuous bands, or a *matairua* "double frame" (three parallel lines) may be printed once and then the same three-line stencil overprinted at right angles to create a gridded square or "box frame" (Figure 9.17). In Lau (southeastern Fiji), the resulting box-frame module is called *kamiki.*

Triangles may be established by folding diagonal lines (today by ruling with a pencil). A variety of motifs are created by selectively filling component parts of the frame, and the resulting patterns are differently named. For example, when every alternate triangle is printed solid, resulting in what Kooijman (1972:377) referred to

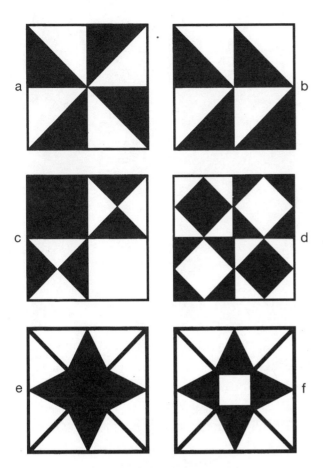

Figure 9.18 *Ceva* ("south wind") family of motifs, Cakaudrove. (a) *ceva*, (b) *ceva musu ti'i dua*, (c) *ceva-i-soni 1*, (d) *ceva-i-soni 2*, (e) *ceva 'ubutawa 1*, (f) *ceva 'ubutawa 2*.

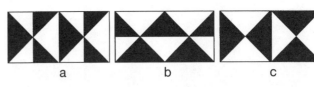

Figure 9.19 *Da'ai* ("bow" or "gun") family of motifs, Cakaudrove. (a) *Da'ai* or *Kubu ni da'ai*, (b) *Da'ai balavu*, (c) *Da'ai musu*.

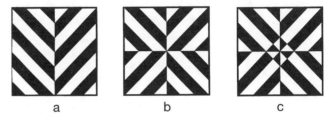

Figure 9.20 Chevrons, called *drau ni niu* ("coconut leaf") family of motifs, Cakaudrove. (a) *Drau ni niu,* (b) *Drau ni niu musu,* (c) *Drau ni niu ceva.*

as a "vane swastika," it is called *bika ni kamiki* (divided frame motif) or *boko ni kamiki* (blocked frame motif).[11]

In Cakaudrove the identical pattern is called *ceva* (pronounced *theh-vuh*), an enigmatic name that refers to a certain southerly wind. However, then starts the notational naming, with a whole sequence of variant forms based on the box-frame module classified as types of ceva (Figure 9.18). First is the *ceva musu ti'i dua*,[12] which means "single component of chopped ceva." As can be seen, the component is one-half of the ceva that, instead of being rotated, is merely repeated. The *ceva i soni* apparently derives from the verb for making small incisions (*soni-ta*), a reference to the ceva motif being "diced up." This quality becomes obvious on the printed cloth, since this motif is always repeated two dimensionally, making a very intricate, "busy" pattern. Finally, the ceva *'ubutawa* appears to mean "ceva motif full of projections," which it clearly is!

Another such name family exists for *da'ai*, a word

that originally meant "bow" and by association was applied to guns when these were introduced. The motif that is called simply *da'ai* is also referred to as *kubu ni da'ai* ("gunstock"), but this was probably a later elaboration. The visual elements of the motif are actually far closer to the ceva motif than to any representational resemblance to either a bow or a gun. However, the ceva series already contained sufficient motifs to test the memory, and following the argument advanced above, that the names were an aide-mémoire, a case clearly existed for a further classificatory title—ergo the da'ai name family. Visual associations were established between at least three motifs, *da'ai* or *kubu ni da'ai* ("bow/gun" or "gunstock"), *da'ai musu* ("chopped da'ai"), and *da'ai balavu* ("long da'ai") (Figure 9.19).

Yet another name family is that of the chevron figure (Figure 9.20), which is arranged in glide reflection and called generically *drau ni niu* ("coconut leaf"). When this is "chopped" and opposed within the box frame, it is called *drau ni niu musu*. While this literally means "chopped coconut leaf," it is far better understood as "chopped drau ni niu motif." A version of it also bears the small ceva vane swastika in the center of it and is accordingly called *drau ni niu ceva*.

There are many such name families in all of Fiji's masi-making regions, always using names systematically to group motifs that share important visual

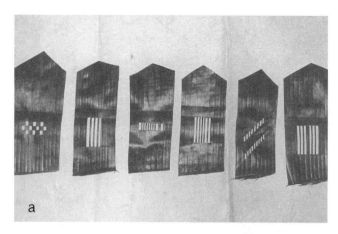

Figure 9.21 (a) "Straight line" stencils made from banana leaves, Moce Island, Lau, 1985. (b) Printing with a banana-leaf stencil, Natewa, Cakaudrove, 1984.

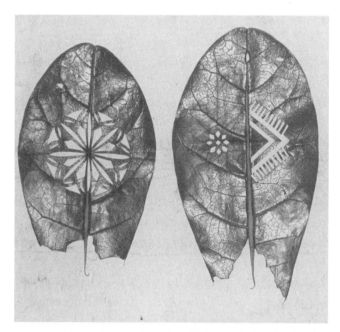

Figure 9.22 Complex stencils made with leaves of a beach-growing tree. Moce Island, Lau, 1985.

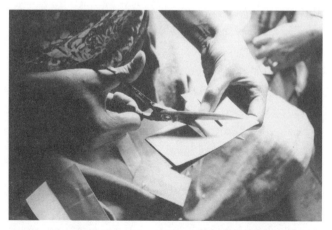

Figure 9.23 Cutting a stencil in light cardboard with scissors, Vatulele Island, 1985.

elements and/or technical procedures for making stencils or printing motifs. With frequently very great differences between individual motifs within a given name family, it is implausible that the makers have convinced themselves that they all resemble, or are visual metaphors for, the object that designates the name family, even something as amorphous as a wind!

Stencil Motifs

All of the Cakaudrove motifs illustrated here have reflection symmetry within the structure of the motif itself, and most show rotation symmetry. Most were not originally stencil motifs but until the last half century were produced by direct painting. This involved careful drafting out of the cloth and then painting in the black and red areas with small brushes made of swabs of masi, using the edge of a coconut leaflet as a frisket or mask. The name given to the technique is *bolabola,* which means "to divide up (generally into equal parts)" and refers to the preliminary drafting, which is far more extensive than is necessary with stencil printing. This was originally done by a process of folding the cloth to create a seam, running a paint swab along it, then folding it again in a different direction. The resulting cloth is therefore properly called *masi bola* (Ewins 1982a:16, n. 58), as distinct from the generic term *masi kesa* applied to stenciled cloth. A sort of symmetry was thus inherent in the process of dividing up the cloth, but the carrying through of this to figuring masi bola was a deliberate design strategy. Today, because of its relative ease and speed, the stenciling process has widely supplanted this

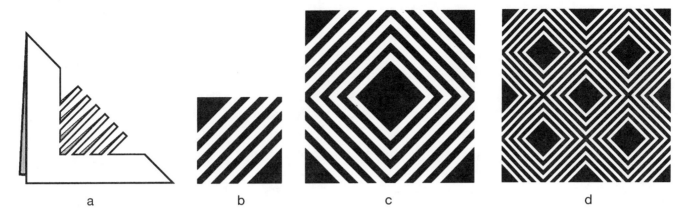

a b c d

Figure 9.24 Stenciling a composite image: (a) method of folding the stencil material to cut symmetrical image, (b) resulting print, (c) composite image, stencil printed four times, (d) large composite image, stencil printed sixteen times.

technique, both for printing bola motifs (such as those illustrated above and many others—see the plates and drawings in Crowe and Nagy [1992] for a representative selection) and for some motifs that were imported, along with the technology, from other regions.

While virtually all Pacific peoples made and figured barkcloth, stenciling was unique to Fiji. Originally, banana and pandanus leaves were used to make stencils for rectilinear motifs because of the ease of slitting with a lemon thorn along their parallel venation (Figure 9.21a), while stencils for more complex forms were made by cutting large fleshy leaves with sharp shells (Figure 9.22). Today stout paper, cardboard, and x-ray film are used, first because they can be kept from one printing session to the next without curling or shriveling and second because they are easier to cut with scissors (Figure 9.23). When paper or thin cardboard are used, the symmetry inherent in most motifs facilitates the method of cutting. Almost invariably, the paper is folded and half of the design cut, in exactly the manner of making paper-chain figures. When the paper is unfolded, the full stencil is revealed (Figure 9.24). The method is less suitable for x-ray film, which retains any creases made in it.

The majority of stencil motifs tend to be printed repetitively in horizontal or vertical rows, exploiting translation, reflection, and glide reflection symmetries. However, some motifs employ rotation symmetry and sometimes reflection within themselves. Still others occur most often as components of two-dimensional patterns (e.g., Figure 9.24).

Conclusion

Sociologists as early as Hume and Durkheim noted that societies order the world of things according to the same patterns and structures they use to organize their societies. Kopytoff (1986:90) sums up that societies "mentally construct" objects simultaneously with, and according to the same rules they use for, constructing people. Durkheim traced this to the "ensemble of mental habits" societies have, which Durand has termed "imaginaries"—ideas about how the cosmos and the natural world is ordered and accordingly how they believe they should order their own social constructions and material inventions.

This chapter has asserted that for Fijians, symmetry is such an overarching idea. It is made manifest in their visual art, particularly in their very important barkcloth or masi, which is pervaded in every aspect by symmetry, from the rectangular shape of all of the different types of cloth through to its figuration, including the design layout, patterns, and even the structure of individual motifs.

Such a dedication to the principle of symmetry, and its consistency and pervasiveness in Fijian two-dimensional art, goes far beyond aesthetic style or convention. Masi, in fact, stands as a physical symbol of the principle of symmetry and references, at least indirectly, all things Fijian that are based on it. The degree to which social structures are similarly structured has been discussed here in terms of kinship relationships and the rituals that celebrate and perpetuate these while simultaneously facilitating social transitions from past to present and present to future. The illustration used here is the lifting of mourning ceremony, the activities of which embody both mirroring and glide reflection. These two symmetries are represented in this chapter as configuring the social interactions in the ritual and nonritual life of Fijians.

The way meaning is carried and transmitted has been analyzed here using a sociosemiotic approach. It has been shown that masi carries perhaps the greatest range of signs of any Fijian artifact. By the process of "mythification" described by Barthes, the particularity of the meanings in the patterns, designs, and motifs in the figuration has been largely subsumed within the overall myth of "Fijianness," but masi's sign value has been strengthened, not diminished. Traditionally the clearest role of masi was as a group identity marker, the uniqueness of each sign shown here to have been achieved through a combination of the particular motifs used by each group and the overall design organization of the figuration. Indeed, the latter was what imparted the greatest particularity to the sign.

Thus, what Saussure termed the syntagmatic or contextual relations of the elements is critically important. The *paradigmatic* axis of meaning, dependent on similarity, which is so important in Western representational or metaphorical art, functions differently in Fijian abstract two-dimensional art. Here similarity and contrast relate not to the external natural world, but operate through repetition and symmetry of elements, in a manner similar to the parallelism Jakobson noted for poetry. This particular form of associative relations carries through into the naming of motifs and patterns, with names being developed as systems of relationships that permit classification of the visual forms to which they are appended.

Today there is much cultural and social interchange between regions, which in precolonial Fiji had little intercourse. One result of this is that the regional group-identifying motifs and design layouts of the masi are, in most areas, being supplemented with, or even supplanted by, those from other areas. Gradually a single homogeneous Fiji-wide masi style is emerging as Fijians redefine their identities in terms of a common ethnicity rather than their regional group particularities.[13] While there is inevitably some loss of aesthetic diversity associated with such a process, the norm of symmetry remains as pervasive in structuring and figuring this new cloth as it was in the original regional types it has incorporated. I contend that this nexus between aesthetic and semiotic comprehension is the major element in the remarkable durability of masi as a current and relevant art form. While retaining its essential elements, it is proving to be sufficiently flexible to carry changed meanings during rapidly changing times. ■

Notes

1. The term *tapa* is of Austronesian linguistic origin. Ling and Ling (1963) point out that in the aboriginal language of Taiwan, the word for *barkcloth* is *tap*. That root form has been modified in other languages that are descended from proto-Austronesian to signify particular types or aspects of barkcloth. This includes several Polynesian languages, whence sailors adopted it as a generic term. However, to use *tapa* as the generic term for Fijian barkcloth is inappropriate since that word has a specific and limited meaning in Fiji, as it does in Tonga and Samoa (Ewins 1982a:5; Thomas 1995:131).

2. The terms *figured, figuring,* and *figuration* are commonly used by artists but less often by anthropologists, who often blur niceties of artistic terminology. The terms are used here because they broadly describe intentionally applying two-dimensional forms to the surface of an object and the visually perceptible result of such action. Each of the terms *design, pattern,* and/or *motif* has a more particular meaning that will emerge in the detailed discussion that follows. *Print(ing)* and *paint(ing)* describe specific and distinct technical processes and the product of these. Finally, *decoration* is not used since it does not suggest (in fact among artists has often been held to specifically exclude) the transmission of meaning, which is argued here to inhere in both the act of figuring and the resultant figuration of barkcloth.

3. The word *design* is used throughout this chapter in the sense normally understood by artists, as an intentional action of visual organization or the output resulting from that action. This usage includes but is not limited to symmetric designs as stipulated in Washburn and Crowe (1988:52).

4. The terms and notations used here are those given in Washburn and Crowe (1988) and summarized in Crowe and Nagy (1992).

5. This term is borrowed from Riggins (1994) and Gottdiener (1995), whose work makes an important contribution to highlighting and overcoming many of the inadequacies of earlier semiotic approaches, as well as symbolic interactionism and postmodern theory/culture studies, in dealing with the social life of material culture. The brief remarks made on theories of semiotics in this chapter are acknowledged as being only superficial notes on particular aspects of what are complex and nuanced theories. For instance, though there are important differences between how Saussure conceived of semiology and Peirce of semiotics, in this discussion they will be treated as broadly consonant and semiotics used throughout. Similarly avoided are arguments about the relative appropriateness of a Saussurean "dyadic" or Peircean "triadic" system, though the discussion here makes it clear that context is critical to meaning. Readers who may not be familiar with semiotics are referred to the succinct Internet article "An Introduction to Semiotics," by English academic Daniel Chandler (1994). Deeper semiotic analyses that are of particular relevance to art may be found in Thibault (1991) and Gottdiener (1995).

6. De Saussure's name is customarily used without the *de* qualifier, given simply as *Saussure* or *Saussurean.*

7. For a broader discussion of the methods of figuring and uses of Fijian masi, see Ewins (1982a:5–21) and Kooijman (1972, 1977). Note that "red" is the color designated by Fijians for the red-brown or brown paint they use, the color deriving either from bark, iron-bearing clays, or both. Not only linguistic but also conceptual continuities exist for Fijians between the golden dye of turmeric, the red of vermilion, and the red-brown of hematitic clay. All are numinous (Geraghty 1993).

8. Jakobson (1960) restyled these terms *metonymic* and *metaphoric* respectively. The Peircean terms sometimes used are indexical and iconic, but even these are not exactly analogous, first because they are two parts of a tripartite rather than a dual system and second because Peirce's definition of *index* and *icon* is closer to the distinction drawn between above between *denotation* and *connotation.*

9. Prehistoric Fijian two-dimensional art, evident on potsherds and petroglyphs, is also principally abstract. The one clear prehistoric exception is the human faces and other representations of fish, birds, and a sailing canoe painted on a limestone cliff in Vatulele Island (Ewins 1995). While these have certain affinities with other Pacific art, there are no evident connections between them and Fijian two-dimensional art in the historical period.

10. A detail of Cakaudrove masi design was also used for the dust jacket of *Symmetries of Culture* (Washburn and Crowe 1988) and other examples illustrated on pages 102 and 177.

11. Kooijman (1977:52, 55) mistakenly recorded this "swastika" as kamiki, but the people of Moce and elsewhere are adamant that *kamiki* refers to the box frame, and *bika ni kamiki* is merely one of the possible elaborations. The word *kamiki* is a now-obsolete name for a type of strong vine used for lashing structures together (its leaves also have medicinal value), today generally called *komidri.* It is unclear why that name was chosen, unless it is an elliptical reference to the shared integrative structural quality of vine and frame.

12. The apostrophe so frequently occurring in the Cakaudrove language represents a glottal stop where the letter *k* would occur in Standard Fijian. A similar linguistic form occurs in Samoan.

13. Whether the reassertion of geopolitical regionalism that has occurred among Fijians in the turbulent wake of the coups of 1987 and 2000 will reverse this trend and result in a return to regional identity markers in masi remains to be seen.

References Cited

Adams, Laurie Schneifer
1996   *The Methodologies of Art.* Icon Editions, HarperCollins, New York.

Barber, Elizabeth Wayland (editor)
1994   *Women's Work: The First 20,000 Years. Women, Cloth and Society in Early Times.* Norton, New York.

Barrow, Terence
1972   *Art and Life in Polynesia.* A. H. & A. W. Reed, Wellington, New Zealand.

Barthes, Roland
1972   *Mythologies.* Jonathan Cape, London, UK.

Baudrillard, Jean
1981   *For a Critique of the Political Economy of the Sign.* Telos Press, St. Louis, MO.

Bloch, Maurice
1977   The Past and the Present in the Present. *Man* n.s.:278–292.

Boissevain, J. (editor)
1996   *Coping with Tourists: European Reactions to Mass Tourism.* Berghahn Books, Providence, RI.

Bourdieu, Pierre
1992   *Distinction: A Social Critique of the Judgment of Taste.* Routledge, London, UK.

Chandler, Daniel
1994   Semiotics for Beginners. http://www.aber.ac.uk/~dgc/semiotic.html, accessed August 1999.

Chomsky, Noam
1977   *Essays on Form and Interpretation.* North-Holland, New York.

Clifford, James
1988   *The Predicament of Culture: Twentieth-Century Ethnography, Literature, and Art.* Harvard University Press, Cambridge, MA.

Crowe, Donald W.
1991   Cakaudrove Patterns. Colloquia Mathematica Societatis János Bolyai, Szeged (Hungary). Special Issue: *Intuitive Geometry* 63:78–84.

Crowe, Donald W., and Dénes Nagy
1992   *Cakaudrove-Style Masi Kesa of Fiji. Ars Textrina*, 18:119–155.

Culler, Jonathan
1986   *Ferdinand de Saussure.* Cornell University Press, Ithaca, NY.

Daily Post (electronic edition).
2000   Local Cloth Makes It Big for Reef. http://www.fijilive.com/news/, accessed February 2, 2000.
de Saussure, Ferdinand

1974   [1916] *Course in General Linguistics.* Fontana, London, UK.

Douglas, Mary
1973   *Natural Symbols: Explorations in Cosmology.* Penguin, Harmondsworth, UK.
1994   The Genuine Article. In *The Socialness of Things: Essays on the Socio-Semiotics of Objects,* edited by S. H. Riggins, pp. 9–22. Mouton de Gruyter, Berlin and New York.

Durand, Gilbert
1999   [1960] *The Anthropological Structures of the Imaginary.* Boombana Publications, Brisbane, Australia.

Durkheim, Emile
1976   [1912] *The Elementary Forms of the Religious Life.* George Allen & Unwin, London, UK.

Durkheim, Emile, and Marcel Mauss
1963   [1903] *Primitive Classification.* University of Chicago Press, Chicago.

Eco, Umberto
1973   Social Life as a Sign System. In *Structuralism: An Introduction,* edited by D. Robey, pp. 57–72. Clarendon Press, Oxford, UK.
1979   *A Theory of Semiotics.* University of Indiana Press, Bloomington.

Ewins, Rod
1982a   *Fijian Artefacts: The Tasmanian Museum and Art Gallery Collection.* Tasmanian Museum and Art Gallery, Hobart, Tasmania.
1982b   *Matweaving in Gau, Fiji.* Fiji Museum, Suva, Fiji.
1987   Bark-Cloth and the Origins of Paper. In *1st National Paper Conference: Post-Conference Papers,* edited by P. Wells, pp. 11–15. Papermakers of Australia, Hobart, Tasmania.
1995   Proto-Polynesian Art? The Cliff-Paintings of Vatulele, Fiji. *Journal of the Polynesian Society* 103:1–51.

Geraghty, Paul
1993   Pulotu, Polynesian Homeland. *Journal of the Polynesian Society* 102:343–384.

Gittinger, Mattiebelle (editor)
1989   *To Speak with Cloth: Studies in Indonesian Textiles.* University of California Press, Los Angeles.

Goodman, Nelson
1976   *Languages of Art.* Hacket Publishing, Indianapolis.

Gottdiener, Mark
1995   *Postmodern Semiotics: Material Culture and the Forms of Postmodern Life.* Blackwell, Oxford, UK.

Hagen, Margaret A.
1986   *Varieties of Realism: Geometries of Representational Art.* Cambridge University Press, Cambridge, UK.

Hanson, F. Allan, and Louise Hanson
1983   *Counterpoint in Maori Culture.* Routledge & Kegan Paul, London, UK.

Hocart, A. M.
1952   *The Northern States of Fiji.* Royal Anthropological Institute

of Great Britain and Ireland, London, UK.

Hume, David
1986   [1777] *Enquiries Concerning Human Understanding and Concerning the Principles of Morals.* Oxford University Press, Oxford, UK.

Jakobson, Roman
1960   Closing Statement: Linguistics and Poetics. In *Style in Language,* edited by T. A. Sebeok. Massachusetts Institute of Technology Press, Cambridge, MA.

Jules-Rosette, Benetta
1984   *The Messages of Tourist Art: An African Semiotic System in Comparative Perspective.* Plenum Press, New York.

Kiparsky, Paul
1983   Roman Jakobson and the Grammar of Poetry. In *A Tribute to Roman Jakobson 1896–1982,* edited by M. Halle, pp. 27–38. Mouton Publishers, Berlin, Germany.

Kooijman, Simon
1972   *Tapa in Polynesia.* Bishop Museum Press, Honolulu.
1977   *Tapa on Moce Island, Fiji.* E. J. Brill, Leiden, Netherlands.

Kopytoff, Igor
1986   The Cultural Biography of Things: Commoditization as Process. In *The Social Life of Things: Commodities in Cultural Perspective,* edited by A. Appadurai, pp. 64–91. Cambridge University Press, Cambridge, UK.

Leach, Edmund R.
1989   *Claude Lévi-Strauss.* University of Chicago Press, Chicago.

Lewis, Justin
1991   *The Ideological Octopus: An Exploration of Television and Its Audience.* Routledge, New York.

Ling, Shun-Sheng, and Mary Man-Li Ling
1963   *Bark-Cloth, Impressed Pottery and the Inventions of Paper and Printing.* University of Taipei, Taipei, Taiwan.

Mauss, Marcel
1969   [1925] *The Gift: Forms and Functions of Exchange in Archaic Societies.* Cohen & West, London, UK.

Maybury-Lewis, David
1989   Introduction: The Quest for Harmony. In *The Attraction of Opposites: Thought and Society in the Dualistic Mode,* edited by D. Maybury-Lewis and U. Almagor, pp. 1–17. University of Michigan Press, Ann Arbor.

Nagy, Dénes
1993   Symmetric Patterns and Ethnomathematics in the South Pacific: Inspiring Research and Helping Education. *Symmetry: Culture and Science* 4:419–428.

Paivio, Allan
1986   *Mental Representations: A Dual Coding Approach.* Oxford University Press, New York.

Peirce, Charles S.
1955   *The Philosophical Writings of Peirce.* Dover, New York.

Riggins, Stephen Harold (editor)
1994   *The Socialness of Things: Essays on the Socio-Semiotics of Objects.* Mouton de Gruyter, Berlin and New York.

Sayes, Shelley-Ann
1982   Cakaudrove: Ideology and Reality in a Fijian Confederation. Unpublished Ph.D. dissertation, Australian National University, Canberra.

Shott, S.
1976   Society, Self and Mind in Moral Philosophy: The Scottish Moralists as Precursors of Symbolic Interactionism. *Journal of the History of the Behavioural Sciences* 12:39–46.

Sperber, Dan
1975   *Rethinking Symbolism.* Cambridge University Press, Cambridge, UK.

Thibault, Paul J.
1991   *Social Semiotics as Praxis: Text, Social Meaning Making, and Nabokov's Ada.* University of Minnesota, Minneapolis.

Thomas, Nicholas
1995   *Oceanic Art.* Thames & Hudson, London, UK.

Toren, Christina
1998   Cannibalism and Compassion: Transformations in Fijian Concepts of the Person. In *Common Worlds and Single Lives: Constituting Knowledge in Pacific Societies,* edited by V. Keck, pp. 163–183. Berg, Oxford, UK.

Washburn, Dorothy, and Donald Crowe
1988   *Symmetries of Culture.* University of Washington Press, Seattle.

Weiner, Annette B., and Jane Schneider (editors)
1989   *Cloth and Human Experience.* Smithsonian Institution Press, Washington, DC.

Williams, Thomas, and James Calvert
1982   [1858] *Fiji and the Fijians.* Fiji Museum, Suva, Fiji.

Contributors

Rod Ewins, Centre for the Arts, University of Tasmania, Tasmania, Australia

Ed Franquemont, Institute of Andean Studies, New Haven, Connecticut [deceased]

F. Allan Hanson, Department of Anthropology, University of Kansas, Lawrence, Kansas

Diane Humphrey, Department of Psychology, King's College, London, Ontario

Michael Kubovy, Department of Psychology, University of Virginia, Charlottesville, Virginia

Anne Paul, Allée des Vergers, Villers-lés-Nancy, France [deceased]

Peter Roe, Department of Anthropology, University of Delaware, Newark, Delaware

Lars Strother, Department of Psychology, University of Virginia, Charlottesville, Virginia

Dorothy K. Washburn, Research Associate, Laboratory of Anthropology, Museum of New Mexico, Santa Fe, New Mexico

Thomas Wynn, Department of Anthropology, University of Colorado, Colorado Springs, Colorado

Index

Note: Page numbers for figures appear in bold.